PORTRAITS OF SPIRITUAL AUTHORITY

RELIGIONS IN
THE GRAECO-ROMAN WORLD

EDITORS

R. VAN DEN BROEK   H.J.W. DRIJVERS
H.S. VERSNEL

VOLUME 137

PORTRAITS OF SPIRITUAL AUTHORITY

Religious Power in Early Christianity, Byzantium and the Christian Orient

EDITED BY

JAN WILLEM DRIJVERS

AND

JOHN W. WATT

BRILL
LEIDEN · BOSTON · KÖLN
1999

This series Religions in the Graeco-Roman World presents a forum for studies in the social and cultural function of religions in the Greek and the Roman world, dealing with pagan religions both in their own right and in their interaction with and influence on Christianity and Judaism during a lengthy period of fundamental change. Special attention will be given to the religious history of regions and cities which illustrate the practical workings of these processes.
Enquiries regarding the submission of works for publication in the series may be directed to Professor H.J.W. Drijvers, Faculty of Letters, University of Groningen, 9712 EK Groningen, The Netherlands.

This book is printed on acid-free paper.

Library of Congress Cataloging-in-Publication Data

Portraits of spiritual authority : religious power in early Christianity, Byzantium, and the Christian Orient / edited by Jan Willem Drijvers and John W. Watt
    p.   cm. — (Religions in the Graeco-Roman world, ISSN 0927-7633 ; v. 137)
    Includes bibliographical references and index.
    ISBN 9004114599
    1. Authority—Religious aspects—Christianity—History of doctrines—Early church, ca. 30-600—Congresses. I. Drijvers, Jan Willem. II. Watt, John W. III. Series.
    BT88.P67   1999
    262'.8'09015—dc21   99-045650
                                                     CIP

Die Deutsche Bibliothek - CIP-Einheitsaufnahme

Portraits of spiritual authority Religious Power in Early Christianity, Byzantium and the Christian Orient / ed. by Jan-Willem Drijvers and John Watt. – Leiden ; Boston ; Köln : Brill, 1999
   (Religions in the Graeco-Roman world ; Vol. 137)
   ISBN 90–04–11459–9

ISSN 0927-7633
ISBN 90 04 11459 9

PRINTED IN THE NETHERLANDS

CONTENTS

ABBREVIATIONS

ACW	Ancient Christian Writers
AHR	*American Historical Review*
Anal. Boll.	*Analecta Bollandiana*
ANRW	*Aufstieg und Niedergang der römischen Welt*
ASS	*Acta Sanctorum*
BSOAS	*Bulletin of the School of Oriental and African Studies*
CAH	*The Cambridge Ancient History*
CCSL	Corpus Christianorum, Series Latina
CSCO	Corpus Scriptorum Christianorum Orientalium
CSEL	Corpus Scriptorum Ecclesiasticorum Latinorum
DOP	*Dumbarton Oaks Papers*
GCS	Die griechischen christlichen Schriftsteller der ersten drei Jahrhunderte
GRBS	*Greek, Roman and Byzantine Studies*
HTR	*Harvard Theological Review*
JbAC	*Jahrbuch für Antike und Christentum*
JECS	*Journal of Early Christian Studies*
JEH	*Journal of Ecclesiastical History*
JHS	*Journal of Hellenic Studies*
JRS	*Journal of Roman Studies*
JTS	*Journal of Theological Studies*
OCA	Orientalia Christiana Analecta
OCP	*Orientalia Christiana Periodica*
OLP	*Orientalia Lovaniensia Periodica*
PG	Patrologia Graeca, ed. J.P. Migne
PO	Patrologia Orientalis
RAC	*Reallexikon für Antike und Christentum*
RE	*Real-Encyclopädie der classischen Altertumswissenschaft*
RHE	*Revue d'Histoire Ecclésiastique*
RHR	*Revue de l'Histoire des Religions*
RSR	*Recherches de Science Religieuse*
SC	Sources Chrétiennes
TRE	*Theologische Realenzyklopädie*
Vig. Chr.	*Vigiliae Christianae*
ZDMG	*Zeitschrift der deutschen morgenländischen Gesellschaft*
ZDPV	*Zeitschrift des deutschen Palästina-Vereins*
ZPE	*Zeitschrift für Papyrologie und Epigraphik*

PREFACE

Late Antiquity is frequently characterised as an age which placed undue emphasis on authority, and because in this period Christianity grew to become the major religious entity in Europe and the Near East, the development of spiritual authority in the Christian church is often considered to have been heavily influenced by the authoritarian society of the Late Roman Empire. All too conscious as we are in our days of the harm wrought by state orthodoxy or arbitrary and excessive religious power, the term can have a chilling ring to it. But spiritual authority is not always arbitrary or unchecked, and the history of the struggle for the attainment and exercise of authority in early Christianity in its manifold variations reflects important issues in the development of Christian thought and in the interaction of Christianity with the culture of the society in which it eventually became so powerful.

The articles collected in this book are all concerned with figures of spiritual authority in Christianity (or its immediate religious environment), and through individual studies of a number of figures across a span of time, the volume is intended to illuminate the way in which the struggle for religious influence developed with the changing relationships between church and society from the early years to the end of antiquity. The papers were all originally delivered at a workshop on the subject in Cardiff during May 1998, part of an ongoing collaborative research project on the transition from Classical to Christian culture involving members of the Research Institute for Classical, Oriental, Medieval and Renaissance Studies (COMERS) in Groningen and the Religious Studies and Classics Departments in Cardiff and Swansea respectively. The project is particularly concerned with the transition from antique to medieval culture in the East (Byzantium and the Christian Orient), and this provided an eastward-running thread for the contributions dedicated to the later part of our period. The articles therefore offer a panorama of the struggle for spiritual influence in Christianity from the early years to the eighth century.

All the contributors consider themselves in a broad sense to be historians, and would like to know about the figures with whom they

deal "how they really were". For all of them, also, the sources to
which they naturally turn for evidence to answer that question are
the literary texts of the period. But running through the volume is
an awareness of the problem of the relationship between the literary representation of a figure and the "reality outside the text",
between the rhetorical strategies of the texts with which we deal and
the persons of spiritual authority to whom these texts refer. Thus
although, for example, many *Lives* of holy men and women appear
in the following pages, the goals of the hagiographers claim as much
attention as the "real lives" of their subjects. The problem of history and literature in the study of early Christianity is explicitly raised
in a general form in the essay on "Rewriting Early Christian History"
which introduces this collection, and is exemplified there by an analysis of one of the best known of all early Christian writings, the
Confessions of Augustine. The issue, however, runs through the entire volume. What are offered here, therefore, are *portraits* of spiritual authority across a span of about six centuries, portraits which, presented
in various ways in histories, *Lives*, panegyrics or epistles, are themselves purposely designed to propagate religious authority.

    In the early part of our period, visionary and prophetic figures
loom large, and claims to religious authority were often based on
powerful spiritual experiences and charisma. In the second and third
centuries AD the development of authority within Christianity cannot be understood without consideration of the claims of those religious figures whose authority was, in one way or another, ultimately
repudiated in the developing Christian tradition. This volume looks
in particular at some representative figures from the spiritual worlds
conventionally designated by the terms Gnosticism and Montanism,
exploring how these visionaries and prophets sought to establish their
authority among their followers, and gauging their impact on the
rise of clerical over against charismatic authority in the developing
catholic tradition (Logan). Not least among the issues of the early
years was the defining of the "heretical" woman, and it remains
uncertain whether that figure portrayed by Firmilian of Caesarea
was a real individual or a literary construct (Trevett). Augustine's
mother Monica was certainly a real individual, but in the analysis
offered here of the Monica portrayed in the *Confessions*, it is argued
that the "life" we have of her is moulded by literature to reflect the
goal of Augustine's philosophy: a Socratic scorning of worldly things
and fearlessness in the face of discomfort or death (Clark). Elsewhere

in the fourth and fifth centuries we see again the power of literature being employed by Christian writers to represent an ideal and
impose its authority upon their readers. The ideal of sanctity and
the manner of the divine presence in the lives of the martyrs is the
central theme governing two stories of martyrs in *Ecclesiastical Histories*,
one of Origen in Eusebius, the other of Lucian of Antioch in Philostorgius. The two anecdotes epitomise differing constructions of sanctity and dramatise an abiding tension in early Christianity: in one
case the body of the saint himself is the tangible sanctuary of the
divine, while in the other the sanctuary is enclosed by the surrounding
company of disciples (Williams). With Gregory of Nyssa's *Life of
Gregory Thaumaturgus* we apparently return to the Cappadocian territory converted from paganism to Christianity in the third century
by the efforts of Firmilian and Gregory Thaumaturgus. It is, however, the ideals of the fourth century Cappadocian fathers that are
represented in the *Life*, not the struggles of the third, and the portrait it paints is their vision, not just of a local saint, but of a highly
educated scion of a wealthy family making his mark on the doctrine
of the church. That was not the end of the story, however, for its
translator, Rufinus, by emphasising in his Latin version the miraculous, at the expense of the rhetorical and biblical moralising of the
original, ensured its fame and influence among less sophisticated
readers in the West (Mitchell). In the East, too, the power of literature to promote religious authority can be observed not only on
synods of bishops through creeds and panegyrics, but also being exercised by bishops themselves on wider audiences through miracle stories. The authority of sees as well as creeds and persons can be
advanced through texts and legends, as evidenced in this volume by
the analysis of Cyril of Jerusalem's use of stories concerning the symbol of the Cross and Jerusalem (Jan W. Drijvers).

By the time of Cyril, good relations with the emperor were of
crucial importance in propagating power within Christianity and the
Church, and Cyril's promotion of Jerusalem against the claims of
Caesarea echoes the earlier use of the imperial cult by local pagan
elites in advancing their status against neighbouring rivals. Christianity
could now look to bishops with ties to the imperial house and theologians well trained in Greek rhetoric and philosophy as potential
bearers of spiritual authority, as well as to holy men. In some individuals these categories overlapped. Spiritual authority and secular
power are strikingly combined in the activity of Rabbula of Edessa,

whose life was also marked by asceticism and care for the urban poor. His visit to Jerusalem around 400 A.D. and his enthusiasm for the *Legend of the True Cross* highlight features he shared with Cyril: a concern for Christian sacred history and a shrewd sense for the realities of secular power. The Syriac *Life* of Rabbula presents him in a highly propagandist way; more a panegyric than a *Life*, it is also a defence of its hero in the tense and "chaotic" period between 436 and 449 (Han J.W. Drijvers). The ability of Syriac authors to employ the techniques of Greek panegyric and hagiography to propagate an ideal of spiritual authority and pure doctrine can also be seen in the two following contributions concerned with portraits of holy men by monastic authors living in Roman and Sasanian domains respectively. John bar Aphtonia, son of a rhetor at Edessa, led the monks of St. Thomas at Seleucia after the death of Anastasius to the new foundation at Qenneshre on the Euphrates, on account of their opposition to the dyophysite Christology supported by the new emperor Justin; while about a century later, across the border in Persia, Mihr-Mah-Gushnasp-George met his death through being denounced to Chosroes II as an apostate from Zoroastrianism by his monophysite rival, the court physician Gabriel of Sinjar. For both men there appeared panegyrists who painted portraits of their subjects as paradigms of spiritual authority and heroes of their faith: the one of the ideal abbot who, with the authority appropriate to the monastery, not that of the world, led his monks by divine wisdom and righteous example to the safety of Qenneshre (Watt); the other, from the pen of Babai the Great, of the holy martyr who died for presenting a pure "Nestorian" confession of faith before the Shah (Reinink). Our panorama closes in Constantinople at the end of the eighth century, where the holy men who had exercised such a profound influence on Christian life over the previous centuries are no longer able to wield spiritual authority. Anecdotes of Origen and Lucian of Antioch had pointed to the conviction of a powerful divine indwelling in the holy person himself or within the sphere of disciples around him, but those of Philaretos the Merciful and Stephen the Younger point to their spiritual powerlessness and isolation. They were men out of their times (Hatlie). In figures such as George and Babai the spiritual authority of the holy man experienced its final flowering. By the end of the eighth century, the boundary had been crossed between Antiquity and the Middle Ages, and one world view had given way to another.

We acknowledge with thanks the financial support given to the Workshop by Cardiff University (Elizabeth James Fund), the University of Wales (Inter-Collegiate Research Support Fund) and the University of Groningen (COMERS), and we wish to express our gratitude to Geoffrey and Marina Greatrex for their assistance in the organisation of the symposium. A special word of thanks is due to the scholars who came from beyond South Wales or Groningen and whose contributions so enlivened the proceedings. While none of the articles presented here is an exact historical record of the lecture delivered at the time, the volume is nevertheless a recognisable portrait of a stimulating conference.

Cardiff/Groningen, Spring 1999

Jan Willem Drijvers
John W. Watt

PART ONE

PEOPLE AND PORTRAITS

REWRITING EARLY CHRISTIAN HISTORY; AUGUSTINE'S REPRESENTATION OF MONICA

Elizabeth A. Clark

Duke University, Durham, N.C.

I. *The End of "History"?**

Some of my fellow historians are sounding the death knell for our discipline. Thus Peter Novick, at the end of his massive book, *That Noble Dream: The "Objectivity Question" and the American Historical Profession*, solemnly proclaims that "[a]s a broad community of discourse, as a community of scholars united by common aims, common standards, and common purposes, the discipline of history" has "ceased to exist".[1] Georg Iggers in his survey of *Historiography in the Twentieth Century*, entitles one chapter, "The 'Linguistic Turn': The End of History as a Scholarly Discipline".[2] Joyce Appleby, Lynn Hunt and Margaret Jacob in their still more negative assessment of theory's impact on the discipline of history, *Telling the Truth About History*, pronounce that there can be "no postmodern history".[3] What are these solemn obituaries about, we may ask?

Peter Novick's *That Noble Dream* provides a good starting point for assessing "the end of history". The phrase "noble dream" in his title refers to the hope that inspired several generations of American historians, copying (or so they imagined) their German predecessors, that they might attain historical "objectivity".[4] Persisting as a goal

---

* A longer, more detailed version of this essay appears in *Theology and the New Histories. The Annual Publications of the College Theology Society* 45 (Maryknoll, N.Y., 1999). I thank the editor, Gary Macy, for permission to publish a shorter version here.

[1] Peter Novick, *That Noble Dream: The "Objectivity Question" and the American Historical Profession* (Cambridge, 1988), p. 628.

[2] Georg G. Iggers, *Historiography in the Twentieth Century: From Scientific Objectivity to the Postmodern Challenge* (Hanover, N.H./London, 1997; original German edition, 1993), ch. 10.

[3] Joyce Appleby, Lynn Hunt, and Margaret Jacob, *Telling the Truth about History* (New York/London, 1994), p. 237.

[4] Novick takes the phrase "noble dream", originally derived from Theodore Clarke Smith, as the frontispiece of his book. Smith's essay, "The Writing of American History in America from 1884 to 1934", *AHR* 40 (1935), was mocked by Charles

for many historians to the present, the creed of historical objectivity contained several interrelated propositions. As Novick summarizes them, they are: that the past is real; that historical truth is reached when it corresponds with that reality; that there is a sharp separation between fact and value, the knower and the known, history and fiction; that historical facts exist prior to interpretation, and are "found", not "made"; that "[t]ruth is one, not perspectival"; that historians, as historians, are disinterested judges, not "advocates or propagandists". To be sure, Novick concedes, in recent years historians have nuanced these desiderata and are more likely to claim, for example, that interpretations are tested by facts, not derived from them. Such concessions, however, have required minimal modifications of the objectivist creed.[5]

As is evident, historians had derived their model from early modern and modern notions of scientific objectivity, and from the philosophical assumption, widely-held since the time of Descartes, that there was "an Archimedean point upon which knowledge could be grounded".[6] With the introduction of relativity theory in physics early in the twentieth century, the bulwark of foundationalism that historians had sought in the sciences crumbled. Concurrently, avant-garde literary and artistic experiments that employed multiple perspectives and voices shook the intellectual world. Yet, Novick argues, these developments had little effect on the historical profession; no one tried to write history à la James Joyce.[7] The model for historical narrative remained that of the nineteenth (not the twentieth)-century English novel.[8] The unsettling effects of these shifts in scientific and literary paradigms impressed themselves on the minds of historians

---

Beard's response, "That Noble Dream", in the next issue of *AHR* (41 [1935]). Commentators note that the American dream of "objectivity" lacked the Hegelian overtones of Leopold von Ranke's construal of the historian's mission; see, for example, Martin Bunzl, *Real History: Reflections on Historical Practice* (London/New York, 1997), p. 3; Iggers, *Historiography*, pp. 25–6; Leonard Krieger, *Ranke: The Meaning of History* (Chicago/London, 1977), ch. 2.

[5] Novick, *That Noble Dream*, pp. 1–2.

[6] Ibidem, ch. 1; p. 538.

[7] Ibidem, pp. 139–44. See also Hannah Arendt, "The Concept of History: Ancient and Modern", in Hannah Arendt, *Between Past and Future: Six Exercises in Political Thought* (New York, 1961), p. 50: why do historians hold onto a notion of determinable truth, when philosophers and natural scientists abandoned it long ago; historians seem fixed in practices of an older notion of "science".

[8] Hayden White, "The Burden of History", in Hayden White, *Tropics of Discourse: Essays in Cultural Criticism* (Baltimore/London, 1978; original of this essay, 1966), pp. 43–4.

much later—for many, not in a decisive way until recent years.

For a profession that struggled to establish itself as a serious science, the implication that history was basically "like" literature was unwelcome: such an allegation might be made against the amateurs who wrote histories for a larger lay public before the late nineteenth century, but could not be leveled against the professionals with Ph.D.s who employ the techniques of archival research.[9] Given that nineteenth-century historians struggled to escape literature's marriage to history, its return in the late twentieth century seemed most unwelcome to many historians. As historian David Harlan has expressed it, "after a hundred-year absence, literature has returned to history, unfurling her circus silks of metaphor and allegory, misprision and aporia, trace and sign, demanding that historians accept her mocking presence right at the heart of what they had once insisted was their own autonomous and truly scientific discipline".[10]

To cite but one example, Roland Barthes' now-familiar claim that the narrative form employed in historical writing did not substantially differ from the "imaginary narration" of the novel or drama was not well-received by the community of historians.[11] The response of the distinguished ancient historian Arnaldo Momigliano to Barthes probably typifies the view of many in the profession: history writing, Momigliano rejoined, is differentiated from other types of literature in "its being submitted as a whole to the control of evidence. History is no epic, history is no novel, history is not propaganda because in these literary genres control of the evidence is optional, not compulsory".[12] Momigliano's contention, in turn, was dimly received

---

[9] Novick, *That Noble Dream*, ch. 2, p. 600; cf. Robert E. Berkhofer, Jr., *Beyond the Great Story: History as Text and Discourse* (Cambridge/London, 1995), pp. 63, 135, and ch. 4.

[10] David Harlan, "Intellectual History and the Return of Literature", *AHR* 94 (1989), p. 581.

[11] Roland Barthes, "The Discourse of History", transl. Stephen Bann, *Comparative Criticism: A Yearbook*, vol. 3, ed. E.S. Shaffer (Cambridge, 1981; French original of this essay, 1967), pp. 7–20. In Linda Orr's view, the most "consistent critique of history is still performed by the novel: fiction evokes the other history that history refuses to write, preferring its traditional fictions". Yet Orr continues, history performs a highly useful service for fiction in that it establishes "the baseline of verisimilitude so that fiction can take flight with a protective netting underneath"; Linda Orr, "The Revenge of Literature: A History of History", *New Literary History* 18 (1986), p. 19.

[12] Arnaldo Momigliano, "The Rhetoric of History and the History of Rhetoric: On Hayden White's Tropes", *Comparative Criticism: A Yearbook*, vol. 3, ed. E.S. Shaffer (Cambridge, 1981), p. 261.

by scholars who by the 1980s had digested the arguments of Hayden White and Paul Veyne.

Likewise, a philosophical line of critique joined that leveled by literary and other theorists. I am glad that historian Peter Novick himself concedes that what historians do worst is reflect on epistemology,[13] so that I do not appear too mean-spirited when I chide my fellow historians on this point. Although all historians now admit that the remains of the past are fragmentary, that our knowledge of it is partial, that all written records ("documents" as well as "literary" productions) are conveyed in language, such considerations seem to have done little to upset the epistemological equanimity of those whom Robert Berkhofer calls the "normal historians". The admission by such "normal historians" that they "cannot capture the fullness of past experience", that "they only have the traces or the residues of the past, and their accounts are necessarily partial"[14] is viewed as sufficient concession to the arguments of the alleged "relativists". The more troubling epistemological questions raised by these concessions about "reality" in relation to representation and historians' criteria for assessing "truth" are either not broached, or are reduced to the observation that since multiple and varying historical sources witness to past events, more than one story needs to be told.[15] Yet to concede that every historical statement must be qualified by the addition "from the so-and-so point of view" suggests (so argues philosopher of history William Dray) that historians themselves admit that they deal in "mere appearances"—a view that if taken seriously would mean that "historians would have to give up all claim to tell how the past really was".[16] The problem occasioned by historians' fusion of representation and referentiality—what Robert Berkhofer calls the "referential illusion"—is scarcely noted.[17]

Historians rather settled for the goal of capturing at least a part of the past's fullness. Building up a context—"thick description", in historical guise—would rescue the day. On this account, the problem facing the historian centered on the relative plentitude or paucity

---

[13] Novick, *That Noble Dream*, p. 15.
[14] Appleby, Hunt, and Jacob, *Telling the Truth About History*, p. 234.
[15] Ibidem, p. 256.
[16] William H. Dray, "Point of View in History", in William H. Dray, *On History and Philosophers of History*. Philosophy of History and Culture 2 (Leiden, 1989), p. 65; original of this essay published in *Clio* 7 (1978), pp. 265–83.
[17] Berkhofer, *Beyond the Great Story*, p. 60.

of documents: were there enough to tell a story? The task of the historian, it was assumed, was "to make the structure of interpretation appear to be (the same as) the structure of factuality".[18] The epistemological and ontological issues involving "the past" and "facts" in relation to the historian's representation of them remained relatively unexamined.

A "strong" challenge to these claims argues rather that since the past is preserved only as written history, is constituted only in a present-day text, there can be no appeal to a "past" aside from this linguistically-constituted record.[19] On this view, it is an illusion of realist historiography to represent what are structures of interpretation as factuality/actuality.[20] Since facts as well as their contexts are interpretive constructs, it is misguided for historians to claim that their interpretations refer to some "actual past realities outside the text"; facts are not already "there" to "coerce" historians' representations.[21]

Roger Chartier frames the problem sharply: "The pertinent question is what criteria permit us to hold possible the relationship that historical writing institutes between the representing trace and the practice represented".[22] Historians, it appears, have not been able to supply these criteria to the satisfaction of their more philosophically-minded colleagues, even those with historians' credentials, such as Chartier. And it is a classicist, not a contemporary theorist—Paul Veyne—who coined the witty but ungenerous phrase to describe his colleagues in the historical profession: that many exhibit themselves as survivals of "the paleoepistemological era".[23]

II. *Rewriting Early Christian History*

One complaint leveled by scholars who oppose the impingement of "theory" on the study of history is that their theoretically-minded colleagues have not actually produced "non-objectivist" historical writing. To these opponents, those most eager to press theoretical

---

[18] Ibidem, p. 60.
[19] Ibidem, p. 14.
[20] Ibidem, p. 63.
[21] Ibidem, pp. 70–1.
[22] Roger Chartier, *Cultural History: Between Practices and Representations*, transl. Lydia G. Cochrane (Ithaca, 1988; French original of this essay, 1987), pp. 65–6.
[23] Paul Veyne, *Writing History: Essay on Epistemology*, transl. Mina Moore-Rinvolucri (Middletown, Conn., 1984; French original, 1971), p. 91.

considerations indulge in "an extravagant appeal to new theories and approaches", yet in the end have nothing more to show for their rhetorical efforts than "a new formalism or textual prudence".[24] Even those who applaud the effort "to escape from a baneful positivism" charge that although colleagues aiming to write intellectual history from a post-structuralist perspective "celebrate bold theories", they end by "revel[ing] in cautious truisms".[25] Critics of theoretically sophisticated historians such as Joan Scott allege that the latter have not incorporated post-structuralist critique into their actual historical practice,[26] and that their experimentations with "voice" and narrative technique (such as Simon Schama's in *Dead Certainties*) result only in "cacophony" and disturbing disjunctions that confuse the reader.[27] Thus it seems imperative for historians in any field—say, early Christian history—who urge their colleagues to register the claims of twentieth-century theory to illustrate in their own work how our century's intellectual shifts might affect their own scholarly writing.

Here, I think historians of early Christianity are in a more advantageous position than historians of some later periods who rely heavily on documentary and archival evidence. Scholars of early Christianity, who can be categorized as intellectual historians, work with *texts*—and texts that are very often self-consciously literary and ideological through and through. Although numerous classicists have in varying ways acknowledged that *their* texts must be looked at primarily as literary products,[28] this view has only slowly and somewhat reluctantly been conceded by patristics scholars.

How historians of Christianity might proceed if they understood their sources as literary texts remains to be seen, because the intellectual problems disturbing the wider historical discipline seem to

---

[24] Russell Jacoby, "A New Intellectual History?", *AHR* 97 (1992), p. 419.

[25] Ibidem, p. 424.

[26] A charge directed at Joan Scott's *Gender and the Politics of History* (New York, 1988), by historian Claudia Koonz in "Post Scripts", *Women's Review of Books* 6 (1989), p. 19. See now Joan Scott's *Only Paradoxes to Offer: French Feminists and the Rights of Man* (Cambridge/London, 1996).

[27] Cushing Strout, "Border Crossings: History, Fiction, and *Dead Certainties*", *History and Fiction* 31 (1992), pp. 156–8.

[28] For ancient history itself as a literary enterprise, see, for example, G.W. Bowersock, *Fiction as History: Nero to Julian*, Sather Classical Lectures 58 (Berkeley/Los Angeles/London, 1994), p. 12; T.J. Luce, *The Greek Historians* (London/New York, 1997), p. 4; various essays in Averil Cameron (ed.), *History as Text: The Writing of Ancient History* (Chapel Hill/London, 1989); and especially A.J. Woodman, *Rhetoric in Classical Historiography: Four Studies* (London/Sydney/Portland, 1988).

have gone unregistered by many students of late ancient Christianity. If we adopted Roger Chartier's arguments that historical work should be an exercise in analyzing the process of representation,[29] and that historians should refocus their task to examine the function of ideas in ideological systems,[30] what might our work look like?

Since this paper represents the beginning of a new project, I have reached no firm position in relation to views such as Chartier's. But I have made two forays in that direction. My first study appeared in the March 1998 issue of *Church History* under the title, "The Lady Vanishes: Dilemmas of a Feminist Historian After the Linguistic Turn". There, after surveying some of the problems that literary theory has posed for feminist historians, I attempted an analysis of texts written by Gregory of Nyssa about his sister Macrina. Here, I would like to explore a different set of materials, Augustine's representation of his mother Monica in the *Confessions* and the Cassiciacum *Dialogues*. I turn now to this subject.

III. *Augustine and Monica*

A half century ago, scholars optimistically mined the *Confessions* to reconstruct Augustine's chronological and intellectual history. They built on earlier studies that had traced Augustine's philosophical ancestry and had variously charted his "conversion" to Platonism or to Christianity. Scholars today claim less: it is now conceded there are many aspects of Augustine's early life about which we learn next to nothing from the *Confessions* (for instance, we would not guess from this work that he had at least one sister).[31] If the *Confessions* is removed from the category of autobiographical reportage and viewed as a literary construct that artfully builds its case through intertextual allusions to classical literature and Scripture,[32] we doubtless lose what we may have imagined as "the real Augustine", but we find instead his literary—and retrospective—self-representation.[33] Augustine the

---

[29] Chartier, *Cultural History*, pp. 13–4.
[30] Ibidem, p. 34.
[31] This we know from Augustine's *Epist.* 211 and from Possidius' *Vita Augustini*.
[32] Pierre Courcelle's *Recherches sur les Confessions de Saint Augustin* (Paris, 1968; 2nd ed.), with its trenchant analysis of the "literariness" of the *Confessions*, provoked an uproar among historians and theologians who believed that Courcelle had erased the "historicity" of the work.
[33] On the problems of understanding Augustine as a "retrospective" self-creation,

rhetorician leaves us no avenue by which to secure an "objective" historical narrative from the literary construction that he here weaves. As James O'Donnell puts it, scholars must rather look to "the rhetorical and exegetical strategies of the *Confessions* themselves".[34] In O'Donnell's view—a view with which I concur—the allegedly "narrative" first nine books of the *Confessions* are "anything but narrative in their construction; their distinctive feature is not the lively biographical interest they evoke, but rather the complexity of the confessional mode, the allusiveness, and the indirectness of the text's construction".[35]

If such is the case, how are we to assess Augustine's treatment of one of the book's star characters, his mother, Monica? Augustine's representation of her provides a fruitful test case through which to explore the literary constructedness of the *Confessions*. On the surface, we have in the *Confessions* (especially in Book 9) one of the fullest extant portraits of an early Christian woman. The supposition that we have here a "life" of an early Christian woman—so relatively rare in patristic writing—itself commends the text to us as precious. Can we not gain insight into other early Christian women from examining her story? Perhaps, but probably not in the straightforward way that we might at first assume, for Monica, too, is a literary representation. We can, however, trace in Augustine's representation of Monica some strands of the "theological logic" of the text, how he shaped his story of Monica to bring home moral and theological points that we can detail in his other early writings. Even if we abandon the quest for "the real Monica", we still can identify many significant "Monica-functions".

To begin: the *Confessions*, despite its extended discussion of Augustine's childhood, is not a "family story" in any straightforward sense.[36] That Augustine seems considerably less fond of his father, Patricius, than of his mother, has often been remarked. In the *Confessions*, Augustine does not even note his father's death until, rather casually, two years after the fact[37]—and shortly thereafter in the text addresses God as

---

see the now-classic article by Paula Fredriksen, "Paul and Augustine: Conversion Narratives, Orthodox Traditions, and the Retrospective Self", *JTS* 37 (1986), pp. 3–34.

[34] James O'Donnell, *Augustine. Confessions*, 3 vols. (Oxford, 1992), vol. 1, p. xxi.

[35] Ibidem, vol. 3, p. 154.

[36] For a discussion of the late ancient family, using Augustine's as an example, see Brent D. Shaw, "The Family in Antiquity: The Experience of Augustine", *Past and Present* 115 (1987), pp. 3–51.

[37] Augustine, *Confessiones* 3.4.

"Father" in the vocative voice for the first time.[38] Moreover, Augustine reveals to his readers that Monica endeavored to substitute God the Father as a paternal parent for him in place of Patricius.[39] And although throughout the *Confessions* Augustine casts himself as the Prodigal Son who goes astray,[40] he returns not to a human father who welcomes him, as in the Biblical parable "literally" read, but to a divine Father.[41] It strikes me that from the *Confessions* Freud might have derived an interesting example of a "family romance"; here, Augustine's own, inadequate father is replaced with a wondrously adequate substitute.

Yet it is not just Patricius who is "replaceable": more surprising, so is Monica herself. In various subtle ways, Augustine dissociates himself from *both* his parents in the *Confessions*. One theme that suggests this dissociation surfaces in his discussion of human conception. Augustine, we must assume, was not ignorant of "where babies come from" when he claims that it is not parents who produce their children, but God.[42] Humans do not know how they are conceived,[43] he writes, or where the "I" was before it enters earthly life.[44] We simply take it "on faith" that our parents are those who identify themselves as such. Here, Augustine uses children's ignorance of their bodily origin to score the epistemological point that if humans do not believe many things without firm proof, they would "accomplish absolutely nothing in life".[45] We have unassailable knowledge that our origin is from God; confidence that human parents are "ours", by contrast, illustrates a lower-level, "everyday" order of trust that Augustine believes is nonetheless necessary for our bodily sojourn in this world.

Another way in which Augustine delicately effaces Patricius and Monica in their paternal and maternal roles is his claim that they stand as his "brother and sister" in the faith, "fellow citizens" with him in the heavenly Jerusalem. Just as Augustine replaces Patricius

---

[38] Augustine, *Confessiones* 3.6.
[39] Augustine, *Confessiones* 1.12.
[40] Augustine, *Confessiones* 1.18, 3.6, 4.16, 8.3.
[41] "The theme of the prodigal son is as much about fathers and estrangement as it is about sons...."; O'Donnell, *Augustine. Confessions*, vol. 2, p. 71.
[42] Augustine, *Confessiones* 1.6.
[43] Augustine, *Confessiones* 9.13.
[44] Augustine, *Confessiones* 1.6.
[45] Augustine, *Confessiones* 6.5. Such a claim echoes Augustine's earlier uneasiness with the Sceptical Academy's position regarding the withholding of assent to sense perceptions; see his *Contra Academicos* for his major discussion of this theme.

with God the Father, so he here substitutes for Monica "our Catholic mother the Church".[46] Later in the *Confessions*, Augustine reaffirms this point: *his* beloved mother is Jerusalem above, the abode of peace.[47] (Augustine here alludes to Paul's allegory of the earthly and heavenly Jerusalems in Galatians 4; that the "Jerusalem above", represented by Sarah, is enjoined in the words of Isaiah 54:1 to "rejoice" as a barren woman, adds further intertextual depth to his displacement of physical maternity.) Such literary dislodgements, I would argue, are not surprising, since Augustine, like other early Christians, seeks to substitute a new spiritual family for his actual physical family. In the new family, he claims, we all equally become "infants in Christ", familial hierarchy—so pronounced in ancient kinship structures—having been erased.[48] The maternal role of Monica is here again occluded.

Likewise, when Lady Continence beckons Augustine to embrace a Christianity marked by sexual renunciation, she is depicted "not as barren but as a fruitful mother of children, of joys born of you, O Lord, her Spouse". She, with the "countless boys and girls surrounding her", lures Augustine to the celibate life, away from the "toys of toys" (*nugae nugarum*) who tempt him to sexual pleasure.[49] Through his portrayal of Lady Continence, Augustine suggests that celibacy is more "fruitful", more "productive" than physical maternity. Motherhood, once again, is deemed of dubious value.

Although literary critic Françoise Lionnet does not pose as an Augustine scholar, she offers some suggestive reflections of "the maternal/the female" in the *Confessions*. Whereas many previous readers of the *Confessions* have been (understandably) puzzled by its structure (what purpose do the final books serve, seemingly "tacked on" to the narrative of Augustine's early life?), Lionnet understands Books 11–13 as integral to the work's structure. In Books 1–9, Augustine focuses on his sinful self, both on his sexual sin and on his transgression as a "seller of words", but Books 11–13 promise a new self which, eventually, will conquer sin.[50] On her account, Books 11–13 *also* concern the act of Augustine's self-creation, albeit in allegorical form.[51]

---

[46] Augustine, *Confessiones* 9.13.
[47] Augustine, *Confessiones* 12.16.
[48] Augustine, *Confessiones* 8.2.
[49] Augustine, *Confessiones* 10.11.
[50] For Augustine's reflections on those who "traffic in literature", become "word-merchants", see *Confessiones* 1.13.
[51] Françoise Lionnet, *Autobiographical Voices: Race, Gender, Self-Portraiture* (Ithaca/London,

In Lionnet's reading, "woman" represents for Augustine the prime aspect of the sinful self that must be erased[52]—not only his sexual relations as depicted in the first nine books, but also "the female" as represented in his allegory of creation in Book 13. There, "woman" denotes not only Eve, but the "lower" force within the soul (*man's* soul) which must be subject to the reasoning power of the mind,[53] an association which early Christian writers borrowed from Philo[54] and which Origen made standard.[55] In Lionnet's reading, the unruly passions, coded as female, here represent the negative aspect of the self, the negative "internal other", which needs displacing—and indeed *is* displaced by a "positive self". Augustine explicates this "positive self" in his elaboration of man's creation in "the image of God", i.e., as a rational being. Yet as Lionnet notes, the "feminine" dimension is not simply erased, since Augustine's *God* appropriates attributes of "woman", the "receptive, nurturing, maternal... qualities usually coded as feminine in Western culture".[56] It is thus no accident, she concludes, that Augustine identifies God with the "place of rest, of absolute peace"—that is, with the maternal.[57]

For Lionnet, it is essential for Augustine to position his depiction of Monica's death in the *Confessions* in between his recounting of his old sinful self and his vision of the new, saved self. The death of his mother, Lionnet writes, "is the culmination of his narrative of a life of sin and marks his liberation from earthly and bodily connections. It is necessary for his earthly mother to die in order for Augustine to get closer to God...".[58] On this reading, all the necessary "maternal" qualities Augustine assigns to the culminating vision of bliss can be found in God, not in a "real" human woman. Here,

---

1989), p. 45, p. 64. Lionnet is here also concerned to stress that Augustine gives up his old self as writer (and we might add, public orator) to become the consummate "reader" of the "transcendent Other" (p. 56). Exegetic reading becomes "redemption" (p. 39).

[52] Ibidem, p. 32.

[53] Augustine, *Confessiones* 13.32, 13.34.

[54] See Richard A. Baer, Jr., *Philo's Use of the Categories of Male and Female*, Arbeiten zur Literatur und Geschichte des hellenistischen Judentums 3 (Leiden, 1970).

[55] Origen, *Hom. 1 Gen.* 15; *Hom. 10 Exod.* 3; *Comm. Matt.* 12.4; *Hom. 4 Gen.* 4; *Hom. 5 Gen.* 6; *Hom. 2 Exod.* 1; *Hom. 22 Num.* 1.

[56] Lionnet, *Autobiographical Voices*, p. 32.

[57] Ibidem, p. 44.

[58] Ibidem, p. 56. See likewise Brian Stock, *Augustine the Reader: Meditation, Self-Knowledge, and the Ethics of Interpretation* (Cambridge/London, 1996), p. 121; earlier in the *Confessions* (4.7), the death of Augustine's friend is recounted to illustrate the transitoriness of human life; Monica's death, conversely, concerns eternal life.

"the embodied self, born of an earthly mother", is transfigured and transcended.[59]

Yet even if Monica's role as "real mother" of Augustine is so often occluded, as a character she nonetheless plays an indispensable role in Augustine's account. What are the "Monica-functions" that Augustine constructs? To start with the obvious, Monica offers an exemplary paradigm for Augustine's depiction of appropriate wifely behavior. Although Augustine claims that all women, including Monica, bear the sinful legacy of Eve,[60] Monica nonetheless sets a pattern of spousal virtue for other Christian matrons. Her obedience to Patricius, Augustine claims, was in truth obedience to God's law—presumably the "law" of the New Testament Household Codes that enjoins the submission of wives as divinely-ordained female behavior.[61] He posits that his mother escaped the beatings that other women suffered from their husbands by never arguing with Patricius when he was angry— and that she reminded her friends that the Roman marriage contract put them in subjugation to their husbands. They were, in Augustine's rendition of Monica's claim, *ancillae*—slave-girls—to their husbands, who stand as lords (*domini*).[62] Monica is, as Kim Power has recently phrased it, "the epitome of obedient subordination".[63] That such a picture of wifehood recommends itself to many of us much less enthusiastically than it did to Augustine goes without saying. His portrayal, it should be noted, is consistent with his approach to women's status elsewhere in his writings.[64]

A second way in which Monica serves a useful purpose for Augustine lies more strictly in the realm of theology and ethics: she is the "faithful servant", indeed, "the handmaid", of God.[65] (That Augustine here uses the word *ancilla* for his mother may well have reminded his readers of another *ancilla Domini*, the Virgin Mary who humbly submits to the angel's announcement of her impending pregnancy

---

[59] Ibidem, pp. 65–6.

[60] Augustine, *Confessiones* 5.8.

[61] Augustine, *Confessiones* 1.11.

[62] Augustine, *Confessiones* 9.9.

[63] Kim Power, *Veiled Desire: Augustine on Women* (New York, 1996), p. 76.

[64] Elizabeth A. Clark, "Theory and Practice in Late Ancient Asceticism: Jerome, Chrysostom, and Augustine", *Journal of Feminist Studies in Religion* 5 (1989), pp. 25–46; for a more positive view of Augustine and women, see Gerald Bonner, "Augustine's Attitude to Women and 'Amicitia'", *Homo Spiritalis: Festgabe für Luc Verheijen OSA*, eds. Cornelius Mayer, Karl Heinz Chelius (Würzburg, 1987), pp. 259–75.

[65] Augustine, *Confessiones* 2.3.

[Luke 1:38].) Throughout the *Confessions*, Augustine sounds the theme that God uses people as his servants, even without their knowledge, to bring about the conversion and reformation of others.

Notably, Monica herself plays the role of God's servant in Augustine's conversion, imploring God with her tears and prayers for the rescue of her son. If God had raised *his* own Son from the dead, could not Monica's son be similarly lifted up?[66] Augustine here cites Psalm 144:7, "You sent down your help from above" (a verse that Christian exegetes often interpreted as referring to the Incarnation) to suggest Monica's role: because of her pious prayers and tears, God had reassured her in a dream that Augustine would come to stand on the same "rule" as she did.[67] Monica is here depicted as playing a semi-salvific role in Augustine's conversion.

Most important, and the "Monica-function" on which I wish to concentrate, Augustine's representation of his mother as "manly" in her faith, despite her "weak women's body", borrows the *topos* of woman-as-wisdom familiar from other early Christian writings, such as Gregory of Nyssa's portrayal of his sister Macrina. Two representations of Monica have often been unproblematically read by those eager to exalt Augustine's depiction of his mother: his accounts of Monica in the Cassiciacum *Dialogues*, and of their discussion at Ostia at the moment of their so-called "vision".[68] These scenes, to certain readers, show that Monica had untapped philosophical potential. I would like to argue for another reading: first, that Augustine's depiction of Monica in the Cassiciacum dialogues serves certain *theological* purposes; and second, that Augustine's portrayal of Monica at the Ostia "vision" represents a fleshing out of the definition of philosophy he had formulated in those dialogues—philosophy in story form, if you will. Unpacking the "theological logic" of these texts is an enlightening exercise.

In the Cassiciacum dialogues, written shortly after Augustine's conversion, and a decade or more before the *Confessions*, Monica is depicted as present on the country estate at which Augustine and his younger students and friends had gathered for intellectual retreat.

---

[66] Augustine, *Confessiones* 9.4; cf. 3.11, 6.1.

[67] Augustine, *Confessiones* 3.11.

[68] The scholarly debates as to whether the experience at Ostia should properly be called "mystical" are summarized by J. Kevin Coyle in "In Praise of Monica: A Note on the Ostia Experience of *Confessions* IX", *Augustinian Studies* 13 (1982), pp. 87–90.

In two of these treatises, *De beata vita* and *De ordine*, Monica emerges as more central to the philosophical conversation than we might have expected. She intervenes not only to ask questions, but also to express her opinion. She is represented as arriving at the same definition of happiness as had Cicero in the *Hortensius*.[69] Augustine throughout his treatise *On the Happy Life* praises her astuteness and even claims that she upstaged his argument, beating him to the trenchant point he had reserved for his final triumphant proof.[70] Do we not have here a representation of "woman-as-wisdom"? Yet there is much in these two treatises, *On the Happy Life* and *On Order*, to challenge such a claim.

First of all, Augustine makes clear that Monica is uneducated; he even leaves it doubtful whether she can read or write at all.[71] Augustine himself remarks that despite his praise for his mother, he does not wish to misrepresent the case: Monica, for all her insight, "could not easily acquire a mode of expression that would be free from defect of pronunciation and diction". (Augustine confesses that he himself— the aspiring orator—had been faulted in Italy for his ["North African"?] pronunciation.) Augustine here claims that "the assurance that comes from theory"—men's province—"is one thing", while "that gained by native ability"—such as Monica's—"is quite different".[72] However much Augustine admires Monica's abilities, he himself does not exaggerate her learning.

Interestingly, Augustine in these dialogues does not stress the point we might expect on the basis of his later writings, namely, that the Holy Spirit had infused Monica's heart and mind to enable her to "learn wisdom", a commonplace found in much monastic literature that seeks to explain the theological and moral erudition of the uneducated. Rather, at this early stage in Augustine's theological development, Monica's abilities are described in ways that suggest Augustine here resorts to a type of "natural theology" that he later would imbue with a more distinctively Christian coloration: like the Gentiles of Romans 1, Monica, despite her lack of education, possesses some innate knowledge of God that merely needs drawing out.

Similarly, in *On the Happy Life* and in *On Order*, Augustine offers

---

[69] Augustine, *De beata vita* 2.10; Augustine notes that her understanding corresponds with that of Cicero in his (lost) treatise, *Hortensius*.
[70] Augustine, *De beata vita* 4.27.
[71] Augustine, *De ordine* 1.8.26; cf. 1.11.31.
[72] Augustine, *De ordine* 2.17.45.

two examples of uneducated men—uneducated either through their own lack of effort or because they belong to the working classes—with whom observant readers might profitably compare the case of Monica. The first example: Augustine claims that his uneducated male relatives present at Cassiciacum, despite their lack of even elementary literary training, are able to participate in the discussion because of their "common sense";[73] this concession provides Augustine with the space to imply that Monica, as well, may join the all-male discussants. A second example: Augustine informs the group that there were learned men in the past (read: the *pagan* past), who although shoemakers or workers of similarly low status, were able to achieve wisdom[74]—and so, he seems to suggest, with Monica. Augustine confesses that he will entrust himself to her as a "disciple" in the pursuit of wisdom, so advanced is her understanding.[75] What is the meaning of such a claim?

Here, I accept Kim Power's suggestion that one function of Monica is to provide Augustine with an alternative model of piety to that of educated men. Although Augustine claims that his male friends at Cassiciacum considered Monica as "a great man in their midst",[76] it seems more likely that Augustine uses Monica to illustrate a second means to faith: not the approach through study that he enjoys, but a way of holiness that simple people of no education can embrace.[77] She represents, in effect, the great mass of untutored Christian lay people, who nonetheless are sons and daughters of the Church: Monica, like them, has not read philosophical books, but nonetheless has access to truth.[78] Although Augustine informs his mother that some women of old did indeed engage in philosophical discussion with men,[79] he assures her that if she steadfastly participates in the "sacred mysteries", that is, in the sacraments, and continues her virtuous mode of life, this lower path will be good enough for her—and for God. There is no need for her to trouble her brain with the problems of theodicy, the origin of evil, or the eternity of the world—

---

[73] Augustine, *De beata vita* 1.6.

[74] Augustine, *De ordine* 1.11.31.

[75] Augustine, *De ordine* 1.11.32.

[76] Augustine, *De beata vita* 2.10.

[77] Power, *Veiled Desire*, p. 88.

[78] Augustine, *De beata vita* 4.27. I thank Rowan Williams for reinforcing the point during the conference discussion that Monica can now, for the baptized Augustine, "stand in for" the community of baptized Christians.

[79] Augustine, *De ordine* 1.11.31.

these points, Augustine implies, can be reserved as discussion topics for educated men such as himself.[80]

What then does Augustine mean when, instructing Monica on the etymology of the Greek word *philosophia*, he calls her a true "lover of wisdom", that is, a "philosopher"?[81] The Cassiciacum dialogues supply two interrelated answers, both of which, I posit, are given narrative form in Augustine's later description of the "vision" (perhaps more accurately described as an "audition")[82] at Ostia in the *Confessions*. A first manifestation of Monica's "wisdom" in the Cassiciacum dialogues is that she does not fear discomfort or death, thus showing that she has achieved (in Augustine's words) "the stoutest stronghold of philosophy".[83] Here, Augustine alludes to Socrates' claim in the *Phaedo* that those who rightly engage in philosophy "study only dying and death".[84] Is this not what Monica is also represented as doing? Can she not be counted as a latter-day "female Socrates"?

Moreover, Augustine claims that true philosophers will experience a vision of Oneness and Beauty, and will be united to the object of their love, the Beautiful. Augustine implies in the dialogue *On Order* that Monica in her own way has found this Beauty, for she has experienced the manifestations of God's order in the world.[85] And these claims lead us back to the *Confessions*' description of the "vision" at Ostia, the most dramatic portrayal of Monica as a "philosopher" in the entire Augustinian corpus. Here, the two attributes of the true philosopher that Augustine has accorded to Monica in the Cassiciacum dialogues (not fearing death; experiencing Oneness and Beauty) are given narrative form. Yet some problems attend our understanding of Monica as a "philosopher" in this scene as well.

Augustine's rendition of his and Monica's discussion at Ostia, although it appears to cast Monica into a philosophical role similar to Augustine's, is colored through and through with allusions to Plotinus' treatises "On Beauty" and "On the First Three Hypostases",

---

[80] Augustine, *De ordine* 2.17.46. For a discussion of similar themes, see Phillip Cary, "What Licentius Learned: A Narrative Reading of the Cassiciacum Dialogues", *Augustinian Studies* 29 (1998), pp. 160–1.

[81] Augustine, *De ordine* 1.11.32.

[82] O'Donnell, *Augustine Confessions*, vol. 3, p. 133.

[83] Augustine, *De ordine* 1.11.32.

[84] Plato, *Phaedo* 9 (64A).

[85] Augustine, *De ordine* 2.19.51–20.52.

as Paul Henry demonstrated some years ago.[86] These, obviously, are not books that Monica had read—but thanks to the research of twentieth-century scholars, we can claim with some degree of confidence that Augustine had done so.[87] The Ostia "vision" is Augustine's own lightly-Christianized version of Plotinian notions of the soul's ascent. However much Monica is represented as joining in the dialogue equally with Augustine, we should not, I think, imagine her as expressing these Plotinian sentiments—and Augustine himself, in depicting the scene a decade or so later, concedes that they did not speak in these "exact words".[88]

The Ostia vision seems manifestly linked to the goal of philosophy that Augustine posits in the Cassiciacum treatises *On Order* and *Soliloquies*. The achievement of Oneness, the union with what one loves in a vision of Beauty, is the summit of the philosopher's quest, Augustine argues in *De ordine*.[89] In the *Soliloquies*, he asks what lover of wisdom, what philosopher, will be able to gaze on and "embrace Wisdom", with no veil between them—"naked, as it were". To achieve this union with Beauty and Wisdom, the lover must forsake the things of sense. Disengaging the "wings" of his soul from the sticky lime of the body, conceived as a prison, his soul can soar free. Augustine here avers that he does not begrudge this love of Beauty to others. In fact, since those who enjoy this love in common with him will become all the dearer, he urges "many" to share it with him.[90]

At the time he wrote the *Soliloquies*, Augustine claimed that there is more than one road to wisdom; some, he writes, are able to look at the sun directly, but others cannot and need assistance of a different sort.[91] Later, in his *Retractions*, written at the end of his life, Augustine worries that from this passage in the *Soliloquies* some readers might infer that Christ was *not* the only route to wisdom—an interpretation contradicted by Jesus' pronouncement in John 14:6, "I am the way".[92] In retrospect, Augustine wishes to correct any misimpression he might earlier have given by his phrase, "more than one way to

---

[86] Paul Henry, *La Vision d'Ostie: Sa place dans la vie et l'oeuvre de Saint Augustin* (Paris, 1938); also see discussion in Courcelle, *Recherches sur les Confessions*, p. 222.

[87] See Courcelle, *Recherches sur les Confessions*, pp. 156–7, referring to Paul Henry, *Plotin et l'Occident* (Louvain, 1934), pp. 78–119, 128.

[88] Augustine, *Confessiones* 9.10.

[89] Augustine, *De ordine* 22.18.48, 2.19.51.

[90] Augustine, *Soliloquia* 1.13.22–1.14.24.

[91] Augustine, *Soliloquia* 1.13.23.

[92] Augustine, *Retractiones* 1.4.3.

wisdom".[93] Yet at the time Augustine composed the *Soliloquies*, I posit, he may not have been so much pondering whether there can be truth *apart* from Christ, but rather the dual paths for the educated and the uneducated, the "more than one road" that leads to God's truth. Monica's way, that of the uneducated who nonetheless are faithful Christians, also leads to a heavenly home.

The *Confessions* thus portrays Monica, with all her educational deficiencies, as fully worthy to participate in the experience at Ostia with Augustine. As son and mother here ponder what the eternal life of the saints might be like, they reach out in thought and together touch the eternal wisdom, as Augustine puts it.[94] The scene in the *Confessions* depicting the Ostia "vision" represents in story form the Cassiciacum dialogues' injunction to "embrace Wisdom": here, Monica, despite her lack of education, achieves the summit of the philosopher's quest.

Significantly, the discussion continues with Monica's admission that she no longer clings to the world, that she is ready for death; she does not even care where her body is to be buried, as long as Augustine will remember her "at God's altar". After Monica's death, Augustine's friends report that she had confessed to them at Ostia that she despised life and welcomed death; even if her death were to come while she was on foreign soil, she trusted that God would be able to find her body at the time of the general resurrection.[95] Thus, it seems, the Ostia scene, and Monica's confession, are framed to mirror perfectly the goal of philosophy that Augustine had set out in his Cassiciacum dialogues: her scorning of worldly things, her fearlessness—like Socrates'—in confronting "either discomfort or death".[96] Likewise, Augustine at Cassiciacum had written that when the vision of Beauty appears to the worthy, it will erase from their minds disturbing intellectual problems.[97] In the "vision" at Ostia, Augustine shared that knowledge of Beauty (now, in the *Confessions*, more closely identified with God) with his mother, true philosopher at heart.

---

[93] We might wonder whether Augustine, in the interim, had read (or learned of from reading Ambrose's rejoinders) the Third *Relatio* of Symmachus, pagan senator and literary afficianado, who had used as one of his arguments for the retention of the Altar of Victory in the senate house that "there is not one road to truth". The *Soliloquies* were written a few years after the conflict over the Altar of Victory, but the event is not reported in Augustine's early writings.

[94] Augustine, *Confessiones* 9.10.

[95] Augustine, *Confessiones* 9.10–11.

[96] Augustine, *De ordine* 1.11.32.

[97] Augustine, *De ordine* 2.19.51.

Yet, as Camille Bennett has suggested, it is not Augustine's old "carnal" mother who is here represented, the mother so eager for her son's worldly success and advancement, but a new "spiritual" mother who emerges in the *Confessions* only after Augustine leaves her weeping on the shores of North Africa as he sails away to Italy. Once Monica could renounce her all-too-human desire for long life, and for Augustine to marry and have children (the physical route to immortality), she could become a new, spiritualized mother. She is now fit to share the vision at Ostia with Augustine and to be represented as engaging in philosophical discussions with him and his friends. She has been born to a new life and, more importantly for future readers, she has been granted a new representation.[98]

Is there then no "real" Monica—or for that matter, no "real" Augustine? We are reduced to this option only if we cling to the notion that ancient treatises are transparent to the events and people they depict. But if we abandon that view, and accept, with literary theorists, that there is no such thing as "transparent" literature, we still have a "life" of Monica, but one whose representation is itself molded by literature. This does not, I posit, make it less of a "life"—although, to be sure, it is a "life" of a different sort, a "textualized life", a "life" different from that which we are used to encountering in church history textbooks.

Has then this "lady (Monica) vanished"? If this means, "can we recover her pure and simple from texts?", my answer is "no". But that is not the last word: she leaves her "traces", through whose exploration, as they are imbedded in a larger social-linguistic framework, she lives on. "Afterlife" comes in different forms—or so we should know from the study of Christian history and theology.

BIBLIOGRAPHY

Appleby, Joyce, Hunt, Lynn and Jacob, Margaret, *Telling the Truth about History* (New York/London, 1994).
Arendt, Hannah, "The Concept of History: Ancient and Modern", in Hannah Arendt, *Between Past and Future: Six Exercises in Political Thought* (New York/London, 1961), pp. 41–90.
Baer, Jr., Richard A., *Philo's Use of the Categories of Male and Female*, Arbeiten zur Literatur und Geschichte des hellenistischen Judentums 3 (Leiden, 1970).

---

[98] Camille Bennett, "The Conversion of Vergil: The Aeneid in Augustine's Confessions", *Revue des Études Augustiniennes* 34 (1988), pp. 63–4.

Barthes, Roland, "The Discourse of History", transl. Stephen Bann, *Comparative Criticism: A Yearbook*, vol. 3, ed. E.S. Shaffer (Cambridge, 1981; French original of this essay, 1967), pp. 7–20.

Beard, Charles, "That Noble Dream", *AHR* 41 (1935), pp. 74–87.

Bennett, Camille, "The Conversion of Vergil: The Aeneid in Augustine's Confessions", *Revue des Études Augustiniennes* 34 (1988), pp. 47–69.

Berkhofer, Jr., Robert E., *Beyond the Great Story: History as Text and Discourse* (Cambridge/London, 1995).

Bonner, Gerald, "Augustine's Attitude to Women and 'Amicitia'", *Homo Spiritalis: Festgabe für Luc Verheijen OSA*, eds. Cornelius Mayer, Karl Heinz Chelius (Würzburg, 1987), pp. 259–75.

Bowersock, G.W., *Fiction as History: Nero to Julian*, Sather Classical Lectures 58 (Berkeley/Los Angeles/London, 1994).

Bunzl, Martin, *Real History: Reflections on Historical Practice* (London/New York, 1997).

Cameron, Averil (ed.), *History as Text: The Writing of Ancient History* (Chapel Hill/London, 1989).

Cary, Phillip, "What Licentius Learned: A Narrative Reading of the Cassiciacum Dialogues", *Augustinian Studies* 29 (1998), pp. 141–63.

Chartier, Roger, *Cultural History: Between Practices and Representations*, transl. Lydia G. Cochrane (Ithaca, 1988; French original of this essay, 1987).

Clark, Elizabeth A., "The Lady Vanishes: Dilemmas of a Feminist Historian After the Linguistic Turn", *Church History* 67 (1998), pp. 1–31.

———, "Theory and Practice in Late Ancient Asceticism: Jerome, Chrysostom, and Augustine", *Journal of Feminist Studies in Religion* 5 (1989), pp. 25–46.

Courcelle, Pierre, *Recherches sur les Confessions de Saint Augustin* (Paris, 1968; 2nd ed.)

Coyle, J. Kevin, "In Praise of Monica: A Note on the Ostia Experience of *Confessions* IX", *Augustinian Studies* 13 (1982), pp. 87–96.

Dray, William H., "Point of View in History", in William H. Dray, *On History and Philosophers of History*, Philosophy of History and Culture 2 (Leiden, 1989), pp. 54–72; original of this essay published in *Clio* 7 (1978), pp. 265–83.

Fredriksen, Paula, "Paul and Augustine: Conversion Narratives, Orthodox Traditions, and the Retrospective Self", *JTS* 37 (1986), pp. 3–34.

Harlan, David, "Intellectual History and the Return of Literature", *AHR* 94 (1989), pp. 581–609.

Henry, Paul, *Plotin et l'Occident* (Louvain, 1934).

———, *La Vision d'Ostie: Sa place dans la vie et l'oeuvre de Saint Augustin* (Paris, 1938).

Iggers, Georg G., *Historiography in the Twentieth Century: From Scientific Objectivity to the Postmodern Challenge* (Hanover, N.H./London, 1997; original German edition, 1993).

Jacoby, Russell, "A New Intellectual History?", *AHR* 97 (1992), pp. 405–24.

Krieger, Leonard, *Ranke: The Meaning of History* (Chicago/London, 1977).

Lionnet, Françoise, *Autobiographical Voices: Race, Gender, Self-Portraiture* (Ithaca/London, 1989).

Luce, T.J., *The Greek Historians* (London/New York, 1997).

Momigliano, Arnaldo, "The Rhetoric of History and the History of Rhetoric: On Hayden White's Tropes", *Comparative Criticism: A Yearbook*, vol. 3, ed. E.S. Shaffer (Cambridge 1981), pp. 259–68.

Novick, Peter, *That Noble Dream: The "Objectivity Question" and the American Historical Profession* (Cambridge, 1988).

O'Donnell, James, *Augustine. Confessions*, 3 vols. (Oxford, 1992).

Orr, Linda, "The Revenge of Literature: A History of History", *New Literary History* 18 (1986), pp. 1–22.

Power, Kim, *Veiled Desire: Augustine on Women* (New York, 1996).

Scott, Joan, *Gender and the Politics of History* (New York, 1988).

————, *Only Paradoxes to Offer: French Feminists and the Rights of Man* (Cambridge/London, 1996).

Shaw, Brent D., "The Family in Antiquity: The Experience of Augustine", *Past and Present* 115 (1987), pp. 3–51.

Smith, Theodore Clarke, "The Writing of American History in America from 1884 to 1934", *AHR* 40 (1935), pp. 439–49.

Stock, Brian, *Augustine the Reader: Meditation, Self-Knowledge, and the Ethics of Interpretation* (Cambridge/London, 1996).

Strout, Cushing, "Border Crossings: History, Fiction, and *Dead Certainties*", *History and Fiction* 31 (1992), pp. 154–62.

Veyne, Paul, *Writing History: Essay on Epistemology*, transl. Mina Moore-Rinvolucri (Middletown, Conn., 1984; French original, 1971).

White, Hayden, "The Burden of History", in Hayden White, *Tropics of Discourse: Essays in Cultural Criticism* (Baltimore/London, 1978; original of this essay, 1966), pp. 27–50.

Woodman, A.J., *Rhetoric in Classical Historiography: Four Studies* (London/Sydney/Portland, 1988).

PART TWO

THE STRUGGLE FOR AUTHORITY

MAGI AND VISIONARIES IN GNOSTICISM

Alastair H.B. Logan

University of Exeter

Gnosticism is a notoriously hard beast to define, very much the "Hydra-headed monster" of which Irenaeus complained eighteen centuries ago![1] Scholars have pointed out that the very term is a nineteenth century neologism, and a recent commentator, Michael Williams, has argued very forcefully in his book *Rethinking "Gnosticism"*,[2] that the category as usually defined (e.g. in terms of dualism, anticosmicism, reverse or protest exegesis of the Old Testament, libertine versus ascetic attitudes etc.) is dubious, if not misleading and even false. Instead he prefers to talk of "biblical-demiurgical movements". We may not entirely agree with his diagnosis: I myself have attempted to identify a definite movement which called itself "Gnostic", which Irenaeus, Plotinus and Epiphanius knew, the latter two certainly from personal acquaintance, and which was probably responsible for the Nag Hammadi Library.[3] But one significant contribution Williams makes in his book is to apply the insights of social scientists, particularly those of his university colleague in the University of Washington in Seattle, Rodney Stark, about the nature and dynamics of religious movements to the Gnostic phenomenon.[4] In this paper I would like to expand and develop these insights with reference to the question of authority and figures of authority in Gnosticism (I still prefer and would defend the legitimacy of the term!). I want to look at the figures of magus and visionary in certain Gnostic movements, particularly Simon Magus, Valentinus and Marcus the Magus.

Williams refers primarily to the distinction between church and sect in terms of "ideal types" pioneered by Ernst Troeltsch, a pupil

---

[1] *Adversus Haereses* 1.30.15.

[2] Michael A. Williams, *Rethinking "Gnosticism". An Argument for Dismantling a Dubious Category* (Princeton, 1996).

[3] See Alastair H.B. Logan, *Gnostic Truth and Christian Heresy* (Edinburgh, 1996).

[4] Williams, *Rethinking "Gnosticism"*, pp. 109ff., pp. 219f. etc., with particular reference to Rodney Stark and William Sims Bainbridge, *The Future of Religion. Secularization, Revival, and Cult Formation* (Berkeley/Los Angeles/London, 1985).

of Max Weber.[5] But Troeltsch's "ideal types" with their half a dozen characteristics have proved impossible to use for theorizing. Thus, in a pioneering article, Benton Johnson narrowed down the definitions to a single variable: tension within sociocultural environment; churches accept their social environment, sects reject it.[6] Building on Stark's refining of this categorization in terms of churches being closer to the low tension pole and sects to the high, and the latter's tendency to become more church-like, sparking off new sects desiring greater tension with the social environment, Williams differentiates "sect movements" (e.g. Marcionites and Montanists) from "church movements" (e.g. Valentinians and Basilideans).[7]

Williams also refers to the recent attempt by Alan Scott to make use of the further categorization by Stark and William Sims Bainbridge of the cult as distinct from church and sect. The latter define a sect as a schismatic deviant movement which has broken off from another religious body to revive or re-establish an old faith, while they define cults as nonschismatic deviant groups which are innovatory, introducing an alien (external) religion or inventing a new indigenous one. They proceed to distinguish three types of contemporary cult: audience cults, client cults and cult movements. The first are literary, involving no formal organization or group commitment to a dogma (e.g. astrology etc.); the second involve a therapist-client relationship (e.g. psychoanalysis etc.), while only the third are genuinely religious, seeking to satisfy all the religious needs of believers and in extreme forms excluding membership in other groups.[8]

Scott suggests that the "Sethian" Gnostic sect Hans-Martin Schenke and others claim to have identified from a number of Nag Hammadi and related treatises[9] is more like an audience cult, based on texts

---

[5] E. Troeltsch, *The Social Teaching of the Christian Churches* 1 (London, 1931), pp. 331–43.

[6] B. Johnson, "On Church and Sect", *American Sociological Review* 28 (1963), pp. 539–49 esp. p. 542.

[7] Williams, *Rethinking "Gnosticism"*, pp. 109ff.

[8] Stark, Bainbridge, *The Future of Religion*, pp. 24–30.

[9] Cf. H.-M. Schenke, "Das sethianische System nach Nag-Hammadi-Handschriften", *Studia Coptica*, ed. P. Nagel (Berlin, 1974), pp. 165–73; idem, "The Phenomenon and Significance of Gnostic Sethianism", *The Rediscovery of Gnosticism*, vol. 2: *Sethian Gnosticism*, ed. Bentley Layton (Leiden, 1981), pp. 588–616; J.D. Turner, "Sethian Gnosticism: A Literary History", *Nag Hammadi, Gnosticism, and Early Christianity*, eds. C.W. Hedrick, R. Hodgson Jr. (Peabody MA, 1986), pp. 55–86. For a critique of this thesis see particularly F. Wisse, "Stalking Those Elusive Sethians", *The Rediscovery of Gnosticism*, vol. 2: *Sethian Gnosticism*, ed. Bentley Layton (Leiden, 1981), pp. 563–78.

as objects of individual meditation, than a cult movement or sect.[10] While Williams admits the validity of Scott's application of the term "cult" to *some* of the relevant circles, he objects to Scott's characterization of Sethian and other groups as highly deviant and in high tension with their environment, appealing to "church movements" like the Valentinians.[11]

However, neither Williams nor Scott have sufficiently taken in the full import of the Stark-Bainbridge definitions: Williams still treats his biblical-demiurgical movements as basically sects, of which some are more churchlike than others, rather than as cults, which I will argue is more accurate, certainly as far as my examples go. And Scott has overlooked the communal, exclusive and sacramental—in a word essentially religious—character of groups such as the Sethians, whom I prefer to call Gnostics, and their library. Indeed one simply has to ask the question in terms of the Stark-Bainbridge definitions of sect and cult to see that "cult movement" seems most appropriate. To supporters of the majority view that Gnosticism emerged from Judaism,[12] and of the minority opinion which sees it as an offshoot of Christianity,[13] one has to pose the question: is it then a schismatic, revival movement harking back to the past (a sect), or not rather a new religious movement or movements, offering new answers to old problems (a cult)? Here the comparison with Marcionitism is particularly revealing: Marcionitism is clearly sectarian, a protest movement within Christianity harking back to the pure message of Jesus and his Father, the God of Love, and to Paul's understanding of the faith. No wonder Marcion was excommunicated and expelled from the Church! Valentinus, on the other hand, even if Tertullian at one point lumps him in with Marcion as "once

---

[10] Alan B. Scott, "Churches or Books? Sethian Social Organization", *JECS* 3 (1995), pp. 109–22. Cf. also F. Wisse, "The Nag Hammadi Library and the Heresiologists", *Vig. Chr.* 25 (1971), pp. 205–23.

[11] Williams, *Rethinking "Gnosticism"*, p. 113.

[12] Cf. e.g. K. Rudolph, "Randerscheinungen des Judentums und das Problem der Entstehung des Gnostizismus", *Kairos* 9 (1967), pp. 105–22; idem, *Gnosis. The Nature and History of Gnosticism* (Edinburgh, 1984), pp. 276ff.; G.W. MacRae, "The Jewish Background of the Gnostic Sophia Myth", *Novum Testamentum* 12 (1970), pp. 86–101; G.A.G. Stroumsa, *Another Seed. Studies in Gnostic Mythology*, Nag Hammadi Studies 24 (Leiden, 1984); Henry A. Green, *The Economic and Social Origins of Gnosticism*, SBL Dissertation Series 77 (Atlanta, 1985); Pheme Perkins, *Gnosticism and the New Testament* (Minneapolis, 1993), esp. Part 1.

[13] Cf. e.g. S. Pétrement, *A Separate God. The Christian Origins of Gnosticism* (London, 1991).

and again cast out (*semel iterum ejecti*)" of the Church,[14] he never unambiguously describes as excommunicate and grudgingly concedes almost became a bishop in Rome.[15] However I do think Stark and Bainbridge are wrong when they describe Manichaeism as a sect movement.[16] Although Mani was expelled from his Jewish-Christian baptizing sect, his was a new religion, not a revival of an old. What began as a cult became a world religion, as does sometimes happen.

How then can these insights be applied to the subject of my paper, magi and visionaries in Gnosticism? Williams has appealed to their value in illuminating an ancient religious phenomenon or phenomena, and with the usual caveats and reservations I suggest they may illuminate my topic too. Naturally Stark and Bainbridge's suggestions remain models and hypotheses, and the evidence about Gnosticism is notoriously thin, elusive and partial, but the value of applying their analysis will lie in the explanatory power of the models. Elsewhere in their book Stark and Bainbridge identify three models of cult formation: the *psychopathological*, the *entrepreneurial* and the *subcultural-evolutionary*.[17] The *psychopathological* model, used by many anthropologists and ethnopsychiatrists, sees cults as novel cultural responses to forms of personal and societal crisis. New cults are invented by individuals suffering from forms of mental illness. Typically—and this will be important later—these individuals achieve their novel visions during psychotic episodes in which the individual invents a new package of compensators to meet his own needs.[18] The individual's illness commits them to their new vision, either because their hallucinations appear to demonstrate its truth or because compelling needs demand immediate satisfaction. After the episode the individual will be most likely to succeed in forming a cult around their vision if the society contains many others with similar problems. Not surprisingly, such cults most often succeed in periods of crisis in society. This model, of course, is supported by the traditional Freudian view of all religions as mere projections of neurotic wish fulfilment or psychotic delusions!

---

[14] *Praesc. haer.* 30.
[15] Cf. *Adv. Val.* 4; C. Markschies, *Valentinus Gnosticus? Untersuchungen zur valentinianischen Gnosis mit einem Kommentar zu den Fragmenten Valentins* (Tübingen, 1992), p. 307.
[16] Stark, Bainbridge, *The Future of Religion*, p. 113.
[17] Ibidem, pp. 171–88.
[18] A compensator is the belief that a reward will be obtained in the distant future or in some other context which cannot be immediately verified; ibidem, p. 6.

In a famous paper in 1956, Anthony Wallace suggested that perhaps all major religions, which he classes as *revitalization movements*,
originated according to this model. Indeed he goes on to claim that:

> With very few exceptions, every religious revitalization movement with
> which I am acquainted has been originally conceived in one or more
> hallucinatory visions by a single individual. A supernatural being appears
> to the prophet-to-be, explains his own and his society's troubles as
> entirely or partly the result of a violation of certain rules and promises
> the individual and society revitalization if the injunctions are followed
> and rituals practised, but personal and social catastrophe if not.[19]

However, social scientists have had to admit that not all cult founders
have been ill or mad, so alternative models are required. Stark and
Bainbridge propose as a second model the *entrepreneur* model. The
chief ideas of this, they suggest, are that cults are businesses which
provide a product for their customers and receive payment in return.
These products are novel or at least repackaged to appear new. Such
a process requires a supply to be manufactured and sold, the work
of entrepreneurs, motivated by profit. People enter the cult business
because they see how profitable it can be, particularly if they have
been involved in a successful cult already. Successful entrepreneurs
require skills and experience, most easily gained by previous cult
experience. Since the most successful sales are of existing compo-
nents in new configurations or further developed, cults tend to cluster in lineages, linked by individual entrepreneurs who begin in one
cult and leave to found their own, and such cults bear strong "family resemblances". Ideas for new products can come from any cultural source or personal experience, but the skilful entrepreneur
experiments carefully and only incorporates new products if market
response is favourable.[20]

While the first two models stress the individual, the third model,
again Stark and Bainbridge's own, the *subculture-evolution* model, emphasizes group interaction processes. It suggests that cults can emerge
without authoritative leaders, achieving radical developments by many
small steps. Stark and Bainbridge maintain that cults are expressions
of novel social systems, usually small, but composed of a few intimately interacting individuals. They are the result of sidetracked or

---

[19] A.F.C. Wallace, "Revitalization Movements", *American Anthropologist* 58 (1956),
pp. 273–82.
[20] Stark, Bainbridge, *The Future of Religion*, pp. 178–82.

failed collective attempts to obtain scarce or nonexistent rewards.
This results in their generating and exchanging compensators. If this
exchange of rewards and compensators becomes sufficiently intense,
the group will in extreme cases socially implode. Once separated to
some degree from external control, the evolving cult develops and
consolidates a new culture, energized by the need to facilitate the
exchange of rewards and compensators, and inspired by essentially
accidental factors. The end point of successful cult evolution is a
novel religious culture embodied in a distinct social group which has
to cope with the problem of winning new members.[21] I have tried
to simplify the social scientific jargon, not perhaps with great success!

So what has this got to do with magi and visionaries, with Simon,
Valentinus and Marcus? Quite a lot in fact! All three, I would suggest, are best seen as cult founders, and the three models outlined,
which Stark and Bainbridge insist are compatible and not mutually
exclusive, can help illuminate the sketchy and fragmented picture of
the three we get from the heresiologists. Of course Simon and Marcus
have the nickname "*magos*", but we should not be misled by that. On
the one hand one would expect some magical claim from any self-
respecting religious leader in the ancient world, from Moses onwards,[22]
and equally the charge of magic against opponents from Christian
heresiologists. It is perhaps significant that Irenaeus (or his heresiological source) depicts the followers of Simon, Basilides and Carpocrates
in remarkably similar fashion as adepts of magic.[23] However, although
the term "*magos*" may not have been Simon or Marcus' own self-
designation, but a device of their opponents to discredit them, it may
nevertheless, as Filoramo suggests, retain something of the truth, hint-
ing at the charismatic power of such figures, ancient and modern.[24]

But can the claim that Simon *founded* the Simonian cult be sub-
stantiated in the light of the meagre and biased evidence? Certainly
Acts suggests his enormous influence on the Samaritans (cf. 8:9–11),
and Justin Martyr, a near neighbor in Samaria, probably got his

---

[21] Ibidem, pp. 183–8.
[22] Cf. Exod. 7:1–8:20.
[23] Cf. *Adv. Haer.* 1.23.4, 24.5, 25.3. See below for similar charges levelled at
Marcus and his followers (1.13.5). Their pagan contemporary, Lucian, levels similar
charges against Alexander of Abonoteichos and his admirer and teacher (*Alexander*, 5).
On the later view of Simon's full-blown magical, indeed divine powers, cf. Ps. Clem.
Rec. 2.5, 9; 3.47f.
[24] Giovanni Filoramo, *A History of Gnosticism* (Oxford, 1990), pp. 153f. John Fowles'
novel, *The Magus*, suggests a modern equivalent.

information about Simon being worshiped as a god in Rome, statue and all, from Simonians there.[25] And although Origen claims not to be able to find more than thirty Simonians in the whole world, with very few in Palestine,[26] Eusebius of Caesarea refers to his followers practising baptism and insinuating themselves into the Church, as well as cultivating Simon and Helen's images and possessing written oracles.[27] The survival of the movement thus seems reasonably attested, and if Simon himself did not found it, who else would have done so after his death and failure to rise again, something he had apparently claimed he would do?[28] And why would the claim, probably as early as Justin, that he was father of all Christian heresies have arisen if he and his followers had not come into contact and competition with the nascent Christian movement?

On the other hand, the way he is portrayed does not imply that he is some kind of Samaritan heretic or schismatic, founding a revivalist sect, claiming to be the Messiah. Rather he is presented as a charismatic, prophetic figure making the claim to be God ("the Great Power") himself, and offering his followers salvation, perhaps even immortality. His location in Samaria, where no one religion seems to have been predominant, would also fit the Stark-Bainbridge thesis that cults tend to develop where organized religion is weak and where large numbers of people have drifted away from all ties to it.[29] Proponents of the psychopathology model would have a field day with Simon and consider him psychotic, although of course we have no evidence that he saw visions.[30] However, if we accept that the picture in Acts has some verisimilitude, Simon's attempt to buy the power of the Holy Spirit from the apostles suggests the entrepreneur model. Certainly Simon's promise of salvation, even immortality, as reward for worshiping him, is the ultimate religious prize, what Stark and Bainbridge would call the most general religious

---

[25] Cf. *1 Apol.* 26.1–3; 56; *2 Apol.* 15; *Dial.* 120.

[26] *Contra Cels.* 1.57. His figure may be a garbled recollection of the Simon-Dositheus tradition (cf. Ps. Clem. *Hom.* 2.23f.). See also 6.11 (only 30 Dositheans!) and 5.62, attesting Celsus' knowledge of the existence of Simonians.

[27] Eusebius, *Hist. Eccl.* 2.1.11f., 13.1, 6f.

[28] Cf. Ps. Hipp. *Ref.* 6.20.3. Note the claim of Menander, Simon's successor, in Justin, *1 Apol.* 26.4.

[29] Cf. Stark, Bainbridge, *The Future of Religion*, pp. 396f., p. 445 etc.

[30] However the later view of Simon in the Ps. Clementines has him deceived by demonic phantasms in his claim to see spiritual beings, cf. *Rec.* 2.16f., and appealing to imagination as a vehicle of cognition of the divine, cf. *Rec.* 2.71.

compensator, and it is not surprising that his cult should have reached Rome, centre and magnet of the Empire.

Max Weber's concepts of "charisma" and the charismatic leader[31] have been much criticized by social scientists, but interestingly enough in his description of the charismatic prophet he gives a word-for-word picture of Simon Magus, as a magician with power to raise the dead and even rise himself. After his death the development proceeds without and beyond him. If he is to live on in some manner he must himself become the object of a cult, which means the incarnation of a god.[32] And Stark and Bainbridge allow that charisma as "an unusual capacity to influence others, to inspire intense liking and respect" might be the most useful definition of the term if used at all to describe cult founders. They can only succeed if they have unusual social skills. Indeed simple arithmetic, say Stark and Bainbridge, reveals that the vast majority of cult founders must have been extremely skilled at building strong interpersonal ties with others, and in this sense deserve to be called charismatic.[33] Surely Simon Magus belongs in this category as charismatic, as a skilled entrepreneur with dazzling rewards and compensators to offer. But finally, the fact that his failure to rise after death does not seem to have destroyed his cult movement perhaps suggests elements of the third model, of *subculture-evolution*, whereby the followers interact to generate new rewards and compensators, develop a myth (i.e. of Simon and Helen) and produce a new movement. Menander, on the other hand, would seem to be an entrepreneur who left Simon's cult to found his own similar one.

What, second, of Valentinus? There is no evidence of him being described as a magus or practising magic, but, according to the author of the *Refutatio* (Hippolytus, or rather Pseudo-Hippolytus),[34] he was a visionary.[35] The author records how Valentinus saw a small

---

[31] See M. Weber, *Economy and Society. An Outline of Interpretive Sociology*, eds. G. Roth, C. Wittich (Berkeley/Los Angeles/London, 1978), e.g. ch. III sections IV and V of vol. 1, part 1.

[32] Ibidem, p. 467.

[33] Stark, Bainbridge, *The Future of Religion*, pp. 356f.

[34] Allen Brent, *Hippolytus and the Roman Church in the Third Century. Communities in Tension before the Emergence of a Monarch-Bishop*, Supplements to *Vigiliae Christianae* 31 (Leiden, 1995). Esp. chs. 4 and 5, argues persuasively that the author of the *Refutatio* is not Hippolytus, the author of the *Contra Noetum*, but an earlier member of his school, and that the *Refutatio* was completed around 218, before the death of Callistus.

[35] Cf. G. Quispel, "The Original Doctrine of Valentine", *Vig. Chr.* 1 (1947), p. 47.

child, newly born, and asked him who he was, and he answered that he was the Logos.[36] Then he added to this an imposing myth and on this, says Ps.-Hippolytus, he wants to base the "sect" (*hairesis*) that was founded by him.[37] Filoramo rightly compares Valentinus' vision, as an internal spiritual experience and decisive turning point, to that of Paul; a meeting with Christ, which radically transforms his life.[38] The "imposing myth" Ps.-Hippolytus mentions is, I believe, the myth of Irenaeus' Gnostics (or Barbelognostics and Ophites) and of the *Apocryphon of John* and related texts from Nag Hammadi, of the Naassenes of Ps.-Hippolytus, of the group responsible for the *hypogeum* under the Viale Manzoni in Rome with its initiation chamber and fascinating wall paintings,[39] and the Christian group or *hairesis* which attended Plotinus' lectures in Rome in the 260s. Like a smart entrepreneur Valentinus adopted and adapted an existing successful cult myth. And the reference to a vision seems entirely plausible in the light of the psychopathological model and the comments of Anthony Wallace.

But we need not consider Valentinus ill or mad. In a more recent paper discussing the three models and criticizing the tendency of social scientists to explain religious innovation in terms of illness, Stark has argued that there is room for revelations involving neither craziness nor corruption.[40] Thus there is very little empirical evidence

---

On visions in this period see R. Lane Fox, *Pagans and Christians in the Mediterranean World from the Second Century A.D. to the Conversion of Constantine* (Harmondsworth, 1988), ch. 8.

[36] Cf. A.F.J. Klijn, "Jewish Christianity in Egypt", *The Roots of Egyptian Christianity*, Studies in Antiquity and Christianity, eds. Birger A. Pearson, James E. Goehring (Philadelphia, 1986), pp. 169f., on the Logos Christology rooted in Jewish Wisdom he finds in four early Egyptian Christian texts: *Epistula Apostolorum, Sibylline Oracles, Testimony of Truth* (NHC IX,3) and *Apocalypse of Peter*—all probably later than Valentinus.

[37] *Ref.* 6.42.2.

[38] Filoramo, *History of Gnosticism*, p. 156. Valentinus' psalm (*Ref.* 6.37.6–8) evidently reflects another visionary experience.

[39] See W.H.C. Frend, *The Archaeology of Early Christianity* (London, 1996), pp. 209–11; C. Cecchelli, *Monumenti cristiano-eretici di Roma* (Rome, 1944); J. Carcopino, *De Pythagore aux Apôtres. Études sur la conversion du Monde Romain* (Paris, 1956); G. Wilpert, "Le pitture dell'ipogeo di Aurelio Felicissimo presso il Viale Manzoni in Roma", *Atti della Pontificia Accademia Romana di Archeologica* 3.1.2 (Rome, 1924), pp. 1–43. But Paul Corby Finney, "Did Gnostics make Pictures?", *The Rediscovery of Gnosticism*, vol. 1: *The School of Valentinus*, ed. Bentley Layton (Leiden, 1980), p. 447, denies Gnostic provenance.

[40] Rodney Stark, "How sane people talk to the gods: A rational theory of revelations", *Innovation in Religious Traditions*, eds. Michael A. Williams, Collett Cox and Martin S. Jaffee (Berlin/New York, 1992), pp. 19–34, quote p. 21.

to support (1) the psychopathological model, and as regards (2) the entrepreneurial model, very few of apparently sane recipients of revelations are crooks, while (3) the subculture-evolution model is incapable of filling the gaps. Thus Stark's thesis is that normal people can, through entirely normal means, have revelations, if not sufficiently profound to serve as the basis of new religions. But then, he continues, "enter genius". Unusually creative individuals, he argues, will sometimes create profound revelations and will externalize the source of this new culture. Novel revelations will most likely come to persons of deep religious concerns who perceive shortcomings in the conventional faiths, something that increases during periods of social crisis. During such periods the numbers of people who receive novel revelations and the number willing to accept them is maximized. The more reinforcement the recipient receives, the more likely they are to have more revelations. And the interaction between successful founder and their followers tends to amplify heresy. The result of these processes and interactions is more radical revelations. As Stark notes, this model of revelations is now linked to the subcultural-evolution model.[41]

Now this scenario corresponds very strikingly, I suggest, to the picture of Valentinus and his followers given both by the heresiologists and by primary Valentinian texts like Ptolemy's *Letter to Flora*. From the fragments Valentinus comes over as a very attractive and creative personality, the author not only of letters, homilies and books, but also of one of the most evocative myths of all time, if building on an existing, but much less sophisticated Gnostic one. Stark and Bainbridge rightly point to the higher educational level of those founding and attracted to cult movements.[42] And Valentinus has been rightly considered a pioneer of the assimilation of Christianity to the most sophisticated philosophical movement of the time, Platonism.[43] Yet he does not strike one as a forceful, magnetic, charismatic, entrepreneurial figure like Simon Magus, but as a winning, charming personality concerned to interact with his disciples and correspondents. Now what is striking about Valentinus and the

---

[41] Ibidem, pp. 22–9.
[42] Stark, Bainbridge, *The Future of Religion*, pp. 405ff.
[43] Cf. Irenaeus, *Adv. Haer.* 2.14.3; Tertullian, *Praesc. Haer.* 7, 30; *Carn.* 20; Ps. Hipp. *Ref.* 6.21.1, 29.1, 37.1; G.C. Stead, "In Search of Valentinus", *The Rediscovery of Gnosticism*, vol. 1: *The School of Valentinus*, ed. Bentley Layton (Leiden, 1980), pp. 75–102; Markschies, *Valentinus*, Excursus V.

Valentinians is not only the large number of them we know by name compared to other groups, but also the fertility of their imaginations, ever producing new variants on Valentinus' original system.[44] Yet oddly enough they do not tend to break away to form new spinoff cults; Valentinus' original myth with its Pleroma of thirty aeons and system of male-female syzygies remains paramount or at least always recognisable behind the ever more complex and daring speculations of his pupils.

But what were the shortcomings in the conventional faiths or the societal crisis posited by Stark that might have given rise to Valentinus' revelations and cult movement? Notice that Valentinus came from Alexandria and went to Rome, cities where again, as with Samaria, there was no dominant religion. Further, and more importantly, in Alexandria, Diaspora Judaism (including Jewish-Christian groups)[45] had evidently been all but wiped out by the ruthless crushing of the messianic uprising of Jews in Cyrenaica, Egypt and Cyprus of A.D. 115–117.[46] And, as Stark and Bainbridge have also pointed out, increasingly secularized Jews, of whatever era, are strikingly more liable to join cult movements.[47] The crisis among Jews over another failure of their God to send a messiah who would save his people, coupled with a related crisis of faith among Christians, victims of persecution both by Jews for their messianic beliefs and by pagans for their similarity to Jews and finding it increasingly difficult, a difficulty spectacularly highlighted by Marcion, to reconcile the God of the Old Testament and of the Jews with the loving Father of Jesus Christ, may have been the final catalyst which provoked Valentinus' vision of the unknown God and his revealer, the heavenly Christ. Certainly the system of Basilides, Valentinus' older Alexandrian contemporary, as pictured by Irenaeus, is evidently and deliberately hostile to the Jews, their law, their prophets and their

[44] Cf. Irenaeus, *Adv. Haer.* 1.11.1–12.3.

[45] On the likely Jewish-Christian character of early Egyptian Christianity see e.g. C.H. Roberts, *Manuscript, Society and Belief in Early Egyptian Christianity*, Schweich Lectures 1977 (London, 1979), esp. ch. 3.

[46] Cf. Eusebius, *Hist. Eccl.* 4.2–4; Dio Cassius, *Epitome*, 68.32.1–3; Appian, *Bell. civ.* 2.90; M. Hengel, "Messianische Hoffnung und politischer 'Radikalismus' in der 'jüdisch-hellenistischen Diaspora': Zur Frage der Voraussetzungen des jüdisches Aufstandes unter Trajan 115–117", *Apocalypticism in the Mediterranean World and the Near East*, ed. D. Hellholm (Tübingen, 1983), pp. 655–86; J.M.G. Barclay, *Jews in the Mediterranean Diaspora: From Alexander to Trajan (323 B.C.E.–117 C.E.)* (Edinburgh, 1996), pp. 78–81, pp. 225–8.

[47] Stark, Bainbridge, *The Future of Religion*, pp. 400–3.

God, and Basilides' dig at the Jewish God's desire to subjugate the other nations to his own people and their consequent alienation from the Jews seems best interpreted as an allusion to the revolt of 115–117.[48]

But Valentinus, although also showing traces of hostility, is more concerned to fill the vacuum left by the eclipse of Jewish and Jewish-Christian views of God as Creator, Lawgiver and Redeemer of his people, by stressing instead the Pauline understanding of the Father of Jesus Christ, the God of grace and election, and synthesizing that with more philosophical, Platonic views of God and the cosmos.[49] Indeed Valentinus may have been one of the first to champion Paul and Pauline theology in Egypt.[50] We noted Filoramo's apt comparison of Valentinus' vision to that of Paul, and a case has been made to see esoteric exegesis of Romans in particular as a—if not the—key to Valentinianism.[51] Thus the Old Testament God is not demonized but demoted to an ignorant and arrogant Platonic Demiurge, the God of creation and law. And I think some support for this interpretation can be found, not only in the allusive fragments of Valentinus as echoed in the *Excerpta ex Theodoto* and the account of Ps. Hippolytus,[52] but also in the more sophisticated argument of the *Letter to Flora* of Valentinus' Roman pupil, Ptolemy, preserved by Epiphanius.[53] For the problem highlighted by Ptolemy (who makes

---

[48] Cf. Irenaeus, *Adv. Haer.* 1.24.3–6. Note his reference to the Christ and revealing comment "no longer Jews . . .".

[49] On the new opportunities offered Christians by the crushed revolt see Roberts, *Manuscript*, pp. 58f. On Valentinus as a "biblical Platonist" see Stead, "In Search of Valentinus", esp. p. 78.

[50] Cf. Roberts, *Manuscript*, pp. 45, 62, 71, on the dearth of Pauline writings among the earliest papyri. Markschies, *Valentinus*, 200, notes a direct citation of Rom. 2:14f. in frg. 2. The *Gospel of Truth* (NHC I), even if not by Valentinus himself, is permeated with Pauline echoes, and Klijn, "Jewish Christianity", p. 174, notes that all four of his early Egyptian post-Valentinus Christian writings are concerned with Paul.

[51] Cf. Elaine H. Pagels, "The Valentinian Claim to Esoteric Exegesis of Romans as Basis for Anthropological Theory", *Vig. Chr.* 26 (1972), pp. 241–58.

[52] Cf. frg. 1 (Clem. Alex. *Strom.* 2.36.2–4: fear of man by his angelic creators and their marring of his creation, implying, against Markschies' thesis, the Gnostic myth and a more negative view of the Demiurge); *Exc. ex Theod.* 33.3–4; 37–8 (the roughness and weakness of Topos, the Demiurge, subdued by Jesus); Ps. Hipp. *Ref.* 6.33 (the ignorance, foolishness and exclusivist arrogance of the Demiurge); *ValExpos* (NHC XI) 37.32–38.39. Conversely, frgs. 2 (Clem. Alex. *Strom.* 2.114.3–6) and 6 (*Strom.* 6.52.3–4) suggest the more Pauline themes of the grace of God and the law written on the heart.

[53] Cf. Epiphanius, *Haer.* 33.3.1–7.10.

significant reference to Paul)[54] and wrestled over by second century Jews and Christians, such as Barnabas, Ignatius, Basilides, Marcion, Carpocrates, Justin and Trypho, was precisely the nature and authority of the Jewish Law and of its divine Lawgiver.

Philo of Alexandria had shown one way for educated Diaspora Jews to preserve monotheism and retain the authority of the Law, namely to give the Pentateuch a Platonizing allegorical interpretation. But that rather rarefied approach and accommodation to Hellenism did not seem to appeal to all Jews, particularly perhaps the local Jews of Alexandria after their catastrophe, and certainly not to many early Christians. The evidence, such as it is, suggests that the latter preferred typology, evinced a simple faith in the concrete figures of Jesus and his Father, the God of love and judgment, acting directly in history, were decidedly ambiguous over the continuing validity of the laws of the Pentateuch and claimed to be the new or true Israel of God.[55]

From the text of the Old Testament interpreted in the light of the words of Jesus, and with passing appeal to Paul as authority, Ptolemy argues that the source of the Law is neither the perfect God and Father of Jesus Christ, nor the Devil, but an intermediate deity, the creator God of righteousness, and that the Law itself is in three parts, one from the Lawgiver, one from Moses and one from the traditions of the elders. Further, the Law given by the Lawgiver is in three parts, the pure legislation fulfilled by the Savior, the law interwoven with injustice, to be destroyed, and the ceremonial law, to be given a spiritual (i.e. allegorical) interpretation. Ptolemy promises a future explanation of how the three types of natures thus revealed derived from a single principle, namely an exposition of the Valentinian myth, when Flora is properly initiated, "counted worthy of the apostolic tradition which we also have received by succession, because we can prove all our statements from the teaching of the Savior."[56]

The Valentinian approach illustrated in Ptolemy, unlike the sectarian rejection of Marcion, might thus appeal to disillusioned, secularized Diaspora Jews as much as to Christians, allowing the former

---

[54] Cf. Idem, 33.5.15, 6.6.

[55] Cf. e.g. the attitudes underlying Stephen's speech in Acts 7 and the *Epistle of Barnabas*. The views of the author of Hebrews may be more Philonic in their Platonic colouring and use of allegory, but they are not representative and no more sympathetic to Philo's defence of the Law.

[56] Epiphanius, *Haer.* 33.7.9.

to preserve the Old Testament as scripture, while relieving them of the awkwardness of the ceremonial law and primitive code of retribution, and solving the problem of the apparent impotence of their God and his latest messiah. In his recent book, *The Rise of Christianity*, Stark intriguingly argues that Jews did not cease to be attracted to Christianity after the first century, but continued as a significant source of Christian converts as late as the fourth century.[57] Conversely, Valentinus' "biblical Platonism" and appeal to Paul's theological program as an alternative to the more Jewish-Christian tendencies of earlier Egyptian Christianity offered a new perspective to Christians disowned by Jews and devastated by Jewish persecution. Valentinus' myth may thus have allowed both Diaspora secularized Jews and Christians, wrestling with each other and with the crudities of the Old Testament God compared to the God of Jesus and the Platonists, a new way forward.[58] The message Valentinus worked out in Alexandria he took with him and spread in the more promising territory of Rome and the West.

Finally I would like to say a brief word about the figure of Marcus, not only dubbed a magus, like Simon, but a visionary, the purported recipient of divine revelation, like Valentinus.[59] As regards his claim to be a *magos* or wonder worker, Irenaeus attributes to Marcus himself what Ps. Hippolytus explains as well-known tricks of magicians or alchemists such as changing the color of wine and filling larger cups to overflowing from smaller.[60] Further he insinuates that it is by demon possession that Marcus is able to prophesy, encouraging his female followers to do the same, to the extent apparently of indulging in *glossolalia*.[61] His final charge as regards magic is that Marcus practises administering love potions and aphrodisiacs to some of his female followers and has sex with them.[62] Although this might be put down to heresiological propaganda since it echoes the charge

---

[57] Rodney Stark, *The Rise of Christianity. A Sociologist Reconsiders History* (Princeton, 1996), ch. 3.

[58] Cf. the similar strategy of Justin, another biblical Platonist arguing with liberal Jews over the proper interpretation of the LXX concerning God, Christ and the Law.

[59] Cf. Irenaeus, *Adv. Haer.* 1.13.1, 14.1.

[60] Irenaeus, *Adv. Haer.* 1.13.2; Ps. Hipp. *Ref.* 6.39.2–3, 40.3–4, with reference either to a lost book, *kata Magon*, or to a lost section of book 4. Cf. also 4.28.13, and Lucian, *Alexander*, 5–7, 12–15.

[61] Irenaeus, *Adv. Haer.* 1.13.3. Irenaeus' picture of Marcus as a precursor of the Antichrist and false prophet has echoes of Paul's denunciation of the *magos* and false prophet Barjesus/Elymas of Acts 13:6–10.

[62] Irenaeus, *Adv. Haer.* 1.13.5.

against the followers of Simon and Carpocrates found in the heresiological catalogue at the end of his first book,[63] Irenaeus does claim that this information has been divulged by Catholic women led astray by Marcus, on their return to "the church of God".[64] Rather like Simon and the contemporary pagan Alexander of Abonoteichos, Marcus comes over as a powerful, charismatic figure, perhaps even a charlatan, with his magic tricks, prophetic claims and way of attracting educated religious women.

As regards Marcus' claim to be a visionary, Irenaeus describes him as "passing himself off as the womb and receptacle of the Sige [the supreme female Valentinian aeon] of Colorbasus [a pupil of Valentinus]". Marcus recounts how Sige descended on him in female form and revealed to him its nature, disclosing to him alone the origin of all things, which it never before had revealed to anyone, either of the gods or men.[65] And Marcus has to go one better than Valentinus: two supreme heavenly female revealers are clearly better than one lower male figure! So we find that Sige reveals another supreme Valentinian female aeon, Truth, who utters the name of Jesus Christ. This is then given a very elaborate exegesis by Sige, not just an *angelus interpres* figure, as is usual in examples of this revelatory genre such as *The Shepherd* of Hermas, but in characteristic Gnostic fashion a form of the supreme divinity itself.[66] As Filoramo points out, both the vision of Marcus and that of Valentinus thus present certain significant features: "they are not allegorical but direct; the auditory element is important; the nature of the soteric [sic!] message is fundamental".[67]

In the light of Irenaeus' account of his views and those of his followers, which comprise a very elaborate speculative expression in terms of letters and numbers of the central themes of Valentinian theology, cosmology and Christology, Marcus has traditionally been considered a disciple of Valentinus,[68] but I consider him sufficiently distinct to treat separately. He seems the classic example of an entrepreneurial cult founder, utilizing material from all sorts of quarters, including earlier successful cult movements, particularly Valentinianism, and attracting high-born, well-educated women, a phenomenon

---

[63] Cf. Irenaeus, *Adv. Haer.* 1.23.4, 25.3.
[64] Irenaeus, *Adv. Haer.* 1.13.5.
[65] Irenaeus, *Adv. Haer.* 1.14.1.
[66] Irenaeus, *Adv. Haer.* 1.14.3ff.
[67] Filoramo, *History of Gnosticism*, p. 237 n. 22.
[68] Cf. Irenaeus, *Adv. Haer.* 1.13–21; Tertellian, *Adv. Val.* 4 etc.

characteristic of cult movements, in that such women tend to be socially isolated and relatively deprived while at the same time being members of the social elite.[69] His vision may have an artificial and borrowed air, and display all too clearly his entrepreneurial skills, but it does suggest the value he and his contemporaries assigned to visions and auditions as sources of authority. Certainly his elaborate speculations, with their deliberate echoes of Pythagorean and mystical Jewish interpretations of letters and numbers, seem to have exercised a considerable hold on various educated but spiritually hungry and rootless groups and individuals, particularly in the urban and populous centres of ancient Mediterranean society.

As a friend of mine who has just completed a dissertation on Marcus recently remarked to me, he is a syncretist, who flits from idea to idea, who ten or twenty years after would be teaching something entirely different. Indeed my friend thinks the closest thing to Marcus today can be found in New Age religious movements, and Marcus' system seems to have had in his time the kind of attraction that pseudo-scientific cults like Scientology have for Western urban society today. And that brings us full circle, back to Stark and Bainbridge on contemporary sects and cults, suggesting, whatever detailed criticisms one may have of Stark's interpretation of early Christianity, the considerable fruitfulness of the social scientific approach to religion in the case of Gnostic figures like Simon, Valentinus and Marcus.

BIBLIOGRAPHY

Barclay, J.M.G., *Jews in the Mediterranean Diaspora: From Alexander to Trajan (323 B.C.E.–117 C.E.)* (Edinburgh, 1996).
Brent, Allen, *Hippolytus and the Roman Church in the Third Century. Communities in Tension before the Emergence of a Monarch-Bishop*, Supplements to *Vigiliae Christianae* 31 (Leiden, 1995).
Carcopino, J., *De Pythagore aux Apôtres. Études sur la conversion du Monde Romain* (Paris, 1956).
Cecchelli, C., *Monumenti cristiano-eretici di Roma* (Rome, 1944).
Filoramo, Giovanni, *A History of Gnosticism* (Oxford, 1990).
Finney, Paul Corby, "Did Gnostics make Pictures?", in *The Rediscovery of Gnosticism*, vol. 1: *The School of Valentinus*, ed. Bentley Layton (Leiden, 1980), pp. 434–54.
Frend, W.H.C., *The Archaeology of Early Christianity* (London, 1996).
Green, Henry A., *The Economic and Social Origins of Gnosticism*, SBL Dissertation Series 77 (Atlanta, 1985).

---

[69] Stark, Bainbridge, *The Future of Religion*, pp. 413–17.

Hengel, M., "Messianische Hoffnung und politischer 'Radikalismus' in der 'jüdisch-hellenistischen Diaspora': Zur Frage der Voraussetzungen des jüdisches Aufstandes unter Trajan 115–117", *Apocalypticism in the Mediterranean World and the Near East*, ed. D. Hellholm (Tübingen, 1983), pp. 655–86.

Johnson, B., "On Church and Sect", *American Sociological Review* 28 (1963), pp. 539–49.

Klijn, A.F.J., "Jewish Christianity in Egypt", *The Roots of Egyptian Christianity*, Studies in Antiquity and Christianity, eds. Birger A. Pearson, James E. Goehring (Philadelphia, 1986), pp. 161–75.

Lane Fox, Robin, *Pagans and Christians in the Mediterranean World from the Second Century A.D. to the Conversion of Constantine* (Harmondsworth, 1988).

Logan, Alastair H.B., *Gnostic Truth and Christian Heresy* (Edinburgh, 1996).

MacRae, G.W., "The Jewish Background of the Gnostic Sophia Myth", *Novum Testamentum* 12 (1970), pp. 86–101.

Markschies, C., *Valentinus Gnosticus? Untersuchungen zur valentinianischen Gnosis mit einem Kommentar zu den Fragmenten Valentins* (Tübingen, 1992).

Pagels, Elaine H., "The Valentinian Claim to Esoteric Exegesis of Romans as Basis for Anthropological Theory", *Vig. Chr.* 26 (1972), pp. 241–58.

Perkins, Pheme, *Gnosticism and the New Testament* (Minneapolis, 1993).

Pétrement, S., *A Separate God. The Christian Origins of Gnosticism* (London, 1991).

Quispel, G., "The Original Doctrine of Valentine", *Vig. Chr.* 1 (1947), pp. 43–73.

Roberts, C.H., *Manuscript, Society and Belief in Early Christian Egypt*, Schweich Lectures 1977 (London, 1979).

Rudolph, K., "Randerscheinungen des Judentums und das Problem der Entstehung des Gnostizismus", *Kairos* 9 (1967), pp. 105–22.

———, *Gnosis. The Nature and History of Gnosticism* (Edinburgh, 1984).

Schenke, H.-M., "Das sethianische System nach Nag-Hammadi-Handschriften", *Studia Coptica*, ed. P. Nagel (Berlin, 1974), pp. 165–73.

———, "The Phenomenon and Significance of Gnostic Sethianism", *The Rediscovery of Gnosticism*, vol. 2: *Sethian Gnosticism*, ed. Bentley Layton (Leiden, 1981), pp. 588–616.

Scott, Alan B., "Churches or Books? Sethian Social Organization", *JECS* 3 (1995), pp. 109–22.

Stark, Rodney, "How Sane People talk to the Gods: A Rational Theory of Revelations", *Innovations in Religious Traditions*, eds. Michael A. Williams, Collett Cox and Martin S. Jaffee (Berlin, 1992), pp. 19–34.

———, *The Rise of Christianity. A Sociologist Reconsiders History* (Princeton, 1996).

———, Bainbridge, William Sims, *The Future of Religion: Secularization, Revival, and Cult Formation* (Berkeley/Los Angeles/London, 1985).

Stead, G.C., "In Search of Valentinus", *The Rediscovery of Gnosticism*, vol. 1: *The School of Valentinus*, ed. Bentley Layton (Leiden, 1980), pp. 75–102.

Stroumsa, G.A.G., *Another Seed. Studies in Gnostic Mythology*, Nag Hammadi Studies 24 (Leiden, 1984).

Troeltsch, E., *The Social Teaching of the Christian Churches* 1 (London, 1931).

Turner, J.D., "Sethian Gnosticism: A Literary History", *Nag Hammadi, Gnosticism, and Early Christianity*, eds. Charles W. Hedrick, Robert Hodgson Jr. (Peabody MA, 1986), pp. 55–86.

Wallace, A.F.C., "Revitalization Movements", *American Anthropologist* 58 (1956), pp. 273–82.

Weber, Max, *Economy and Society. An Outline of Interpretive Sociology*, eds. G. Roth, C. Wittich (Berkeley/Los Angeles/London, 1978).

Williams, Michael A., *Rethinking "Gnosticism". An Argument for Dismantling a Dubious Category* (Princeton, 1996).

Williams, Michael A., Cox, Collett, and Jaffee, Martin S. (eds.), *Innovations in Religious Traditions* (Berlin, 1992).

Wilpert, G., "Le pitture dell'ipogeo di Aurelio Felicissimo presso il Viale Manzoni in Roma", *Atti della Pontificia Accademia Romana di Archeologica* 3.1.2 (Rome, 1924), pp. 1–43.
Wisse, Frederik, "The Nag Hammadi Library and the Heresiologists", *Vig. Chr.* 25 (1971), pp. 205–23.
———, "Stalking Those Elusive Sethians", *The Rediscovery of Gnosticism*, vol. 2: *Sethian Gnosticism*, ed. Bentley Layton (Leiden, 1981), pp. 563–78.

SPIRITUAL AUTHORITY AND THE "HERETICAL" WOMAN: FIRMILIAN'S WORD TO THE CHURCH IN CARTHAGE

CHRISTINE TREVETT

Cardiff University

This study concerns three people: two of them men of authority who were Christian bishops and the third, an unnamed Christian woman, whose claims to authority were presented as a problem. Her provenance, indeed her existence as an individual rather than as a literary device, is uncertain.

The account of the woman is given briefly in *Epistle* 75 of the Cyprianic corpus (bishop Firmilian of Caesarea to bishop Cyprian of Carthage) and it brings us into the debates about orthodoxy and heresy, the relation of charismatic to clerical authority, women and the sacraments and the process of defining the "heretical" woman. Firmilian's little-studied presentation of this woman is of interest for the aforesaid things. I shall suggest that probably it was also a thrust in a debate about which we have almost no evidence. In this debate she was used as the foil for toleration. Her actions, as Firmilian described them, became reminders of unacceptable consequences if certain dangers were not acknowledged. "She" may even have been a composite of various stereotypes and projected fears with regard to the kinds of teachers and teachings she was used to represent.

I have inferred this element of propaganda in the letter. It is not made explicit in the text that the section devoted to her had as one of its functions being ammunition in a particular war about a certain view of spiritual authority. But I shall argue that in the war the battle lines had not been drawn as rigidly in some geographical areas as in others. In addition, this inference serves to plug a small hole in a remarkable gap of silence about the Carthaginian church situation.

Little attention has been paid to this account, perhaps because it appears as one element in one letter of a series in the Cyprianic corpus which addresses "greater" questions. In any case, scholarly consideration of second- and third-century Christian womankind has been "patchy", despite attention to the stories and story-tellers of the Apocryphal Acts, to females and the feminine in Gnostic groups, to women in the martyrologies and the New Prophecy/Montanism, and despite much heart-searching about methodology when studying all things gender-related.[1] Relatively few writers have trawled the extensive second and early third century material for an overview of what was happening to Christian women, including the catholic kind, in various settings, in this important period of self-definition for the church.[2]

Cyprian of Carthage is associated with a corpus of 81 letters written and received between 249 and 258 c.e. (the year of his death). *Epistle* 75 (no. 74 in some editions) is a long letter from Firmilian, written in 256 c.e. in reply to a letter from Cyprian (not extant). It contained a refutation of the views of bishop Stephen and the Roman Christians on the baptism of heretics,[3] with Firmilian supporting Cyprian's own view about the matter.[4]

The main issue in the letter was whether or not heretics' baptism conferred remission of sins and consequently whether re-baptism was necessary when they sought acceptance by the catholics. Firmilian told Cyprian of experiences and catholic decisions in his own region and it was in that context that he introduced the story of a Christian woman who had been in Cappadocia more than twenty years previously.

The unnamed woman had been active publicly in the late 230s

---

[1] A few examples must suffice: S.L. Davies, *The Revolt of the Widows. The Social World of the Apocryphal Acts* (Carbondale, 1980); V. Burrus, *Chastity as Autonomy. Women in the Stories of Apocryphal Acts*, Studies in Women and Religion 23 (Lewiston, 1987); E. Pagels, *The Gnostic Gospels* (London, 1979); D.L. Hoffman, *The Status of Women and Gnosticism in Irenaeus and Tertullian* (Lampeter/New York, 1995); S.G. Hall, "Women among the Early Martyrs", *Martyrs and Martyrologies*, Studies in Church History 30, ed. D. Wood (Oxford, 1993), pp. 1–22; B.D. Shaw, "Body, Power, Identity: Passions of the Martyrs", *JECS* 4 (1996), pp. 269–312; C. Trevett, *Montanism. Gender, Authority and the New Prophecy* (Cambridge, 1996); B. Brooten, "Early Christian Women and Their Cultural Context. Issues of Method in Historical Reflection", *Feminist Perspectives on Biblical Scholarship*, ed. A.Y. Collins (Chico, 1985), pp. 65–91; E.A. Clark, "Ideology, History and the Construction of 'Woman' in Late Ancient Christianity", *JECS* 2 (1994), pp. 155–84; E.A. Clark, H. Richardson (eds.), *Women and Religion* (San Francisco, 1996, rev. ed.), ch. 1.

[2] M.Y. Macdonald, *Early Christian Women and Pagan Opinion. The Power of the Hysterical Woman* (Cambridge, 1996); A. Jensen, *God's Self-Confident Daughters. Early Christianity and the Liberation of Women*, transl. by O.C. Dean Jr. (Kampen, 1996).

[3] Eusebius, *Hist. Eccl.* 6.4. Cyprian, *Epist.* 75. 7–10, *S. Thasci Caecili Cypriani Opera Omnia*, CSEL 3.2, ed. W. von Hartel (Vienna, 1871), pp. 814–5. The most recent edition is G.F. Diercks, *Sancti Cypriani Episcopi Epistularium*, CCSL IIIC (Turnhout, 1994). On the date cf. G.W. Clarke, *The Letters of St. Cyprian*, ACW 43, 44, 46, 47, 4 vols. (New York, 1984–89), vol. 4, p. 256 n. 7.

[4] On the baptism of heretics and schismatics: *Epistles* 69ff. A. Jilek, *Initiationsfeier und Amt. Ein Beitrag zur Struktur und Theologie der Ämter und der Taufgottesdienstes in der frühen Kirche* (Frankfurt, 1979), pp. 248–62.

C.E., in the time after Alexander Severus.[5] After a period of quiet under Alexander, Firmilian reported, there had been "many conflicts and oppressions" for people of all kinds. Christians were confused at the turn of events and in addition severe earthquakes in the region had made them scape-goats for public fear (*Epist.* 75.10).[6] Consequently some of them were fleeing from the localised persecution when this woman came into the area.

Firmilian described her as prophesying from a state of ecstasy, teaching, baptising those she had taught, sanctifying bread and celebrating eucharist. She acted, he wrote, as though possessed by the Holy Spirit. She had uttered sayings about earthquakes, or "promised to make the earth tremble" as he put it. In some way (described vaguely) she claimed association with Judea and Jerusalem and said that she planned to return there. She suffered no ill-effects from walking barefoot, even in snow in hard winter and she performed remarkable deeds (*admiribilia quaedem et portentosa perficiens; Epist.* 75.10).

The woman seemingly was enjoying a successful mission, but Firmilian was presenting all these actions in an unflattering light. Her words on earthquakes, gaining followers, even being saved from frostbite, were evidence of demonic power. She had indeed baptised "many", he conceded, "using the customary and legitimate words of interrogation". But she was a deceiver who had led astray even church officials and she had been sexually predatory.

A number of interesting questions are raised by this account. What kind of Christianity would such a woman have represented? Was she to be regarded as a heretic? What light may this account from Cappadocia shed on debates in and about the church in Carthage? What does it say of the shifting presentation of women and of women's authority?

With what kind of Christianity was this woman (real or devised) aligned? Either catholic or New Prophecy/Montanist have been the options addressed by writers in the past and they seem the most plausible ones. Anne Jensen and others have assumed her to be a catholic.[7] I think this is possible, though it is not the view I hold.

---

[5] Declared Caesar by Elagabalus in 221, d. 235 C.E. Her period was that of Maximinus Thrax. See A. Lippold, "Maximinus Thrax und die Christen", *Historia* 24 (1975), pp. 479ff. and Eusebius, *Hist. Eccl.* 6.28, citing works of Origen.

[6] Cf. Tertullian's maxim in *Apol.* 40.2 and Augustine, *Civ. Dei* 2.3.

[7] Jensen, *God's Self-Confident Daughters*, pp. 182–6; P. Labriolle, "Mulières in ecclesia taceant. Un aspect de la lutte antimontaniste", *Bulletin d'Ancienne Littérature et d'Archéologie Chrétienne* 1 (1911), pp. 1–24, pp. 103–22, pp. 292–8, especially p. 121, n. 2;

It is important to bear in mind, nevertheless, that non-catholic and non-orthodox are not interchangeable terms. It would be short-sighted to suppose that any second or even early third-century account suggestive of women baptising or celebrating eucharist must point to a non-catholic and therefore heretical group at work.

The developing catholic tradition was not uniform nor were its loyalists wholly obedient to emerging norms. Anne Jensen did not fail to take account of the fluidity and diversity in developing orthodox Christianity. She took this baptising, eucharist making, prophesying, sign-performing, perhaps ascetic female leader to be catholic. One thing in particular seems in favour of this reading. It is the woman's familiarity with correct (in Firmilian's terms) liturgy. He acknowledged as valid the "invocation" she used to sanctify the bread. She said the usual eucharistic prayer.[8] Her baptismal practice was impeccable—all things considered *ut nihil discrepare ab ecclesiastica regula uideretur.*

By contrast, I am suggesting that she was not a catholic but belonged to the New Prophecy.[9] It seems to me that everything points to this, and indeed that Firmilian's description of this woman as an example of the unacceptable, as also his choice of keywords in that description of her, were conditioned by his desire to draw the attention of Cyprian to the potential for disruption and error which he saw in the New Prophecy.

The fact that she was familiar with catholic liturgy does not gainsay her being a New Prophet. Only if one assumes that they were something wholly distinct from the prevailing church tradition, or were the kind of wild-eyed hysterics of some writers' imaginations, should one be surprised that in many respects they did what catholics did. Several other things point to the woman being representative of the New Prophecy.

— The geographical setting, i.e. Cappadocia, is right for the New
   Prophecy. Originating in Phrygia about seventy years previously,

---

P. Labriolle, *La Crise Montaniste* (Paris, 1913), pp. 483–7; P.H. Lafontaine, *Les conditions positives de l'accession aux ordres dans la première législation ecclésiastique (300–492)* (Ottawa, 1963), pp. 11–2.

   [8] Since Labriolle's 1913 edition of the sources for Montanism a number of writers have inserted a negative in the text, which seems to demand it, the thrust of the passage being that she did nothing liturgically incorrect and it was not *sine sacramento solitae praedicationis offerret.*

   [9] I gave only very brief consideration to this account in my *Montanism*, pp. 170–1. *Cataphrygians* was another name for the New Prophets, based on the area of their beginnings.

it had spread with great rapidity. It would have been a relatively short step to Cappadocia.

— Firmilian mentioned the woman's ecstasy in association with her prophecy. The relation between the two had been a bone of contention between the New Prophets and their early opponents. In Carthage Tertullian had addressed the issue of ecstasy at length in his lost treatise *De Ecstasi*, and ecstasy was found in churches there decades later. But in Firmilian's context ecstasy was a word to trigger alarm.

— Firmilian reported negatively on her mode of prophesying, which was using what I take to be prophetic "I" sayings, here in relation to natural disaster and probably in association with eschatological threat or promise. This was a common prophetic practice, to judge from the Hebrew Bible and the Revelation of John, and it was one employed by the New Prophets, as a careful reading of some of the extant "oracles" indicates.[10]

— Firmilian told of reference to Judea and returning to Jerusalem, making out that she had come from there. Itinerants in the New Prophecy got around, and even in the second century Christian visitors made their way to Jerusalem. Still another explanation presents itself, which aligns the presentation with that of a New Prophet. She had come from "Jerusalem". The earliest anti-Montanist writers reported that the New Prophets labelled their own communities "Jerusalem", even when they were in unprepossessing villages in Phrygia.[11]

---

[10] Trevett, *Montanism*, p. 171; C. Trevett, "Eschatological Timetabling and the Montanist Prophet Maximilla", *Studia Patristica* 31, ed. E.A. Livingstone (Louvain, 1997), pp. 218–24. When Firmilian said she had promised she would make the earth shake he may have meant utterances of the kind "thus saith the Lord 'I will shake . . .'", in echo perhaps of something like Psalm 60:2f., and in line with New Prophet practice. On prophecy and ecstasy Trevett, *Montanism*, pp. 86–95. On "I" and other prophetic forms, *Montanism*, pp. 77–86, pp. 163–70 and S.E. McGinn, "The 'Montanist' Oracles and Prophetic Theology", *Studia Patristica* 31, ed. E.A. Livingstone (Louvain, 1997), pp. 128–35. E.M. Boring, *Sayings of the Risen Jesus. Christian Prophecy in the Synoptic Tradition* (Cambridge, 1982), pp. 128–32 (on "Sentences of Holy Law" and prophetic "I" sayings), also D. Hill, *New Testament Prophecy* (London, 1979); D.E. Aune, *Prophecy in Early Christianity and the Ancient Mediterranean World* (Grand Rapids, 1983); S. Elm, "Montanist Oracles", *Searching the Scriptures*, vol. 2, *A Feminist Commentary*, ed. E.S. Fiorenza (London, 1994), pp. 131–8; A. Stewart-Sykes, "The original condemnation of Asian Montanism", *JEH* 50 (1999), pp. 1–22. Cf. for possible parallel forms Origen, *Contra Celsum* 7.9.

[11] Eusebius, *Hist. Eccl.* 5.18.2 [Apollonius]; Cyril of Jerusalem, *Catechesis* 16 [*De spiritu sancto* 1.8]; Augustine, *De Haer.* 27; cf. Epiphanius, *Pan.* 49.1.

— Finally, Firmilian's letter actually refers to Cataphrygian (New Prophecy) teaching. He told of catholic brethren who had been open to receiving those who "appear to recognise the same Father and Son with us" (*Epist.* 75.7 and 19) and it was in the light of those discussions about reception of the already baptised that the example of this woman was introduced (*Epist.* 75.10). She was not said explicitly to be a Cataphrygian.

All things considered, it seems to me that she was one of those "who are called Cataphrygians and attempt to employ new prophecies" (*Epist.* 75.7), i.e. a Montanist.[12]

Received wisdom held (until recent decades, at least) that from the outset the New Prophecy was heretical, though always a few dissenting voices pointed to the fact that the evidence was to the contrary. Cyprian *Epistle* 75 (from Firmilian) is part of the body of material which casts doubt on such assumptions about its heretical nature in the early stages, though it is not the clearest example of the kind.

Cataphrygian teaching is less evidently heresy in this letter than are other errors, even though in Cappadocia Firmilian would surely have heard the word heresy used to describe it. It may have been so included among heresies in *Epistle* 75.7, but then elsewhere in the letter Firmilian was refusing to toy with distinctions between heresy and false prophecy, saying that each was as bad as the other. "There is no difference between a false prophet and a heretic", Firmilian opined (*Epist.* 75.9), a judgement which immediately preceded the description of the unnamed woman (*Epist.* 75.10). At first sight, then, her condemnation was still to be on grounds of false prophecy rather than heresy proper,[13] and Firmilian reported that an exorcist had confronted her possessing demons (*Epist.* 75.10).[14]

---

[12] The term *Montanism*, still the most common designation for this teaching, is not found in Christian writings until the fourth century. On her Montanism see also K. Aland, "Bemerkungen zum Montanismus und zur frühchristlichen Eschatologie", *Kirchengeschichtliche Entwürfe* (Gütersloh, 1960), pp. 116–7; R.H. Fischer, "Die antimontanistischen Synoden der 2. und 3. Jahrhunderte", *Annuarium Historiae Conciliorum* 6 (1974), p. 268; F.C. Klawiter, *The New Prophecy in Early Christianity*, unpublished PhD thesis (University of Chicago, 1975), p. 172; S. Elm, "Perceptions of Jerusalem Pilgrimage as Reflected in Two Early Sources on Female Pilgrimage", *Studia Patristica* 20, ed. E.A. Livingstone (Louvain, 1989), pp. 221–2.

[13] The New Prophecy was just that, prophecy. Opposition was to its form and its content. Some Asians diagnosed it as false prophecy, demonic and characterised by ecstasy. The word heresy was also used, as Firmilian surely knew (cf. Eusebius,

Other passages in *Epistle* 75 support the view that even in Asia it had been not Cataphrygian unorthodox theology but rather its pneumatology, emanating in prophecy and challenges to church authority, which had alienated the catholic side. Only with the passage of more time still, and the fragmentation of "Montanism", should we speak of heresy proper. In fact Firmilian never used the word heretic of this woman, though he was working to equate false prophecy with suspect Trinitarianism and heresy.

His language shows that debate had existed in Asia as to whether Cataphrygian Christian converts might indeed be received and their baptisms acknowledged, not least because they were observed to "recognise the same Father and Son with us" (*Epist.* 75.19). For his part Firmilian was quite clear on the matter. He would have no truck with the New Prophecy, regarding false prophecy as on a par with heresy. But in Carthage, I suggest, the situation was quite different, and it was due to that difference that the "heretical" woman here described had been created.

In his own writing on the re-baptism debate Cyprian does not seem to have addressed the question of the Cataphrygians. Marcionism, Patripassianism, the Valentinians and others were referred to in his letters, and in *Epist.* 75.5 Firmilian too mentioned Marcion, Apelles and Valentinus, though he cited the Cataphrygians also. If Cyprian had indeed been silent on the matter, then that is interesting. We can not be certain of his silence, of course, for his letter to Firmilian is not extant. But Firmilian was far from silent, and about things which had taken on considerable significance in Asian catholic circles.

The "heretical" woman prophet, I suggest, served as a valuable device in reminding Carthage of what some Asian Christians saw as unpalatable truths. Firmilian advised Cyprian of catholic discussions which had taken place at Iconium (*Epist.* 75. 7.4 and 19.4)[15] and

---

Hist. Eccl. 5.16.8 [Anon.]; Epiphanius *Pan.* [his early, anonymous probably Asian source] 48.1–3; 49.12–11). In Rome, and probably in Carthage, the debates about it were rather different: Trevett, *Montanism*, pp. 55–65 (Rome), pp. 66–76 (Carthage), pp. 94–5, pp. 141–50.

[14] An exorcist faced her bravely (*fortiter*), aided by the exhortations of brave (*fortes*) brethren. The few accounts of attempted exorcism in anti-Montanist sources all concern women. The exorcist showed the spirit to be "wicked" but it is not clear that she ceased her activities. Here exorcist appears for the first time as a rank in the church. See R. Seagraves, *Pascentes cum Disciplina. A Lexical Study of the Clergy in the Cyprianic Correspondence* (Fribourg, 1993), pp. 155–65.

[15] See Fischer, "Die antimontanistischen Synoden", pp. 265–7; J.E. Merdinger, *Rome and the African Church in the Time of Augustine* (London, 1997), pp. 43–9.

Asian refusal of the validity of Cataphrygian prophecy. But Firmilian
shows us how the debate had been broadened, so as to bring it into
a sphere in which heresy might in due course be a proper allegation.

The argument ran as follows. Those who sought "to employ new
prophecies" and understood God to have sent "the Spirit that speaks
by Montanus and Prisca" (*Epist.* 75.8) lacked a proper understanding of the Spirit and of God. Moreover those who continued in false
prophecy against the faith of Christ's church clearly did not possess
Christ either (*Epist.* 75.7). Thus the basis for rejection of their baptism could be made doctrinal.[16] False prophecy and heresy were one.

On such grounds the woman might well be regarded as a heretic
as well as a false prophet (if one accepted that Cataphrygian prophecy,
properly subject to *diakrisis*, was false). Not a few Asian Christians
would have seen it that way and Firmilian, I suggest, did not want
it thought, least of all by Cyprian, that New Prophets might be
indulged as relatively harmless charismatics. So he provided a "dangerous female" example of what the New Prophecy stood for.

Despite her use of the same Christian Trinitarian language and
ritual as her catholic hearers and the fact that in every respect (*Epist.*
75.10–11) she seemed not to have made a false move, such tradition-
alism could not excuse her overweening error. Not only was she one
of the Cataphrygians—judged suspect for false prophecy, "Jerusalem"
communities and ecstasy—but "this woman" had celebrated eucharist
and baptised. "What shall we say?" he demanded with regard to the
issue in question (that of the validity of baptism by those not of the
catholic fold). What of the fact that a wicked demon had baptised
"by means of a woman"? Had sins been remitted under the circumstances? Was not the power of remitting sins accorded to the apostles and by them to churches established and to bishops over them?
(*Epist.* 75.16). To these final questions, at least, Cyprian would have
given an affirmative reply.

The introduction of the story of a woman of the Cataphrygians
was, I suggest, a ploy to stigmatise the New Prophecy in the light
of discussions about it in that part of the world (Asia Minor) where

---

[16] The growing scholarly consensus about Cataphrygian orthodoxy: S. McGinn-
Moorer, *The New Prophecy of Asia Minor and the Rise of Ecclesiastical Patriarchy in Second
Century Pauline Traditions*, unpublished PhD dissertation Northwestern University
(Evanstone Ill., 1989), ch. 2. Firmilian's view about the Trinity accords broadly
with Cyprian's in other letters, but Cyprian, so far as we know, had not addressed
the implications of *Cataphrygian pneumatology*.

it had started. Firmilian's "keywords" pointed to his knowledge of Cataphrygian self-definition and Asian catholic response—ecstasy, false prophecy (and perhaps heresy), Jerusalem, demons, woman, spoke eloquently of the view of some Asian catholics. And his questions about her baptism should be regarded as "trump cards" in this presentation. They need to be read in association with his affirmation (*Epist.* 75.7) that those who "separate from God's church" can not possess authority and grace, for such things have been deposited "in the church where the elders preside (*ubi praesident maiores*), who also possess the authority of baptising, imposition of hands and ordaining".

Nevertheless the statement about separation (*sciderant*) from the church was not applicable to the New Prophecy in every place. It spoke of the Asian situation, rather than the African, for example. Likewise other things in Firmilian's description of the female prophet spoke of Asian concerns, rather than those in Carthage, as we shall see.

We do not know whether Cyprian had initiated the discussion about New Prophets in an earlier letter to Firmilian or whether in mid third-century Cappadocia the anomalous position of the Carthaginians with regard to them was mulled over regularly. Anomalous it probably was. In Rome, after some vacillation and debate about the claims to prophetic authority (not least by women) and about the Paraclete, the New Prophecy had been deemed unacceptable and the word "heresy" started to be used there of the "Phrygians", despite Hippolytus' acknowledgement that "they speak correctly concerning the origin and creation of the universe, and they have not accepted strange teachings about Christ".[17] In Carthage, so far as we know, this was not so. Indeed Douglas Powell put the matter succinctly:[18]

> there is no unambiguous statement of the excommunication of the Tertullianists by the Church, no more is there one of excommunication of the Church by Tertullianists . . . Mutual accusations of heresy undoubtedly formed part of the repudiation of the former *societas sententiae*,[19] but there is no hint that this involved also a repudiation of the *communio sanctorum*.

---

[17] *Refut. Omn. Haer.* 10.25. R. Heine, *The Montanist Oracles and Testimonia* (Macon, 1989), p. 57. Some "Phrygians" in Rome were allegedly Modalist in theology; Hippolytus, *Refut. Omn. Haer.* 8.19, 10.26). We do not know how many, or even whether this was a calumny, but in any case Modalism was common at this time. See Trevett, *Montanism*, pp. 55–66.

[18] D. Powell, "Tertullianists and Cataphrygians", *Vig. Chr.* 29 (1975), pp. 33–54, pp. 36–7.

[19] Cf. Tertullian, *De Pud.* 1.10.

Firmilian, then, may have felt there were good reasons for introducing the matter of the danger of the New Prophecy—and not for-
getting its women—into a discussion about authority and the re-baptism
of heretics. It would have been a word dropped into one of a number
of remarkable silences in anti-Montanist sources, because little is
known about the New Prophecy in North Africa in the period following its introduction there. This may have been in the 190s or at
the turn of the third century. Tertullian embraced the New Prophecy
and half a century later Cyprian held Tertullian in high regard.
Moreover in recent decades it has become almost a commonplace
of scholarship that the New Prophecy (probably associated with the
so-called "Tertullianist" group in Carthage) was well-integrated in
Carthaginian congregations, and was neither heretical nor schismatic. Rather it represented what Powell had designated an *ecclesiola in
ecclesia*.[20] In fact there is silence except for the writings of Tertullian,
and nothing to indicate its presence in Carthage at all.

But the situation of toleration which is posited for Carthage would
surely not have been comprehensible or acceptable to Firmilian and
many other bishops. Consequently this letter to Cyprian, if part of
its purpose was indeed to furnish evidence of the unacceptability of
Cataphrygian behaviour and of some claims to spiritual authority,
offers a shaft of light into an otherwise dark situation. It would be
evidence not just for the New Prophecy in Carthage but for a debate
about its presence there in churches beyond North Africa.

The fact was that the forms of the New Prophecy in Asia and in
Carthage were probably somewhat different. To judge from the evidence of Tertullian (and it is hazardous to regard him as in any
way "typical" of an adherent of the New Prophecy), the African
kind, though rigorous (denouncing digamy, advocating self-denial)
and charismatic (recognising as authoritative visions, utterances of
the New Prophecy's founders and encounters with angels who guided
on matters of practice and belief) seems to have been less at odds
with mainstream catholics and does not seem to have countenanced,
for example, itinerant prophetic women. Indeed the New Prophecy
sisterhood in Carthage seems to have involved an extremely orderly

---

[20] No schism in Carthage: Trevett, *Montanism*, 68–76; D. Rankin, *Tertullian and
the Church* (Cambridge, 1995) and the classic study by Powell, "Tertullianists and
Cataphrygians".

if visionary crew. In any case, some of the matters cited in Firmilian's keywords would scarcely have troubled Cyprian.

Firmilian's question about the remission of sins in relation to the prophetic woman's baptism was rhetorical. He and Cyprian alike knew the answer as to whether or not baptism by a woman would be legitimate. Tertullian's Montanist dictum about remission of sins, penned in respect of another context, had said that it was the church of the spirit which held the power to remit, and by means of the spiritual individual—*non ecclesia numerus episcoporum* (*De Pud.* 21). But this did not mean that he approved of a female, even one of New Prophecy persuasion, baptising, celebrating eucharist or pronouncing forgiveness.[21] In Carthage not even "Tertullianist" women would have done so.

In all likelihood, then, Firmilian was crying danger about a door which was firmly closed in North Africa. Nevertheless he would have been confident that Cyprian would deplore those aspects of her activity and to that end he provided a colourful and pointed reminder of the multifarious possibilities associated with the New Prophecy.[22]

It was not just the danger of women and priestly rites that was being driven home. The references to prophecy and ecstasy would have been very important in the Asian context. Yet these are unlikely to have had a chilling effect on the African bishop. Cyprian seems not to have shared Asian hostility to the association of these two things. Indeed Carthage was an exceptional place in Christian terms. Congregational prophecy, ecstasy and the receipt of visions were still common there in the mid-third century.[23] To Firmilian, of course,

---

[21] Tertullian acknowledged the Spirit in the first New Prophets male and female (e.g. *De Pud.* 21) but his views on women shifted only a little with Montanism. As with Paul, Tertullian's teachings about women are complex. See Hoffman, *The Status of Women and Gnosticism*, pp. 175–82; K.J. Torjeson, *When Women Were Priests. Women's Leadership in the Early Church and the Scandal of their Subordination in the Rise of Christianity* (San Francisco, 1993), pp. 158–76.

[22] *Sacerdos*: J.D. Laurance, *"Priest" as Type of Christ. The Leader of the Eucharist in Salvation History according to Cyprian of Carthage* (New York, 1984), pp. 195–215; Seagraves, *Pascentes cum Disciplina*, pp. 41–8.

[23] Cyprian on ecstasy: *Epist.* 16.41—"innocent young boys" had visions and "filled with the Holy Spirit and in ecstasy they see with their eyes and they hear and then speak the words of warning and instruction". The last book of Tertullian's *De Ecstasi* was written to refute the writings of Apollonius in Asia (Jerome, *De Vir. Ill.* 40). On Carthage: A. von Harnack, "Cyprian als Enthusiast", *Zeitschrift für die Neutestamentliche Wissenschaft und die Kunde der älteren Kirche* 3 (1902), pp. 177–91; Seagraves, *Pascentes cum Disciplina*, pp. 245–53; C.M. Robeck, *Prophecy in Carthage. Perpetua, Tertullian and*

being of the Cataphrygian persuasion made the woman a false prophet, and suspect doctrinally too.

The usurpation of priestly rights and rites underlies Firmilian's hostile presentation of the woman. Bishop Cyprian, he knew, was much concerned with catholicity, so in *Epistle* 75 Firmilian wrote of errorists who were "enemies of the one, catholic church in which we are", the adversaries "of us who have succeeded the apostles" and who asserted "unlawful priesthoods".[24] He was probably hoping to implicate the unnamed woman of his devising in the threat to catholic continuity (*Epist.* 75.16).

Some weapons had become increasingly important in Christianity's battles for the hearts and tolerance of those beyond the churches. Continuity (succeeding the apostles), sound teaching and authority structures involving men of standing in the community were among them. The church, if presented as a trustworthy environment, would seem to non-Christians in due course to contain "people like us". Women, however, if too visible, and claiming "false priesthoods", would be a disruptive element in such a vision of recognisably ordered community comprehensible to the non-Christian world. Heresy was disorder.[25]

Firmilian's subsuming of false prophecy under the category of heresy was bringing together two forces of disorder, *viz.* women (for prophecy had always been a mode of Christian expression open to them) and heresy. Thus his demonically-inspired female prophet, a "worst-case scenario", was designed, I suggest, to put into perspective Cyprian's sanguine response to Cataphrygians. He was casting into the pot the most contentious and suspect characteristics of the new cult, and as they were associated with the more suspect sex. For while in general Firmilian was wholly at one with Cyprian's views on heretics, it was his belief that New Prophets too were to be so regarded.

Nevertheless Cyprian would not have been alone in failing to associate the New Prophecy with serious error. From its outset, and even

---

Cyprian (Cleveland, 1992); G. Schöllgen, *Ecclesia Sordida? Zur Frage der sozialen Schichtung frühchristlicher Gemeinden am Beispiel Karthagos zur Zeit Tertullians, JbAC* Ergänzungsband 12 (Münster, 1984).

[24] Torjeson's one reference to this woman in *When Women Were Priests*, p. 115 makes her a female presbyter.

[25] See the essays of R. Williams, "Heresy" and W. Wischmeyer, "The Sociology of Pre-Constantine Christianity" in *Christendom*, ed. A. Kreider, forthcoming.

in Asia, there had been "prophetic" types who failed to discourage Montanus (Eusebius, *Hist. Eccl.* 5.16.8) and who were dismissed by some as far from "the true faith". Carthage had its share of such "prophetic" people, indeed Cyprian was among them. So Firmilian's propagandist account, which even acknowledged the traditional liturgical and trinitarian language of his New Prophetess, was designed instead to show that (perhaps contrary to Carthaginian experience) not even some element of rectitude was guarantee that a New Prophet was not, in reality, offensive and a threat to the properly constituted authority of the church.

Tertullian should have been there at that hour. The real reason for catholics' (psychics) opposition to the New Prophecy, he maintained, was not to do with orthodoxy or "because Montanus, Prisca and Maximilla preach another God, nor because they dismiss Jesus Christ, nor because they overturn some rule of faith or hope". No, said Tertullian, taking his stand on the moral high ground as usual, it all came down to the guts and genitals of the psychics (*De Ieiunio* 1). Catholics resented the fact that New Prophets were spiritual high-flyers, advocates of discipline, rigorists who were teaching that "our fasts ought to be more numerous than our marriages"! Tertullian would certainly have found ludicrous any suggestion that such purists needed re-baptism![26]

Firmilian, by contrast, had been weaned on Asian catholic opposition to more than just the increased discipline of the New Prophecy. He moved to equate it with heresy and unacceptable freedoms for women. One trump card was the claim of this woman's sexual misdemeanour.[27] The prophetess had been discovered to have deceived/seduced and had association with (*commiscerentur*) a deacon and even a rustic presbyter (or perhaps one called Rusticus). I have chosen to interpret this verb *commisceo* with that ambiguity implied in Seagraves's lexical study of the Cyprianic corpus.[28] There he translated the accusation as "slept with". Many translators have opted for the more clear

---

[26] Probably Cyprian did not encounter itinerant female New Prophets around Carthage, where the New Prophecy was a relatively tame affair, its female loyalists well-disciplined. The question of "Montanist" baptism or re-baptism would not have arisen, for such people were *within* the churches there.

[27] Sexual misconduct is not otherwise an accusation in early anti-Montanist sources but comes later: C. Trevett, "Gender, Authority and Church History. A Case Study of Montanism", *Feminist Theology* 17 (1998), pp. 9–24.

[28] Seagraves, *Pascentes cum Disciplina*, p. 164.

cut "had intercourse with" and we must look at this final accusation
in the light of all else we are told about her.

Here was an itinerant, prophesying, teaching ascetic, a loyalist of
an idealised "Jerusalem" community. She is likely to have been celibate, so I would posit that Firmilian was making a hostile reference
to the vexed practice of *virgines subintroductae*—i.e. the cohabitation,
even shared beds (and the subsequent scandal which might emerge)
of dedicated celibates. Such a prophet may indeed have "slept with"
men. More significantly, however, Firmilian probably knew that
Cyprian would look negatively on this, as well on as some other
aspects of her behaviour. Cyprian was familiar with the *virgines subintroductae* and he and others in Carthage had condemned virgins who
shared their beds but nevertheless pleaded their chastity.[29] Nevertheless
he did not label them heretics.

Firmilian, then, had colored carefully the picture of the New
Prophecy, filtering it through the image of a female claiming spiritual authority who might prove (in his terms) out of control near
poorly defended boundaries. His decision to do this may have owed
something either to Cyprian's letter to him or to Asian catholics'
discussions (of which we know nothing) about the African New
Prophecy/"Tertullianism". Eastwards in the empire that Prophecy
had given rise to all manner of fears among its catholic opponents.
In north Africa, I suggest, the danger had not seemed acute. Hence
this portion of Firmilian's letter illuminates the darkness which otherwise shrouds the New Prophecy in Carthage after Tertullian's lifetime and I infer from it (a) that Cataphrygianism was indeed present
there and (b) that it was probably tolerated to a degree not countenanced in some other parts of the Christian world.

Finally, the account of the woman is interesting not just because
it confirms some of what we think we know about the New Prophecy
but also for the pointer it provides to the developing Christian
definition of propriety and impropriety in female behavior. The
unnamed female prophet was already being described in categories
which would in due course come to be markers of the heretical
woman proper,[30] and the reverse image of that compliant orthodox

---

[29] Cyprian, *Epist.* 4 (*Epist.* 61 in some editions, *To Pomponius*). On Firmilian and
the examination of Paul of Samosata: Eusebius, *Hist. Eccl.* 7.4–5, 7.27–30. Achelis,
Labriolle and Clark have made useful studies of *virgines subintroductae*.

[30] Cf. V. Burrus, "The Heretical Woman as Symbol in Alexander, Athanasius,
Epiphanius and Jerome", *HTR* 84 (1991), pp. 230ff.

woman that the church had been promoting. She had been, according to Firmilian in the public and not the private sphere, behaving disorderly and disrupting ordered community,[31] demonically wily and deceitful, usurping the rites of men, and sexually predatory. Yet not many decades previously, and still doing such things, she might simply have been a prophet. In some parts of the Christian world at least, one such as Firmilian's prophetess might have been viewed as a successor of prophetic and didactic leaders, male and female, whose pedigree stretched back to the Apostles. Paul had acknowledged women as prophets,[32] some prophetic women had reputations in the public (Christian) sphere as teachers, travellers and so on.[33] Now a prophetic woman's activities might be tested and not only judged false (as had always been the case) but heretical, thereby easily robbing her of other ministries.

Such judgements had come to the fore in the debates about the early New Prophecy in Asia, where Cataphrygians were described in terms both of false prophecy and heresy.[34] That was the school of thought to which, half a century on, Firmilian belonged also. Less hostile analysis might have conceded that a prophet's eschatological warnings, her probable "I" form of prophetic speech, her "signs", her teaching, her itinerant ascetic lifestyle, even her chastity-threatening co-habitation (if that is what it was) did align her with Christian prophets of the past, including the prophets of the New Testament and the *Didache*. These were evidence of spiritual authority, though prophetic eccentricities had seemed scandalous to some.[35] And of

---

[31] Williams, "Heresy", forthcoming.

[32] Paul also knew women co-workers, patronesses, apostles, deacons and so on; Torjeson, *When Women Were Priests*, pp. 23–30; J.-A. McNamara, *A New Song. Celibate Women in the First Three Christian Centuries* (New York, 1983), ch. 6.

[33] Prophets and apostles of New Testament and *Didache* were poor. The New Prophet Priscilla travelled considerable distances, like some of the women in stories of the Apocryphal Acts. Firmilian's female ecstatic was an itinerant prophet whose barefootedness suggests ascetic poverty or a "sign" indicative of mourning in a time of crisis (cf. 2 Sam. 15:30; Isa. 20:2f.; Ezk. 24:17, 23; Mic. 1:8).

[34] Sources preserved by Eusebius: *Hist. Eccl.* 4.27 [Apolinarius]; 5.16.22 [Anonymous]; 5.18.1 [Apollonius] cf. Hippolytus, *Refut. Omn. Haer* 8.19 in Rome.

[35] *Didache* 11.11 accepts enacting "a worldly mystery of the church", perhaps meaning co-habitation (cf. Hosea 1:2f.? Eph. 5:21–31?). The Coptic and Ethiopic redactions of this passage indicate that cohabitation was a problem. S.J. Patterson, "DIDACHE 11–13: The Legacy of Radical Itinerancy in Early Christianity", *The Didache in Context*, ed. C.N. Jefford (Leiden, 1995), pp. 313–29; K. Niederwimmer, "An Examination of the Development of Itinerant Radicalism in the Environment and Tradition of the Didache", *The Didache in Modern Research*, ed. J.A. Draper

course such things would have aligned her with those prophetic and teaching women to which the New Prophets looked back.[36] None of these things concerned Firmilian.

Christianity was changing. Issues of charisma, office, and spiritual and clerical authority had come to a head in the crisis of the New Prophecy, though they were not new.[37] Such freedom for women could not remain uncontained and the kind of women—catholic, New Prophet, other—whose real Christian lives were the stuff from which Firmilian built his picture of the earth-shaking baptiser, could not remain for long out of the ranks of (at best) the marginalised and (at worst) the heretics. Firmilian and his like would see that it was so. Cyprian was under pressure, I suggest, to acknowledge and act upon the dangers seen to be inherent in the New Prophecy. He was otherwise renowned as the champion of proper clerical office. He would soon be dead.

BIBLIOGRAPHY

Achelis, H., *Virgines Subintroductae. Ein Beitrag zum VII Kapital des I Korintherbriefs* (Leipzig, 1902).
Aland, K., "Bemerkungen zum Montanismus und zur frühchristlichen Eschatologie", *Kirchengeschichtliche Entwürfe* (Gütersloh, 1960), pp. 105–48.
Aune, D.E., *Prophecy in Early Christianity and the Ancient Mediterranean World* (Grand Rapids, 1983).
Boring, E.M., *Sayings of the Risen Jesus. Christian Prophecy in the Synoptic Tradition* (Cambridge, 1982).
Brooten, B., "Early Christian Women and Their Cultural Context. Issues of Method in Historical Reflection", *Feminist Perspectives on Biblical Scholarship*, ed. A.Y. Collins (Chico, 1985), pp. 65–91.

(Leiden, 1996), pp. 328–9; R. Rader, *Breaking Boundaries. Male/Female Friendship in Early Christian Communities* (New York, 1983), pp. 62–73. For a critique of this and other interpretations of *Did.* 11:11 and of "too flashy and flighty" itinerant prophets A. Milavec, "Distinguishing True and False Prophets. The Protective Wisdom of the Didache", *JECS* 2 (1994), pp. 132–4.

[36] Trevett, *Montanism*, pp. 33–4. Eusebius, *Hist. Eccl.* 3.31.3; 3.39.9; 5.24.2 (Polycrates); Epiphanius, *Pan.* 49.1–2; Origen, *Catenae* on I Cor. 14:34–5. They looked back to (among others) the unnamed daughters of Philip in Caesarea and in Ephesus and Hierapolis, Ammia in Philadelphia (Eusebius, *Hist. Eccl.* 5.17.2–4 [Anon.]). The traditions about Philip(s) and prophetesses in Asia are as confused as those about John(s). See W. Tabbernee, *Montanist Inscriptions and Testimonia. Epigraphic Sources Illustrating the History of Montanism* (Macon, 1997), pp. 502–8.

[37] C. Trevett, "Prophecy and Anti Episcopal Activity: A Third Error Combated by Ignatius?" *JEH* 34 (1983), pp. 1–18; idem, "Charisma and Office in a Changing Church", *Christendom*, ed. A. Kreider, forthcoming.

Burrus, V., *Chastity as Autonomy. Women in the Stories of Apocryphal Acts*, Studies in Women and Religion 23 (Lewiston, 1987).

————, "The Heretical Woman as Symbol in Alexander, Athanasius, Epiphanius and Jerome", *HTR* 84 (1991), pp. 229–48.

Clark, E.A., "Ideology, History and the Construction of 'Woman' in Late Ancient Christianity", *JECS* 2 (1994), pp. 155–84.

————, "John Chrysostom and the Subintroductae", *Ascetic Piety and Women's Faith. Essays on Late Ancient Christianity* (Lewiston/Queenston, 1986), pp. 265–90.

————, Richardson H., (eds.), *Women and Religion* (San Francisco 1996, rev. ed.).

Clarke, G.W., *The Letters of St. Cyprian*, ACW 43, 44, 46, 47 (New York, 1984–89).

Davies, S.L., *The Revolt of the Widows. The Social World of the Apocryphal Acts* (Carbondale, 1980).

Diercks, G.F., *Sancti Cypriani Episcopi Epistularium*, CCSL IIIC (Turnhout, 1994).

Elm, S., "Perceptions of Jerusalem Pilgrimage as Reflected in Two Early Sources on Female Pilgrimage", *Studia Patristica* 20, ed. E.A. Livingstone (Louvain, 1989), pp. 219–23.

————, "Montanist Oracles", *Searching the Scriptures*, vol. 2, *A Feminist Commentary*, ed. E.S. Fiorenza (London, 1994), pp. 131–8.

Fischer, R.H., "Die antimontanistischen Synoden der 2. und 3. Jahrhunderte", *Annuarium Historiae Conciliorum* 6 (1974), pp. 241–73.

Hall, S.G., "Women Among the Early Martyrs", *Martyrs and Martyrologies*, Studies in Church History 30, ed. D. Wood (Oxford, 1993), pp. 1–22.

Harnack, A. von, "Cyprian als Enthusiast", *Zeitschrift für die Neutestamentliche Wissenschaft und die Kunde der älteren Kirche* 3 (1902), pp. 177–91.

Hartel, W. von (ed.), *S. Thasci Caecili Cypriani Opera Omnia*, CSEL 3 2 (Vienna, 1871).

Heine, R., *The Montanist Oracles and Testimonia* (Macon, 1989).

Hill, D., *New Testament Prophecy* (London, 1979).

Hoffman, D.L., *The Status of Women and Gnosticism in Irenaeus and Tertullian* (Lampeter/New York, 1995).

Jensen, A., *God's Self-Confident Daughters. Early Christianity and the Liberation of Women*, transl by O.C. Dean Jr. (Kampen, 1996).

Jilek, A., *Initiationsfeier und Amt. Ein Beitrag zur Struktur und Theologie der Ämter und der Taufgottesdienstes in der frühen Kirche* (Frankfurt, 1979).

Klawiter, F.C., *The New Prophecy in Early Christianity. The Origin, Nature and Development of Montanism A.D. 165–220*, unpublished PhD dissertation (University of Chicago, 1975).

Labriolle, P., "La polémique antimontaniste contre la prophétie extatique", *Revue d'histoire et de littérature religieuses* 11 (1906), pp. 97–145.

————, "Mulières in ecclesia taceant. Un aspect de la lutte antimontaniste", *Bulletin d'ancienne littérature et d'archéologie chrétienne* 1 (1911), pp. 1–24, 103–22, 292–8.

————, *La crise Montaniste* (Paris, 1913).

————, *Les sources de l'histoire du Montanisme. Textes grecs, latins, syriaques* (Paris, 1913).

————, "Le Mariage Spirituel dans l'Antiquité Chrétienne", *Revue Historique* 137 (1921), pp. 204–25.

Lafontaine, P.H., *Les conditions positives de l'accession aux ordres dans la première législation ecclésiastique (300–492)* (Ottawa, 1963).

Laurance, J.D., *"Priest" as Type of Christ. The Leader of the Eucharist in Salvation History according to Cyprian of Carthage* (New York/Bern, 1984).

Lippold, A., "Maximinus Thrax und die Christen", *Historia* 24 (1975), pp. 479–92.

Macdonald, M.Y., *Early Christian Women and Pagan Opinion. The Power of the Hysterical Woman* (Cambridge, 1996).

McGinn-Moorer, S.E., *The New Prophecy of Asia Minor and the Rise of Ecclesiastical Patriarchy in Second Century Pauline Traditions*, unpublished PhD dissertation Northwestern University (Evanstone Ill., 1989).

McGinn, S.E., "The 'Montanist' Oracles and Prophetic Theology", *Studia Patristica* 31, ed. E.A. Livingstone (Louvain, 1997), pp. 128–35.

McNamara, J.-A., *A New Song. Celibate Women in the First Three Christian Centuries* (New York, 1983).

Merdinger, J.E., *Rome and the African Church in the Time of Augustine* (London, 1997).

Milavec, A., "Distinguishing True and False Prophets. The Protective Wisdom of the Didache", *JECS* 2 (1994), pp. 117–36.

Niederwimmer, K., "An Examination of the Development of Itinerant Radicalism in the Environment and Tradition of the Didache", *The Didache in Modern Research*, ed. J.A. Draper (Leiden, 1996), pp. 321–39.

Pagels, E., *The Gnostic Gospels* (London, 1979).

Patterson, S.J., "DIDACHE 11–13: The Legacy of Radical Itinerancy in Early Christianity", *The Didache in Context*, ed. C.N. Jefford (Leiden, 1995), pp. 313–29.

Powell, D., "Tertullianists and Cataphrygians", *Vig. Chr.* 29 (1975), pp. 33–54.

Rader, R., *Breaking Boundaries. Male/Female Friendship in Early Christian Communities* (New York, 1983).

Rankin, D., *Tertullian and the Church* (Cambridge, 1995).

Robeck, C.M., *Prophecy in Carthage. Perpetua, Tertullian and Cyprian* (Cleveland, 1992).

Schöllgen, G., *Ecclesia Sordida? Zur Frage der sozialen Schichtung frühchristlicher Gemeinden am Beispiel Karthagos zur Zeit Tertullians*, *JbAC* Ergänzungsband 12 (Münster, 1984).

Seagraves, R., *Pascentes cum Disciplina. A Lexical Study of the Clergy in the Cyprianic Correspondence* (Fribourg, 1993).

Shaw, B.D., "Body, Power, Identity: Passions of the Martyrs", *JECS* 4 (1996), pp. 269–312.

Stewart-Sykes, A., "The original condemnation of Asian Montanism", *JEH* 50 (1999), pp. 1–22.

Torjeson, K.-J., *When Women Were Priests. Women's Leadership in the Early Church and the Scandal of their Subordination in the Rise of Christianity* (San Francisco, 1993).

Tabbernee, W., *Montanist Inscriptions and Testimonia. Epigraphic Sources Illustrating the History of Montanism* (Macon, 1997).

Trevett, C., "Prophecy and Anti Episcopal Activity: A Third Error Combated by Ignatius?" *JEH* 34 (1983), pp. 1–18.

———, *Montanism. Gender, Authority and the New Prophecy* (Cambridge, 1996).

———, "Eschatological Timetabling and the Montanist Prophet Maximilla", *Studia Patristica* 31, ed. E.A. Livingstone (Louvain, 1997), pp. 218–24.

———, "Gender, Authority and Church History: A Case Study of Montanism", *Feminist Theology* 17 (1998), pp. 9–24.

———, "Charisma and Office in a Changing Church", *Christendom*, ed. A. Kreider, forthcoming.

Williams, R., "Heresy", ib.

Wischmeyer, W., "The Sociology of Pre-Constantine Christianity", ib.

TROUBLED BREASTS: THE HOLY BODY
IN HAGIOGRAPHY

ROWAN WILLIAMS

Cardiff University

In the last couple of decades, we have all become a great deal better attuned to the subtlety and many-sidedness of the constructions of sanctity in the early Christian world. We have learned from Peter Brown and his pupils to recognise the novel social meanings of holiness, the ways in which access to sacred power is coded and organised in the ascetic and the hierarch in their significantly different modes.[1] We have learned to observe the codes carried by holy bodies in their distinctive social spaces. Recent research has examined the various concordats between hierarchical and ascetical holiness[2] in the process of defining a standard Catholic piety in the post-Constantinian Church, the attempts to move away from a risky focus upon the inspired individual so as to make available a socially intelligible image of holiness, at once non-elitist and subject to certain kinds of communal control. David Brakke's work on Athanasius and asceticism is an excellent example of such study in the last few years,[3] and it is noteworthy that he has lately chosen to write about the significance for Athanasius and Antony (the Antony, at least, of the literary tradition) of body and locality. My intention in this essay is to offer some reflections on these themes as they interact with some larger themes of fourth and fifth century theology, reflections beginning from two anecdotes about saintly figures, superficially not dissimilar, but on

---

[1] The seminal works are P. Brown's *The Body and Society. Men, Women and Sexual Renunciation in Early Christianity* (New York, 1988) and, to a lesser extent, *The Cult of the Saints. Its Rise and Function in Latin Christianity* (Chicago/London, 1981). An important recent study is Caroline Walker Bynum, *The Resurrection of the Body in Western Christianity, 200–1336* (New York, 1995). Despite the title, the early chapters have valuable discussion of Greek and Syriac material.

[2] For a brief discussion, see Rowan Williams, *Arius. Heresy and Tradition* (London, 1987), especially pp. 82–91.

[3] D. Brakke, *Athanasius and the Politics of Asceticism* (Oxford, 1995); idem, "'Outside the Places, Within the Truth': Athanasius of Alexandria and the Localization of the Holy", *Pilgrimage and Holy Space in Late Antique Egypt*, ed. David Frankfurter (Leiden, 1998), pp. 445–81.

further examination suggesting a helpful typology in writing about holy bodies in the fourth century. In reading these texts, we should be able to unpick some significant strands in the mesh of imagination and anxiety that surrounds the topic at this period.

The first of these anecdotes is pretty well-known. Eusebius, in his summary of Origen's career in the sixth book of the *Ecclesiastical History*,[4] records that Origen's father, Leonides, would often stand over his young son as he lay sleeping and "uncover his breast, as if a divine spirit were enshrined therein, and kissing it with reverence count himself happy in his goodly offspring". This touching vignette seems to belong with a fairly substantial body of partly oral tradition about Origen current in Palestine, and probably also in Alexandria, whose roots go back a few decades before Eusebius himself. It has echoes of another well-known passage, more nearly contemporary with Origen, the testimony of Gregory Thaumaturgus in his *Panegyric* to the conviction among Origen's students that his guardian angel was no less than the "angel of Great Counsel" of Isaiah 9:6 (in the Septuagint)—that is, the Logos himself.[5] This latter passage has often been compared with Porphyry's statement that Plotinus' disciples believed the master's *daimon* to be a god.[6] Both Eusebius' childhood anecdote and Gregory's reminiscence imply a strong doctrine of divine indwelling in the holy person: the presence of God or the spirit of God is immediate and personal, to the extent that the body of the saint can be spoken of as a shrine of divine habitation. By implication at least, this divine indwelling is depicted as exceptionally deep and long-lasting.

My second story is less familiar. In his edition of Philostorgius' *Ecclesiastical History*, Bidez published as an appendix a number of texts to do with the martyrdom of Lucian of Antioch, mostly from a hitherto unpublished *Life of Constantine* and from the hagiographical work of Symeon Metaphrastes.[7] The correspondence of some of this material to what Photius reports as contained in Philostorgius' chronicle points clearly to a fairly early *passio* of Lucian standing behind

---

[4] Eusebius, *Hist. Eccl.* 6.2.11.
[5] Gregory Thaumaturgus, *Pan. logos* 4.42.
[6] *Vita Plotini* 10.
[7] *Philostorgius Kirchengeschichte. Mit dem Leben des Lucian von Antiochien und den Fragmenten eines arianischen Historiographen*, ed. Joseph Bidez, 3rd ed., revised by Friedhelm Winkelmann (Berlin, 1981), appendix VI, pp. 184–201.

both Philostorgius and the later hagiographical tradition.[8] Philostorgius has every reason to be interested in Lucian: for this so-called "Arian" historian, the heroes of his narrative are, in the first generation, Lucian and the circle around Eusebius of Nicomedia, and at later stages the Anomoians who could claim intellectual and spiritual parentage in this circle. Philostorgius is notoriously lukewarm about Arius himself, whose doctrinal errors are noted.[9] What is more, the martyrdom material is directly associated with Lucian's favourite pupil, Antony or Antoninus, who was later to be one of the teachers of Aetius—a crucial link in the "apostolic succession" of anti-Nicene theology.[10] It must be overwhelmingly likely that the original *passio* of Lucian originated in the Eusebian circle and was first current in anti-Nicene groups.

The story itself, in Photius' summary and in the longer version preserved by Symeon,[11] describes an incident occurring shortly before Lucian's death. He is in prison, being subjected to slow starvation, and his disciples believe the end is near; but the feast of the Epiphany is approaching (this is, incidentally, one of the earliest references to the feast we possess, assuming the narrative to derive from substantially contemporary sources) and Lucian prophesies that he will live to celebrate the feast with his friends. The day arrives; there is no possibility of erecting an altar in the cell, before the eyes of Lucian's guards, and the saint says, "Let my breast be your altar; I do not think it is less worthy for God than a table of soulless matter. And you can be a holy shrine [*naos*] for me, closing me in on every side". The disciples surround him as he instructs them, and place on his chained and immobilised body "the symbols of the holy rite". He looks heavenwards and, "hardly managing to get the words out", utters the "accustomed prayers". His disciples share with him in the sacrament, unseen by the unbelievers around; and Lucian dictates to Antoninus a last letter to his pupils describing these events. We are to suppose that this letter is the source for the anecdote.[12]

At first sight, these two stories seem to point to a similar idea. The breast of the holy man is holy ground; the body of the saint

---

[8] For a discussion of the textual background and a proposed stemma, see ibidem, pp. cxlvii–cl.

[9] Ibidem, p. 14 (2.3 of Philostorgius' *Hist. Eccl.*).

[10] Ibidem, pp. 44–6 (3.5 of Philostorgius' *Hist. Eccl.*).

[11] Ibidem, p. cxlix on the inadequacy of the published text of Symeon.

[12] Ibidem, pp. 195–6; p. 196.15–17 on Antoninus and the letter.

is a tangible sanctuary for the divine. But a more careful reading rapidly brings out the differences. As already noted, the Origen material presupposes a model of holiness in which the holy man is in a pretty literal sense the tabernacle of the divine spirit. The saint's living body is the place in which God dwells and acts, a place where heaven and earth meet. Something similar could be said about the body of the consecrated virgin in Methodius' *Symposium* (VIII.1.171). But in the Lucian anecdote, the stress is different: the martyr's body is *not* itself a shrine, a dwelling place for God. The saint's life as an ensouled body certainly—as Lucian says—makes that body a worthy site for the action of God in the sacrament, but that action is not as such internal to the saint's embodied being.. The *naos* is the surrounding company of disciples, forming the enclosure in which the divine presence is invoked by prayer—the *accustomed* prayer, which we must assume is some sort of liturgical formula. It is not that the holy man's suffering body is in any way a source for divine power flowing into the world; it is the focus of a corporate and regulated activity of supplication to God. The contrast to the eucharistic imagery of some earlier martyrological literature is marked. Ignatius notoriously imagines his body being ground like grain by the teeth of the beasts in the arena so as to become bread for the Church;[13] Polycarp appears to be uttering a sort of eucharistic anaphora over his own body before it is burned, and his burning flesh at the stake is like bread baking.[14] But Lucian's martyrdom is a soberer affair: attention is drawn to the impending "dissolution of his body", and this body is clearly the site, not the substance, of the eucharistic event.

The two stories are unlikely to be separated by more than a few decades, and it is difficult to see them straightforwardly as representing any kind of progression in martyrological thought. They do, however, give some sense of distinct poles, even perhaps of themes that may be emphasised as correctives to each other. At the simplest level, the Lucian material seems to reflect the kind of process so well described by Brakke and others, the process by which the exemplary doer and sufferer for Christ's sake is increasingly seen as enclosed by a corporate life under visible authority, so that such a person ceases to be in any way an independent focus or source of

---

[13] Romans 4.
[14] *Mart. Pol.*, pp. xiv–xv.

sacred power. Yet we also have abundant evidence—again admirably chronicled by Brakke—of wariness about a depersonalising of sacred power by means of the cult of relics, and a corresponding stress upon the role of the divine spirit in the *living saint*.[15] Athanasius is certainly concerned about the regularising of holiness within a hier-archical system, but is equally sceptical about holiness inhering in the bodies of martyrs as such—especially given the practice of some of his Melitian and Arian enemies of exposing the bodies of mar-tyrs in or near their churches as a token of legitimacy, and encour-aging the belief that contact with these relics secures miraculous cures.[16] If the living saint is potentially a threat to good order because of claims to the indwelling spirit, the dead saint may be equally problematic. The martyr's body and the saint's living flesh are both dangerous "sites".

But how exactly does this relate to our two anecdotes? Origen's world is one in which the created spirit attains its destiny by a kind of immersion in the eternal activity of the Logos. The incarnate Christ is precisely a pre-existent spirit utterly at one with the Word, and, as Origen says in one passage, to be at one with the Logos is to be "one spirit" with him.[17] This suggests that fidelity to Christ brings us into the same relation to the eternal Word as is enjoyed by the spirit of Jesus. When Gregory Thaumaturgus says that Origen has the Logos as a guardian angel, he is making a theologically rather awkward but quite intelligible move within this frame of ref-erence. Origen's own attunement to the divine Word is so perfect that it needs no mediation or assistance from lower spiritual powers such as are at hand to help ordinary mortals. He is well on the way to becoming, if not (in the language of later debate) *isochristos*,[18] then at least one in whom the *kind* of union that exists between Jesus and the Logos is significantly echoed. The Origenian universe is one in

---

[15] See *Vita Ant.* 90.1–21 and *Ep. Fest.* 41.

[16] *Ep. Fest.* 41, 42.

[17] *Contra Celsum* 2.9; cf. *de Princ.* 2.6.3. St. Paul says in I Cor. 6:17 that the believer is ἐν πνεῦμά with the Lord; this is obviously the supreme form of union between the Logos and creation, and so is the form of union supremely realised in the incar-nate Christ.

[18] The Origenist monks of sixth century Palestine were called *isochristoi* by their opponents because of their alleged belief that there would be no eschatological dis-tinction between Christ and believers. The view is condemned in the thirteenth anathema of the fifth Council. See John Binns, *Ascetics and Ambassadors of Christ. The Monasteries of Palestine, 314–631* (Oxford, 1994), pp. 212–4.

which there is, so to speak, space for the created spirit to move on
into such a degree of assimilation to Christ and union with the
Logos. As Origen's critics were not slow to point out, the mode of
union that exists between God and humanity in Christ is not wholly
different from the mode of union that may come to exist in any
saint.[19]

However, the more this union is understood in terms of the mediation of the sacramental life of the community, the more the holiness of the saint has to be seen as different in kind from the Saviour's.
Christ alone is perfectly united with the Logos; for the rest of us,
there is only the action of grace upon our lives. Gregg and Groh,
in their well-known and controversial essay on *Early Arianism*, quite
rightly noted the emphasis in the *Life of Antony* ascribed to Athanasius
upon the priority of what Christ does "in" Antony;[20] exactly the same
emphasis is to be found in the texts recently discussed by Brakke
from Athanasius' hand.[21] Any suggestion of a fusion between the
action of the Saviour and the action of the saint is minimised in
favour of the picture of grace triumphing in and over the saint's
mortal frailty. In *this* context, the saint's body is not so much the
tabernacle of a stable and persisting power that has become "native"
to the holy body as the site of a struggle between divine and human
will, a site marked by the cost and wounds of that struggle. Divine
presence and power are woven into the narrative of the holy person's
spiritual warfare.

Only in Christ is the flesh fully and lastingly saturated with indwelling divine power: hence the immense significance of the Eucharist
as transmitting that perfect power and immortal life to the believer's
flesh. The risen and glorified body of Christ continues, in the sacramental life of the Church, to be the carrier for a plenary and effective
divine presence. This, of course, is the heart of much of what we
think of as Alexandrian Christology: if the Logos in the flesh is fully
present only in Christ, and if Christ's glorified flesh is present in
the Eucharist, holiness is to be found primarily in this reality and
only derivatively—though still importantly—in the body of the holy

---

[19] Something like this is presumably behind the charge to which Pamphilus'
Apology attempts to respond, that Origen taught that Christ was *purus homo*.
[20] Robert Gregg, Dennis Groh, *Early Arianism—A View of Salvation* (Philadelphia/
London, 1981), ch. 4.
[21] *Ep. Fest.* 42; cf. *Vita Ant.* 37, 48, 56, etc.

person.[22] The holy body becomes so because of its participation in the ecclesial body, sacramental and communal, where "accustomed" prayer may be relied upon to make present that unique holy flesh which is Christ's. Any claim to holiness independent of this becomes immediately suspect; we can see in the early monastic literature, and in the comments of those not too friendly to the monks, how monastic attitudes to the Eucharist could become matters of contention.[23] In short, Lucian's celebration of the sacrament on the altar of his body offers a vivid and telling image of the relation between the saint and the power of God as it was conceived in circles that were cautious about Origenian indwelling: the saint has merited the presence of God here in this place and time, but the relation between saint and God remains strictly speaking a relation between two distinct agents.

Perhaps paradoxically, this more detached model for the relation of God and the holy body is the one that fosters a more reverential attitude to relics. In the "Origenian" picture, no particular sanctity can attach to the flesh independently of the indwelling Logos or divine spirit; when the flesh dies, the spirit, united to the Logos, continues its life elsewhere, in closer spiritual proximity to the eternal truth. To think of a persisting divine power in the discarded and inherently ambiguous flesh would make no sense. Thus Origen's followers remained unsympathetic to a cultus of holy places and objects; we might think here of Eusebius' ambivalent feelings about the Holy Land and its sacred sites.[24] What may surprise us more is the degree to which Athanasius seems to share such an Origenian approach— and what we know of Antony suggests that he shared Athanasius' reservations. It is significant that Antony in his letters exhorts the monk to make his body an altar; but he goes on to interpret this in terms of Elijah's sacrifice in the biblical narrative, in which the material on which the sacrifice is laid is consumed by fire from

---

[22] Henry Chadwick's celebrated essay on "Eucharist and Christology in the Nestorian Controversy", *JTS* 2 (1951), pp. 145–64, remains a point of orientation in considering this subject.

[23] Apart from the quite well-known anxieties expressed by the Synod of Gangra, there is material in the *Apophthegmata patrum* suggesting that monastic eucharistic practice was an awkward area for later generations of ascetics. See Samuel Rubenson, *The Letters of St. Antony. Monasticism and the Making of a Saint* (Minneapolis, 1995), pp. 155–7, on a tradition relating to Antony himself.

[24] Well discussed in P.W.L. Walker, *Holy City, Holy Places? Christian Attitudes to Jerusalem and the Holy Land in the Fourth Century* (Oxford, 1990).

heaven.[25] The body lifts itself Godward, holding up before God the thoughts of the heart, and is then "consumed" by the "great invisible fire" that is God's gift—prior to the refreshing rain of the Holy Spirit falling in comfort on the soul. Even if, in the world of Athanasius and Antony, the presence of the holy in the saint's body is a presence articulated in a history of struggle rather than a steady radiance of indwelling, the association of this with particular places and objects remains suspect. Control is exercised by the forms of loyal and regular common life in communion with the bishop rather than by the possession of holy things—because holy things can be owned and deployed in a semi-private way. However, by the last quarter of the fourth century, bishops have learned to deploy the ownership of relics as part of the working of hierarchical authority, and to gather relics into approved, central locations. Ambrose and Augustine in the West are the obvious examples,[26] but there are Eastern sources from the period displaying all sorts of interest in the location of relics. The vicissitudes of the remains of the martyr Babylas tell us a lot about this;[27] likewise the fact that Gregory of Nyssa is concerned to bury members of his family in proximity to the graves of notable local saints.[28]

It is not exactly that relics were not thought of as possessing *power* before the late fourth century (the North African evidence is striking here;)[29] but it is certainly the case that by this period they had come

---

[25] Letter 6.73ff.; Rubenson, *The Letters of St. Antony*, p. 221.

[26] On Ambrose's discovery of the relics of Gervasius and Protasius, see Paulinus' *Vita* 14; on Augustine's promotion of the cultus connected with the relics of St. Stephen, see his own *de miraculis S. Stephani*, and note the mention (1.7) of the placing of relics in a former Donatist church as a symbol of its "Catholicising".

[27] Sozomen, *Hist. Eccl.* 5.19, Chrysostom, *Homilia de S. Bab. contra gentes*, and other sources describe the transfer of the relics of this Antiochene martyr initially to a site near a noted shrine of Apollo, then at the instigation of the Emperor Julian to a church in the city, and later to a new basilica.

[28] *Orat. 3 in xl. mart.*; this is presumably not only a bid to secure the patronage and intercession of the saints in question, but also an attempt to associate a leading clerical dynasty with a particular sacred place. Not only bishops show an interest in relics as guarantors of power and legitimacy: Constantius' translation of the remains of Andrew, Luke and Timothy to Constantinople, recorded by Jerome (*Contra Vigilantium*) is clearly another case of using holy bodies to reinforce a particular sovereign authority—in this instance, to gain something of a sacred aura for a new city, short of indigenous holy bodies.

[29] We may recall the martyrdom of Cyprian, with cloths and handkerchiefs being laid before him as he goes to his death; and the notorious case of Lucilla and her personal and private relic at the beginning of the Donatist controversy—a good example of the problems faced also by Athanasius in relation to relics being deployed *against* local clerical authority.

to be seen pretty universally as not simply sacred things but specifically the occasion of miracle, the locus of divine activity. Touched by God, and so marked for good, the holy body that was once the site of divine action may be expected to continue to be such, a tangible link among earthly things with the Creator's power. The language may be a little extravagant, but it would not be too far wrong to say that the holy body in this context is a kind of *theatre* in which the same dramatic action may be "played" in death as in life, precisely because the agent is the immortal God rather than the human saint in isolation; and the action is authoritative and recognisable in virtue of the holy body's incorporation into the ecclesial body, by its location, its role in ecclesial devotion and ecclesial self-identification. We have already all the ingredients that will before too long lead to the placing of relics in or under the altars of all churches.

But let us return for a moment to the earlier point about the relation between divine indwelling in Christ and divine indwelling in the saints. As we noted, Origen's scheme suggests that, ultimately, there is not too much difference between the two kinds of indwelling, even if it is amply conceded that the indwelling in Christ is unique in duration and unbroken intensity. Shall we then speak of Christ's body as a *naos* for the Logos? Origen does so—though not often. But this at once poses a question about the sacramental participation of the believer in Christ's body: in an Origenian system, the point of communion in the material sacramental rite is essentially, even solely, to assist the growth of spiritual maturity. It is a necessary bridge into the interiority of Jesus, but its intrinsic significance for our material life is minimal. This scheme proved increasingly unattractive to the Alexandrian Church, as the concern for some kind of *physical* transformation as part of the redemptive event became more prominent. We do not find the language of Christ's body as shrine in Alexandrian theology after 300: the body becomes the vehicle and source of powers that will transfigure the believers' material body, and the language of a physical shrine, a container for the independent life of the divine spirit, cannot do justice to such a conviction. But precisely because this language allows a clear conceptual differentiation between the indwelling power and the enveloping humanity—even if the latter is deserving of love and reverence because of the former—it offers a promising tool for any theology concerned to guard against the compromising of divine transcendence in the incarnation. The Arian debates had brought into clear relief the potential difficulty of reconciling the full divinity of an impassible Logos with its presence in genuinely vulnerable human flesh: the language of the humanity as *naos* was apparently a way of avoiding unacceptable implications, and it was to become widespread among Syrian and Asian writers in the fourth and fifth centuries, a hallmark, in fact, of the "Antiochene" Christology.[30]

Alexandrian critics of this theology were quick to point out that this should entail the impossibility of the communication of divine life through the Eucharist.[31] If the humanity is only the envelope of the divine, remaining substantially unaffected by the presence of the Logos, what exactly is going on when that humanity is sacramentally re-presented and shared with us? Antiochene theologians do not seem to have formulated a standard reply to this charge. But it may be that their approach to the Eucharist does indeed reflect a certain following-through of the possible implications of their Christology. Theodoret, in the *Eranistes*, has a passage in which he tries to suggest what a "figural" doctrine of Christ's presence in the Eucharist might mean, a presence that amounted to something comparable with the presence of the fulfilled divine revelation in the narrative foretype (as the history of Christ's redeeming work on the cross is "present" in the story of Abraham and Isaac).[32] Theodore of Mopsuestia in his liturgical commentaries gives the first signs of the Eucharist being interpreted as a kind of "passion play", its details corresponding to the earthly life of the Lord.[33] In both these theologies, the sacramental body of Christ is not in any way an intrinsically holy object—a "tenseless" bit of glorified matter, embodying and transmitting divine power; it is the presence of a narratively defined humanity, a history achieved. It merits a response of awe and terror— the characteristic Syrian contribution to the rhetoric of sacramental devotion, as so many modern liturgists have pointed out[34]—just as

---

[30] As early as Eustathius of Antioch, who varies the metaphor by calling the humanity of Jesus a "throne" for the Logos; the same language appears in the anti-Manichaean *Acta Archelai* as a touchstone of orthodoxy. Ignatius (*Ephesians* 9) sets *naophoroi* and *christophoroi* side by side, but it must be doubtful whether he intends any specific Christological point by this.

[31] The point is already made by Cyril in his third letter to Nestorius (7) and elsewhere.

[32] *Eranistes* II, col. 165ff.

[33] See his *Catechetical homilies* 15 and 16.

[34] The "novel idea" of approaching the consecrated elements with terror may, writes Gregory Dix, *The Shape of the Liturgy* (London, 1945), p. 480 have "found a specially congenial soil in Syria, where, since time immemorial "the holy" had also meant in some way 'the dangerous'".

much as the relic of the holy person merits veneration and may be expected to manifest divine action. But the theological picture behind it is strictly comparable with the "Lucianic" model I have been attempting to sketch: here is the *site* of God's activity—but not in any sense that will bind God to or identify God with this particular phenomenon, or will threaten to compromise the transcendence of the unchanging divine person who is at work.

The point of this rather complex and laboured discussion of the Eucharist is to furnish a reminder that doctrinal accounts of the union between God and humanity in Christ are not constructed in abstraction from what is being said and thought about holiness and the possibilities of divine power inhering in some agent in the created order, or being in some way bound to a specific locus in that order. The Antiochene theology we have been examining struggles to preserve the essential integrity and transcendence of the holy; it is present on earth only in a relationship that is in some sense dialogical or dramatic in respect of created agency. Even in Christ, we have to hold on to a model of two essentially dissimilar sources of agency at work—even if we say that one consistently, even uninterruptedly, dominates the other. And this is entirely in accord with a picture of holiness that is wary of anything like a fusion between the fully and unambiguously holy on the one hand and the created human agent on the other.

This point is further borne out by looking at the Syrian traditions represented by the Pseudo-Macarian homilies, in which the language of "indwelling" is quite frequently found.[35] Here the human spirit may be indwelt by Christ or the Holy Spirit while at the same time being indwelt by passion or sin: distinct powers, in other words, may be at work in the spirit of a human being on the way to holiness. When sin or passion has finally been evicted, as something that has no natural affinity with the human spirit in its proper dignity as made by God, the Spirit or the Bridegroom may come to take up lasting residence and to "occupy" more and more of the human spirit's life in perceptible, tangible ways. In his fine monograph on the Pseudo-Macarians, Columba Stewart establishes the continuity of this cluster of images with other texts of Syrian provenance, especially the

---

[35] It is discussed at length in Columba Stewart, *"Working the Earth of the Heart"*. *The Messalian Controversy in History, Texts, and Language to A.D. 431* (Oxford, 1991), pp. 203–23.

writings of Ephraem and the *Liber graduum*, making it clear that the
stress on indwelling language and the description of the created spirit
as a shrine for the divine visitant represent a distinctively Syrian style
of talking about holiness; these idioms are rarer in the Greek literature of the period.[36] It is worth noting too that in this milieu the
imagery of the heart as an altar has some currency: the altar of the
heart, upon which is offered the sacrifice of perfect, Spirit-inspired
devotion, is the reality to which the outward forms of the liturgy
point.[37] The Lucian narrative reads almost like a parabolic summary
of this theological trope.

In the world of the Origenian anecdote, the flesh contains a spirit
that is virtually indistinguishable from the divine Logos, in the sense
that it is immersed in the Logos' action. In the world of the later
Syrian material, the created agent as a whole becomes the *naos* in
which another agency is at work—initially struggling alongside evil
impulses, finally triumphing in the achievement of a steady partnership between created and uncreated. The living saint as shrine—or,
indeed, the humanity of Jesus as shrine—has a notably different sense
from what it might mean in the Origenian context. Lucian's body
is not a shrine but the focus of a shrine; and even when *naos* language clearly reappears as a metaphor for holiness, it carries with it
implications of ontological separateness that would have been alien
to Origen's world. Yet (to reiterate the paradox) it is this theology
of ontological separation that sits the more comfortably with the
association between divine power and specific items in the world—
because the power does not depend upon the free agency, the concrete present activity of the created partner. Long vistas open up
from this point on to the turbulent landscape of debate over grace
and freedom; and there is another trajectory to be followed in the
Eastern Christian theology of holy images, which, in its mature form,
depends heavily on the idea of a transparency in created reality to

---

[36] Ibidem, pp. 208–10 on Greek usage; pp. 216–23 on the *Liber graduum* and the
Macarians.

[37] *Liber graduum* cols. 288–9, 292; Stewart, *"Working the Earth of the Heart"*, pp. 218–9;
cf. 52.2.3 in Collection I of the Macarian material. The parallel with the imagery
in Antony's sixth letter (above, n. 25) is worth noting, though the "fire from heaven"
element is not found in quite this form in the Macariana (but cf. 25.9 in Collection
II); the allusion to Elijah calling down fire from heaven in 20.1.4 of Collection III
makes a different point. Ephrem has some passages where the Elijah metaphor is
used, as in Hymn 10 on Faith (CSCO 154/5, Script. Syri 73/74, p. 51, transl. p. 35),
where the allusion is to the Eucharist.

divine power—but also upon the conviction that divine *energeia* really absorbs and transfigures created reality.

The iconodule theology, of course, presupposes not only Chalcedon but the refinements of Chalcedon laboured over by theologians of the sixth and seventh centuries. As I have already hinted, the Christological settlement (if that is the right term for it) arrived at by the end of the fifth century draws upon more than just narrowly Christological debate, and to make full sense of it we need to be aware of these ambient problems about locating the holy. Chalcedon sought the elusive balance between a holiness that always remains alien to the created order and a holiness that cuts through the narratives and mediations of the created order by appealing to a direct absorption of the created soul into uncreated Mind. The tight antitheses of the Chalcedonian *Definitio* reflect anxieties that were not at all abstract.

They were not abstract because they had to do with human power as well as divine. The relative innocence or optimism of the Origenian picture, in which there is an unproblematic continuity between God's indwelling in Christ and his presence in the saints, is inevitably eroded by conflicts over authority. Athanasius and Antony stand halfway between Origen and Lucian, in the typology I have been proposing: highly suspicious of individual claims to authority at an angle to the public life of a hierarchically governed church, they are still disposed to locate the divine indwelling in the living *saint*. But the living saint needs to be incorporated fully into an orderly community; and, even so, the emphasis is already shifting towards the action of the divine *in* the saint, rather than the synergy of human and divine. A distance opens up between divine and human agency which allows for a far more robust emphasis upon struggle and progress in the saint's historical experience. Once this element has become dominant, as happens in the Syrian tradition in its various ramifications, it is easier to treat the holy body as a tool for divine activity, which may be used practically independently of the continuing living action of the holy person. And, just as Athanasius is eager to incorporate exceptional forms of holy life within the Catholic community, and tends to regard local cults of relics as one more threat to this, the generation that followed discovered that relics too could be used as part of a consolidating episcopal strategy. The body of the holy man or woman now becomes the bearer of a double significance: it reminds the believer of the victorious, impassible, transcendent power of God precisely *by* being a passive and materially powerless object. The relentless pushing back of the boundaries of the physically bearable, characteristic especially of Syrian asceticism, could be seen as a sustained attempt to render visible the body's destiny as a passive tool for God, a site for the action of an Other.[38] The holy body becomes significant *because* it is empty, passive and subject to alien will. The Egyptian heirs of Origen in the monastic settlements of the desert had, theoretically, what we should probably regard as a "lower" doctrinal valuation of the material body; but they were pretty consistently less interested in ascetic gymnastics. If the inner life was advancing towards its proper maturity, this might well be visible in the body (as when Antony emerges from his long solitude); but the testing to the limit of the body as an act designed to display the sovereignty of the converted will is not a regular part of their ascetical strategy. The whole of this convoluted subject should warn us against the more prevalent *clichés* about "positive" and "negative" valuations of the body in early Christianity.[39]

In sum, then, I have been suggesting that the stories with which we began dramatise for us an abiding tension in early Christianity, especially from the end of the third century onwards. How is God present in the world? Evidently and uncontroversially in the lives of the saints, above all the martyrs. But is this presence a simple union with the activity of the created spirit or a more dialectical affair in which divine power wrestles with and "holds down" created will, so that this created will may in turn subdue the material body? Issues about sacramental theology and Christology are inextricably bound up with these questions, since Christ is the supreme case of holiness enfleshed; and the risks associated with some ways of understanding holiness in general are manifestly connected with the risks perceived in certain kinds of discourse about the saints and their bodies. The lines of differentiation do not run uniformly between two clearly and coherently defined theologies, and the later Byzantine accounts of the holy in the material represent elements of both of the "primitive" models with which we started. Dialectical models move towards

---

[38] Theodoret's *Historia Religiosa* is the classic source for accounts of the extremism of some Syrian ascetical exploits.

[39] Walker Bynum, *The Resurrection of the Body*, p. 92, n. 125 has a simple and telling observation on this matter: "disciplining [the body] during life and honoring it after death are not contradictory (as they would be if asceticism were a kind of Platonic denial of the body) but complementary".

a functional equivalence with simpler accounts of divine indwelling, as in the theology of iconography; but they only arrive there by way of a highly sophisticated interpretation of what the presence in action of the divine might mean. Less dialectical ways of talking still presuppose a much more radical dualism between bodies as such, as material and passive, and the realm of transcendent meaning—but may equally (and precisely because of this dualism) reflect less anxiety or conflict over the body at some levels. The underlying issues can be read as one more reflection of Christian theology's perennial effort to find a satisfactory balance between what I have elsewhere (following Jonathan Smith) called the "locative" and the "utopian" in Christian language—the recognition of the concreteness of the holy within the contingent order, always undercut by the disruptive, discontinuous elements in a narrative which is inescapably one of exile and alienation, loss and death.[40]

BIBLIOGRAPHY

Binns, John, *Ascetics and Ambassadors of Christ. The Monasteries of Palestine, 314–631* (Oxford, 1994).
Brakke, D., *Athanasius and the Politics of Asceticism* (Oxford, 1995).
———, "'Outside the Places, Within the Truth': Athanasius of Alexandria and the Localization of the Holy", *Pilgrimage and Holy Space in Late Antique Egypt*, ed. David Frankfurter (Leiden, 1998), pp. 445–81.
Brown, P., *The Cult of the Saints. Its Rise and Function in Latin Christianity* (Chicago/London, 1981).
———, *The Body and Society. Men, Women and Sexual Renunciation in Early Christianity* (New York, 1988).
Chadwick, Henry, "Eucharist and Christology in the Nestorian Controversy", *JTS* 2 (1951), pp. 145–64.
Dix, Gregory, *The Shape of the Liturgy* (London, 1945).
Gregg, Robert, Groh, Dennis, *Early Arianism—A View of Salvation* (Philadelphia/London, 1981).
Philostorgius Kirchengeschichte. Mit dem Leben des Lucian von Antiochien und den Fragmenten eines arianischen Historiographen, ed. Joseph Bidez, 3rd ed., revised by Friedhelm Winkelmann (Berlin, 1981).
Rubenson, Samuel, *The Letters of St. Antony. Monasticism and the Making of a Saint* (Minneapolis, 1995).
Stewart, Columba, *"Working the Earth of the Heart". The Messalian Controversy in History, Texts, and Language to A.D. 431* (Oxford, 1991).
Walker, P.W.L., *Holy City, Holy Places? Christian Attitudes to Jerusalem and the Holy Land in the Fourth Century* (Oxford, 1990).

---

[40] See Rowan Willams, "Does it make sense to speak of pre-Nicene orthodoxy?", *The Making of Orthodoxy. Essays in Honour of Henry Chadwick*, ed. Rowan Williams (Cambridge, 1989), pp. 6ff.

Walker Bynum, Caroline, *The Resurrection of the Body in Western Christianity, 200–1336* (New York, 1995).

Williams, Rowan, *Arius. Heresy and Tradition* (London, 1987).

————, "Does it make sense to speak of pre-Nicene orthodoxy?", *The Making of Orthodoxy. Essays in Honour of Henry Chadwick*, ed. Rowan Williams (Cambridge, 1989), pp. 1–23.

PROMOTING JERUSALEM:
CYRIL AND THE TRUE CROSS

JAN WILLEM DRIJVERS
University of Groningen

Cyril of Jerusalem is one of the many persons from Antiquity about whom we would like to know more than we actually do.[1] The sources about him are not abundant. The main information about his life and episcopate can be found in the ecclesiastical historians Rufinus, Socrates, Sozomen and Theodoret as well as in Epiphanius and Jerome. There exists one *vita* of Cyril in Armenian but this *vita* is late—it dates from the fifteenth century—and adds nothing to what is already known from earlier sources.[2] Furthermore there are his own writings, most of which date from early in his career as bishop of Jerusalem or perhaps even from before that when he was still a presbyter. His most important work is his *Catechetical Lectures*. He delivered them either in 348/9 when still a presbyter or in 350 or 351 when he was newly appointed bishop.[3] We have his *Sermon on the Paralytic* which he certainly gave before he became a bishop and his *Letter to Constantius* from 351. Cyril's *Mystagogical Catecheses* must be placed at the end of his epicopate, if indeed they are by him; they may well have been delivered by John, Cyril's successor. Over the past decades various works have been discovered and published

---

[1] For Cyril see e.g. J. Mader, *Der heilige Cyrillus, Bischof von Jerusalem in seinem Leben und seinem Schriften* (Einsiedeln, 1891); A. Paulin, *Saint Cyrille de Jérusalem Catéchète* (Paris, 1959); W. Telfer, *Cyril of Jerusalem and Nemesius of Emesa*, The Library of Christian Classics IV (London, 1955); Edward J. Yarnold, "Cyrillos von Jerusalem", *TRE* 8 (1981), pp. 261–6; R.C. Gregg, "Cyril of Jerusalem and the Arians", *Arianism. Historical and Theological Reassessments. Papers from the Ninth International Conference on Patristic Studies, Oxford September 5–10, 1983*, ed. R.C. Gregg (Philadelphia, 1985), pp. 85–109; P.C. Hanson, *The Search for the Christian Doctrine of God. The Arian Controversy 318–381* (Edinburgh, 1988), pp. 398–413; Frances M. Young, *From Nicaea to Chalcedon. A Guide to the Literature and its Background* (London, 1996⁴), pp. 124–33; *The Oxford Dictionary of the Christian Church* (1997, 3rd ed.), pp. 442–3.

[2] E. Bihain, "Une Vie arménienne de saint Cyrille de Jérusalem", *Le Muséon* 76 (1963), pp. 319–48.

[3] See now Alexis Doval, "The Date of Cyril of Jerusalem's Catecheses", *JTS* 48 (1997), pp. 129–32.

which are ascribed to Cyril; however, the authenticity of these works is debatable. Among them a Coptic encomium on Mary Magdalen, a *Sermo acephalus* and the very interesting letter in Syriac on the rebuilding of the Jewish Temple.[4]

Cyril was probably born in Jerusalem, sometime between the years 315 and 320. He was ordained presbyter by Maximus, bishop of Jerusalem, but the exact date is not known. He succeeded Maximus in 349/350 when he was appointed bishop by Acacius, the metropolitan in Caesarea. There is some confusion regarding the circumstances under which Cyril was nominated. While the sources are contradictory on this, it seems that the orthodox Maximus wanted another successor but that Cyril was supported by the Arian Acacius. It has been supposed that early in his career Cyril belonged to the Arian camp. His *Catechetical Lectures* and other writings, however, give no ground for such an opinion. It may have been Cyril's wish to become bishop of Jerusalem that made him opportunistic in christological matters, as a consequence of which Acacius had the impression that Cyril was sympathetic towards Arian views. Already soon after his consecration as bishop he fell out with Acacius—the conflict probably being about jurisdictions between the sees of Jerusalem and Caesarea, as well as Cyril's orthodoxy—and in 357 he was deposed and sent into exile. The immediate cause of this was his misappropriation of church possessions for the benefit of the poor in Jerusalem who suffered from a famine in the mid-350s.[5] He spent his exile in Tarsus but was reinstated by the Council of Seleucia of 359 which was hostile to Acacius. He was deposed and exiled again in 360 by the emperor Constantius who had come round to Acacius' view.[6]

---

[4] R.-G. Coquin, G. Godron, "Un encomion copte sur Marie-Madeleine attribué à Cyrille de Jérusalem", *Bulletin de l'Institut Francais d'Archéologie Orientale* 90 (1990), pp. 169–212; Michel Aubineau, "Un sermo acephalus ineditus—CPG 4272: Sévérien de Gabala?—restitué à Cyrille de Jérusalem", *Vig. Chr.* 41 (1987), pp. 285–9; S.P. Brock, "The Rebuilding of the Temple under Julian. A New Source", *Palestine Exploration Quarterly* 108 (1976), pp. 103–7; S.P. Brock, "A Letter Attributed to Cyril of Jerusalem on the Rebuilding of the Temple", *BSOAS* 40 (1977), pp. 267–86; repr. in idem, *Syriac Perspectives on Late Antiquity* (London, 1984). According to Brock this letter is inauthentic but this view has been contested by Ph. Wainwright, "The Authenticity of the Recently Discovered Letter Attributed to Cyril of Jerusalem", *Vig. Chr.* 40 (1986), pp. 286–93.

[5] Sozomen, *Hist. Eccl.* 4.25.

[6] Epiphanius, *Haer.* 73.37 reports that Cyril had intended to consecrate a new bishop of Caesarea during Acacius' discomfiture after the Council of Seleucia.

When Julian the Apostate became emperor in 361 Cyril was allowed to return. By then he seems to have had considerable influence in Palestine. When Acacius died in 365/366 Cyril succeeded in promoting his own nephew Gelasius to the metropolitan see of Caesarea. In 367 when the emperor Valens reverted to the policy of his predecessor Constantius, Cyril was again forced to go into exile. This third banishment was the longest of all. He only returned to Jerusalem after Valens' death in 378. This last exile probably made Cyril a fierce opponent of the Arian party. His part in the Council of Constantinople of 381 clearly emphasized the orthodoxy of Cyril's views.[7] He died in 386 or 387.

Scholars have devoted much attention to Cyril's christological stand, especially his attitude to Arianism. His theology in connection with the holy places, particularly Jerusalem, has lately been treated and contrasted with that of Eusebius in an admirable study by Peter Walker.[8] Among his writings the *Catechetical Lectures* in particular have been thoroughly studied. Cyril's conflicts with the metropolitan of Caesarea, which were focused on the position of the Jerusalem see, have also not gone unnoticed by students.[9] Less attention has been paid to Cyril's attitude towards the symbol of the True Cross and the use of this symbol in his efforts to advance the status of Jerusalem as a bishopric of prominence in the church province of Palestine and throughout the Christian world. This paper particularly focuses on the question how Cyril made use of the symbol of the cross to promote Jerusalem and add to his own spiritual authority in his conflict with Caesarea.

In the first three centuries of the Christian era Jerusalem, or Aelia Capitolina as it was then usually called, was not a city of great

---

According to Theodoret, *Hist. Eccl.* 2.23 he was exiled again because Acacius had informed Constantius that Cyril had sold a "holy robe" which had been dedicated by the emperor's father Constantine.

[7] Theodoret, *Hist. Eccl.* 5.9.

[8] P.W.L. Walker, *Holy City, Holy Places? Christian Attitudes to Jerusalem and the Holy Land in the Fourth Century* (Oxford, 1990). Also idem, "Eusebius, Cyril and the Holy Places", *Studia Patristica* 20, ed. E.A. Livingstone (Louvain, 1989), pp. 306–14.

[9] J. Lebon, "La position de Saint Cyrille de Jérusalem dans les luttes provoqués par l'Arianisme", *RHE* 20 (1924), pp. 181–210, pp. 357–86; Z. Rubin, "The Church of the Holy Sepulchre and the Conflict between the Sees of Caesarea and Jerusalem", *The Jerusalem Cathedra* 2, ed. Lee I. Levine (Jerusalem/Detroit, 1982), pp. 79–105; Z. Rubin, "The Tenure of Maximus, Bishop of Jerusalem, and the Conflict between Caesarea and Jerusalem during the Fourth Century", *Cathedra* 31 (1984), pp. 31–42 (*non vidi*).

importance for the Christian world. It was mainly seen as a (former) Jewish city. Even though Christians were of course aware of
the fact that Jerusalem played a central role in the Life and Passion
of Jesus, this Gospel tradition was only exploited by the Jerusalem
bishops from the third century onwards. Sometime in this century
a list of successive bishops from earliest times on was constructed,
analogous to those of Rome, Alexandria and Antioch, and it seems
that at the end of the century Jerusalem bishops played prominent
roles at ecclesiastical councils.[10] But it was only during the reign of
Constantine the Great that Jerusalem was raised to a position of
prominence.[11] The building of the Church of the Holy Sepulchre by
the emperor was of great importance in this respect, as was the decision of the Council of Nicaea that the bishop of Jerusalem was to
be the most honoured member after the bishops of Rome, Alexandria
and Antioch, although he remained subordinate to the metropolitan
in Caesarea.[12] By the time Cyril became bishop, Jerusalem had
become one of the most important Christian holy places, attracting
many pilgrims from all over the Roman Empire.[13] As already mentioned, soon after his ordination Cyril entered into conflicts with
Acacius. They were about the interpretation of the seventh canon
of the Nicaean Council which gave Jerusalem prominence except in
its own church province, and about Arianism. Cyril soon claimed
the primacy in Palestine for Jerusalem by arguing that his bishopric
was an apostolic see.[14] His struggle for power and the promotion of
Jerusalem was complicated by the fact that for the greater part of

---

[10] C.H. Turner, "The Early Episcopal Lists II: The Jerusalem List", *JTS* 1 (1900),
pp. 529–53; E. Honigmann, "Juvenal of Jerusalem", *DOP* 5 (1950), pp. 209–79.

[11] See E.D. Hunt, "Constantine and Jerusalem", *JEH* 48 (1997), pp. 405–24 with
references to earlier works on the subject.

[12] For the Church of the Holy Sepulchre as well as other church foundations by
Constantine in Palestine, see Eusebius, *Vita Constantini* 3.25ff., 51. The seventh canon
of Nicaea in: J.D. Mansi, *Sacrorum Conciliorum nova et amplissima Collectio* II p. 672: "Since
custom and tradition have established that the bishop of Aelia be honored, let him
have the succession of honor, safeguarding, however, the domestic right of the
metropolis" (transl. Honigmann, "Juvenal of Jerusalem", p. 212 n. 10).

[13] For the increase of the number of pilgrims see in general E.D. Hunt, *Holy
Land Pilgrimage in the Later Roman Empire A.D. 312–460* (Oxford, 1982). Of interest
with respect to pilgrimages to the Holy Land in Late Antiquity are also Pierre
Maraval, *Lieux saints en pèlerinages d'Orient. Histoire et géographie des origines à la conquête
arabe* (Paris, 1985) and Robert Oosterhout (ed.), *The Blessings of Pilgrimage* (Urbana/
Chicago, 1990).

[14] Sozomen, *Hist. Eccl.* 4.25; Theodoret, *Hist. Eccl.* 2.26.

his episcopate the empire was ruled by the Arian emperors Constantius and Valens, who evidently were on the side of the metropolitan in Caesarea. Jerusalem's position and that of its bishop was further-more complicated by the fact that after the death of Constantine, the interest of the emperors in Jerusalem waned,[15] only increasing again in the time of the Theodosian dynasty.

Cyril's theology, which can be reconstructed mainly from his *Cate-chetical Lectures* and which seems to have been of a practical nature, places Jerusalem in a prominent position. In these instructions to candidates for baptism Jerusalem plays a central role and the im-portance of the city as a place of biblical tradition is particularly em-phasized. Only in Jerusalem could the Holy Places, the witnesses of Christ's Life and Passion, be visited. Golgotha likewise was the cen-tre of the world. In the Jerusalem liturgy, the pinnacles of which are attested by the pilgrim Egeria and which is generally consid-ered to have been developed and organised by Cyril, the city itself again figures prominently. According to Cyril Jerusalem was of particu-lar interest to God and therefore, contrary to Caesarea, it was a holy and pre-eminent city.[16]

In the recent studies of Simon Price and Douglas Edwards it has been convincingly argued that there is a connection between reli-gion and political influence and that religion helps structure the net-works of power.[17] Price has made clear that the Roman imperial cult in the cities of Asia Minor was of importance both for these cities and their local elites in establishing relationships with the imperial house and advancing their own status and influence in competi-tion with other cities and their elites. Furthermore, the imperial cult also enhanced the dominance of the elites over the local populace. A relationship with the imperial house could bring all sorts of advan-tages to a city and its elites, such as easier admission to the emperor and the granting of privileges and benefactions. The imperial cult

---

[15] The only evidence we have for imperial interest in Jerusalem is Cyril's remark (*Catech.* 14.14) that the sons of Constantine were to thank for the gold, silver and precious stones which adorned the Church of the Holy Sepulchre.

[16] For Cyril's attitude to Jerusalem see Walker, *Holy City, Holy Places?*, pp. 311–46.

[17] S.R.F. Price, *Rituals and Power. The Roman Imperial Cult in Asia Minor* (Cambridge, 1984); Douglas R. Edwards, *Religion and Power. Pagans, Jews, and Christians in the Greek East* (New York/Oxford, 1996).

was therefore "a major part of the web of power that formed the fabric of society".[18] Edwards's study also deals with cities in Asia Minor in the first two centuries of our era. In contrast to Price's work, which is confined to the imperial cult, Edwards discusses pagan cults in general as well as Judaism and Christianity. He also emphasizes the importance to local elites of the Greek East of becoming part of various power relationships in the Roman Empire. To negotiate these relationships, cults were of particular importance. Important factors in this respect are the tradition of the cult, its promotion and spread, and the communication with the divine might through power brokers (generally coming from the local elite). In addition to the cult itself, religious symbols associated with it also supplied powerful images for communicating and acquiring or maintaining power and/or prestige.

While the approach of Price and Edwards has enabled us to understand better the role of power relationships in the context of pagan cults of the first centuries c.e., it might also be fruitful when applied to Christianity in the world of Late Antiquity. As has been demonstrated by Peter Brown and others,[19] bishops increasingly took over the role of patron of local elites and became figures of authority in their local communities. These bishops often shared the same social background and the same *paideia* as the secular elite, and it therefore comes as no surprise that politically they operated to a great extent in the same way as these elites. In their endeavours to anchor their city and their see in a power network, or to consolidate or enlarge their influence within power relationships, bishops resorted to cults and religious symbols. One might think here for instance of the various martyr cults which could lend great prestige and authority, if cleverly exploited, to a city and its bishop.[20] Cyril as bishop of Jerusalem clearly aimed at enlarging the prestige and authority of his episcopal see. He sought to make Jerusalem more important than it was in the church province of Palestine, and in the network of power relationships within the Roman Empire. It is not difficult to imagine what Cyril's goals were: the recognition of Jerusalem's

---

[18] Price, *Rituals and Power*, p. 248.

[19] E.g. Peter Brown, *Power and Persuasion in Late Antiquity. Towards a Christian Empire* (Madison, 1992); *CAH* XIII (1998), pp. 269–72.

[20] E.g. Peter Brown, *The Cult of the Saints. Its Rise and Function in Latin Christianity* (Chicago, 1981).

pre-eminence as an apostolic see at least in the church province of Palestine but probably also in the Christian world on the whole, the obtaining of metropolitan rights, as well as the creation of a profoundly Christian Jerusalem. To achieve his goals, religious symbols were employed: Jerusalem itself of course with its many holy sites, and also the symbol of the Cross, which until the reign of Constantine had had relatively little appeal for Christians,[21] but now became a significant means to increase the glory of Jerusalem.

The symbol of the Cross in particular was an important weapon for Cyril in his efforts to gain prominence and power. The Cross has been called the apex of Cyril's theological system[22] and in several of his works it plays a central role. In the *Catechetical Lectures* he refers regularly to the Cross and in these references he plays down the negative aspects usually connected with the Cross and the crucifixion. Instead he emphasizes the glory of the Cross. For Cyril the Cross is the glory of the Catholic Church, a source of illumination and redemption, the end of sin, the source of life, a crown of glory instead of a dishonour, the ground of salvation, the foundation of the faith, the sign of the Second Coming of Christ.[23] The symbolic value of the Cross was enhanced by the fact that the *lignum crucis* was actually present for everyone to see in the Church of the Holy Sepulchre. Three times in his *Catechetical Lectures* Cyril alludes to the material presence of the Cross as well as to the spread of its relics over a wide area. To his catechumens he remarks that "the holy wood of the Cross . . . is here to be seen on this very day, and [that] through those who take [pieces] from it in faith, it has from here already filled almost the whole world".[24] Twice more he mentions that from Jerusalem relics of the Cross are spread all over the world.[25] For Cyril, Jerusalem was evidently central to the cult of the Cross. And through the distribution of relics of the Cross Jerusalem became connected with other parts of the Christian world. In this

---

[21] See e.g. M. Sulzberger, "Le symbole de la Croix et les monogrammes de Jésus chez les premiers Chrétiens", *Byzantion* 2 (1925), pp. 337–448; P. Stockmeier, *Theologie und Kult des Kreuzes bei Johannes Chrysostomos. Ein Beitrag zum Verständnis des Kreuzes im 4. Jahrhundert*, Trierer Theologische Studien 18 (Trier, 1966).

[22] Walker, *Holy City, Holy Places?*, p. 256.

[23] *Catech.* 13.1, 19, 20, 22, 37 (cf. 2–4), 38; 15.22. See Walker, *Holy City, Holy Places?*, pp. 256–7, p. 328.

[24] *Catech.* 10.19 (PG 33, 685–687).

[25] *Catech.* 4.10 (PG 33, 470); 13.4 (PG 33, 777).

way the cult of the Cross increased in status and also the prestige
of Jerusalem as the centre of the cult was enhanced.

On 7th May 351 a strange phenomenon occurred in Jerusalem.[26]
In the sky above Golgotha there appeared a luminous cross which
extended as far as the Mount of Olives. The shining light filled the
sky over Jerusalem for more than a day and everyone there observed
the phenomenon. As a consequence, young and old, men and women,
local folk and strangers, pagans and Christians rushed to the Church
of the Holy Sepulchre to praise and acknowledge the one true God.
We know about this event because soon after its occurrence Cyril
reported it in a letter to the emperor Constantius.[27] In the letter
Cyril argues that the manifestation of the celestial Cross was conclu-
sive proof of the divine support for Constantius' reign and for his
campaigns against his enemies; Cyril refers here to the usurper
Magnentius against whom Constantius was about to launch a military campaign. Even the favours which God had endowed on
Constantius' father Constantine were surpassed. Constantine had
been given a mere earthly sign—a reference to the discovery of the
relics of the Cross—whereas Constantius was shown a sign from
heaven. By this the prophecy in the Gospel of Matthew (24:30) was
fulfilled announcing that a sign would appear in heaven heralding
the Son of Man. The celestial cross thus announces the final return
of God at the end of time and the establishment of His reign.
Constantius' reign is compared here with the divine kingdom. What
objective was Cyril attempting to achieve in sending this letter? It
was already observed half a century ago by J. Vogt that the letter
was one of the tactics he employed in his conflict with Acacius of
Caesarea.[28] This may well be the case. It was sent by way of first
fruits from Cyril to Constantius, implying that a relationship between
Jerusalem and the emperor was desired.[29] The letter was evidently

---

[26] On the date see H. Chantraine, "Die Kreuzesvision von 351—Fakten und
Probleme", *Byzantinische Zeitschrift* 86/7 (1993/4), pp. 430–41.

[27] For the letter see E. Bihain, "Épitre de Cyrille de Jérusalem à Constance sur
la Vision de la Croix (BHG3 413)", *Byzantion* 43 (1973), pp. 264–96. An English
translation is given in Telfer, *Cyril of Jerusalem and Nemesius of Emesa*, pp. 193–9. The
letter was also translated into Armenian, Georgian and Syriac; for the Syriac version see J.F. Coakley, "A Syriac Version of the Letter of Cyril of Jerusalem on the
Vision of the Cross", *Anal. Boll.* 102 (1984), pp. 71–84.

[28] J. Vogt, "Berichte über Kreuzeserscheinungen aus dem 4. Jahrhundert n. Chr.",
Annuaire de l'Institut de Philologie et d'Histoire Orientales et Slaves 9 = Mélanges Henri
Grégoire I (1949), pp. 593–606.

[29] *Letter to Constantius* 1 = Telfer, *Cyril of Jerusalem and Nemesius of Emesa*, p. 193.

designed to draw the emperor's attention to the city of Jerusalem and the see of its bishop. No evidence is available that Constantius, vis-à-vis his father, was particularly interested in Jerusalem. This letter had to change that. In practice the emperor was head of the Church; it was therefore important for Cyril and Jerusalem to have close connections with the emperor as in the days of Constantine. Cyril presented himself as the messenger of good tidings for the emperor and as the emissary of God to communicate and interpret a divine sign. It is not without significance that this sign was a Cross, a symbol so central to Cyril's theology, and that it appeared in Jerusalem. The letter had to emphasize that Jerusalem was in God's view a pre-eminent and holy city, a view which also the emperor should hold. It is noticeable in this respect that Cyril mentions in this short letter the city of Jerusalem as many as seven times. Cyril's purpose in sending the letter was evidently to negotiate a power relationship between Jerusalem and the emperor in order to obtain benefits and privileges, such as a favourable position for Jerusalem and its epicopal see in the conflict with Caesarea.[30] Unfortunately for Cyril, however, Constantius remained indifferent to the claims of Jerusalem and its bishop, and in the conflict between Jerusalem and Caesarea he took sides with the Arian Acacius.

In the beginning of the 360s Cyril was confronted with a completely different situation. For the first time in his life the Roman Empire was ruled by a pagan emperor. Although Julian the Apostate reigned only for some twenty months (361–363), Jerusalem was directly faced with the new religious policy of the emperor. Julian, who considered the Jews as his natural allies in his efforts to de-christianize the Roman Empire, decided to rebuild the Jewish Temple. Although the project, which started somewhere in the first months

---

The remark about first fruits implies that Cyril had not been bishop for very long, which is an argument for dating his nomination in 350.

[30] Vogt, "Berichte über Kreuzeserscheinungen", p. 601: "Das besondere Anliegen des Briefschreibers besteht aber deutlich darin, dass er Jerusalem, die Kirche und den Bisschofstuhl dieser Stadt, dem Kaiser nahebringen will." Cyril does not refer to the other famous celestial cross which appeared to Constantine in 312 on the evening before his battle with Maxentius. Vogt (p. 604) thinks that Cyril was deliberately reticent about this appearance since it was described by Eusebius, former metropolitan in Caesarea. Others think that Cyril may not have been familiar with Constantine's vision of the Cross; see Chantraine, "Die Kreuzesvision von 351", pp. 440–1. For Cyril's motives, see also T.D. Barnes, *Athanasius and Constantius. Theology and Politics in the Constantinian Empire* (Cambridge [Mass.], 1993), pp. 107–8.

of 363, was a complete failure, the Christian reaction to it was vehement. Gregory of Nazianzus, Ephraem Syrus, the ecclesiastical historians and others in their descriptions of the rebuilding of the Temple
are utterly reproachful of Julian and the Jews and ascribe the failure of the event to God's intervention.[31] Though the restoration of
the Temple was an attempt to undermine the position of Jerusalem
as a Christian holy place, a position for which Cyril fought hard,
strangely enough there is no reaction from the bishop of Jerusalem,
except for his alleged remark mentioned by the ecclesiastical historians with reference to Jesus' prophecy in Matthew 24:2 that the
Jews would never be able to put one stone upon another.[32] There
is of course Cyril's most interesting letter in Syriac on the event, but
its authenticity is debated. All sources, genuine or not, agree that
the restoration was abandoned because of earthquakes, storms and
fires sent by God. As a symbol of the Christian victory and God's
power, a luminous cross appeared in the sky above Jerusalem. Those
who witnessed this miracle had the sign of the cross burnt into their
clothes and when afterwards they spoke about this miracle, the cross
on their bodies became fluorescent. The descriptions of the failure
of the restoration of the Temple demonstrate again the special relationship between Jerusalem and the symbol of the cross. But who is
responsible for this miraculous story about the celestial cross? This
matter, with which as far as I know nobody has concerned himself,
is of some interest, especially since there was a fully developed story—
in Ephraem Syrus and Gregory of Nazianzus—about the failure of

---

[31] Gregory Nazianzus, *Orat.* 5.3–4; Ephraem Syrus, *HcJul.* 4.18–23; Rufinus, *Hist.*
Eccl. 10.38–40; Socrates, *Hist. Eccl.* 3.20; Sozomen, *Hist. Eccl.* 5.22; Philostorgius,
Hist. Eccl. 7.9; Theodoret, *Hist. Eccl.* 5.22.

[32] Rufinus, *Hist. Eccl.* 10.38; Socrates, *Hist. Eccl.* 3.20. On the rebuilding of the
temple see e.g. M. Adler, "Kaiser Julian und die Juden", *Julian Apostata*, ed. R. Klein
(Darmstadt, 1978), pp. 48–111 (transl. of "The Emperor Julian and the Jews", *The
Jewish Quarterly Review* 5 (1893), pp. 591–651); F. Blanchetière, "Julien. Philhellène,
philosémite, antichrétien. L'affaire du Temple de Jérusalem (363)", *Journal of Jewish
Studies* 31 (1980), pp. 61–81; D. Levenson, "Julian's Attempt to rebuild the Temple:
An Inventory of Ancient and Medieval Sources", *Of Scribes and Scrolls. Studies on the
Hebrew Bible, Intertestamental Judaism, and Christian Origins presented to John Strugnell on
the occasion of his sixtieth birthday*, eds. Harold W. Attridge, John J. Collins, Thomas
H. Tobin (Lanham/New York/London, 1990), pp. 261–79; Jan Willem Drijvers,
"Ammianus Marcellinus 23.1.2–3: The Rebuilding of the Temple in Jerusalem",
Cognitio Gestorum. The Historiographic Art of Ammianus Marcellinus, Koninklijke Nederlandse Akademie van Wetenschappen Verhandelingen, Afd. Letterkunde, Nwe. Reeks,
vol. 148, eds. J. den Boeft, D. den Hengst, H.C. Teitler (Amsterdam, 1992), pp.
19–26.

the Temple's restoration shortly after the project was abandoned and Julian's death on 26th June 363. Could it be that Cyril himself created the story to demonstrate God's special care for Jerusalem by sending the victorious sign of the Cross? Could it be that Cyril cleverly exploited the failed rebuilding of the Temple by emphasizing Jerusalem's pre-eminent position as a Christian city? In other words, did Cyril make use of the dramatic events of 363 to promote his own episcopal see? Did he turn an event which could have had disastrous consequences for Christian Jerusalem into a victory by creating this story about a victorious celestial cross? Unfortunately the sources do not yield an affirmative answer to these questions, but the assumption is not unlikely considering the fact that Cyril had some special interest in celestial crosses and was apparently well versed in composing stories in which the symbol of the Cross and Jerusalem are prominent (see below). In one of his *Catechetical Lectures* Cyril had already referred to the coming of the Antichrist and the rebuilding of the Temple, as well as to the failure of the restoration which would be accompanied by God's sending of "pretended signs and wonders".[33] In 363 Cyril apparently saw his chance to realise his own remarkable prediction of 349 for the benefit of Jerusalem and his own position.

The symbol of the Cross was also prominent in the liturgy of Jerusalem. It is generally held that Cyril was responsible for the development and organisation of Jerusalem's liturgical cycle.[34] Part of this liturgy is described in the *Itinerary of Egeria*. Egeria visited Jerusalem in the early 380s and celebrated Holy Week there. The climax of these festivities was of course Good Friday, when the community of Jerusalem and the pilgrims who happened to be present assembled at the Church of the Holy Sepulchre. The bishop took his seat behind a table on which a gold and silver box was placed containing the wood of the Cross. One by one the believers went past the table and they touched the wood with their forehead, then with their eyes and then kissed it.[35] As is evident from Egeria's description, the Cross, thanks to Cyril, played a prominent role in the Jerusalem

---

[33] *Catech.* 15.15.

[34] E.g. John Wilkinson, *Egeria's Travels to the Holy Land* (Jerusalem/Warminster, 1981, 2nd rev. ed.), pp. 54–5. For the Jerusalem liturgy of Late Antiquity see John F. Boldovin, *Liturgy in Ancient Jerusalem* (Nottingham, 1989).

[35] *It. Eger.* 37.1–3.

liturgy. Possibly the relics of the Cross were also shown during the
Encaenia, the date on which the Church on Golgotha was consecrated. This date coincides with that of the discovery of the Cross.[36]
It is finally time to have a closer look at the story of the discovery
of the Cross and the possible role of Cyril in its creation.

Cyril referred regularly to the material presence of relics of the
Cross in the Church of the Holy Sepulchre. In his letter to Constantius
he explicitly states that these relics had been found in the reign of
Constantine. But no story yet existed in the early years of Cyril's
episcopate about how the cross came to be present in the Church
of the Holy Sepulchre. If there had been one, Cyril would certainly
have referred to it in his lectures for the catechumens and in his
letter to Constantius. Some forty years later, however, there was a
fully developed legend about how the Cross was discovered in Jerusalem by Helena, the mother of Constantine.[37] It tells the story of
how the pious Helena travelled to Jerusalem to search for the Cross.
A heavenly sign showed her the spot where it was buried. She tore
down the temple of Aphrodite which was built on that spot and
found deep beneath the rubble three crosses. The True Cross was
identified with the help of Macarius, Jerusalem's bishop at the time.
Through praying and by bringing the crosses into contact with a
mortally ill woman, the Cross of Christ was eventually recognised.
At the place where it was found Helena built a marvellous church,
i.e. the Church of the Holy Sepulchre. Part of the Cross was left in
Jerusalem and part was sent to Constantine, who also received the
nails with which Christ's body was attached to the Cross.[38] In this

---

[36] *It. Eger.* 48.1–2.

[37] For the legend of *inventio crucis* see S. Heid, "Der Ursprung der Helenalegende
im Pilgerbetrieb Jerusalems", *JbAC* 32 (1989), pp. 41–71; S. Heid, "Zur frühen
Protonike- und Kyriakoslegende", *Anal. Boll.* 109 (1991), pp. 73–108; S. Borgehammar,
How the Holy Cross was Found. From Event to Medieval Legend (Stockholm, 1991); Jan
Willem Drijvers, *Helena Augusta. The Mother of Constantine the Great and Her Finding of
the True Cross* (Leiden, 1992); H. Heinen, "Helena, Konstantin und die Überlieferung
der Kreuzauffindung im 4. Jahrhundert", *Der Heilige Rock zu Trier. Studien zur Geschichte
und Verehrung der Tunika Christi*, eds. E. Aretz et al. (Trier, 1995), pp. 83–117; Han
J.W. Drijvers & Jan Willem Drijvers, *The Finding of the True Cross. The Judas Kyriakos
Legend in Syriac. Introduction, Text and Translation*, CSCO 565, Subs. 93 (Louvain, 1997).

[38] This short summary is based on Rufinus, *Hist. Eccl.* 10.7–8. This text comes
closest to the lost original of Gelasius of Caesarea (see below). Constantine used the
nails to have a horse's bridle made—thereby fulfilling the Old Testament prophecy
of Zechariah 14:20—and for adding strength to a helmet which he used in battle.

legend not only Helena figures prominently but also Macarius, Jerusalem's bishop at the time the Cross was allegedly found (the mid 320s). By way of a miraculous healing Macarius identified the True Cross from the three crosses which Helena had found on Golgotha. The legend clearly gives expression to the wish for a three-cornered relationship between the imperial house, represented by Helena, Jerusalem and its episcopal see, represented by Macarius. The Cross was the symbol which was meant to cement this relationship. Helena's partition of the Cross—part was left in Jerusalem and another part was sent to Constantine—by which the alliance between Jerusalem and the imperial house was confirmed, is the clearest expression of this. Opinions differ about how this remarkable legend, which became tremendously popular in Late Antiquity and thereafter, came into being.[39] It is certain that the legend of the discovery of the Cross originated in Jerusalem during the episcopate of Cyril and was first put into writing by Gelasius of Caesarea in his now lost *Church History*.[40] This latter work was written at the behest of Cyril, Gelasius' maternal uncle, and appeared around 390. Not much is known about Gelasius but after Acacius' death (*c.* 365) he was made bishop and metropolitan of Caesarea by Cyril. He was, however, prevented from occupying his see until 378. Presumably there existed, in particular from 378 onwards, a close collaboration between Cyril and his nephew. It is not improbable that Cyril was responsible for the origin and composition of the legend of the Cross and that he suggested to Gelasius that he include the story in his *Church History*. The aim of the legend is obviously to sustain the authenticity of the Cross present in Jerusalem but also, and perhaps primarily, to establish a

---

[39] The legend has three versions: 1. the Helena legend included in the Church Historians and related by Ambrose, Paulinus of Nola and Sulpicius Severus; 2. the Protonike legend only known in Syriac (and later also in Armenian) and incorporated in the Edessene *Doctrina Addai*; 3. the Judas Kyriakos legend in which the Jew Judas finds the Cross for Helena. It is especially this third version of the legend which became so popular.

[40] F. Winkelmann, *Untersuchungen zur Kirchengeschichte des Gelasios von Kaisereia*, Sitzungsberichte der deutschen Akademie der Wissenschaften zu Berlin 65.1 (Berlin, 1966); F. Winkelmann, "Charakter und Bedeutung der Kirchengeschichte des Gelasios von Kaisereia", *Byzantinische Forschungen* 1 (1966), pp. 346–85. Winkelmann was able to reconstruct the contents of Gelasius' *Church History*. Fragment 20 of this reconstruction deals with the legend of the Cross. Rufinus' version of the legend (*Hist. Eccl.* 10.7–8) resembles that of Gelasius to a great extent; see Drijvers, *Helena Augusta*, pp. 100ff.

relationship between Jerusalem, its bishop and the imperial rule of
Rome. In that respect the purpose of the legend is remarkably consistent and comparable with that of Cyril's *Letter to Constantius*. It was
the perfect myth to promote Jerusalem.

During Cyril's episcopate Jerusalem lived in conflict with Caesarea.
This conflict had a theological/christological aspect but was also
about power and influence in the church province of Palestine. In
the same period connections with the imperial power were strained;
the Arian leanings of Constantius and his successors were certainly
not advantageous to Jerusalem. But it also seems that Constantine's
successors did not have the same interest in Jerusalem as the first
Christian emperor. In these circumstances it was necessary to preserve and extend the prestige and power of Jerusalem as a holy place
and as an apostolic see. Cyril used his spiritual authority to act as
patronus of the local community. He acted in the same way as local
elites in former centuries had done to advance the status of their
city and themselves: he exploited the main cult of Jerusalem, that is
the cult of the Cross—which he himself helped to develop—, to link
himself and his episcopate to power relationships. The connection
with the imperial house was of special importance. In a world of
an imperialized Christianity good relations with the emperor were
extremely profitable. To negotiate his access to power networks Cyril
used miracles (the celestial crosses), texts (his *Letter to Constantius* and
the legend of *inventio crucis*) and the Cross itself (the relics) as his
ticket. One may wonder whether Cyril's policy was successful. I think
it was. His conflict with Caesarea was resolved by the nomination
of his own nephew Gelasius as metropolitan. Even though theoretically Cyril was subordinate to Gelasius, Cyril actually was the bishop
with the greater authority; the list of participants at the Council of
Constantinople of 381, where Cyril's name is at the top of the list
of bishops of Palestine and Gelasius is mentioned second, is proof
of this.[41] Gelasius must have accepted the primacy of Jerusalem over
that of Caesarea, otherwise he would never have included in his
Church History the narrative about the discovery of the Cross in which
empress and bishop cooperate so closely and in which Jerusalem is

---

[41] C.H. Turner, "Canons Attributed to the Council of Constantinople, A.D. 381.
Together with the Names of the Bishops, from two Patmos MSS ROB'RO'", *JTS*
15 (1914), pp. 161–78, p. 168.

so central.[42] The relationship with the imperial house greatly improved during the last years of Cyril's episcopate and thereafter. The Theodosian dynasty showed increasing interest in the Holy Land and in Jerusalem. Female members of the imperial family visited Palestine and were not averse to being presented as new Helenas.[43] Cyril had evidently succeeded in his efforts to promote Jerusalem. By cleverly using the symbol of the Cross Cyril had made Jerusalem and its bishop into an important participant in the power networks of the late antique Roman Empire.

BIBLIOGRAPHY

Adler, M, "Kaiser Julian und die Juden", *Julian Apostata*, ed. R. Klein (Darmstadt, 1978), pp. 48–111; transl. of "The Emperor Julian and the Jews", *The Jewish Quarterly Review* 5 (1893), pp. 591–651.

Aubineau, Michel, "Un sermo acephalus ineditus—CPG 4272: Sévérien de Gabala?—restitué à Cyrille de Jérusalem", *Vig. Chr.* 41 (1987), pp. 285–9.

Barnes, T.D., *Athanasius and Constantius. Theology and Politics in the Constantinian Empire* (Cambridge [Mass.], 1993).

Bihain, E., "Une Vie arménienne de saint Cyrille de Jérusalem", *Le Muséon* 76 (1963), pp. 319–48.

———, "L'Épitre de Cyrille de Jérusalem à Constance sur la Vision de la Croix (BHG3 413)", *Byzantion* 43 (1973), pp. 264–96.

Blanchetière, F., "Julien. Philhellène, philosémite, antichrétien. L'affaire du Temple de Jérusalem (363)", *Journal of Jewish Studies* 31 (1980), pp. 61–81.

Boldovin, John F., *Liturgy in Ancient Jerusalem* (Nottingham, 1989).

Borgehammar, S., *How the Holy Cross was Found. From Event to Medieval Legend* (Stockholm, 1991).

Brock, S.P. "The Rebuilding of the Temple under Julian. A New Source", *Palestine Exploration Quarterly* 108 (1976), pp. 103–7.

———, "A Letter Attributed to Cyril of Jerusalem on the Rebuilding of the Temple", *BSOAS* 40 (1977), pp. 267–86; repr. in idem, *Syriac Perspectives on Late Antiquity* (London, 1984).

Brown, Peter, *The Cult of the Saints. Its Rise and Function in Latin Christianity* (Chicago, 1981).

———, *Power and Persuasion in Late Antiquity. Towards a Christian Empire* (Madison, 1992).

---

[42] After Cyril's death Jerusalem's position waned again and the bishop of Caesarea once again became the more powerful. During the episcopate of Juvenal (422–458) Jerusalem achieved official and permanent metropolitan status and did become a patriarchate; see Honigman, "Juvenal of Jerusalem".

[43] Hunt, *Holy Land Pilgrimage*, pp. 155ff., pp. 221ff.; K.G. Holum, *Theodosian Empresses. Women and Imperial Dominion in Late Antiquity* (Berkeley/Los Angeles/London, 1982), pp. 184ff., pp. 217ff.; Jan Willem Drijvers, "Helena Augusta: Exemplary Christian Empress", *Studia Patristica* 24, ed. E.A. Livingstone (Louvain, 1993), pp. 85–90; Leslie Brubaker, "Memories of Helena: Patterns in Imperial Female Matronage in the Fourth and Fifth Centuries", *Women, Men and Eunuchs. Gender in Byzantium*, ed. Liz James (London/New York, 1997), pp. 52–75.

Brubaker, Leslie, "Memories of Helena: Patterns in Imperial Female Matronage in the Fourth and Fifth Centuries", *Women, Men and Eunuchs. Gender in Byzantium*, ed. Liz James (London/New York, 1997), pp. 52–75.

Chantraine, H., "Die Kreuzesvision von 351—Fakten und Probleme", *Byzantinische Zeitschrift* 86/7 (1993/4), pp. 430–41.

Coakley, J.F., "A Syriac Version of the Letter of Cyril of Jerusalem on the Vision of the Cross", *Anal. Boll.* 102 (1984), pp. 71–84.

Coquin, R.-G., Godron, G., "Un encomion copte sur Marie-Madeleine attribué à Cyrille de Jérusalem", *Bulletin de l'Institut Français d'Archéologie Orientale* 90 (1990), pp. 169–212.

Doval, Alexis, "The Date of Cyril of Jerusalem's Catecheses", *JTS* 48 (1997), pp. 129–32.

Drijvers, Jan Willem, *Helena Augusta. The Mother of Constantine the Great and Her Finding of the True Cross* (Leiden, 1992).

———, "Ammianus Marcellinus 23.1.2–3: The Rebuilding of the Temple in Jerusalem", *Cognitio Gestorum. The Historiographic Art of Ammianus Marcellinus*, Koninklijke Nederlandse Akademie van Wetenschappen Verhandelingen, Afd. Letterkunde, Nwe. Reeks, vol. 148, eds. J. den Boeft, D. den Hengst, H.C. Teitler (Amsterdam, 1992), pp. 19–26.

———, "Helena Augusta: Exemplary Christian Empress", *Studia Patristica* 24, ed. E.A. Livingstone (Louvain, 1993), pp. 85–90.

Drijvers, Han J.W. & Drijvers, Jan Willem, *The Finding of the True Cross. The Judas Kyriakos Legend in Syriac. Introduction, Text and Translation*, CSCO 565, Subs. 93 (Louvain, 1997).

Edwards, Douglas R., *Religion and Power. Pagans, Jews, and Christians in the Greek East* (New York/Oxford, 1996).

Gregg, R.C., "Cyril of Jerusalem and the Arians", *Arianism. Historical and Theological Reassessments. Papers from the Ninth International Conference on Patristic Studies, Oxford September 5–10, 1983*, ed. R.C. Gregg (Philadelphia, 1985), pp. 85–109.

Hanson, P.C., *The Search for the Christian Doctrine of God. The Arian Controversy 318–381* (Edinburgh, 1988).

Heid, S., "Der Ursprung der Helenalegende im Pilgerbetrieb Jerusalems", *JbAC* 32 (1989), pp. 41–71.

———, "Zur frühen Protonike- und Kyriakoslegende", *Anal. Boll.* 109 (1991), pp. 73–108.

Heinen, H., "Helena, Konstantin und die Überlieferung der Kreuzauffindung im 4. Jahrhundert", *Der Heilige Rock zu Trier. Studien zur Geschichte und Verehrung der Tunika Christi*, eds. E. Aretz et al. (Trier, 1995), pp. 83–117.

Holum, K.G., *Theodosian Empresses. Women and Imperial Dominion in Late Antiquity* (Berkeley/Los Angeles/London, 1982).

Honigmann, E., "Juvenal of Jerusalem", *DOP* 5 (1950), pp. 209–79.

Hunt, E.D., *Holy Land Pilgrimage in the Later Roman Empire A.D. 312–460* (Oxford, 1982).

———, "Constantine and Jerusalem", *JEH* 48 (1997), pp. 405–24.

Lebon, J., "La position de Saint Cyrille de Jérusalem dans les luttes provoqués par l'Arianisme", *RHE* 20 (1924), pp. 181–210.

Levenson, D., "Julian's Attempt to rebuild the Temple: An Inventory of Ancient and Medieval Sources", *Of Scribes and Scrolls. Studies on the Hebrew Bible, Intertestamental Judaism, and Christian Origins presented to John Strugnell on the occasion of his sixtieth birthday*, eds. Harold W. Attridge, John J. Collins, Thomas H. Tobin (Lanham/New York/London, 1990), pp. 261–79.

Mader, J., *Der heilige Cyrillus, Bischof von Jerusalem in seinem Leben und seinem Schriften* (Einsiedeln, 1891).

Maraval, Pierre, *Lieux saints en pèlerinages d'Orient. Histoire et géographie des origines à la conquête arabe* (Paris, 1985).
Oosterhout, Robert (ed.), *The Blessings of Pilgrimage* (Urbana/Chicago, 1990).
Paulin, A., *Saint Cyrille de Jérusalem Catéchète* (Paris, 1959).
Price, S.R.F., *Rituals and Power. The Roman Imperial Cult in Asia Minor* (Cambridge, 1984).
Rubin, Z., "The Church of the Holy Sepulchre and the Conflict between the Sees of Caesarea and Jerusalem", *The Jerusalem Cathedra* 2, ed. Lee I. Levine (Jerusalem/Detroit, 1982), pp. 79–105.
———, "The Tenure of Maximus, Bishop of Jerusalem, and the Conflict between Caesarea and Jerusalem during the Fourth Century", *Cathedra* 31 (1984), pp. 31–42.
Stockmeier, P., *Theologie und Kult des Kreuzes bei Johannes Chrysostomos. Ein Beitrag zum Verständnis des Kreuzes im 4. Jahrhundert*, Trierer Theologische Studien 18 (Trier, 1966).
Sulzberger, M., "Le symbole de la Croix et les monogrammes de Jésus chez les premiers Chrétiens", *Byzantion* 2 (1925), pp. 337–448.
Telfer, W., *Cyril of Jerusalem and Nemesius of Emesa*, The Library of Christian Classics IV (London, 1955).
Turner, C.H., "The Early Episcopal Lists II: The Jerusalem List", *JTS* 1 (1900), pp. 529–53.
———, "Canons Attributed to the Council of Constantinople, A.D. 381. Together with the Names of the Bishops, from two Patmos MSS ROB'RO'", *JTS* 15 (1914), pp. 161–78.
Vogt, J., "Berichte über Kreuzeserscheinungen aus dem 4. Jahrhundert n. Chr.", *Annuaire de l'Institut de Philologie et d'Histoire Orientales et Slaves* 9 = Mélanges Henri Grégoire I (1949), pp. 593–606.
Wainwright, Ph., "The Authenticity of the Recently Discovered Letter Attributed to Cyril of Jerusalem", *Vig. Chr.* 40 (1986), pp. 286–93.
Walker, P.W.L., "Eusebius, Cyril and the Holy Places", *Studia Patristica* 20, ed. E.A. Livingstone (Louvain, 1989), pp. 306–14.
———, *Holy City, Holy Places? Christian Attitudes to Jerusalem and the Holy Land in the Fourth Century* (Oxford, 1990).
Wilkinson, John, *Egeria's Travels to the Holy Land* (Jerusalem/Warminster, 1981, 2nd rev. ed.).
Winkelmann, F., *Untersuchungen zur Kirchengeschichte des Gelasios von Kaisereia*, Sitzungsberichte der deutschen Akademie der Wissenschaften zu Berlin 65.1 (Berlin, 1966).
———, "Charakter und Bedeutung der Kirchengeschichte des Gelasios von Kaisereia", *Byzantinische Forschungen* 1 (1966), pp. 346–85.
Yarnold, Edward J., "Cyrillos von Jerusalem", *TRE* 8 (1981), pp. 261–6.
Young, Frances M., *From Nicaea to Chalcedon. A Guide to the Literature and its Background* (London, 1996⁴).

PART THREE

THE REPRESENTATION OF AUTHORITY

THE LIFE AND *LIVES* OF GREGORY THAUMATURGUS

STEPHEN MITCHELL

University of Wales, Swansea

The most familiar church leader from third century Asia Minor is Gregory, formerly known as Theodorus, later known as Thaumaturgus, bishop of the Pontic metropolis of Neocaesarea from about 240 to 270. This is largely due to the work of his namesake, Gregory of Nyssa, who wrote a panegyrical *Life of Gregory* around 380. Famously the panegyric remarks that when Gregory took up office, reluctantly, as Neocaesarea's first bishop, there were only seventeen Christians in the city; when he died only seventeen pagans remained unconverted. His spiritual authority was interpreted as the decisive factor in the transformation of the Pontic region from a pagan to a Christian world.

I. *The Life*

The historical basis for reconstructing Gregory's career is notoriously insecure. Recent studies of Gregory of Nyssa's *Life of Gregory* have shown that most of the work is no more than pious fiction. We are in a better position to judge than is often the case with hagiographic enquiry, in that we do possess a few authentic works of Gregory himself, and these suffice to show that much of what Gregory of Nyssa wrote was, quite simply, factually wrong. We must begin with these.

Our main sources for the authentic Gregory are his own writings. Works ascribed to him fill nearly 225 columns of the *Patrologia Graeca*, but this tally contracts to half on closer scrutiny.[1] Supposedly authentic are a version of the Creed, quoted in Gregory of Nyssa's *Life* from

---

[1] Evagrius, *Hist. Eccl.* 3.9 comments on the spurious attributions of works to Gregory Thaumaturgus. For the work *Ad Theopompum*, preserved in a Syriac version and ascribed to Gregory, see L. Abramowski, "Die Schrift Gregors des Lehrers 'ad Theopompum' und Philoxenus von Mabbug", *Zeitschrift für Kirchengeschichte* 89 (1978), pp. 273–90; repr. in eadem, *Formula and Context. Studies in Early Christian Thought* (Aldershot, 1992).

a copy which he claimed was still to be seen in Gregory's church at Neocaesarea (PG 46, 912d–913a);[2] the *Canonical Letter*, sent to another senior churchman, perhaps a neighbouring bishop, with instructions how to deal with Christians who had compromised themselves during the Gothic raids on the Pontus during the 250s;[3] a speech of farewell and thanks delivered in praise of his teacher Origen;[4] and a paraphrase of the book of Ecclesiastes.[5] We also possess a copy of Origen's reply to Gregory.[6] Rufinus, in the section on Gregory Thaumaturgus which he added to his translation of Eusebius' *Church History* (written in 402/3), mentions the paraphrase of Ecclesiastes and gives a Latin version of his Creed.[7] According to Jerome in the entry for Gregory in his treatise *On Illustrious Men*, the Panegyric and the Metaphrasis were available for inspection in his day, doubtless at Caesarea itself.[8] Jerome, however, was more guarded in his allusion to the popular stories, turned into high art by Gregory of Nyssa, about Gregory's miracles:

> Theodorus, on his departure, wrote a panegyric of thanks to Origen and delivered it before a large assembly. Origen himself was present. The panegyric is extant at the present day. He wrote also a short but very valuable paraphrase on Ecclesiastes and current repute speaks of other epistles of his, but more especially of the signs and wonders, which as bishop he performed to the great glory of the churches.[9]

---

[2] A Declaration of Faith; PG 10, 984–8; PG 46, 912D–13A. English transl. *The Ante-Nicene Fathers* VI, 7.

[3] PG 10, 1019–48; *The Ante-Nicene Fathers* VI, 18–20. K.M. Fouskas, Γρηγορίου Θαυματουργοῦ ἡ κανονικὴ ἐπιστολή (Athens, 1978).

[4] The Oration and Panegyric addressed to Origen: PG 10, 1049–1104; *The Ante-Nicene Fathers* VI, 21–39; P. Koetschau, *Des Gregorios Thaumaturgos Dankrede an Origenes* (Freiburg im Breisgau, 1894); H. Crouzel (ed.), *Grégoire le Thaumaturge. Remerciement à Origène suivi de la lettre d'Origène à Grégoire*, SC 148 (Paris, 1969); P. Guyot, R. Klein, *Gregor der Wundertäter. Oratio prosphonetica ac panegyrica in Origenem/Dankrede an Origenes*, Fontes Christiani 24 (Freiburg im Breisgau, 1996).

[5] Metaphrasis of the Book of Ecclesiastes: PG 10, 988–1018; *The Ante-Nicene Fathers* VI, 9–17; J. Jarik, *Gregorius Thaumaturgos' Paraphrase of Ecclesiastes*, Society of Biblical Literature, Septuaginta and Cognate Studies 29 (Atlanta, 1990).

[6] H. Crouzel (ed.), *Grégoire le Thaumaturge. Remerciement à Origène suivi de la lettre d'Origène à Grégoire*, SC 148 (Paris, 1969), pp. 186–94; English transl. in J.W. Trigg, *Origen*, The Early Christian Fathers (London/New York 1998), pp. 210–3.

[7] Rufinus, *Hist. Eccl.* 7.28.2. This addition to Rufinus' *Church history* was edited by E. Schwarz and T. Mommsen, *Eusebios. Die Kirchengeschichte* II.2, GCS (1908), pp. 952–6.

[8] For Jerome at Caesarea, see J.N.D. Kelly, *Jerome. His Life, Writings and Controversies* (London, 1975), p. 98, p. 135.

[9] Jerome, *De Vir. Ill.* 65. Jerome, *Comm. in Eccl.* 4; *Epist.* 70.4 remarks that "books

The contents of the panegyric of Origen, the first surviving Christian speech in this genre,[10] confirm the testimony of Jerome, that it was delivered on the occasion of Gregory's departure from his teacher. It contains invaluable biographical information, and also provides the fullest description from any source of Origen's profession as a teacher of Christian philosophy.[11] Biographically the most important section of the panegyric is paragraph 5, in which Gregory explains his own conversion and how he had originally become Origen's pupil.

Gregory recounts that he had been brought up in his father's house as a pagan. His father died when he was fourteen, and from that time, as his own powers of reason were reaching maturity, he began to receive visits from the Sacred Word, urging him towards conversion. His mother made him attend the lessons of a teacher of public speaking. During this studentship an event which Gregory attributed to the appearance of his providential guardian suggested to one of his teachers that Gregory be instructed in Latin and then in Roman law. This, his teacher pointed out, would be Gregory's passport to a career (ἐφόδιον), whether he intended to become an advocate in the courts or follow another liberal profession. The study of law led from Pontus to Berytus, "a city not far distant from this territory (i.e. Caesarea), somewhat latinized, and credited with a school for these legal studies."[12] At this time Origen himself had moved from Alexandria to Caesarea. Gregory even then might have gone to Rome, but for the governor of Palestine suddenly commanding that Gregory's sister's husband come to Caesarea and join his staff. The husband sent for his wife to follow him, and Gregory was required to escort her. A military escort provided sufficient extra tickets for the imperial transport system, and by this chance Gregory came to Palestine to study Roman law at Berytus.[13] The whole section

---

survive of Theodorus, who was afterwards called Gregorius, a man with the character and virtues of the apostles."

[10] George A. Kennedy, *Classical Rhetoric and its Christian and Secular Tradition from Ancient to Modern Times* (London, 1980), pp. 140–1.

[11] P. Nautin, *Origène, sa vie et son oeuvre* (Paris, 1977), pp. 183–97, contests the ascription of the *Panegyric of Origen* to Gregory, but there are no strong grounds for scepticism. The case for the traditional attribution is restated by H. Crouzel, "Faut-il voir trois personnages en Grégoire le Thaumaturge?", *Gregorianum* 60 (1979), pp. 287–320.

[12] πόλις Ῥωμαϊκωτέρα πως, καὶ τῶν νόμων τούτων εἶναι πιστευθεῖσα παιδευτήριον; PG 10, 1065C.

[13] J. Modrzejewski, "Grégoire le Thamaturge et le droit romain: à propos d' une édition récente", *Revue du Droit* 49 (1971), pp. 313–24; F. Millar, "Culture grecque

lucidly illustrates the career opportunities available to aspiring and able members of the provincial gentry in the third and fourth centuries.[14]

More information comes from the beginning of the speech. It begins conventionally with a highly elaborate declaration of the speaker's inability to do justice to the subject before him. For eight years, Gregory says, he had no opportunity to create or deliver an oratorical exercise in the Greek manner. Instead he had been pre-occupied with philosophical dialectic which was concerned not with form but with content. To make matters worse he had also had to devote himself to another language altogether, Latin, in order to master the language of the Roman laws:

> Moreover another branch of learning occupies my mind completely, and the mouth binds the tongue if I should desire to make any speech, however brief, with the voice of the Greeks: I refer to those admirable laws of our sages by which the affairs of all the subjects of the Roman Empire are now directed, and which are neither composed nor learnt with difficulty. These are wise and exact in themselves, and manifold and admirable, and, in a word, thoroughly Grecian; and they are expressed and committed to us in the Roman tongue, which is a wonderful and magnificent sort of language, and one very aptly conformable to royal authority, but still difficult to me.[15]

Thus, Gregory's handling of the conventional formula, which begins the speech, provides us with splendid evidence of three aspects of the high culture of the Roman Empire—Greek rhetoric, Greek philosophy, and Roman law—all within the compass of an able, aspiring and upwardly mobile member of the civic and landed elite of an east Anatolian family.

It is worthwhile pausing over the account of Gregory's conversion. The *Menologium Graecum* observes rather confusingly that he was the son of Hellenes (pagans), but himself born a Christian.[16] Gregory

---

et culture latine: le foi et la loi", *Les Martyrs de Lyon (177)*, Colloques Internationaux du Centre National de la Recherche Scientifique 575 (Paris, 1978), pp. 187–93.

[14] R. Lane Fox, *Pagans and Christians in the Mediterranean World from the Second Century A.D. to the Conversion of Constantine* (Harmondsworth, 1986), pp. 517–28.

[15] PG 10, 1052C–1053A.

[16] *Menologium Graecum*, ad diem 17 Nov. "Memorial of Gregorius, bishop of Neocaesarea, called Thaumaturgus, who is among the saints of Our Father. He lived in the time of the emperor Aurelian, being a son of pagans (Hellenes). He himself was born Christian, and was instructed in the mysteries of the faith through a vision of the most saintly Theotokos and of John the Evangelist." The last reference alludes to Gregory of Nyssa's account of the revelation of the Creed.

himself referred to his πάτρια ἔθη τὰ πεπλανημένα, that is to his father's (or his ancestors') erroneous beliefs. He had no hope of Christian salvation while he was still a child of a father who feared the old gods (δεισιδαίμων). Yet after the latter died, when he was fourteen he underwent a conversion experience, the prompting of the Holy *Logos* which began to visit him. This he later considered to be a sign of the working of divine Providence. When he was studying under teachers of Greek rhetoric he took it as another intervention by "his divine instructor and true guardian", ὁ θεῖος παιδάγωγος καὶ ἀληθὴς κηδέμων, that one of his teachers thought to instruct him in Roman Law, the first step on the road which led him to law school at Berytus. This act of providence was the secret mechanism, τὰ δὲ μὴ φαινόμενα μέν, ἀληθέστερα δέ, not in appearance but in true reality, which caused the appearance of the soldier with free tickets for the imperial transport service, which brought him to Palestine. Then, once Gregory was in Berytus, it was his providential divine angel, ὁ θεῖος ἄγγελος, which led him on to his final stopping-point, Caesarea.[17]

Gregory's own account, which we must accept as truthful, describes an organic transition not a sudden change. It shows Gregory as one who was ready for conversion at a very young age, and who recognised God's hand behind the chances and opportunities of his teenage years. What sort of a pagan had he been? He and his brother had both been given religious names by their parents, Athenodorus and Theodorus, respectively gift of Athena and gift of god. By the third century A.D. Theodorus, a name later very commonly used by Christians, should in many instances be taken not as a non-specific reference to any pagan god, but as an allusion to the supreme god. It is plausible to think that Gregory's family inclined to henotheistic belief in a supreme deity, although this did not exclude their recognition of the daimonic or angelic status of conventional pagan gods, as is shown by the theophoric name of their second son. Indeed belief in divine angels, to which Gregory confesses, was characteristic of such religious views. Moreover, we may compare the language which Gregory used to describe his father's "erroneous" beliefs with Gregory of Nazianzus' later description of his father, who had been a worshipper of Theos Hypsistos, a cult which combined strains of Judaism with pagan monotheism. The latter was "a shoot from a lamentable stock, which sprang from a mixture of pagan error and adherence to Jewish law", one of the hypsistarians, who worshipped a single divinity, revered as "pantokratôr." I have argued elsewhere that these "hypsistarians" are to be identified with the "god-fearers" of New Testament and later texts, and as such were one of the prime "target groups" for Christian conversion.[18] The allusions in this biographical section of the *Panegyric of Origen* amount to circumstantial evidence, therefore, that Theodorus and his family were on the road to Christian belief even before the call to reawakening which was acknowledged in the change of name to Gregorius.

Origen himself moved from Alexandria to Caesarea around 234, remaining until his death in the 250s.[19] This provides a *terminus ante quem* for Gregory's own arrival there, when he was perhaps in his later teens. We may assume that he was born between 210 and 220. The eight years in which he had refrained from practising Greek rhetoric should correspond to his student career at Berytus, although later writers, including Eusebius, contract this period to five.[20] During this time he must have been a frequent visitor to Origen, as also to his sister and brother-in-law at Caesarea, but Berytus perhaps served as his main place of residence. Probably before 245 Gregory left again for his native Neocaesarea. The bulk of the panegyric is a full as well as a fulsome account of Origen's teaching methods, dialectical studies embracing geometry and astronomy, the works of philosophers and other pagan writers, Origen's "preparation for the Gospel", which was the prelude to an exhaustive examination of Scripture.[21]

Not much of the teacher's influence can be made out in Gregory's own work, but Jerome's testimony that he knew of the surviving

---

[18] S. Mitchell, "Wer waren die Gottesfürchtigen?", *Chiron* 28 (1998), pp. 55–64; idem, "The Cult of Theos Hypsistos between Pagans, Jews and Christians", *Pagan Monotheism in Late Antiquity*, eds. P. Athanassiadi, M. Frede (Oxford, 1999), pp. 81–148.

[19] Nautin, *Origène*, pp. 410, 431–2; Trigg, *Origen*, p. 36.

[20] Eusebius, *Hist. Eccl.* 6.30; Jerome, *De Vir. Ill.* 65; Suda, s.v. Gregorius, which derives entirely from Jerome. There may be a way to reconcile the two traditions. Eusebius (*Hist. Eccl.* 6.27) says that from 235–8 Origen had to leave Caesarea for Cappadocia. During this period he was in contact with Firmilianus. It is conceivable that Origen used this connection to advise or organise Gregory's return to Pontus as bishop. If so, it would provide some factual basis for Gregory of Nyssa's claim, that Firmilianus had steered Gregory in the direction of Origen (PG 46, 905C).

[21] Trigg, *Origen*, pp. 36–8.

paraphrase of Ecclesiastes, which he must have seen in Caesarea, confirms that this work was written during Gregory's period of study there, and the choice of genre, if not the intellectual content, reflects the influence of Origen's own homilies on books of the Bible. Both the translator for the *Ante-Nicene Fathers* collection and recently Robin Lane Fox have roundly castigated Gregory's effort as a turgid and systematic misrepresentation of the Old Testament book.[22]

Gregory's return to Pontus, and also that of his brother Athenodorus, are recorded by Eusebius in his *Church History*, the only testimony to his life that survives from the period between his death and the evidence of the Cappadocian fathers. Eusebius says that the most distinguished pupils of Origen at Caesarea were

> Theodorus—who was none other than that most illustrious bishop of my own day, Gregorius—and his brother Athenodorus. They were passionately devoted to Greek and Roman studies, but he implanted in them a love of true philosophy and induced them to exchange their old enthusiasm for a theological training. Five whole years they spent with him, making such remarkable progress in theology that while still young both were chosen to be bishops of the churches in Pontus.[23]

The source for most of this information is likely to have been the *Panegyric of Origen*, a copy of which should have been accessible to Eusebius in Caesarea, as it was later to Jerome. However, Eusebius' mistake in reducing the eight years of Gregory's own account to five, and the details about his brother Athenodorus, suggest that he may have been drawing on a more informal local tradition. Eusebius thereafter names Gregory and his brother as the two leaders of the Pontic church in 260,[24] and says that they were members of the synod which condemned Paul of Samosata at Antioch in 265.[25] On the other hand neither was present in 270 at the second Antioch synod which excommunicated Paul.[26] The anonymous Latin *Life* of

---

[22] S.D.F. Salmond, the translator, in the *Ante-Nicene Fathers* V, p. 9 n. 2 remarks, "The wise benevolence of our author is more apparent than his critical skill. No book is more likely to puzzle a pagan enquirer than this: so the metaphrase gives it meaning and consistency; but over and over again, not Solomon's meaning, I am persuaded." At more length see Lane Fox, *Pagans and Christians*, pp. 522–4.

[23] Eusebius, *Hist. Eccl.* 6.30.

[24] Idem, 7.14.

[25] Idem, 7.28.

[26] Idem, 7.30; *contra* Photius, *Synod. Vet.* 27 which includes Gregory at this meeting, presided over by Helenus, bishop of Tarsus.

Gregory ends with the statements that he flourished in the time of the Roman emperor Gallienus (260–68) and in the time of the Roman pope Dionysius (259–69), and that he and his brother took part in the synod which deposed Paul of Samosata, information which was surely derived from Eusebius.[27] It seems likely that Gregory had died by 270.[28]

The only unimpeachable historical document from Gregory's episcopacy is the so-called *Canonical Letter* written in the aftermath of barbarian raids in northern Asia Minor in the middle of the third century. It dealt with the problems of Christians who had wittingly or otherwise eaten sacrificial meat, of girls who had been raped by the invaders, and most of all local people who had exploited the anarchic situation to seize property from their neighbours or even joined the barbarians themselves. It also illustrates as neatly as could be wished how a church leader before Constantine, equipped by his training both in Roman law and in biblical knowledge, turned exclusively to the latter for guidance in the cases which came before him.[29]

The raiders themselves are designated as "Northmen and Goths", Βοράδοι καὶ Γότθοι (Canon 3), and this provides a historical context in the 250s, when Gothic attacks on Asia Minor are extensively, although not always clearly documented.[30] The sixth century Byzantine historian Zosimus, who probably drew on the third century Athenian writer Dexippus, refers to an unsuccessful attack by "Borani" on Pityus in Colchis and then to a successful raid on Pityus and Trapezus, which occurred in the middle 250s.[31] The latter of these episodes is a plausible context for the events that are implied in Gregory's letter, and it has been assumed, perhaps rightly, that Gregory's addressee

---

[27] For details of this *Life*, see below p. 133.

[28] The *Menologium Graecum*, 17 November, claims that he lived in the time of the emperor Aurelian; the Suda entry places him under Julian!

[29] See Lane Fox, *Pagans and Christians*, pp. 539–42.

[30] The bibliography is extensive. See in particular M. Salamon, "The Chronology of Gothic Incursions in Asia Minor in the 3rd century A.D.", *Eos* 59 (1971), pp. 109–39; B. Scardigli, "Die gotisch-römischen Beziehungen im 3. und 4. Jhdt. n. Chr. Ein Forschungsbericht 1950–1970", *ANRW* II.5.1 (1976), pp. 238–58.

[31] Zosimus 1.32–3; see D. Braund, *Georgia in Antiquity. A History of Colchis and Transcaucasian Iberia* (Oxford, 1994), pp. 262–3. Zosimus tells us that during the raid on Trapezus many inhabitants had come in from the countryside to seek protection from the troops who were stationed within the city walls. The garrison was overwhelmed and fled by sea, while the barbarians, having taken the city against expectations, took possession of much plunder and many prisoners, and destroyed temples and other buildings. They also made incursions into the surrounding territory.

was a leading figure of the church at Trapezus.[32] It has been suggested that Gregory's letter and Zosimus' account should be further harmonised by emending the former's term Βοράδοι to the latter's Βοράνοι, but this is surely unnecessary. Gregory and his fellow inhabitants of Pontus coined their own name for these menacing barbarians, and it need not have been identical to the form used by other contemporaries.

The *Canonical Letter* has many individualities of language, especially the terminology relating to the church, which confirms its authenticity as a product of the third century before the firm hierarchical organisation of the post-Constantinian church had emerged. The letter was a reply to an unnamed churchman, addressed as ἱερώτατε πάππα, "most holy father", without formal indication of rank. The church official called Euphrosynus, whom Gregory sent to help his correspondent, and who was to impose church discipline according to the precedents established in Gregory's own region, was simply called a "brother and fellow-elder".[33] The Christian community and its leaders are defined as τὸν λαόν and τοὺς προεστῶτας (canon 2), precisely the terminology which we encounter in third century Christian inscriptions from Phrygia.[34] Some local Christians had actually used force to detain fugitives from the barbarians. Gregory gave orders only that "some persons" (τινας), not named officials, should be sent to deal with them (canon 6).[35] Persons who "forgot that they were both people of Pontus and Christians and joined the barbarians in their crimes", were to be given no hearing by the church until their cases should be heard by "an assembly of the saints", corresponding to what would later have been an episcopal synod.[36] These details

---

[32] P. Heather, J.F. Matthews, *The Goths in the Fourth Century*, Translated Texts for Historians 11 (Liverpool, 1991), pp. 1–11. For the letter see also S. Mitchell, *Anatolia. Land Men and Gods in Asia Minor*, II: *The Rise of the Church* (Oxford, 1993), p. 56.

[33] Canon 5, τὸν ἀδελφὸν καὶ συγγέροντα.

[34] See the reference to οἱ πρεσβύτεροι λαοῦ πρεστάμενοι in a Christian epitaph from the Upper Tembris Valley in Phrygia (E. Gibson, *The "Christians for Christians" Inscriptions of Phrygia* [Missoula, 1978], no. 29) and the phrases λαοῦ προστάμενον and πατρίδος προιστάμενος which occur on other texts from the same region (cited by Gibson, p. 91). The phrase has its origins in NT terminology, Matt. 26:24, 27:1.

[35] The translated version in *The Ante-Nicene Fathers* VI, 19 renders them as "commissioners", echoed in Heather, Matthews, *The Goths*, p. 9 n. 19: "a commission of enquiry", but this introduces an inappropriate note of formal organisation.

[36] Canon 7: τοὺς μὲν οὖν ἐγκαταλεχθέντας τοῖς βαρβάροις καὶ μετ᾽ αὐτῶν ἐν αἰχμαλωσίᾳ ἐπελθόντας, ἐπιλαθομένους ὅτι ἦσαν Ποντικοὶ καὶ Χρηστιανοί, ἐκβαρβαρωθέντας δὲ ὡς καὶ φονεύειν τοὺς ὁμοφύλους ἢ ξύλῳ ἢ ἀγχόνῃ, ὑποδεικνύναι δὲ ἢ

authenticate the substance of the letter. They imply that the church organisation was informal and at a primitive stage, as it was in third century Phrygia, with no mention of the hierarchy of bishops, priests and deacons which was to be standard a century later. The *Canonical Letter*, for all its brevity and the exceptional nature of its subject matter, gives an authentic glimpse of the workings of the Pontic church in the third century, some of whose features can also be made out in the epigraphy of other parts of Asia Minor.

Even so, the letter does not come down to us in its original form. We may suspect tampering by a later editor, who subdivided the original continuous text into separate canons.[37] The final, eleventh, canon, which indicated grades of penitence precisely with reference to the architectural divisions of churches of the fourth and later centuries, contrasts abruptly with the informal structures of the rest of the letter, and is undoubtedly a later addition.[38]

II. *The Creed of Gregory Thaumaturgus and Gregory of Nyssa in Pontus*

Gregory's Creed is only known to us on the authority of Gregory of Nyssa, the rest of whose *Life of Gregory* is largely fiction. We are told that the text in all its details was revealed to Gregory by a divine vision of an elderly man and a woman, who identified themselves in mutual conversation as John the Evangelist and the Virgin Mary. The creed which they expounded was inscribed in Gregory's own autograph and put on display in the church at Neocaesarea,

---

ὁδοὺς ἢ οἰκίας ἀγνοοῦσι τοῖς βαρβάροις, καὶ τῆς ἀκροάσεως ἀπεῖρξαι δεῖ, μέχρις ἂν κοινῇ περὶ αὐτῶν δόξῃ συνελθοῦσι τοῖς ἁγίοις, καὶ πρὸ αὐτῶν τῷ ἁγίῳ Πνεύματι. The use of the word ἅγιοι is reminiscent of the Montanists, as well, of course, as Constantine's famous Address to the Saints in his Good-Friday Sermon. For Montanist ἅγιοι see W. Tabbernee, *Montanist Inscriptions and Testimonia. Epigraphic Sources Illustrating the History of Montanism* (Macon, 1997), nos. 75, 80, 83, 84, 85, 86, 88, with commentary on p. 493.

[37] Heather, Matthews, *The Goths*, p. 5 point out that the division of the subject matter into eleven "canons" is arbitrary. This is also the view of V. Ryssel, *Gregorius Thaumaturgus. Sein Leben und seine Schriften* (Leipzig, 1880), pp. 29–31 and P.-P. Ioannou, *Discipline Générale Antique.* II: *Les Canons des Pères Grecques* (Rome, 1963), pp. 17–30 (which I have not seen). This editorial intervention presumably occurred after the time of Basil of Caesarea, who was unaware of any written documentation relating to Gregory's episcopate in Pontus. See below pp. 109–10.

[38] Canon 11 mentions εὐκτήριον, νάρθηξ and ναός. Lane Fox, *Pagans and Christians*, pp. 539–45 pleads for authenticity, but the argument cannot be sustained; see Heather, Matthews, *The Goths*, pp. 4–5, p. 10.

just as God's revelation of the Law to Moses enabled him to lead the people of Israel to recognition of God.[39] It contains a notably full exposition of the nature of Father, Son and Holy Spirit, and of the indivisibility of the Trinity.

The authenticity of the document, however, has been definitively refuted in a fine study by Luise Abramowski.[40] It was not known to Basil when he wrote the *De Spiritu Sancto* around 375, and referred to Gregory's form of the doxology, which incorporated the controversial formula "with the holy spirit."[41] In the same year Basil was involved in a bitter controversy with Atarbius, then bishop of Neocaesarea, who advocated a strongly unitarian view of the nature of God, which Basil construed as a revival of the heresy of Sabellius. In a letter sent to the clergy of Neocaesarea Basil defended his own theological views, which were under attack, by claiming that they derived from Gregory and had been inculcated in him by his grandmother Macrina.[42] A second letter contains a defence of the practice of psalm-singing, which appears to have been introduced to Neocaesarea with Basil's blessing by monks. The clergy had alleged that these practices were not observed in the time of Gregory, to which Basil replied that they had preserved none of the customs of their founder's church, not even the current litanies.[43] Evidently Basil had no knowledge of any version of Gregory's Creed when he made these arguments. Even more revealing is a third letter to the leading persons of Neocaesarea, in which he refutes the accusation that Gregory himself had uttered the Sabellian view, that Father and Son, although in thought two, were a single hypostasis. This, said Basil, was not a statement of dogma, but had been a claim made agonistically, during the dispute with Aelianus (or Gelianus).[44] As

---

[39] PG 46, 909C–912C. The comparison between Gregory and Moses is a *topos* of the *Life*.

[40] L. Abramowski, "Das Bekenntnis des Gregor Thaumaturgus bei Gregor von Nyssa und das Problem seiner Echtheit", *Zeitschrift für Kirchengeschichte* 87 (1976), pp. 145–66; repr. in eadem, *Formula and Context. Studies in Early Christian Thought* (Aldershot, 1992).

[41] *De Spiritu Sancto* 74. See E. Schwarz, "Zur Kirchengeschichte des vierten Jahrhunderts", *Zeitschrift für die Neutestamentliche Wissenschaft und die Kunde der älteren Kirche* 34 (1935), p. 195, n. 197.

[42] Basil, *Epist.* 204.6.

[43] Basil, *Epist.* 207.4. We should note that this is flatly contradicted by the rhetorical claim of Basil, *De Sancto Spiritu* 74 (cited on p. 121), that all the institutions of the church at Neocaesarea were founded by Gregory.

[44] Basil, *Epist.* 210.5. This work is now lost and the name of Gregory's opponent

Abramowski demonstrates, it is inconceivable that Basil would have argued in this fashion, had the text of Gregory's Creed been available to him.

We should conclude, on the contrary, that the Creed was compiled, almost certainly by Gregory of Nyssa, after 375, surely after Basil's death (see below p. 112). It has all the hallmarks of a document designed to heal the controversy between Basil and Atarbius, for while the first three paragraphs comprise emphatic and careful assertions of the separate natures of God the Father, God the Son, and the Holy Spirit, thus fulfilling the conditions of three hypostases, the final paragraph is an equally emphatic statement of the indivisibility of the Trinity:

> τριὰς τελεία, δόξῃ καὶ ἀϊδιότητι καὶ βασιλείᾳ μὴ μεριζομένη μηδὲ ἀπαλλοτριουμένη. οὔτε οὖν κτιστόν τι ἢ δοῦλον ἐν τῇ τριάδι, οὔτε ἐπείσακτον, ὡς πρότερον μὲν οὐχ ὑπάρχον, ὕστερον δὲ ἐπεισελθόν· οὔτε γὰρ ἐνέλιπέ ποτε υἱὸς πατρί, οὔτε υἱῷ πνεῦμα, ἀλλ' ἄτρεπτος καὶ ἀναλλοίωτος ἡ αὐτὴ τριὰς ἀεί.

There is a perfect Trinity, in glory, eternity and sovereignty neither divided or estranged. Wherefore there is nothing either created or in servitude in the Trinity, nor is anything superinduced, as if at some former period it was non-existent and at some later period it was introduced. And thus neither was the Son ever wanting to the Father, nor the Spirit to the Son; but without variation, and without change, the same Trinity abideth for ever.[45]

We can be certain that this final section of the Creed was in circulation by 380, for it is quoted almost word for word in Gregory of Nazianzus' sermons on the Holy Spirit and on Holy Baptism, which belong to 380 or 381.[46] In the first of these passages, the for-

---

is uncertain. See H. Crouzel, "Grégoire le Thaumaturge et le 'Dialogue avec Élien'", *RSR* 51 (1963), pp. 422–31. The letter is referred to by Facundus, bishop of Hermia, lib. X c. 6, inter Opp. Sirmondi, "St. Basil defended the great Gregorius", who took the cognomen "worker of miracles", so that he was and is called Thaumaturgus by the Greeks, not only from the error of the Arians, who say that the Son is a creature and made, but also on the opposite side from that of the Sabellians, who say that the substance of the Father and the Son is one, even though Gregorius seems to have said this in his preaching. Thence did the same St. Basil, while speaking about certain persons who strove to excuse their own treachery by quoting the authority of Gregorius himself, say, "They sent in . . .".

[45] PG 46, 913A; transl. *The Ante-Nicene Fathers*, 7.

[46] Greg. Naz., *Or.* 28.28: θεότητα μίαν, δοξῇ καὶ τιμῇ καὶ οὐσίᾳ καὶ βασιλείᾳ μὴ μεριζομένην, ὥς τις τῶν μικρῷ πρόσθεν θεοφόρων ἐφιλοσόφησεν. *Or.* 40.42: οὐδὲν τῆς

mula is attributed to an unnamed theologian, who had written shortly before (μικρῷ πρόσθεν). There is every reason to identify the theologian as Gregory of Nyssa. Gregory of Nazianzus probably learned its terms directly from the author, rather than from reading or hearing the *Life of Gregory Thaumaturgus*, and this may explain why he does not trace its origin back to the original Gregory.

The allusions by Gregory of Nazianzus supply a *terminus post quem* for the production of the Creed and are the main reason why the composition of the *Life of Gregory Thaumaturgus* is commonly dated around 380.[47] Furthermore, the theological spirit of the Creed is precisely in tune with the efforts of the leaders of the eastern churches to find a credal formula, which updated Nicene orthodoxy with contemporary trinitarian thinking. This was precisely the task which Theodosius enjoined on his clergy after his accession in 379 and which was to determine the agenda of the Ecumenical Council of Constantinople in 381.[48]

These argument are strong ones, but they can be reinforced and made more precise with detailed information about Gregory of Nyssa's movements at this period. Gregory had been reluctantly installed as bishop of Nyssa in 371 but was expelled from the see in 375 at the instigation of the hard-line *vicarius* of Pontica, Demosthenes, presumably acting on the instructions of the emperor Valens. He was reinstated to his post by 378 and attended the council of Antioch in 379.[49] His subsequent journey to Pontus and his activities there are recounted in two of his letters, *Epist.* 19 to Ioannes, a cleric in Antioch, and the letter sent to various addressees which recounted the life and described the death of his sister Macrina.[50]

τριάδος, ὦ οὗτοι, δοῦλον οὐδὲ κτιστὸν, οὐδὲ ἐπείσακτον ἤκουσα τῶν σοφῶν τινος λέγοντος.

[47] G. May, "Die Chronologie des Lebens und Werke des Gregor von Nyssa", *Écriture et culture philosophique dans la pensée de Grégoire de Nysse*, ed. M. Harl (Leiden, 1971), pp. 56–9.

[48] E. Schwarz, "Zur Kirchengeschichte des vierten Jahrhunderts", pp. 196–213.

[49] H. Dörrie, "Gregor III (Gregor von Nyssa)", *RAC* 12 (1983), 867–8; G. May, "Gregor von Nyssa in der Kirchenpolitik seiner Zeit", *Jahrbuch der österreichischen Byzantinistik* 15 (1966), pp. 105–32.

[50] G. Pasquali's edition of the letters of Gregory of Nyssa has been re-issued in W. Jaeger, *Gregorii Nysseni Opera* VIII.2 (Leiden, 1959); I have used V.W. Callahan's edition of the *Life of Macrina* in W. Jaeger, *Gregorii Nysseni Opera* VIII.1 (Leiden, 1952). See too P. Maraval, *Grégoire de Nysse. Vie de Ste Macrine*, SC 178 (Paris, 1971) and his edition of the letters in the same series: *Grégoire de Nysse, Lettres* (Paris, 1990).

In the latter Gregory reports that a council convened in Antioch in the ninth month, or a little later, after the death of Basil, an event which is usually dated to 1 January 379.[51] That would be September 379. The primary business of this important council, which was attended by 153 bishops, following the succession of the emperor Gratian after the death of the emperor Valens in 378 and the accession of Theodosius in the following year, was to reconcile the theological views of most of the eastern Church with the trinitarian views of the Cappadocian fathers, which were to become enshrined orthodoxy two years later at Constantinople.[52] Gregory returned from Antioch to Anatolia to be received with worrying news of his sister Macrina's health at her retreat at Annisa. He immediately undertook a ten-day journey, which brought him to her bedside the day before her death.[53] In the *Life of Macrina* he says that he felt the urgent need to travel to see her, after an interval of almost eight years, before the year had passed.[54] This implies a decision taken late in the travelling season, during the same autumn, plausibly in October 379. Gregory certainly made his way by a direct route across Asia Minor from Tarsus through the Cilician Gates to Pontus, without visiting his home see, Nyssa. His choice of route had caused him to miss his brother Peter, who had set out to find him four days before his arrival at Annisa, when their sister's con-

---

[51] The date has been put earlier by P. Maraval, "La date du mort de Basile de Césarée", *Revue des études augustiniennes* 34 (1988), pp. 25–38, but the most recent discussion, by P. Rousseau, *Basil of Caesarea* (Berkeley/Los Angeles/London, 1994), pp. 360–3 remains agnostic. As will be seen from what follows, the evidence of Gregory of Nyssa's letters provides no reason to abandon the traditional date.

[52] C.J. Hefele, H. Leclercq, *Histoire des Conciles* 1.2 (Paris, 1907, repr. Hildesheim, 1973), p. 985. See G. Bardy, "La concile d'Antioche (379)", *Revue Bénédictine* 45 (1933), pp. 196–213; E. Schwarz, "Zur Kirchengeschichte des vierten Jahrhunderts", pp. 198–201, and "Über die Sammlung des Cod. Veronensis LX", *Zeitschrift für die Neutestamentliche Wissenschaft und die Kunde der älteren Kirche* 35 (1936), pp. 1–23; R. Staats, "Die römische Tradition im Symbol von 381 (NC) und seine Entstehung auf der Synode von Antiochien 379", *Vig. Chr.* 44 (1990), pp. 209–21.

[53] *Epist.* 19.10: ἐπειδὴ τοίνυν ἐπέστην παρ' ὑμῖν τοῖς Καππαδόκαις· εὐθὺς τις ἀκοὴ περὶ αὐτῆς διετάραξε. δέκα δὲ ἦν ἡμερῶν ἡ διὰ τοῦ μέσου ὁδός, καὶ ταύτην πᾶσαν διὰ τῆς ἐνδεχομένης ἐπείξεως διανύσας γίνομαι κατὰ τὸν Πόντον καὶ εἶδον καὶ ὤφθην. Note that the entire return journey from Antioch is described as the entrance to his home city, Neocaesarea (ταυτά μοι τῆς Πατρίδος ... τὰ εἰσιτήρια).

[54] *Life of Macrina*, W. Jaeger, *Gregorii Nysseni Opera* VIII.1, 386–7: καὶ ἐπειδὴ πάλιν πρὸς τὴν ἑαυτοῦ ἕκαστος ἀπελύθημεν, πρὶν τὸν ἐνιαυτὸν παρελθεῖν, ἐνθύμιον ἐμοὶ τῷ Γρηγορίῳ γίνεται πρὸς αὐτὴν διαβῆναι. ... οὐκ ὀλίγον ἐφαίνετο τὸ διάστημα ὀκτὼ μικροῦ δεῖν παραμετρούμενον ἔτεσιν.

dition appeared critical, but had taken another road, evidently the direct cross country route towards Nyssa.[55] Gregory, but not Peter, was present at his sister's death.

On the third day after his arrival, and after Macrina's burial, he withdrew from Annisa. Before he had digested his misfortunes, his neighbours from Galatia required him to deal with the usual conflicts with heretics in their country. Their knowledge of his whereabouts is indicative that the main purpose of his visit was not a personal one, to see his dying sister, but was concerned with church politics.[56] Then other troubles crowded in on him.[57] He received a petition from the entire people of the nearby town of Ibora, whose bishop had recently died, asking him to ensure the succession of a suitable candidate.[58] It is clear that this mass embassy confronted him at Neocaesarea, which lay close to Ibora.[59] The whole population can hardly have travelled to a more distant provincial centre to find him. We know from the *Life of Macrina* that enormous crowds travelled from the surrounding area to attend her funeral, including Araxius, bishop of a neighbouring city.[60] Similar, but apparently separate dealings are reported in *Epist.* 19: "Since he happened to be in Pontus taking care of matters according to the appropriate procedure for the Church there", he received embassies from the people

---

[55] *Life of Macrina*, W. Jaeger, *Gregorii Nysseni Opera* VIII.1, p. 387: φήσαντος δὲ πρὸς ἡμᾶς αὐτὸν ἐξωρμηκέναι καὶ τετάρτην ἡμέραν ἄγειν, συνεὶς ὅπερ ἦν, ὅτι δι' ἑτέρας ὁδοῦ γέγονεν αὐτῷ πρὸς ἡμᾶς ἡ ὁρμή, . . .

[56] *Epist.* 19.11, εἶτά μοι, πρὶν καταπεφθῆναι τὴν συμφοράν, οἱ πρόσχωροι τῆς ἐμῆς ἐκκλησίας Γαλάται, τὸ σύνηθες αὐτοῖς περὶ τὰς αἱρέσεις ἀρρώστημα πολλαχοῦ τῆς ἐμῆς ἐκκλησίας κατὰ τὸ λεληθὸς ὑποσπείραντες, ἀγῶνα παρέσχον οὐ μικρόν, . . . For Galatian heresies, specifically at Ancyra, see Mitchell, *Anatolia* II, pp. 91–5.

[57] *Epist.* 19.10: ἡμέρᾳ τρίτῃ κηδεύσας ὑπέστρεφον. . . . Maraval takes ὑπέστρεφον to imply that Gregory returned to Nyssa at this point, but it only means that he had withdrawn from Annisa, evidently to Neocaesarea.

[58] *Epist.* 19.12: εἶτα ἐπὶ τούτοις ἄλλα . . . πανδήμει πρὸς ἡμᾶς ἐπρεσβεύσαντο.

[59] The location of both Annisa and Ibora was established by G. de Jerphanion, "Ibora. Gazioura?", *Mélanges de l'Université St. Joseph de Beyrouth* 5 (1911), pp. 333–54, summarised by H. Leclercq, "Ibora", *Dictionnaire d'Archéologie Chrétienne et de Liturgie* 7, cols. 4–9 and W. Ruge, "Ibora", *RE* 9 (1914), col. 816. He places Annisa at Sunisa (which preserves the ancient name), west of the confluence of the rivers Iris and Lycus, and Ibora to the east, south of the Lycus, near Herek.

[60] *Life of Macrina*, W. Jaeger, *Gregorii Nysseni Opera* VIII.1, p. 407: ἐπειδὴ ὄρθρος ἐγένετο, τὸ μὲν πλῆθος τῶν ἐκ πάσης τῆς περιοικίδος συρρυέντων ἀνδρῶν ἅμα καὶ γυναικῶν ἐπεθορύβει ταῖς οἰμώγαις τὴν ψαλμῳδίαν. . . . ὡς δὲ προσῄει κατ' ὀλίγον ἡ ἡμέρα καὶ ἐστενοχωρεῖτο πᾶς ὁ περὶ τὴν ἐσχατιὰν τόπος τῷ πλήθει τῶν συρρυέντων, παραστὰς ὁ τῶν τόπων ἐκείνων διὰ τῆς ἐπισκοπῆς προεστώς, Ἀράξιος ὄνομα αὐτῷ (παρῆν γὰρ σὺν παντὶ τῷ τῆς ἱερωσύνης πληρώματι), ...

of Sebaste, asking him to forestall a heretic take-over.[61] The language which Gregory uses here betrays the central purpose of his trip. He was on a mission, which had evidently been enjoined on him at the Antioch council, to settle disputes in the bishoprics of Pontus and establish the unity of the Church. Macrina herself alluded to this in her reported death-bed conversation with her brother, in which she contrasted his international renown with the more modest forensic and sophistic achievements of their father:

> Our father enjoyed considerable renown for his education in those former times, but his fame extended only to the courtrooms of his native land. Later, when he led the rest on account of his sophistic skills, his reputation did not go beyond the boundaries of Pontus, although his renown in his fatherland was dear to him. But your name is well known in cities, peoples and provinces; churches send you to make alliances and to put things to rights, and churches invite you to do so.[62]

The nature and location of Gregory's activities become clearer from the next passage of *Epist.* 19. Gregory was responsible for registering votes cast in the election to the vacant bishopric of Sebastia by the other bishops who had been summoned for this very purpose. To his dismay he found that he had been elected himself.[63] We are dealing with an electoral synod held under the presidency of a bishop of a neighbouring province, precisely as the canons of the Council of Antioch of 341 had enjoined.[64] This business would certainly have been conducted at a major regional centre, the metropolis of the province of Pontus Polemonianus, Neocaesarea, and this inference is confirmed by Gregory's allusion in the following sentence to the

---

[61] *Epist.* 19.13: ἐπειδὴ γὰρ ἐγενόμεθα κατὰ τὸν Πόντον καὶ κατὰ τὸν προσήκοντα τύπον τῆς παρ᾽ αὐτοῖς ἐκκλησίας ἐπεμελήθημεν συνεργίᾳ θεοῦ, εὐθὺς ἡμᾶς ἐπὶ τοῦ τόπου καταλαμβάνουσιν ὁμοιότροποι πρεσβεῖαι παρὰ τοῦ πληθοῦς τῶν Σεβαστηνῶν φθάσαι τὴν τῶν αἱρετικῶν ἐπιδρομὴν ἀξιούντων.

[62] *Life of Macrina*, W. Jaeger, *Gregorii Nysseni Opera* VIII.1, p. 394: σὺ δέ, φησί, πόλεσι καὶ δήμοις καὶ ἔθνεσιν ὀνομαστὸς εἶ καὶ σὲ πρὸς συμμαχίαν τε καὶ διόρθωσιν ἐκκλησίαι πέμπουσι καὶ ἐκκλησίαι καλοῦσι. . . . We need to remember that these words, as they stand, are Gregory's own, not Macrina's.

[63] *Epist.* 19.15: ἀλλὰ γὰρ κατὰ τὴν ἀκολουθίαν γίνομαι μετὰ τῶν λοιπῶν ἐπισκόπων τῶν εἰς αὐτὸ τοῦτο συγκεκλημένων ὡς ψήφους ὑπὲρ χειροτονίας δεξόμενος, ἡ ψῆφος δὲ ἤμην ἐγὼ καὶ ἠγνόουν ὁ δείλαιος τοῖς ἐμαυτοῦ πτεροῖς ἁλισκόμενος.

[64] Hefele, Leclercq, *Histoire des Conciles* 1.2, p. 718 canon 14, which provided for the introduction of bishops of the neighbouring province to take part in the debate when there was an internal division. Canon 19 laid down that episcopal appointments were to take place in the presence of the metropolitan and a majority of the other provincial bishops; compare canons 4 and 6 of the Council of Nicaea.

presence of the provincial governor and the troops under his command, who intervened in the disturbance and appear even to have taken him into custody, before he was extricated from the situation.[65] In fact another of Gregory's letters should evidently be related to this context. In *Epist.* 22, addressed to "the bishops", Gregory compares his plight to that of Jonah in the belly of the whale. He had spent three days confined in the bowels of the beast among the unrepentant Ninevites, a reference which can be placed alongside the reference in *Epist.* 19 to the forces of authority committing him to the evils of Babylon.[66] The letter was evidently written from prison on this occasion, a plea to his fellow bishops to pray for his deliverance.

The sequence of events which we can reconstruct from Gregory's two accounts allows us to date this synod to the late autumn of 379, very plausibly to November.[67] We can probably fix the exact day. The Latin *Life* of Gregory Thaumaturgus, which may be dated to the beginning of the fifth century (pp. 134–5), ends with a paragraph which states that his date of burial was *XV Kalendarium Decembrium*, that is November 17. This is confirmed by the much later *Menologium Graecum*. These sources are clearly independent of one another and the information has to be treated as reliable. The anniversary of Gregory Thaumaturgus' death, November 17th, was surely the occasion for the composition of the panegyric.

Gregory of Nyssa's task in the metropolitan church itself was to heal the doctrinal rift between the single hypostasis unitarianism of Atarbius and the trinitarian position. Basil himself, in his first letter to the clergy of Neocaesarea in 375, had proposed to them that

---

[65] *Epist.* 19.16: στάσεις ἐπὶ τούτοις, ἀνάγκαι, δάκρυα, προσπτώσεις, φυλακαί, τάγμα στρατιωτικὸν καὶ αὐτὸς ὁ ἐπιτεταγμένος αὐτοῖς κόμης ἐφ᾽ ἡμᾶς κινῶν καὶ πᾶσαν ἀφορμὴν πρὸς τὴν τυραννίδα τὴν καθ᾽ ἡμῶν συναγείρων, ἕως ἐναφῆκεν ἡμᾶς τοῖς Βαβυλωνίοις κακοῖς. . . .

[66] *Epist.* 22: τρεῖς ἦσαν ἡμέραι αἱ τὸν προφήτην ἐν τῷ κήτει κατέχουσαι, ἀλλ᾽ ὅμως ὁ Ἰωνᾶς ἠκηδίασεν· ἐγὼ δὲ τοσοῦτον χρόνον ἔχω ἐν τοῖς ἀμετανοήτοις Νινευΐταις, ἐν τοῖς σπλάγχνοις τοῦ θηρίου κρατούμενος, καὶ οὔπω ἐξεμηθῆναι τῆς ἀχανοῦς ταύτης φάρυγγος ἠδυνήθην. εὔξασθε οὖν τῷ κυρίῳ τελειωθῆναι τὴν χάριν, ἵνα ἔλθῃ τὸ πρόσταγμα τὸ τῆς συνοχῆς ταύτης ῥυόμενον καὶ καταλάβω τὴν ἐμαυτοῦ σκηνὴν καὶ ὑπ᾽ αὐτὴν ἀναπαύσωμαι. For Babylon, see the previous note. Maraval in his 1990 edition of the letters interprets the three days as a metaphorical allusion to a supposed three months that Gregory may have spent as bishop of Sebastia.

[67] Canon 20 of the Council of Antioch of 341 laid down that the metropolitan of each province should convoke two annual synods to deal with church business, one to be held in the fourth week after Easter, the other on 15 October. The Pontic synod of autumn 379 may have been scheduled to start on that date.

their differences should be settled by calling a council: "But there are bishops; let appeal be made to them. There is a clergy in each of God's dioceses; let the most eminent be assembled. Let whoso will speak freely, that I may have to deal with a charge not a slander."[68] The reconstruction of Gregory of Nyssa's activities in 379 contains the evidence that this suggestion was realised. The Creed, as we have seen, was tailor-made for this purpose, but it will not have been easy to impose an acceptable compromise. The medium in such a case was as important as the message. Gregory of Nyssa's presentation of the new Creed as a divine revelation to the founder of the Neocaesarean Church, occupying pride of place in the opening section of his long and eloquent *Life of Gregory*, was surely no less important than the formula itself in securing allegiance from the bishops, clergy and people of the Pontic region. Indeed it is plausible to suggest that the entire work, with its astounding and unprecedented elaboration of Gregory's miraculous powers, was designed precisely to confirm the authority of the supposed author of the Creed. The panegyric was delivered to a congregation, assembled to celebrate Gregory Thaumaturgus' name day, which was headed by the entire gathering of Pontic bishops, who had assembled for the electoral synod. Many passages in the speech itself confirm that its rhetoric was designed precisely for such an audience (see section IV).

III. *The Lives and the Miracles*

We move from the life to the legend. The story of Gregory Thaumaturgus was told repeatedly in the churches of antiquity and the early middle ages.[69] As with other famous saints, accounts of his life, and in particular of the miracles he performed, circulated in many languages, the most important of which are listed here.

a) The Greek *life* by Gregory of Nyssa: PG 46. 893–957. Ed. G. Heil in W. Jaeger et al., *Gregorii Nysseni Opera* X.1 (Leiden, 1990).

b) A Latin *life*. Published in *Bibliotheca Casinensis* III, florilegium, 168–79. See A. Poncelet, "La vie latine de Saint Grégoire le thaumaturge", *RSR* 1 (1910), pp. 132–60; and W. Telfer, "The Latin

---

[68] Basil, *Epist.* 204.4; cf. Rousseau, *Basil of Caesarea*, pp. 275–8.

[69] W. Telfer, "The Cultus of St. Gregory Thaumaturgus", *HTR* 29 (1936), pp. 225–344.

Life of St. Gregory Thaumaturgus", *JTS* 31 (1929/30), pp. 142–55, pp. 354–63.

c) A Syriac *life* probably of the sixth century. Published by V. Ryssel, "Eine syrische Lebensgeschichte des Gregorius Thaumaturgus. Nach cod. Mus. Brit. syr. add. 14648 aus dem syrischen übersetzt", *Theologische Zeitschrift aus der Schweiz* 11 (1894), pp. 228–54. See P. Koetschau, "Zur Lebensgeschichte Gregors des Wunderthäters", *Zeitschrift für wissenschaftliche Theologie* 41 (1898), pp. 211–50.

d) Coptic: M. van Esbroek, "Fragments sahidiques du Panégyrique de Grégoire le Thaumaturge par Grégoire de Nysse", *OLP* 6/7 (1975/6), pp. 555–68.

e) Armenian: *Vies et Passions des Saints* I (Venice 1874), pp. 317–31; cf. A. Poncelet, *RSR* 1 (1910), pp. 155–60.

The relationships between these versions and the traditions about Gregory preserved by other sources, Basil, Rufinus, and the *Menologium Graecum*, are shown in the accompanying table (pp. 118–9).

Much scholarly work has been devoted to tracing the connections between these versions. Thus A. Poncelet, discussing the anonymous Latin life, which claims to be a free translation of Gregory of Nyssa's original, argued that it had been compiled in the late fourth or at the beginning of the fifth century, before 402/3, when Rufinus added his original chapters on Gregory Thaumaturgus to his translation of Eusebius' *Church History*.[70] This was disputed by W. Telfer, who claimed that it made use of Rufinus, but was not composed before the eighth century.[71] V. Ryssel, who published the Syriac version from a manuscript in the British Museum, argued that it derived from a short Greek life of the early fourth century, which had been composed before Gregory of Nyssa's well-known version.[72] This was effectively refuted by P. Koetschau, who showed that the Syriac version should be considered a derivative product, probably of the sixth century.[73] A full re-appraisal of the problems which these studies

---

[70] A. Poncelet, "La vie latine de Saint Grégoire le thaumaturge", *RSR* 1 (1910), pp. 132–60, pp. 567–9.

[71] W. Telfer, "The Latin Life of St. Gregory Thaumaturgus", *JTS* 31 (1930), pp. 142–55, pp. 354–63.

[72] V. Ryssel, "Eine syrische Lebensgeschichte des Gregorius Thaumaturgus. Nach cod. Mus. Brit. syr. add. 14648 aus dem syrischen übersetzt", *Theologische Zeitschrift aus der Schweiz* 11 (1894), pp. 228–54.

[73] P. Koetschau, "Zur Lebensgeschichte Gregors des Wunderthäters", *Zeitschrift für wissenschaftliche Theologie* 41 (1898), pp. 211–50.

Life and Miracles of Gregory Thaumaturgus

Episode	Basil	Greg.Nys.	Rufinus	Latin Life	Syriac Life	Armenian Life	Menologium
Prologue		1, 2		1			
Home and upbringing		3, 4		2		1	1
The harlot in Alexandria		5		3	11	2	2
Studies with Origen and return to Pontus		6		4		3	
Consecrated by Phaedimus		7		5		4	3
Revelation of Creed		8		6		5	
Text of Creed		9	4	7		6	
Expels demon from temple and converts the priest		10, 11	3	8	5	8	
Moves a boulder		12		8a		9	4
Converted priest succeeds him as bishop			3a	8b		10	5
Enters Neocaesarea		13		9			
Guest of Musonius		14		10			
Builds earthquake-proof church		15		11			
Dries up lake in brothers' dispute	3	16	1	12	9	11	6
Signs of lake survive		16a		12a			
Stops Lycus flooding	2	17, 18		13	8	12	7
Makes cliff recede to make room for church			2	14			
Consecrates Alexander, charcoal-burner, as bishop of Comana		19, 20		15	10	13–14	
Choice vindicated		21		16		15	

(table cont.)

Episode	Basil	Greg.Nys.	Rufinus	Latin Life	Syriac Life	Armenian Life	Menologium
Festival and plague		30–31		17			
Slays a dragon which ravaged Comana				18			
Punishes two Jews who try to cheat him		22		19	4	16	
Exorcises demon from boy		23		20	12	17	
Flies from city in persecution		24		21	13		
Escapes persecutors in the mountains and converts his pursuer		25		22	14	20–21	
Second sight of Troadius' martyrdom		26		23	6	22	
The Deacon in the haunted bath		27		24	7	22	
Establishes martyrs' festivals		28		25		23	
Only seventeen pagans left at his death		28a		25a	15		8
Gives directions for his burial		29		26		24–5	
An earlier episode: Plague hits the city and relieves the overcrowding of a pagan festival in the theatre		30–31		(17)		23	
Notes omission of miracles		31				26	

Socrates, *Hist. Eccl.* 4.27 comments that Gregorius, while still a layman, healed the sick and cast out devils even by his letters. Pagans were attracted by his actions as well as by his discourse. Sozomen, *Hist. Eccl.* 7.27 tells the story of the punishment of the two Jews, but identifies them only as beggars and says that the story was also told of Epiphanius.

The Armenian version inserts four other episodes: 18 Gregory escapes punishment in a boiling bath; 19a Gregory exorcises the daughter of the Roman emperor; 19b The miraculous transport of a marble column to Cappadocia; 19c Gregory in Sicily; miracle at Mt. Etna.

have raised would be out of the question here. The observations that follow are for the most part concerned with Gregory of Nyssa's *Life* and with the question of the date and origin of the Latin version.

IV. *The Composition of Gregory of Nyssa's Life and its Audience*

The most elaborate version is the best known, the work of Gregory of Nyssa. This has recently been examined by Raymond van Dam,[74] but the expert historical demolition job has been done by Robin Lane Fox.[75] At all points where this account can be measured against information provided in Gregory's own works, it is found wanting. According to Gregory of Nyssa, Gregory is said to have become a Christian only after the death of both parents, not of his father alone (PG 46, 900B). His conversion to Christianity is said to result from his dissatisfaction with the disputes of pagan philosophers (PG 46, 901A–B). He is supposed to have travelled to Alexandria, where he encountered the harlot and performed his first miracle; no mention is made of Caesarea at all (PG 46, 901C–904C). Firmilian, bishop of Caesarea (for Gregory of Nyssa another of the legendary founders of the Cappadocian church), is made into the decisive influence on his life. It was he who sent him to the leading exponent of Christian doctrine, Origen, here mentioned in a single, dismissive sentence (PG 46, 905C). All of this is fancy and in plain contradiction to Gregory's own version of events.[76] Later writers also preferred approximate guesswork to the truth. Socrates, perhaps modelling him on Basil or Gregory of Nazianzus, has him studying in the schools of Athens before going to Berytus,[77] the *Menologium* states that he lived under

---

[74] R. van Dam, "Hagiography and History: The Life of Gregory Thaumaturgus", *Classical Antiquity* 1 (1982), pp. 272–308. The main conclusions of this lengthy article, in particular the claim that "the ambiguity of (Gregory's) position in society remained the basis of his success" (p. 307 and pp. 288–97 *passim*), seem to be unsubstantiated and obscure.

[75] Lane Fox, *Pagans and Christians*, p. 530.

[76] H. Crouzel, "Faut-il voir trois personnages", pp. 312–9 tried to show that passages in Gregory of Nyssa's panegyric show familiarity with Gregory Thaumaturgus' *Panegyric of Origen*. Despite A. Momigliano, "The Life of St. Macrina by Gregory of Nyssa", *Ottavo contributo alla storia degli studi classici e del mondo antico* (Rome, 1987), pp. 333–47, the case is not convincing.

[77] Socrates, *Hist. Eccl.* 4.27 distinguishes Gregory Thaumaturgus from the other later Gregories: "This Gregory's fame is celebrated at Athens, at Berytus, throughout the entire diocese of Pontus, and I might say in the whole world. When he had finished his education in the schools of Athens he went to Berytus to study

Aurelian, the *Suda* under Julian. From the 370s onwards almost everything that was set down about Gregory belongs to the realm of legend and should be analysed as such.

The origin of this legend lay to all appearances with the great fathers of the Cappadocian Church. Before the appearance of Gregory of Nyssa's life Basil referred explicitly to Gregory's miracles, in *De Sancto Spiritu*:

> But where shall I rank the great Gregory, and the words uttered by him? Shall we not place among Apostles and Prophets a man who walked by the same spirit as they; who never through all his days diverged from the footprints of the saints; who maintained, as long as he lived, the exact principles of evangelical citizenship? I am sure that we shall do the truth a wrong if we refuse to number that soul with the people of God, shining as it did like a beacon in the Church of God; for by the fellow-working of the Spirit the power which he had over demons was tremendous, and so gifted was he with the grace of the word "for obedience to the faith . . . among the nations" (Rom. 1:5), that, although only seventeen Christians were handed over to him, he brought the whole people alike in town and country through knowledge to God. He too by Christ's mighty name commanded even rivers to change their course, and caused a lake, which afforded a ground of quarrel to some covetous brethren, to dry up. Moreover his predictions of things to come were such as in no wise to fall short of those of the great prophets. To recount all this wonderful work in detail would be too long a task. By the superabundance of gifts, wrought in him by the Spirit in all power and in signs and marvels, he was styled a second Moses by the very enemies of the Church. Thus in all that he through grace accomplished, alike by word and deed, a light seemed ever to be shining, token of the heavenly power from the unseen which followed him. To this day he is the object of great admiration to the people in his own neighbourhood, and his memory, established in the churches ever fresh and green, is not dulled by length of time. Thus not a practice, not a word, not a mystic rite has been added to the Church besides what he bequeathed to it. Hence truly on account of the antiquity of their institution many of their ceremonies appear to be defective. For his successors in the administration of the Churches could not endure to accept any subsequent discovery in addition to what had had his sanction.[78]

---

civil law." Socrates goes on to say that he met and studied with Origen there, but was recalled soon after by his parents and returned to his country. While still a layman he healed the sick and cast out devils even by his letters. Pagans were attracted by his acts as well as by his discourse. He is mentioned by Pamphilus the martyr in the books he wrote in defence of Origen.

[78] Basil, *De Sancto Spiritu* 74.

Basil assured us he had a good source for these stories, his grand-mother:

> What clearer evidence can there be of my faith, than that I was brought up by my grandmother, blessed woman, who came from you? I mean the celebrated Macrina who taught me the words of the blessed Gregory; which, as far as memory had preserved down to her day, she cherished herself, while she fashioned and formed me, while yet a child, upon the doctrines of piety.[79]

We can recognise here both the concepts and the oral tradition that also inspired Gregory of Nyssa: the comparison of Gregory with Moses; the obvious fiction that there were only seventeen Christians when he arrived at Neocaesarea; and two of the legendary miracles attached to him that were particularly celebrated because the stories were confirmed by local folk-lore surrounding things or places associated with the saint: the dried-up lake-basin which resolved the dispute of two brothers; and the tree which had grown from the staff he had thrust into the bank of the river Lycus to prevent it flooding.

These were the palpable, if questionable links which joined the pioneering years of Gregory's conversion of Neocaesarea with the dominant Christian culture of Pontus and Cappadocia in the 370s and 380s. The torch lit by Gregory was passed down to the bishops who succeeded him, as Basil maintained in another letter to Neocaesarea (*Epist.* 204),

> Next, if it tend towards intimacy to have the same teachers, there are to you and to me the same teachers of God's mysteries, and spiritual fathers, who from the beginning were the founders of your Church. I mean the great Gregory, and all who succeeding in order to the throne of your episcopate, like stars rising one after another, have tracked the same course, so as to leave the tokens of the heavenly polity most clear to all who desire them.[80]

The last of these had been Musonius, whom Basil had commemorated in a letter of consolation to his church, on Musonius' death in 368, in which he used the metaphor of a chain of jewels to describe this episcopal succession (*Epist.* 208):

> That Lord, from the time of Gregory the great champion of your church down to that of the blessed departed, setting over you one

---

[79] Basil, *Epist.* 204.6.
[80] Basil, *Epist.* 204.2.

after another, and from time to time fitting one to another like gem
set close to gem, has bestowed on you glorious ornaments for your
church.[81]

The point is repeated in the last of Basil's polemical letters to the
Neocaesareans:

> There is going on among you a movement ruinous to the faith, dis-
> loyal to the apostolic and evangelical dogmas, disloyal too to the tra-
> dition of Gregory the truly great, and of his successors up to the blessed
> Musonius, whose teaching is still ringing in your ears. For these men,
> who, from fear of confutation, are forging figments against me, are
> endeavouring to renew the old mischief of Sabellius, started long ago,
> and extinguished by the tradition of the great Gregory.[82]

The final rivet in this chain is provided in Gregory of Nyssa's *Life*,
who reveals that the nobleman who provided a home for Gregory
on his return to Neocaesarea from Palestine was none other than a
certain wealthy man called Musonius, a forebear—if he is not an
invention—of the bishop who died in 368 (PG 46, 921b).[83]

Basil and Gregory of Nyssa had a vested interest in Gregory. He
was one of them, a member of one of the wealthy land-owning families of eastern Asia Minor, who had obtained higher education and
aspired to prominent careers in the Roman Empire, and who had
made their mark in the Church. He was also a local saint. Their
family estate, where their sister Macrina created a model monastic
retreat in the 350s, was barely fifty kilometres from Neocaesarea.
The legends that were told were on the lips of the population all
around them. They thus invented a father of the Church according
to their own needs. Many of his characteristics and his activities by
design matched their own.

This view is developed by Van Dam and by Lane Fox, and it is
surely in essence correct. It does not, however, explain the most
striking difference between the archetype and his successors and the
most distinctive aspect of the legendary Gregory, his sobriquet
Thaumaturgus, and the miracles that he is said to have accomplished.

---

[81] Basil, *Epist.* 208.2.
[82] Basil, *Epist.* 210.3.
[83] I suspect that a similar real or invented link between the two eras exists in
the person of Phaedimus, the bishop of Amasea, who supposedly consecrated Gregory
Thaumaturgus (PG 46, 908D–909B). Compare Gregory of Nyssa's fragmentary *Epist.*
23 containing a reference to a contemporary Phaedimus.

Neither Basil nor Gregory of Nyssa, however much they may have wished to emulate the model they had created, claimed to be a worker of miracles. Miracles in Christian discourse became an important way of talking or writing about Christian achievements. They were not, by definition, a component of everyday, contemporary life, even that of mighty bishops. The relation of miracles to the activities of churchmen was analogous to that between myths told about the old Greek gods and the rituals and prayers accomplished by pagan priests and devotees. Miracles, however, being the stuff of legend, did not themselves lead to or achieve conversions directly. Nor, one suspects, were stories about miracles directed at the unconverted. Certainly neither Basil's *On the Holy Spirit* nor Gregory of Nyssa's *Life*, still less the later accounts, preserved in Greek liturgical handbooks such as the *Menologium*, or in Syriac, Coptic or Latin translations, would have reached an audience of non-believers. They were intended to heighten the wonder of existing believers at the power of God and his saints.

Miracles were not, apart from exceptional cases, a phenomenon that explains conversion,[84] nor was their telling designed as a means of conversion. They supply Christianity with its myths, and like all myths they were also stories which had to be told. Miracle stories originate in an oral rather than a written culture, as Basil's reference to his grandmother's story-telling illustrates. Given their place as a component of certain genres of Christian literature, the explication of miracles belongs to a discussion of forms of Christian narrative. Their importance lies more with their role in these narratives than in their relation to reality. The particular importance of the stories surrounding Gregory Thaumaturgus is that their genesis in a

---

[84] For an opposing view see R. MacMullen, "Two Types of Conversion to Early Christianity", *Vig. Chr.* 37 (1983), pp. 174–92 (repr. in idem, *Changes in the Roman Empire. Essays in the Ordinary* (Princeton, 1990), pp. 130–41); and *Christianizing the Roman Empire A.D. 100–400* New Haven/London, 1984), esp. pp. 59–61: "Clearly some very large part of the population, one region in the province of Pontus, was won over to the Church by Gregory the Wonder-Worker in specific and identifiable decades—our only surviving account of any such event, however many others there may or must have been just like it. He succeeded perhaps in part through speaking publicly to groups. He is shown speaking like that, but confirming or instructing. No conversions are said to result. Rather, and expressly, conversions result from his supernatural acts; and, by implication and by position in the narrative, they are presented as the cause of the whole grand picture of his success in his campaigns against daemonic hosts." (p. 61).

local oral culture is precisely documented, while their transformation into a written tradition can be attributed to particular circumstances and to the formative hand of a particular author, Gregory of Nyssa.

Although miraculous tales occur in the Gospels, and acquire an even higher profile in the Apocryphal Acts, which reached their literary form during the second and third centuries, miracle stories do not belong to all forms of Christian literature and they were not present at all periods. The *Church Histories* of Eusebius, Socrates and Sozomen, are not on the whole the places to find miracles, nor are the earlier saints' or martyrs' lives. Martyr acts and Christian biographies written up until the middle of the fourth century focus either on the heroic suffering or on the exemplary asceticism of their Christian heroes. No miracles, for instance, are attributed to Polycarp, Pionius or to the martyrs of Scilli or Lyons. The earliest true hagiographies, the *Life of Antony*, completed around 357, or the *Life of St. Theodotus of Ancyra*, probably written in the time of Julian,[85] emphasise the supernatural power associated with their heroes, and illustrate their ability to cure the sick or their gift of second sight,[86] but they do not contain recognisable miracles comparable to the feats of Gregory Thaumaturgus. There is, therefore, no real precedent for what Gregory of Nyssa produced around 380. The work is a new type of hagiography, and the achievement is signalled by the title, εἰς τὸν βίον τοῦ ἁγίου Γρηγορίου τοῦ θαυματουργοῦ. The last word tells us that we should expect a different sort of Christian life, based on miraculous deeds. We can, moreover, define a specific place, time and milieu, the Pontic countryside around Neocaesarea, the century from 270 to 370, and the Christian population at all levels from the common people to the households of the landed gentry, in which this oral tradition was cultivated, and we can specify the occasion on which and the individuals by whose hands the tradition was transmuted into the high written culture of the Church.

This is not the place for a full literary and rhetorical analysis of Gregory of Nyssa's *Life*. However, it is important to note that the miracle stories, which in many cases had the unassuming character of folk-tales, were set in the framework of a sophisticated literary and homiletic exposition. Gregory of Nyssa affirmed at the outset

---

[85] S. Mitchell, "The Life of Saint Theodotus of Ancyra", *Anatolian Studies* 32 (1982), pp. 106–31.
[86] So, for instance, the *Life of Antony*, 48 and 58.

that his subject constituted an outstanding example of virtue which should assist us in the conduct of our own lives (893A–B), and he expounded the lessons to be learned from Gregory's example at every opportunity. Thus, although the miraculous episodes in the saint's life are the work's most striking feature, they do not dominate it. Gregory of Nyssa begins with an elaborate proem, which avows the difficulties of doing justice to the subject, and gives a distinct and original Christian slant to the conventional theme of the hero's city and origins (896A–900A). The next section covering his education and conversion, which is set largely and fictitiously in Alexandria, contains the first miracle, of the harlot who importuned the young man, was possessed by a demon and then released from its grip at Gregory's intercession (900B–905C). This leads, as Gregory of Nyssa puts it, to "the life itself".[87] A lengthy section concerns his return to Neocaesarea after initially choosing a life of solitude, his ordination by the neighbouring bishop, Phaedimus of Amasia, the introduction of the Creed, the ousting of pagan demons from a temple, and the construction of a church (905C–924C). Three supernatural stories are used to enhance the narrative impact, the vision of John and the Virgin Mary and the revelation of the Creed, the expulsion of the demons from a temple, and the miraculous displacement of a great boulder to remove the doubts of the temple's former priest. There then follow two of the episodes for which he was most famous locally, and which were recalled by Basil in his *De Sancto Spiritu*, the resolution of the feud between two brothers by drying up the lake about which they were in dispute, and the taming of the floods of the river Lycus, by planting his staff on its bank (926A–933A). Then comes his resolution of the dispute over the succession to the bishop-ric of Comana by the nomination of the charcoal-burner Alexander (933B–940A). Two more miracles are inserted, the unsavoury episode of the two Jews, and the exorcism of a demon from a boy (940C–944A), before the "historical" episode of the Decian persecution, during which Gregory fled to the mountains (944A–949D). This provides the context for two miraculous events, the second sight which gave him knowledge of the martyrdom of Troadius and the story of his deacon who overcame a demon in the city's bath-house (950A–953C).

---

[87] PG 46, 905C. The section begins with the rhetorical question, αὐτὸς δὲ ὁ βίος τίς;

Thereafter Gregory introduced martyrs' festivals to replace the events of the old pagan calendar, thus confirming Neocaeasarea as a Christian not a pagan city, before he died (953D–956A). The work ends curiously with another story which the writer says he had passed over before, telling how a plague put an end to an overcrowded pagan festival, and that only Gregory by invoking God's power was able to end the pestilence, thus restoring the victims not only to health but also to the Christian faith (956B–957D). Both introducing and closing this episode Gregory of Nyssa observed that other stories of Gregory's miracles could be told, but that he thought it better to omit them so as not to diminish the credibility of those that he had related.

Parallels to Gregory's life and actions are adduced throughout the work from the Old and New Testament. Gregory's education in Alexandria matched Moses' sojourn in Egypt (901C); his indifference to the harlot recalled Joseph and the wife of Potiphar (905B); Moses' return from the mountain and his revelation of the Law to the people of Israel presaged Gregory's return from the wilderness (908C) and his revelation of the Creed (913B). He resolved the brothers' quarrel as Solomon had settled the dispute between the two women over the child (924D–925B), and caused the lake to disappear as Moses had parted the waters of the Red Sea or as Jesus son of Noah had stayed the waters of the river Jordan (925D, 928D). When he tamed the torrent of the river Lycus he emulated Elisha, who had interrupted the flow of the river Jordan by throwing a sheepskin over it (931D; 2 Kings 2:13–14), and his choice of the humble Alexander to be bishop of Comana was as Samuel's choice of Saul to be king (933D; 1 Samuel 9–12). The punishment of the deceit of the two Jews by death corresponded with that of Ananias who had attempted to deceive Peter over the cost of a piece of land (9421B; cf. Acts 5:1–11). When Gregory hid from his enemies during the persecution, the aid that he gave to those suffering was like that of Moses to the Israelites in their struggle with the Amalekites (949A).

The recourse to these often allusive and obscure parallels implies the presence of an audience, at least some of whom were familiar with the biblical texts. Abramowski's study of the Creed, discussed above, has shown how the composition of "Gregory's Creed", at least, was designed to resolve a major doctrinal dispute which had split the Pontic and Cappadocian bishoprics during the 370s, and attempted to reconcile the position of Basil and of Atarbius of Neocaesarea.

The presentation of this Creed of reconciliation was probably, indeed, the major reason for the entire work. The date, place and context of the delivery of the panegyric, 17 November 379, have been reconstructed from the evidence of Gregory of Nyssa's letters relating to his Pontic journey of that autumn (above pp. 112–5). That conclusion is fully borne out by the manner in which the audience was addressed.

Gregory of Nyssa states at the outset that the great Gregory was the focal point (σκόπος) of the *syllogos* and *synodos* which he was addressing. From internal evidence it becomes clear that this gathering was not simply drawn from the city of Neocaesarea, but from the surrounding provinces of Helenopontus, whose chief city was Amasia, and Pontus Polemonianus, whose chief city was Neocaesarea itself.[88] The long exordium, which contains an elaborate variation on the conventional theme of praising the subject's *patria*, studiously relegates any mention of Gregory Thaumaturgus' actual home city to a subordinate position. Gregory of Nyssa elaborates on the company's communal *patris*, Paradise (895B); "our several fatherlands" (τὰ δὲ ἡμέτερα πάτρια), which do not need the embellishment of pagan myths (895C), and the common origin they share in Pontus, a country whose virtue is made clear by its other name Euxeinos (897B–C). Only then does he mention Neocaesarea, which "in the common judgement of the province is like the peak of the whole surrounding country, the fatherland of Gregory, which was named after Caesar."[89]

The entire work continues to stress Gregory's achievement not within the context of the city but of the whole province. The eyes and expectations of the *ethnos* were on him as he returned from his education (908B). When he began to convert the population the whole *ethnos* was still in the thrall of idols and temples (913D), but was astounded by the report of his miraculous powers (919A). In

---

[88] See Mitchell, *Anatolia* II, p. 159.

[89] PG 46, 897D: τοιούτου δὲ ὄντος τοῦ ἔθνους παντός, ὡς ὅπερ ἄν τις αὐτοῦ μέρος ἐφ᾽ ἑαυτοῦ κατασκέψηται, τῶν ἄλλων προτερεύειν οἴεσθαι· οὐδὲν δὲ ἧττον τῇ κοινῇ κρίσει τοῦ ἔθνους, οἱόν τις κορυφὴ πάσης τῆς περιοικίδος τῶν ἄλλων, ἢ τοῦ μεγάλου Γρηγορίου πόλις ἐστὶν, ἣν βασιλεύς τις ἐπίσημος ... Καῖσαρ τὸ ὄνομα ... ἐπὶ τῷ ἰδίῳ ὀνόματι Νεοκαισαρείαν καλεῖσθαι τὴν πόλιν ἠξίωσεν. For the term κορυφή used to acclaim a capital of a province, compare the acclamation and epigram for Perge in 275: R. Merkelbach et al., *Epigraphica Anatolica* 29 (1997), pp. 69–74 (αὖξε Πέργη ἡ κορυφὴ τῆς Παμφυλίας and εἶπέ με τις κορυφὴν πόλεων κλεινῶν βασιλήων). The term is discussed by J. Nollé, "Pamphylische Studien 11 und 12", *Chiron* 21 (1991), pp. 334ff., and P. Weiss, "Auxe Perge. Beobachtungen zu einem bemerkenswerten städtischen Dokument des späten 3. Jahrhunderts n. Chr.", *Chiron* 21 (1991), p. 378.

conclusion Gregory of Nyssa invited his hearers to wonder at the collective conversion of the entire province from empty beliefs in paganism to recognition of Christian truth.[90] The overcrowded festival which led to the plague and the final miracle was a provincial gathering.[91] The inclusiveness of the approach is reinforced by the stories which involved individuals from other cities of the region: Firmilian, the founder of the church at Cappadocian Caesarea, the dominant see of eastern Anatolia (905C), who put Gregory on the path towards the Christian faith; Phaedimus bishop of Amasia, chief city of the neighbouring province, who was responsible for his consecration (908D–909B); and Alexander, who was chosen by Gregory to be bishop of Comana, a subordinate city within Polemonian Pontus (933D–940B). Each of those episodes corresponded to contemporary diplomatic protocol and would have flattered the ears of appropriate sections of the audience.

In the version that has been transmitted to us, there is some ambiguity about whether the work was simply a speech for declamation or a written document. The initial address and indeed the rhetorical nature of the whole work, which is not without several unpolished or even incoherent passages,[92] suggest the former, a speech prepared in some haste.[93] However, there are also internal references to the work as a written document. At the close he says that he has decided not to add accounts of other miracles to what he has already written, for fear of robbing the work of credibility.[94] Even more clearly at an earlier point he explained that telling all of Gregory's

---

[90] PG 46, 956A–B: τὴν δὲ ἀθρόαν παντὸς τοῦ ἔθνους μετάστασιν ἀπὸ τῆς Ἑλληνικῆς ματαιότητος εἰς τὴν ἐπίγνωσιν τὴν ἀληθείας θαυμαζέτω ἕκαστος τῶν ἐντυγχανόντων τῷ λόγῳ.

[91] PG 46, 956B: πρὸς ταύτην ἅπαν σχέδον συνερρεῖ τὸ ἔθνος.

[92] The whole section covering Gregory's return from Alexandria and his inauguration as bishop is badly constructed. The episode of the deacon and the demon in the bath house is incoherently tacked on to the account of the persecution. It is not difficult to find other examples of sloppy composition, which contrast with the considerable art which has gone into other sections, such as the proem and the whole setting of the revelation of the Creed. It should be clear from the argument why these parts were handled by Gregory with more care.

[93] This is readily understandable, given the circumstances of its composition, when Gregory was being harrassed into assuming the vacant see of Sebastia, and may even have been under arrest. See above p. 115.

[94] PG 46, 957D: ἔστι δὲ καὶ ἄλλα τῇ μνήμῃ μέχρι τοῦ δεῦρο διασωζόμενα τοῦ μεγάλου Γρηγορίου θαύματα, ἅπερ φειδόμενοι τῆς ἀπιστούσης ἀκοῆς, ὡς ἂν μὴ βλαβεῖεν οἱ τὸ ἀληθὲς ἐν τῷ μεγέθει τῶν λεγομένων ψεῦδος οἰόμενοι, τοῖς προγεγραμμένοις οὐ προσεθήκαμεν. Compare 921C for the omission of exaggerated stories.

miracles would require a lengthy history which would exceed the time free for the present speech. Nevertheless, he has decided meanwhile to *write out* one or two of the tales which are still told about him.[95] The impression is of a speech superficially revised after delivery. The author did not polish up weak sections, but hesitated whether to include further miraculous episodes. In most cases he resisted temptation, but not in one, the account of the festival and the plague, which he had left out of the speech but decided to include in the written text.[96] Certainly some of these stories which he suppressed circulated by word of mouth (if not in informal written versions) for they became current in Latin translations within a generation of Gregory of Nyssa's composition (see section V).

V. *The Latin Life*

The inclusion of so many miracles in Gregory of Nyssa's *Life* can be traced to the folkloristic elements in its composition and imply that the congregation that first heard the panegyric contained many ordinary people among whom the stories were current. The stories met with different responses. Some writers played down the miracles. Jerome ends his short and largely factual entry on Gregory, with the simple remark that "current repute speaks of other epistles of his, but more especially of the signs and wonders, which as bishop he performed to the great glory of the churches."[97] Socrates was also unspecific, making only the general remark that Gregory healed the sick and cast out demons even while a layman, and that his actions as well as his words won pagans over.[98] Sozomen re-told a single anecdote, the story of the two beggars, which was ascribed not only to Gregory but also to Epiphanius, but which was, he says, all the more to be taken as a sign of God's power for the repetition.[99]

---

[95] PG 46, 944A: ἄλλα τὸ μὲν πᾶσιν ἐφεξῆς τοῖς παρ' ἐκείνου θαύμασιν ἐπεξιέναι μακρᾶς εἴη συγγραφῆς, καὶ λόγου τὴν παροῦσαν σχολὴν ὑπερβαίνοντος· ἑνὸς δ' ἢ δυοῖν ἔτι τῶν νῦν περὶ αὐτοῦ λεγομένων ἐπιμνησθεὶς ἐν τούτοις περιγράφω τὸν λόγον.

[96] PG 46, 956B: τὸ γὰρ ἐν τοῖς πρώτοις αὐτοῦ τῆς ἱερωσύνης γεγενημένον χρόνοις, ὅπερ πρὸς τὰ λοιπὰ τῶν θαυμάτων ἐπειγόμενος ὁ λόγος παρέδραμε, νῦν ἐπαναλαβὼν διηγήσομαι.

[97] Jerome, *De Vir. Ill.* 65.

[98] Socrates, *Hist. Eccl.* 4.27.

[99] Sozomen, *Hist. Eccl.* 7.27. It seems likely that Sozomen had acquired knowledge of the Epiphanius version while he was in Gaza, and of Gregory's when he was in Constantinople.

However, the miraculous deeds formed the central part of the later tradition about Gregory Thaumaturgus, and the key figure responsible for disseminating them in the West, and perhaps in popularising this style of hagiography, was Rufinus of Aquileia. Although there is no evidence that he ever met any of the Cappadocian Fathers, Rufinus encountered their work in the last decade of the fourth century, translating Basil's *Rules* for the abbot of the monastery of Pinetum near Terracina in 397/8,[100] and sermons of Basil and Gregory of Nazianzus in the following year at Aquileia.[101] In 402/3 he produced his *Church History*, a free translation of Eusebius' work which was brought up to the death of Theodosius by two additional books, 10 and 11, compiled by Rufinus himself. The achievements of Basil and Gregory of Nazianzus are duly described in a long chapter of book 11, which ends with a mention of Basil's younger brothers

> Gregory and Peter, of whom the first so rivalled his brother in doctrinal exposition and the second in works of faith, that either was simply another Basil or Gregory [of Nazianzus]. We also have some excellent short works of the younger Gregory [of Nyssa].[102]

More immediately relevant is the section of book 7, based on Eusebius, about Gregory Thaumaturgus himself (see above p. 105). Eusebius' brief résumée of Gregory's life was expanded into three lengthy chapters. These contain accounts of three of his miracles and the text of the Creed.[103] Rufinus' immediate source was not the *Life* of Gregory of Nyssa as we have it, for only one of the stories, the account of the dispute between the two brothers, is close to Gregory of Nyssa's version. One of the others, the clearing of space for a church to be built, is not to be found there,[104] and the other, the story of the expulsion of the demon from the temple, is told with significant variations. Rufinus does not state what source he used, except to say that the deeds of Gregory *sub orientali et septentrionis axe cunctorum sermone celebrantur*. The phrasing favours the view that Rufinus knew

---

[100] P.R. Amidon, *The Church History of Rufinus of Aquileia. Books 10 and 11* (New York/Oxford, 1997), p. viii.

[101] E.A. Clark, *The Origenist Controversy. The Cultural Construction of an Early Christian Debate* (Princeton, 1992), p. 166.

[102] Rufinus, *Hist. Eccl.* 11.9; transl. Amidon.

[103] Erroneously described as the Creed of the *martyr* Gregory.

[104] Although an element of the story recurs in Gregory of Nyssa's *Life* at PG 46, 917A–B.

these stories by word of mouth and not from a written source, especially as he concludes their telling with a reference to works that he
did know in written form, the Metaphrasis of Ecclesiastes and the
Creed.[105]

There is, in addition, a full-length Latin *Life*. A preface to this,
preserved in only one of the nine manuscript versions, explains that
it was a free version of Gregory of Nyssa's work, and conformed to
the practice of learned men translating the scriptures, who preferred
an idiomatic reproduction of the sense of the original to word-for-
word translation.

> *Sanctarum scripturarum doctores egregii, cum de graeca lingua latinis auribus tradere*
> *aliquid studuerunt, non verbum verbo, sed sensum sensui reddere curaverunt. Et*
> *merito. Nam si latinus sermo graeco idiomati respondere voluerit, et euphoniae sub-*
> *tilitatem et rationis sensum penitus suffocat. Et nos beati Gregorii Thaumaturgi*
> *vitam ex loquela attica transferentes, imitando eam quam sanctus Gregorius Nyssenus*
> *pontifex in peregrina, hoc est in graeca lingua composuit, plurimis additis, plurimis*
> *ademptis, ut ratio utillima postulabat, sensum attendentes latinis viris compediose*
> *curavimus ministrare.*[106]

The work itself confirms the translator's intention. It preserves the
same order of events and narrative structure as Gregory of Nyssa's
original version, but abbreviates and simplifies the rhetorical excursuses. The result is to emphasise the narrative and throw the episodes,
and especially the miracles, into sharper relief. At certain points the
translator has clearly improved on the original. The appended story
of the overcrowded festival and the plague is inserted immediately
after the ordination of Alexander as bishop of Comana. The Latin
version emends the Greek account of Gregory's ordination by Phaedimus, in which the ceremony was carried out in the absence of the
would-be bishop, with a more coherent story in which both Phaedimus
and Gregory separately experienced visions of the one consecrating
the other, and this led the previously reluctant Gregory to accept
his destiny.[107] Details which would have made sense to a local audience but not to a western readership were omitted: the Cappadocian
origin of Firmilian, the fact that the text of the Creed was preserved

---

[105] *Sed et ingenii sui nobis in parvo maxma monumenta dereliquit. Im Ecclesiasten namque
metafrasin iden Gregorius magnificantissime scripsit et catholicae fidei expositionem breviter editam
dereliquit . . .*

[106] Poncelet, "La vie latine de Saint Grégoire", pp. 567–9.

[107] Ibidem, p. 147.

in the church at Neocaesarea, and the name of the river Lycus. On the other hand certain items were added. These include one entire miracle, Gregory slaying a dragon which threatened to devour each month one of the young men of Comana, one of the most distinctively folkloristic fables, which evidently circulated readily in the oral tradition. This is placed after the relocated story of the festival and the plague. The Latin *Life* also contains a number of significant small extra biographical details. It states that Gregory went to study under Origen in the company of his brother Athenodorus, who is never mentioned by Gregory of Nyssa, and that the name of the Roman emperor responsible for the persecution was Gallienus. These two details, one true the other erroneous, are consonant with information recorded in the final paragraph of the Latin *Life*, which contains biographical details entirely lacking in the Greek version: *claruit autem vir iste sanctissimus tempore Gallieni imperatoris et Romani pontificis Dionysii. In synodo etiam quae contra Paulum Samosatenum haereticum episcopum Antiochiae facta est cum Atenodoro fratre suo mirabilis apparuit. Depositus est vero XV kalendarium Decembrium, regnante Domino* ... The source for all this, except for the date of burial, was Eusebius' information about Gregory in the *Church History*.

Two of the items in the Latin *Life* reproduce items from Rufinus' additional chapters to his translation of Eusebius' *Church History* almost word for word. One of these was the version of the Creed, the other the account of the miraculous enlargement of the site for building a church.[108] In the case of the story of the brothers' dispute the Rufinus version is significantly longer than that of the Latin *Life*, but includes extensive verbal correspondences. On the other hand the story of the purging of the demon from the sanctuary is only briefly told by Rufinus, but elaborated at greater length, and with considerable fidelity to Gregory of Nyssa's original in the Latin *Life*.[109]

The two studies which have been devoted to this Latin *Life* have reached opposite views about the relationship between the two Latin versions. Poncelet argued that the full life was earlier than Rufinus and was written at the end of the fourth or very early in the fifth century, before 402. Telfer thought that the dependence was reversed

---

[108] There are three inconsequential differences in the Creed (Rufinus readings first, *Deus/Dominus; quid/quod; antehac/antea*) and two in the miracle (*agerent/aierent; haec/hoc*). See Poncelet, "La vie latine de Saint Grégoire", p. 137.

[109] Telfer, "The Latin Life of St. Gregory Thaumaturgus", pp. 148–55.

and suggested as his own hypothesis that the *Life* was compiled some-where in South Italy, by a writer who wanted to show off his fair but not impeccable knowledge of Greek, between the eighth and eleventh centuries.

Poncelet's view is intrinsically more plausible, for it assumes that the translation was produced at a time when both Rufinus and Jerome attest a lively interest among Latin readers in the stories about Gregory. But the issue may be simplified by the simpler and more dramatic hypothesis, that Rufinus himself was also the author of the Latin *Life*. Rufinus was familiar with and admired the works of Gregory of Nyssa, as he affirmed in *Church History* 11.9. The trans-lation practice which is described in the preface to the *Life*, involv-ing both abridgements and excursuses, corresponds with his own.[110] The historical information at the end of the work comes directly from Rufinus' own translation of Eusebius' *Church History*. The story of Gregory killing the dragon which he adds to the original comes from the writer's additional knowledge of oral (or less likely of writ-ten) sources. We know that Rufinus had access to such material, because the episodes contained in his supplement to Eusebius include an episode which is not to be found in Gregory of Nyssa. Finally, the assumption that Rufinus was responsible for both the surviving Latin versions of Gregory's miracles accounts for the difficulty of deciding the authorial priority of one over the other. Rufinus would have had no compunction transcribing verbatim his own previous effort, nor would he have hesitated to abridge or expand episodes to suit a new context.[111] If this hypothesis about its authorship is correct, it would be simplest to assume that the Latin *Life* was pro-duced after, probably soon after, the translation of Eusebius' *Church History*. Otherwise, there would have been no compelling reason to

---

[110] H. Chadwick, "Rufinus and the Tura papyrus of Origen's *Commentary on Romans*", *JTS* 10 (1959), pp. 10–42; repr. in his *History and Thought of the Early Church* (London, 1982); E.C. Brooks, "The Translation Techniques of Rufinus of Aquileia (343–411)", *Studia Patristica* 17, ed. E.A. Livingstone (Oxford/New York, 1982), 357–64; further bibliography in Amidon, *The Church History of Rufinus*, p. 123.

[111] Telfer, "The Latin life of St. Gregory Thaumaturgus" makes a number of useful points in his close analysis of the relationship of the texts, but none excludes the proposal made here. In the second part of his study (pp. 354–63) there are important observations on faults in the Latin translation, some of which may be ascribed to the fact that the writer was working from a recitation of the Greek text, rather than directly from a written version. If the *Life* is the work of Rufinus, this is useful information about his translation practice.

supply the long excursus on Gregory Thaumaturgus in the latter, and Rufinus would have been likely to mention the version either at that point or when he referred to Gregory of Nyssa in book 11. The excursus, however, shows that Rufinus was conscious of a void that needed to be filled, and it is plausible to think that he took an early opportunity to do so.

In translating the *Life* of Gregory Thaumaturgus into Latin, Rufinus, by privileging the stories and miracles at the expense of the rhetorical and biblical moralising which were at the heart of Gregory of Nyssa's project, helped to shape the form in which it was remembered and became famous. Gregory's version was designed to impress and persuade a conclave of bishops and clergy engaged in theological dispute; Rufinus appealed to a wider and less sophisticated audience. The popular stories which Gregory of Nyssa had incorporated from the Pontic oral tradition reasserted themselves in a version designed for relatively unsophisticated audiences in the Latin West. The process, it is clear, can be observed in the translations into Armenian, Coptic, and Syriac, study of which must be left to those linguistically competent to tackle them. Wittingly or unwittingly it seems that Gregory of Nyssa had established a prototype for a life based on miraculous deeds, which was to become one of the most influential of all hagiographical models thereafter.

BIBLIOGRAPHY

This bibliography contains the literature referred to in the footnotes, complemented with relevant literature on Gregory not mentioned in the notes.

Abramowski, L., "Das Bekenntnis des Gregorius Thaumaturgus bei Gregor von Nyssa und das Problem seiner Echtheit", *Zeitschrift für Kirchengeschichte* 87 (1976), pp. 145–66; repr. in eadem, *Formula and Context. Studies in Early Christian Thought* (Aldershot, 1992).
———, "Die Schrift Gregors des Lehrers "ad Theopompum" und Philoxenus von Mabbug", *Zeitschrift für Kirchengeschichte* 89 (1978), pp. 273–90; repr. in eadem, *Formula and Context. Studies in Early Christian Thought* (Aldershot, 1992).
Amidon, P.R., *The Church History of Rufinus of Aquileia. Books 10 and 11* (New York/Oxford, 1997).
Bardy, G., "La concile d' Antioche (379)", *Revue Bénédictine* 45 (1933), pp. 196–213.
Braund, D., *Georgia in Antiquity. A History of Colchis and Transcaucasian Iberia* (Oxford, 1994).
Brooks, E.C., "The Translation Techniques of Rufinus of Aquileia (343–411)", *Studia Patristica* 17, ed. E.A. Livingstone (Oxford/New York, 1982), 357–64.
Chadwick, H., "Rufinus and the Tura papyrus of Origen's *Commentary on Romans*", *JTS* 10 (1959), pp. 10–42; repr. in idem, *History and Thought of the Early Church* (London, 1982).

Clark, E.A., *The Origenist Controversy. The Cultural Construction of an Early Christian Debate* (Princeton, 1992).

Crouzel, H., "La Passion de l'Impassible. Un essai apologétique du IIIe siècle", *L'homme devant Dieu. Mélanges offerts au Père Henri de Lubac*, vol. 1: *Exégèse et Patristique* (Paris, 1963), pp. 269–79.

——, "Grégoire le Thaumaturge et le 'Dialogue avec Élien'", *RSR* 51 (1963), pp. 422–31.

——— (ed.), *Grégoire le Thaumaturge. Remerciement à Origène suivi de la lettre d'Origène à Grégoire*, SC 148 (Paris, 1969).

———, "L'école d' Origène a Césarée: Postscriptum a une édition de Grégoire le Thamaturge", *Bulletin de littérature ecclésiastique* 71 (1970), pp. 15–27.

———, "Faut-il voir trois personnages en Grégoire le Thaumaturge?", *Gregorianum* 60 (1979), pp. 287–320.

———, "La cristologia di Gregorio Thamaturgo", *Gregorianum* 61 (1980), pp. 745–55.

———, "Gregor I (Gregor der Wundertäter)", *RAC* 12 (1983), cols. 781–93.

———, "Gregory the Thaumaturge", *Encyclopedia of the Early Church* I (1992), p. 368.

Devos, P., "Deux oeuvres méconnues de Pierre sous-diacre de Naples au Xe siècle: la Vie de S. Grégoire le Thaumaturge et la Passion de Ste. Restitute", *Anal. Boll.* 76 (1958), pp. 336–53.

———, "Le manteau partagé: un thème hagiographique en trois de ses variantes", *Anal. Boll.* 93 (1975), pp. 157–63.

Dörrie, H., "Gregor III (Gregor von Nyssa)", *RAC* 12 (1983), cols. 863–95.

Evelyn White, H.G., *The Monasteries of the Wadi'n Natrûn. Part 1. New Coptic Texts from the Monastery of Saint Macarius* (New York, 1926).

Frodevaux, L., "Le symbole de Saint Grégoire le Thaumaturge" *RSR* 19 (1929), pp. 193–247.

Fouskas, K.M., Γρηγορίου Θαυματουργοῦ ἡ κανονικὴ ἐπιστολή (Athens, 1978).

Gibson, E., *The "Christians for Christians" Inscriptions of Phrygia* (Missoula, 1978).

Guyot, P., Klein, R., *Gregor der Wundertäter. Oratio prosphonetica ac panegyrica in Origenem/ Dankrede an Origenes*, Fontes Christiani 24 (Freiburg im Breisgau, 1996).

Heather, P., Matthews, J.F., *The Goths in the Fourth Century*, Translated Texts for Historians 11 (Liverpool, 1991).

Hefele, C.J., Leclercq, H., *Histoire des Conciles* 1.2 (Paris, 1907, repr. Hildesheim, 1973).

Hilgenfeld, H., "Die Vita Gregors des Wunderthäters und die syrischen Acta Martyrum et Sanctorum", *Zeitschrift für wissenschaftliche Theologie* 41 (1898), pp. 452–6.

Ioannou, P.-P., *Discipline Générale Antique. II: Les Canons des Pères Grecques* (Rome, 1963).

Jaeger, W. et al., *Gregorii Nysseni Opera* (Leiden, 1952–).

Jarik, J., *Gregorius Thaumaturgos' Paraphrase of Ecclesiastes*, Society of Biblical Literature, Septuaginta and Cognate Studies 29 (Atlanta, 1990).

Jerphanion, G. de, "Ibora. Gazioura?", *Mélanges de l'Université St. Joseph de Beyrouth* 5 (1911), pp. 333–54.

Kelly, J.N.D., *Jerome. His Life, Writings and Controversies* (London, 1975).

Kennedy, George A., *Classical Rhetoric and its Christian and Secular Tradition from Ancient to Modern Times* (London, 1980).

Knorr, U.W., "Gregor der Wundertäter als Missionär", *Evangelisches Missionsmagazin* 110 (1966), pp. 45–79.

Koetschau, P., *Des Gregorios Thaumaturgos Dankrede an Origenes* (Freiburg im Breisgau, 1894).

———, "Zur Lebensgeschichte Gregors des Wunderthäters", *Zeitschrift für wissenschaftliche Theologie* 41 (1898), pp. 211–50.

Lane Fox, R., *Pagans and Christians in the Mediterranean World from the Second Century A.D. to the Conversion of Constantine* (Harmondsworth, 1986).

Leclercq, H., "Ibora", *Dictionnaire d'Archéologie Chrétienne et de Liturgie* 7, cols. 4–9.

MacMullen, R., "Two Types of Conversion to Early Christianity", *Vig. Chr.* 37 (1983), pp. 174–92; repr. in idem, *Changes in the Roman Empire. Essays in the Ordinary* (Princeton, 1990), pp. 130–41.

———, *Christianizing the Roman Empire A.D. 100–400* (New Haven/London, 1984).

Markschies, C., "Gregorios Thaumaturgos", *Der Neue Pauly* 4 (1998), cols. 1211–2.

Maraval, P., *Grégoire de Nysse. Vie de Ste Macrine*, SC 178 (Paris, 1971).

———, "La date du mort de Basile de Césarée", *Revue des études augustiniennes* 34 (1988), pp. 25–38.

———, *Grégoire de Nysse, Lettres*, SC 363 (Paris, 1990).

May, G., "Gregor von Nyssa in der Kirchenpolitik seiner Zeit", *Jahrbuch der österreichischen Byzantinistik* 15 (1966), pp. 105–32.

———, "Die Chronologie des Lebens und der Werke des Gregor von Nyssa", *Écriture et culture philosophique dans la pensée de Grégoire de Nysse*, ed. M. Harl, (Leiden, 1971), pp. 53–63.

Merkelbach, R. et al., *Epigraphica Anatolica* 29 (1997), pp. 69–74.

Millar, F., "Culture grecque et culture latine: le foi et la loi", *Les Martyrs de Lyon (177)*, Collogues Internationaux du Centre National de la Recherche Scientifique 575 (Paris, 1978), pp. 187–93.

Mitchell, S., "The Life of Saint Theodotus of Ancyra", *Anatolian Studies* 32 (1982), pp. 106–31.

———, *Anatolia. Land, Men, and Gods in Asia Minor*, II: *The Rise of the Church* (Oxford, 1993).

———, "Wer waren die Gottesfürchtigen?", *Chiron* 28 (1998), pp. 55–64.

———, "The Cult of Theos Hypsistos between Pagans, Jews and Christians", *Pagan Monotheism in Late Antiquity*, eds. P. Athanassiadi, M. Frede (Oxford, 1999), pp. 81–148.

Modrzejewski, J, "Grégoire le Thaumaturge et le droit romain: à propos d' une édition récente", *Revue du Droit* 49 (1971), pp. 313–24.

Momigliano, A., "The Life of St. Macrina by Gregory of Nyssa", *Ottavo contributo alla storia degli studi classici e del mondo antico* (Rome, 1987), pp. 333–47.

Moretta, E., "I neologismi nell' orazione al Origine di Gregorio il taumaturgo", *Vetera Christianorum* 8 (1971), pp. 41–56, pp. 209–317; 10 (1973), pp. 59–77; 13 (1976), pp. 81–6.

Nautin, P., *Origène, sa vie et son oeuvre* (Paris, 1977).

Nollé, J., "Pamphylische Studien 11 und 12", *Chiron* 21 (1991), pp. 331–44.

Poncelet, A., "La vie latine de Saint Grégoire le thaumaturge", *RSR* 1 (1910), pp. 132–60, pp. 567–9.

Riedinger, R., "Das Bekenntnis des Gregor Thaumaturgus bei Sophronius von Jerusalem und Macarius von Antiocheia", *Zeitschrift für Kirchengeschichte* 92 (1981), pp. 311–4.

Römer, C.A., "Basilius, Epistula XXII.3 und das Glaubensbekenntnis des Gregor—Thaumaturgos in einem Papyrus aus Antinoe", *ZPE* 123 (1998), pp. 101–4.

Rousseau, P., *Basil of Caesarea* (Berkeley/Los Angeles/London, 1994).

Ruge, W., "Ibora", *RE* 9 (1914), col. 816.

Ryssel, V., *Gregorius Thaumaturgus. Sein Leben und seine Schriften* (Leipzig, 1880).

———, "Eine syrische Lebensgeschichte des Gregorius Thaumaturgus. Nach cod. Mus. Brit. syr. add. 14648 aus dem syrischen übersetzt", *Theologische Zeitschrift aus der Schweiz* 11 (1894), pp. 228–54.

Salamon, M., "The Chronology of Gothic Incursions in Asia Minor in the 3rd century A.D.", *Eos* 59 (1971), pp. 109–39.

Scardigli, B., "Die gotisch-römischen Beziehungen im 3. und 4. Jhdt. n. Chr. Ein Forschungsbericht 1950–1970", *ANRW* II.5.1 (1976), pp. 238–58.

Schwarz, E., "Zur Kirchengeschichte des vierten Jahrhunderts", *Zeitschrift für die Neutestamentliche Wissenschaft und die Kunde der älteren Kirche* 34 (1935), pp. 129–213.

138 STEPHEN MITCHELL

————, "Über die Sammlung des Cod. Veronensis LX", *Zeitschrift für die Neutestamentliche Wissenschaft und die Kunde der älteren Kirche* 35 (1936), pp. 1–23.

Simonetti, M., "Una nuova ipotesi su Gregorio il Taumaturgo", *RSR* 24 (1988), pp. 17–41.

Slusser, M., "Gregor der Wundertäter", *TRE* 14, pp. 188–91.

Staats, R., "Dic römische Tradition im Symbol von 381 (NC) und seine Entstehung auf der Synode von Antiochien 379", *Vig. Chr.* 44 (1990), pp. 209 21.

Tabbernee, W., *Montanist Inscriptions and Testimonia. Epigraphic Sources Illustrating the History of Montanism* (Macon, 1997).

Telfer, W., "The Latin Life of St. Gregory Thaumaturgus", *JTS* 31 (1930), pp. 142–55 and pp. 354–63.

————, "The Cultus of St. Gregory Thaumaturgus", *HTR* 29 (1936), pp. 225–344.

Trigg, J.W., *Origen*, The Early Christian Fathers (London/New York 1998).

Van Dam, R., "Hagiography and History. The Life of Gregory Thaumaturgus", *Classical Antiquity* 1 (1982), pp. 272–308.

Van Esbroek, M., "Fragments sahidiques du Panégyrique de Grégoire le Thaumaturge par Grégoire de Nysse", *OLP* 6/7 (1975/6), pp. 555–68.

————, "The Creed of Gregory Thaumaturgus", *Studia Patristica* 22, ed. E.A. Livingstone (Louvain, 1989), pp. 155–66.

Weiss, P., "Auxe Perge. Beobachtungen zu einem bemerkenswerten städtischen Dokument des späten 3. Jahrhunderts n. Chr.", *Chiron* 21 (1991), pp. 353–92.

RABBULA, BISHOP OF EDESSA: SPIRITUAL AUTHORITY AND SECULAR POWER

Han J.W. Drijvers

University of Groningen

The Syriac *vita* of Rabbula is in many aspects a very remarkable document. It presents a highly laudatory portrait of the Edessene bishop, of his great spiritual authority, his exemplary ascetic lifestyle and of his care for the urban poor, the orphans and widows of Edessa. But there is much the *vita* does not tell us. It is totally silent on the Council of Ephesus of 431 and Rabbula's role there. It does not mention Hiba, Rabbula's adversary in doctrinal and political matters, whom the bishop sent into exile in 433, but who became his successor in 436 after Rabbula's death. We do not hear a word about the plague or famines at Edessa or about the flood of the river Daisan that occurred in 412/13, the very year in which Rabbula was appointed to the metropolitan see of Edessa.[1] The *vita* does not contain any details about urban life at Edessa, let alone about what happened outside this town. Actually it is not a real *vita*, a biography, but rather a panegyric, n'en déplaise Baumstark's very high opinion of it:

> Seine von einem ihm persönlich nahestehenden Edessener abgefasste Biographie ist eines der vorzüglichsten Denkmäler ihrer Gattung, das die syrische Literatur aufzuweisen hat, von dem grossen B. ein mit warmer Liebe geschaffenes Bild von plastischer Schärfe bietend.[2]

The *vita* describes the heroic deeds of Mar Rabbula, bishop of Edessa, the blessed city, as the title of the Syriac text says. Such a title belongs to the genre of the martyrs acts more than to real hagiography. Rabbula's life is related as a witness to Christ, to whom he totally devoted and sacrificed it.[3] As a living witness to Christ Rabbula

---

[1] *Chronicon Edessenum = Chronica Minora* I, ed. and transl. by I. Guidi, CSCO, Script. Syr., ser. 3, tome 4 (Paris, 1903), sub lii: *Anno 724, sub Honorio et Arcadio, invictis imperatoribus, muri Edessae, iam tertio, aquia labefactati sunt*; cf. J.B. Segal, *Edessa "the Blessed City"* (Oxford, 1970), p. 156 for a vivid description of this flood and the destruction it caused.

[2] A. Baumstark, *Geschichte der syrischen Literatur* (Bonn, 1922), pp. 72–3.

[3] The *vita* was published by J.J. Overbeck, *S. Ephraemi Syri, Rabulae episcopi Edesseni,*

is portrayed as a model of spiritual authority; as an aristocratic bishop in fifth century Edessa he also was at times an aggressive bearer of secular power. These two sides of Mar Rabbula confront us with the question of how and by what means spiritual authority was exercised.[4]

"Biography was from its inception a genre that found its home in controversy", and this also applies to the Syriac *vita* of Rabbula.[5] It was written as a propaganda tract in defence of the highly controversial bishop before the *Latrocinium Ephesinum* of 449. Its proper context, together with the *Legend of the Man of God*, was the very tense atmosphere at Edessa, where the adherents of the Rabbula party attacked the then bishop Hiba and stirred up public riots, so that the *comes* Chaereas entered the town with troops to restore law and order.[6] The *vita* is, however, almost the only source for Rabbula's life and his secular and ecclesiastical career. In addition we have the Syriac text of a homily of Rabbula allegedly delivered in the cathedral in Constantinople, and some of his letters from a collection originally containing forty-six.[7] We possess Rabbula's canons for the monks, for the clergy and for the "benay" and "benat qeyama", the Sons and Daughters of the Covenant, an inner circle of ascetics in the Christian community of Edessa.[8] Part of his liturgical poetry on

---

Balaeit aliorumque opera selecta (Oxford, 1865), pp. 159–209; a German transl. by G. Bickell, *Ausgewählte Schriften der syrischen Kirchenväter Aphraates, Rabulas und Isaak von Ninive*, Bibliothek der Kirchenväter (Kempten, 1874), pp. 155–211; on Rabbula see P. Peeters, "La vie de Rabboula, évêque d'Édesse (+ 7 aout 436)", *RSR* 18 (1928), pp. 170–204; F. Nau, "Les 'belles actions' de Mar Rabboula, évêque d'Édesse de 412 au 7 aout 435 (ou 436)", *RHR* 103 (1931), pp. 97–135; G.G. Blum, *Rabbula von Edessa. Der Christ, der Bischof, der Theologe*, CSCO 300, Subs. 34 (Louvain, 1969); Han J.W. Drijvers, "The Man of God of Edessa, Bishop Rabbula, and the Urban Poor: Church and Society in the Fifth Century", *JECS* 4 (1996), pp. 235–48; Peter Bruns, "Bischof Rabbula von Edessa—Dichter und Theologe", *Symposium Syriacum VII*, ed. R. Lavenant, OCA 256 (Rome, 1998), pp. 195–202.

[4] See M. Mann, *Sources of Social Power. A History of Power from the Beginning to A.D. 1760*, vol. 1 (Cambridge, 1986), pp. 300–40: "Ideology transcendent: the Christian ecumene"; Peter Brown, *Power and Persuasion in Late Antiquity. Towards a Christian Empire* (Madison, 1992), pp. 136–58.

[5] Patricia Cox, *Biography in Late Antiquity. A Quest for the Holy Man* (Berkeley/Los Angeles/London, 1983), p. 135.

[6] See Drijvers, "The Man of God of Edessa"; Richard Lim, *Public Disputation, Power, and Social Order in Late Antiquity* (Berkeley/Los Angeles/London, 1995), pp. 138–48 for the background of such public riots.

[7] Overbeck, *S. Ephraemi Syri, Rabulae*, pp. 239–44; Blum, *Rabbula von Edessa*, pp. 131–49; Bruns, "Bischof Rabbula von Edessa", pp. 199–200; the preserved letters of Rabbula: Overbeck, *S. Ephraemi Syri, Rabbulae*, pp. 222–44.

[8] See A. Vööbus, *Syriac and Arabic Documents regarding Legislation relative to Syrian Asceticism*, Papers of the Estonian Theological Society in Exile 11 (Stockholm, 1960),

various subjects, among them the True Cross, is also preserved.[9] Rabbula probably became acquainted with traditions regarding the True Cross when he visited the Holy Land.[10] Some of his liturgical hymns might however be spurious.

Notwithstanding its tendentious character, the *vita* of Rabbula tells us much about its hero, especially when its contents are meticulously analyzed and confronted with the other bits of available information. The anonymous author informs his readers that Rabbula had a Christian mother and a pagan father, a priest, who made sacrifices on behalf of the emperor Julian when the latter started his campaign against the Sassanian king Shapur II in 363. His mother found him a Christian wife and both women tried to convert him to the true belief. He obstinately refused. Rabbula received a traditional education in Greek literature and philosophy and apparently pursued a public career in the imperial administration.[11] The *vita* speaks about it in rather disguised terms—he was presumptuous because of the high and glorious position the emperor had given him—but the somewhat later Greek *Life of Alexander Akoimetes*, in which the *vita* of Rabbula is partly incorporated, calls him an imperial prefect of Qenneshrin.[12] Qenneshrin is Chalcis, situated south-west of Beroea, present-day Aleppo, where the family possessed large estates.[13] There

---

pp. 24–50, pp. 78–86; German transl. by Peter Bruns, "Die Kanones des Rabbula (gest. 435) und ihr Beitrag zur Reform des kirchlichen Lebens in Edessa", *Theologia et Jus Canonicum. Festgabe für Heribert Heinemann*, ed. H.J.F. Reinhardt (Essen, 1995), pp. 471–80; for the Sons and Daughters of the Covenant see G. Nedungatt, "The Covenanters of the Early Syriac-Speaking Church", *OCP* 49 (1973), pp. 191–215, 419–44.

[9] See Bruns, "Bischof Rabbula von Edessa", pp. 196–202; Overbeck, *S. Ephraemi Syri, Rabulae*, pp. 245–8, 364–78.

[10] Overbeck, *S. Ephraemi Syri, Rabulae*, pp. 165, 1–3; Blum, *Rabbula von Edessa*, p. 22; Bruns, "Bischof Rabbula von Edessa", p. 196, n. 14. For pilgrimages in this period see E.D. Hunt, *Holy Land Pilgrimage in the Later Roman Empire A.D. 312–460* (Oxford, 1982).

[11] Overbeck, *S. Ephraemi Syri, Rabulae*, 161, 4–5.

[12] *Vie d'Alexandre l'acémète*, ed. E. de Stoop, PO VI (Paris, 1911), pp. 641–704; German transl. of part of this *vita* in Bickell, *Ausgewählte Schriften*, pp. 212–25; cf. A. Vööbus, *La vie d'Alexandre en grec, un témoin d'une biographie inconnue de Rabbula, écrite en syriaque*, Contributions of the Baltic University 59 (Pinneberg, 1947).

[13] Fergus Millar, *The Roman Near East 31 B.C.–A.D. 337* (Cambridge/London, 1993), p. 238; A.H.M. Jones, *The Cities of the Eastern Roman Provinces* (Oxford, 1971²), pp. 231–2; E. Honigmann, "Historische Topographie von Nordsyrien im Altertum", *ZDPV* 46 (Leipzig, 1923), pp. 176–7; P. Monceaux, L. Brossé, "Chalcis ad Belum. Notes sur l'histoire et les ruines de la ville", *Syria. Revue d'art oriental et d'archéologie* 6 (1925), pp. 339f.

is no reason to doubt this information. Rabbula came from a wealthy family of mixed belief, got a solid education and had a public career. We may, however, detect literary dependence on the *vita* of Ephraem Syrus. Ephraem was born in Nisibis; he had a Christian mother and a pagan priest as father.[14] Another possible literary influence is the so-called Syriac *Romance of Julian*, an Edessene propaganda story intended to justify Julian's defeat and the cession of Nisibis, Ephraem's home town, to the Sassanians. The reason for the cession of this Christian stronghold according to the Edessene story is its supposed paganism. Julian is pictured as the most stubborn pagan, and offering sacrifices on behalf of him is the worst thing one can do.[15]

One day Rabbula was witness to a healing performed by a hermit Abraham who lived near Rabbula's estates in a monastery.[16] That was the beginning of his conversion. His mother brought him to Eusebius, bishop of Qenneshrin, and to Acacius, bishop of Beroea, and they talked to him at great length about truth and error, and of course about the true belief in Christ.[17] It must have almost been a philosophical discussion. Rabbula kept his doubts, however, but promised to visit the chapel of Cosmas and Damian. There he was the witness of another healing miracle, a blind man recovering his eye-sight "through the power of the Cross", as the *vita* records. The greatest miracle was however performed on Rabbula himself. The Lord opened his mouth and he praised God, Father, Son, and Holy Ghost. When the bishops Eusebius and Acacius heard of this miracle they brought him to the monastery of the hermit Marcian, the teacher of Eusebius, and to the afore-mentioned Abraham, and there Rabbula took the vow to dedicate his life to God and to live an ascetic life in a monastery. Rabbula also managed to go to Jerusalem to see the holy places and to be baptised in the river Jordan like

---

[14] Text in C. Brockelmann, *Syrische Grammatik* (Berlin, 1912), pp. 23ff.; *Ephraem Syrus Hymni et Sermones*, 4 vols., ed. T.J. Lamy (Mechliniae, 1882–1902), vol. 2, pp. 3ff. Cf. A. Vööbus, *Literary Critical and Historical Studies in Ephrem the Syrian*, Papers of the Estonian Theological Society in Exile 10 (Stockholm, 1958), pp. 22–4, pp. 46–7.

[15] See Han J.W. Drijvers, "The Syriac Romance of Julian. Its Function, Place of Origin and Original Language", *Symposium Syriacum VI*, ed. R. Lavenant, OCA 247 (Rome, 1994), pp. 201–14.

[16] On the hermit Abraham see Theodoret, *Hist. Eccl.* 4.28.3; idem, *Hist. Rel.* 3.17, SC 234 (Paris, 1977), pp. 279–81; cf. P. Canivet, *Le monachisme syrien selon Théodoret de Cyr* (Paris, 1977), pp. 185–7.

[17] On Acacius and Eusebius see Theodoret, *Hist. Eccl.* 5.4.5; cf. Canivet, *Le monachisme syrien*, pp. 113–5; J. Quasten, *Patrology*, vol. 3 (Utrecht/Antwerp/Westminster, 1960), pp. 482–3.

Jesus. When he rose from the water of the Jordan his white baptismal robe was covered with crosses as red as Christ's blood.[18]

This whole passage on Rabbula's conversion and baptism provides an insight into his religious ideas. The hermit Abraham, as well as the bishops Marcianus, Acacius and Eusebius are prominently recorded in the *Ecclesiastical History* and the *Historia Religiosa* of Theodoret bishop of Cyrrhus.[19] Acacius was Theodoret's main informant on holy monks in the Antiochene area.[20] The chapel of Cosmas and Damian was the main church of Theodoret's diocese Cyrrhus. Moreover all these holy monks and bishops were adherents of the School of Antioch, and Theodoret praised their orthodoxy. The theological school of Antioch, allegedly founded by the martyr Lucian, taught a literal and historical exegesis of the Bible, unlike the allegorical interpretation current in Alexandria, and was strongly influenced by Middle-Platonic philosophy. Its most prominent representative was Theodore bishop of Mopsuestia in Cilicia (d. 428), venerated by the later Nestorian church as "the great exponent of the Scriptures".[21]

The *vita* of Rabbula therefore echoes traditions that were also recorded by Theodoret of Cyrrhus, and relates his conversion to Theodoret's ascetic heroes. It remains to be seen whether the author of the *vita* knew Theodoret's writings, or transmitted more or less faithfully the story of Rabbula's conversion as it was told to or heard by him. In my view the latter possibility is more likely. It ought to be emphasised that Rabbula received his first instruction in Christian belief from adherents of the Antiochene theology, which makes it very likely that he shared their religious concepts. A second point of interest is that Marcianus, Acacius and Eusebius came from aristocratic Syrian families of curial or senatorial rank like Rabbula himself.[22] They all shared the same education and could discuss matters

---

[18] Bickell, *Syrische Kirchenväter*, pp. 170–4.

[19] Theodoret, *Hist. Eccl.* 5.4.5; idem, *Hist. Rel.* 3 (Marcianus), *Hist. Rel.* 3.11, *Hist. Eccl.* 4.13.2–3 (Eusebius).

[20] Theodoret, *Hist. Rel.* 2.9; Canivet, *Le monachisme syrien*, pp. 113–5.

[21] The literature on the School of Antioch and its theology is enormous. D.S. Wallace-Hadrill, *Christian Antioch. A Study of Early Christian Thought in the East* (Cambridge, 1982) is a good introduction; on philosophical influence on the Antiochene theology see R.A. Norris, *Manhood and Christ. A Study in the Christology of Theodore of Mopsuestia* (Oxford, 1963), pp. 1–78.

[22] Canivet, *Le monachisme syrien*, pp. 185ff., esp. pp. 248–53; cf. H. Kennedy, J.H.W.G. Liebeschuetz, "Antioch and the Villages of Northern Syria in the Fifth and Sixth Centuries A.D.: Trends and Problems", *Nottingham Medieval Studies* 32 (1988), pp. 75f. and n. 69.

of truth and error on a philosophical level. Quite apart from all miracle stories, this makes the essential elements of Rabbula's conversion to Christianity more plausible. He belongs to the same category
of ascetic monks as John Chrysostom and many others.[23]

The symbol of the cross plays an important role in Rabbula's *vita*.
Healings were performed through the power of the cross; crosses
appear on his baptismal robe; Rabbula took his cross and followed
Jesus; demons were defeated by the power of the cross. The cross
represents might and power. When Rabbula visited Jerusalem around
400 A.D. he certainly became acquainted with the *Legend of the True
Cross* and he therefore is very probably responsible for the inclusion
of this legend in the form of the Protonike story in the final version
of the *Doctrina Addai*. The *vita* does not say anything about this episode,
but only stresses the power and healing capacity of the cross as does
the *Doctrina Addai*. In this way the *vita* constitutes a link between
Rabbula, i.e. Edessa, and Jerusalem, the main scene of the Christian
sacred history.[24]

When Rabbula dedicated himself to the ascetic life he sold all his
estates and possessions and distributed the money as alms to the
poor.[25] The *vita* relates explicitly that Rabbula's alms even came to
Edessa's saints and poor "through a secret device of Christ" to pave
the way for Edessa's future bishop. The only explanation for this
remarkable information is that there had been no relation whatso-
ever between Rabbula and Edessa and the anonymous author was
rather anxious to construct one. The story of Rabbula's election as
bishop confirms this. After the death of the Edessene bishop Diogenes,
the Antiochene patriarch Alexander and his bishops, among them
Acacius, elected Rabbula as his successor.[26] Christ's Spirit told them
in their hearts: "Rabbula should be elected, because in him I am

---

[23] A.J. Festugière, *Antioche païenne et chrétienne. Libanius, Chrysostome et les moines de
Syrie* (Paris, 1959), pp. 252–62 on Marcian and Eusebius and their philosophical
education.

[24] See Jan Willem Drijvers, "The Protonike legend and the Doctrina Addai",
Studia Patristica 33, ed. E.A. Livingstone (Louvain, 1996), pp. 517–23; idem, "The
Protonike Legend, the *Doctrina Addai* and Bishop Rabbula of Edessa", *Vig. Chr.* 51
(1997), pp. 298–315.

[25] Bickell, *Syrische Kirchenväter*, p. 172; Kennedy, Liebeschuetz, "Antioch and the
Villages of Northern Syria", p. 75 and n. 70; Festugière, *Antioche païenne*, pp. 329–46
on John Chrysostom; Brown, *Power and Persuasion*, pp. 94ff.

[26] Rubens Duval, *Histoire d'Édesse* (Paris, 1892), pp. 168ff.; Bickell, *Syrische Kirchenväter*,
p. 176. On the patriarch Alexander see G. Downey, *A History of Antioch in Syria*
(Princeton, 1961), pp. 457f.

well pleased", in this way making Rabbula into an *alter Christus*. Un-like many others Rabbula did not protest against his election, for in his soul there was a strong desire for this dignity, and the craving for this function did not confuse his heart. Rabbula apparently was very ambitious and career-minded and Edessa was a prestigious see. On the other hand the *vita* emphasises Rabbula's humility, austere asceticism, and heavenly virtues resulting in the *vita angelica*.[27] Like Christ and Saint Anthony he was tempted in the desert, and the *vita* contains further elements that present Rabbula as an *alter Christus*.

Notwithstanding this very lofty picture of the Edessene bishop, Rabbula was a severe and at times even violent man, who was very much feared by his clergy and Edessa's population. Clerics who did not listen to him and passed their time in idleness and useless chat-ter, he subjected to his power through violence. The haughty ones he punished, we may assume with corporeal punishments. He also threatened his clerics with severe penalties to avoid association with women. Clerics who lived with him in the same house during the twenty-four years of his episcopate did not dare enter his room, because he struck enormous fear into them. The wealthy Edessenes did not dare harm the poor for fear of Rabbula, and many were kept from sin by the same fear. Although the author of the *vita* presents a highly laudatory picture of the bishop, these remarks nevertheless provide a more differentiated portrait. Rabbula was a violent man, who used his power relentlessly and at times beat up disobedient priests, like a landed proprietor punishing his slaves.[28] A later writer, Barhadbeshabba 'Arbaya, records that at a synod at Constantinople Rabbula was accused of beating up his clerics. When he argued to defend himself that our Lord did the same in the tem-ple at Jerusalem, Theodore the exegete corrected him and made clear that our Lord did not beat up other human beings but only "cast out all them that sold and bought" (cf. Matthew 21:12–13). From that time Rabbula hated Theodore.[29] Hiba, Rabbula's main opponent at Edessa, also ascribes Rabbula's hate of Theodore to personal

---

[27] Bickell, *Syrische Kirchenväter*, pp. 175–90; cf. Peter Nagel, *Die Motivierung der Askese in der Alten Kirche und der Ursprung des Mönchtums*, Texte und Untersuchungen zur Geschichte der altchristlichen Literatur 95 (Berlin, 1966), pp. 34–48 on the *vita angelica*.

[28] Bickell, *Syrische Kirchenväter*, pp. 180–1, pp. 187–8, pp. 191–2.

[29] Mar Barhadbsabba 'Arbaya, *Cause de la fondation des Écoles*, PO IV.4.18 (Paris, 1907), pp. 380–1.

animosity, since Theodore had once rebuked Rabbula during a session of the synod. This is reported in Hiba's famous *Letter to Mari*, probably Mar Dadisho bishop of Ardashir and one of Hiba's former pupils. The letter was written in 433, still within the period of Rabbula's episcopate, and bitterly complains about the unreliable and unworthy behaviour of Rabbula, the Tyrant of Edessa as Hiba calls him, after the Council of Ephesus of 431.[30] Hiba was head of the School of Edessa, a great scholar and translator of Theodore of Mopsuestia's works from Greek into Syriac.[31] He accompanied Rabbula to the Council of Ephesus in 431, but the two men apparently became enemies soon after this Council. They had a totally different social and intellectual background and education, which certainly contributed to their struggles.[32]

When Rabbula was elected bishop of Edessa his main concern was the behaviour of the local priests and monks. The priests living in community used silver tableware, which Rabbula did not consider appropiate. He sold the silver plates and dishes to support the poor and ordered the priests to use earthen tableware. Reading all Rabbula's admonitions and warnings to his priests, the Edessene clergy must have lead a rather messy and worldly life. They were admonished to avoid association with women and in particular were not allowed to live together with the daughters of their brothers and sisters, i.e. with their nieces. It was apparently a common practice, like hiring a maid to serve them. They should abstain from meat and fowl and especially bathing, except when they were ill. Imagine the smell—"göttliches Wohlgeruch"! Lust for money was strictly forbidden, like fine clothing and nice furniture. They were not permitted to trade in worldly goods and certainly not to involve themselves in lawsuits on behalf of their kinsmen. He gave the same rules to the monks and moreover strictly forbade them to lend money on

---

[30] Hiba's letter was originally written in Syriac. A Greek and Latin translation in E. Schwarz, *Acta Conciliorum Oecumenicorum* II.1.3, 32–34; II.3.3, 39–43; the Syriac version in J. Flemming, *Akten der Ephesinischen Synode vom Jahre 449*, Abhandlungen der Akademie der Wissenschaften in Göttingen, phil.-hist. Kl., neue Folge 15.1 (Göttingen, 1917; repr. 1970), pp. 48–52 is based on the Greek. The letter was one of the "Three Chapters" condemned by the Council of Constantinople in 553; see also A. d'Alès, "La lettre d'Ibas à Marès le Persan", *RSR* 22 (1932), pp. 5–25.

[31] On Hiba see I. Ortiz de Urbina, *Patrologia Syriaca* (Rome, 1965), pp. 99–100; E.R. Hayes, *L'école d'Édesse* (Paris, 1930), pp. 191–208; A. Vööbus, *History of the School of Nisibis*, CSCO 266, Subs. 26 (Louvain, 1965), pp. 15–7.

[32] See Lim, *Public Disputation*, pp. 144–8.

interest. Priests were not allowed to receive presents and in particular were not to accept bribes. In short, Rabbula wanted immaculate priests dedicated only to the service of the church and the urban poor. The reality must have been quite otherwise, in particular when we look at Rabbula's preserved canons and rules, for priests and monks. The *vita*, though, reflects these canons and rules and the anonymous author must have known them. The *vita* therefore indirectly vouchsafes the authenticity of most of the canons and rules that were ascribed to Rabbula.[33]

A few examples may suffice. Monks must take care that women never enter their monasteries. Monks shall not drink wine so that they will not blaspheme. They shall not engage in the business of buying and selling in the monasteries.[34] Monks shall not leave their residence and not undertake lawsuits on behalf of others nor go into the town or to the judges. His commands to priests are even stricter. They shall not live with women and shall not be served by women. They shall not take a bribe from anyone, especially not from litigants in a lawsuit. They shall neither demand a fee nor interest nor profane profits. All the priests shall take care of the poor. They shall not stay in public lodgings or in an inn; they shall keep themselves far from wine and meat, except when they are ill. Those who get drunk or visit a tavern shall be expelled from the church. They shall not undertake a lawsuit for their relatives. No priest shall travel without the permission of the bishop (our permission, says Rabbula's rule) to the imperial court or to any far-off place.[35] All these canons and rules together give a vivid insight into the range of abuses that were common practice among the clergy and monks, and confirm what the *vita* tells us.[36] When Rabbula occupied the see of Edessa, the clergy were apparently a disorderly bunch of people who did as they pleased and enjoyed all the pleasures of the world, using or abusing their clerical status to enrich themselves. They must have caused their bishop a great deal of trouble.

Not only were the clergy in disorder, the Edessene church itself

---

[33] Bickell, *Syrische Kirchenväter*, pp. 178–82; cf. Rabbula's canons and rules in Vööbus, *Syriac and Arabic Documents*, and in Bruns, "Die Kanones des Rabbula".

[34] Cf. canons 3 and 24 of the Council of Chalcedon of 451.

[35] Cf. canon 4 of the Council of Chalcedon of 451.

[36] See in general Charles A. Frazee, "Late Roman and Byzantine Legislation on the Monastic Life from the Fourth to the Eighth Centuries", *Church History* 51 (1982), pp. 263–79.

knew many heretics: Bardesanites, Marcionites, Manichees, and Arians. And outside the church there were still many Jews and pagans. The *vita* records that Rabbula dealt very gently with the heretics and did not use harsh measures to convert them to the true faith.[37] That is an indirect sign of their powerful position, in particular that of the Bardesanites, who belonged to the urban élite. In this long passage about the local heresies there is again a certain influence from Ephraem's *vita*. This does not mean that it is mere traditional material without any relation to the actual situation during Rabbula's episcopacy. Edessa was an intellectual and academic center, where Christian philosophies such as Bardesanism, Marcionism and Manichaeism still flourished. The School of Edessa preserved their writings![38]

When Rabbula, however, had converted all heretics, had made his community into a "harmonious body of the perfect man" and wanted a bit of rest after all these efforts on behalf of orthodoxy, a new danger threatened the church: Nestorius, pupil of Theodore of Mopsuestia. He offended the Mother of God (*theotokos*) and Rabbula started to preach against him.[39] The panegyrist reports that Rabbula was called to Constantinople at that time and refuted there "the error of the new Jews" in the presence of the emperor and his courtiers. They were very grateful to him and wanted to present him with a large amount of gold and precious clothes, which he however refused. The *vita* would have us believe that already before the Council of Ephesus of 431 Rabbula refuted Nestorius' doctrine, and that even the calling of this Council and Nestorius' deposition were due to Rabbula's efforts.[40] The real course of events was different. Perfectly in accordance with Rabbula's early instruction in the true faith, the bishop of Edessa was an ardent reader of Theodore's writings, as Hiba records in his *Letter to Mari*.[41] At Ephesus he took part in the

---

[37] Bickell, *Syrische Kirchenväter*, pp. 195–8.

[38] See Han J.W. Drijvers, "The Persistence of Pagan Cults and Practices in Christian Syria", *East of Byzantium. Syria and Armenia in the Formative Period*, eds. N.G. Garsoïan, T.F. Mathews and R.W. Thompson (Washington D.C., 1982), pp. 35–43.

[39] Bickell, *Syrische Kirchenväter*, p. 199. On Nestorius see Wallace-Hadrill, *Christian Antioch*, pp. 126–32; on his position in the dispute over the title *theotokos*, which had already started before he became bishop of Constantinople A. Grillmeier, *Christ in Christian Tradition*, vol. 1 (Atlanta, 1965), pp. 451–5; J.N.D. Kelly, *Early Christian Doctrines* (London, 1960), pp. 311ff.; Timothy E. Gregory, *Vox Populi. Violence and Popular Involvement in the Religious Controversies of the Fifth Century A.D.* (Columbus, 1979), pp. 88–91; 97–100.

[40] Bickell, *Syrische Kirchenväter*, pp. 201–3.

[41] Flemming, *Akten der Ephesinischen Synode*, p. 51, 16–32.

separate meeting of the bishops of the East chaired by John, patriarch of Antioch, who condemned Cyril of Alexandria and his Twelve Anathemas.[42] But back at Edessa he changed his doctrinal position and became a fervent adherent of Cyril. He even translated some of Cyril's writings into Syriac.[43] Rabbula was probably afraid of losing his prestigious episcopal see. Between 431 and 435 many bishops of the Antiochene party lost their sees and at least seventeen were exiled or otherwise punished. The emperor Theodosius had already abandoned Nestorius shortly after the Council of Ephesus.[44] Hiba, who had accompanied Rabbula to Ephesus, wrote in his *Letter to Mari* that "he, who arrogates to himself all power in the church, dared to condemn publicly him who had converted his town from error to truth", i.e. Theodore of Mopsuestia.[45] We may assume that the various factions were evenly balanced at Edessa and that Rabbula was confronted with heavy opposition. Hiba's *Letter to Mari* is an expression of it. It is therefore not surprising that the bishop sent Hiba into exile in 433[46] and was very much in favour of the Formula of Union between Cyril and the Antiochene bishop John, who in his turn had abandoned Nestorius in that same year. The Formula of Union or Reunion goes back to a credal formula stemming from the eastern bishops assembled round John of Antioch at Ephesus in 431. Its main author was Theodoret of Cyrrhus.[47] Might this be an explanation of the similarities between Rabbula's *vita* and Theodoret's writings? It did not help Hiba that he also was in favour of the Union, as becomes clear from his *Letter to Mari*. His presence at Edessa was a real threat to Rabbula's power. In this tricky situation Rabbula may have travelled to Constantinople to plead his case and to condemn publicly Nestorius' theology. The summary of his sermon preached at Constantinople as preserved in the *vita* shows all the

---

[42] A.H.M. Jones, *The Later Roman Empire 284–602. A Social Economic and Administrative Survey*, vol. 1 (Oxford, 1964), pp. 214–6; Peeters, "La vie de Rabboula", pp. 154–7 gives a correct report of the course of events at Ephesus in 431 based on the official acts of the council.

[43] E.g. Cyril, *De recta fide*, ed. P.E. Pusey (Oxford, 1877), pp. 1–153; cf. Quasten, *Patrology*, vol. III, pp. 126–7.

[44] See Kenneth G. Holum, *Theodosian Empresses. Women and Imperial Dominion in Late Antiquity* (Berkeley/Los Angeles/London, 1982), pp. 179–83.

[45] Flemming, *Akten der Ephesinischen Synode*, p. 51, pp. 25–7.

[46] See Hayes, *L'école d'Édesse*, pp. 191 203; Ortiz de Urbina, *Patrologia Syriaca*, p. 99.

[47] Grillmeier, *Christ in Christian Tradition*, pp. 484–6, pp. 488–95.

theological characteristics of the Formula of Union, trying to reconcile Cyril and the eastern bishops. The separately transmitted and much longer sermon displays in essence the same theology.[48] In the Formula of Union the eastern bishops accepted the term *theotokos*, which therefore plays a prominent role in Rabbula's sermon.[49] In this context it is not really relevant whether the sermon is a genuine one truly delivered in Constantinople or a spurious one ascribed to Rabbula. The sermon functions as a means to keep Rabbula in power in a complicated and dangerous situation. The panegyrist would make us believe that Rabbula long before the Council of Ephesus was an adversary of Nestorius and an adherent of Cyril's victorious party. Whether Rabbula really travelled to Constantinople is hard to say, although certainly not impossible for a man of his rank and aristocratic background. In the fifth century, bishops of an aristocratic background had access to the imperial court and power.[50] It is, however, significant that he explicitly forbade his clerics, priests and deacons to travel to the imperial court without his permission, according to canon 38.[51] Was Rabbula afraid that one of them would accuse him and he would still lose his see? It is only a guess, but a guess that makes some sense. All these travelling bishops, priests and monks spread rumours and were a source of conspiracies in complicated political situations. In any case the sermon allegedly preached in Constantinople and the exile of Hiba are both strategic manoeuvres to safeguard Rabbula's own position.

The *vita* digresses at great length on Rabbula's care of the poor, widows and orphans. He had hospitals built for men as well as for women, the latter constructed with the stones of four(!) pagan temples destroyed at Edessa.[52] When he felt near the end of his life, he

---

[48] Bickell, *Syrische Kirchenväter*, p. 202; the complete text of the sermon in Overbeck, *S. Ephraemi Syri*, pp. 239–44. The sermon with all its theological subtleties deserves a thorough study which locates it in the controversies that occurred after the Council of Ephesus of 431; Blum, *Rabbula von Edessa*, pp. 131–49 offers an unconvincing interpretation and date of the sermon.

[49] See Grillmeier, *Christ in Christian Tradition*, pp. 488–99, esp. p. 498f.

[50] See Brown, *Power and Persuasion*, pp. 136ff.

[51] Vööbus, *Syriac and Arabic Documents*, pp. 45f.: "No one among the priests or deacons or benai qeiama shall travel without our permission to the (imperial) court or to any far off place and leave his church, not even if he has the business of the village or of his church"; cf. canon 4 of Chalcedon.

[52] Bickell, *Syrische Kirchenväter*, pp. 204–7; cf. Blum, *Rabbula von Edessa*, pp. 61–81; Susan Ashbrook Harvey, "The Holy and the Poor: Models from Early Syriac Christianity", *Through the Eye of a Needle. Judeo-Christian Roots of Social Welfare*, eds. E. Albu

distributed the alms he used to give in December as early as June all over the world, even to the saints in the desert near Jerusalem. He remitted all the debts due to him and tore up the debentures. The bishop apparently loaned out great sums of money, a practice he had strictly forbidden to his priests.[53] He gave large presents to his priests, who apparently were allowed to accept these in this situation—in his canons Rabbula had forbidden priests to accept presents![54]—then he prayed, made the sign of the cross and died. Rabbula's death caused great mourning in Edessa among Christians and Jews alike. Next day he was put into a coffin and buried in order to prevent the masses from tearing up his body and using the various parts as relics. His tomb was a place of healing and blessings.[55]

There is no doubt that Rabbula after his conversion lead a life of austere asceticism, fasting, nightly prayer, and abstention from meat, wine and bathing, while wearing the black monk's dress. His way of living was a kind of *imitatio Christi* and had a symbolic and exemplary function in itself. This was the life a true Christian should lead. In this way Rabbula exercised the bishop's spiritual authority over clergy and laymen, trying to make his city into a true Christian one with great care for the poor and sick. There is no doubt that the bishop was driven by a sincere dedication to realize this ideal. According to his *vita* he was the model bishop, and Edessa a model Christian city. In this connection Rabbula's veneration of the True Cross as a symbol of victory over all defects of human life and society finds its place. A true Christian life and community ought to be perfect, and the Cross symbolizes this ideal. But the reality is that human nature and society are defective and obstinate, so that other means ought to be employed to realize perfection. The bishop used all means to eradicate divergence from his Christian ideal: threats, beatings, treason against former partners like Hiba, and all forms of violence.[56] He was at the one time a humble monk and a cruel and shrewd civil servant of the imperial administration.

Hanawalt, C. Lindberg (Kirksville, 1994), pp. 43–66; cf. Drijvers, "The Man of God of Edessa", pp. 246–8.

[53] Vööbus, *Syriac and Arabic Documents*, p. 38, canon 9.

[54] Ibidem, canon 8.

[55] Bickell, *Syrische Kirchenväter*, pp. 207–11; cf. A. Angenendt, *Heilige und Reliquien. Die Geschichte ihres Kultes vom frühen Christentum bis zur Gegenwart* (München, 1997²), pp. 149–66.

[56] Bickell, *Syrische Kirchenväter*, pp. 180–2, 188; cf. R. MacMullen, *Christianity and Paganism in the Fourth to Eighth Centuries* (New Haven/London, 1997), pp. 11–31 on Christian violence in the eradication of nonconformity.

This also explains his unexpected change of mind after the Council of Ephesus of 431. The emperor had abandoned Nestorius, and his obedient servant immediately did the same. "Plus royaliste que le roi", he also let down Hiba and Theodore, although the former had accompanied him to Ephesus and the latter had been one of his favourite authors. Thus he subjected himself to the imperial power and at the same time saved his see. In these actions he could consider himself a true servant of Christ as well as of the emperor, Christ's representative on earth.

This way of exercising spiritual authority, combined with all the means of secular power, was a new phenomenon at Edessa. Rabbula was an outsider, who was parachuted down upon the city in 412. Hiba was a local man educated in the School of the Persians, who partly behaved as a local councillor with all the loyalties that belonged to it. Rabbula served only two lords, Christ and the emperor, and had cut all his family ties. Two worlds in conflict, a conflict that flared up again in the prelude to the *Latrocinium Ephesinum* of 449.

The panegyrist who wrote Rabbula's *vita* sketches a portrait of the bishop's spiritual authority. It had a symbolic function in the period between 436, when Rabbula died, and 449 when the Robber Synod convened. Exercising spiritual authority in its pure form is, however, absolutely impossible. Spiritual authorities were in need of secular power to reach their goals. Rabbula of Edessa combined spiritual authority and secular power, something before this time unheard of at Edessa. This was his tragedy, and consequently he was portrayed as the true Christian caretaker of the urban poor and destitute, and as the Tyrant of Edessa. Both portraits have their own truth and only prove that Rabbula was a real human being, not an angel in human disguise as the panegyrist wishes us to believe.

BIBLIOGRAPHY

d'Alès, A., "La lettre d'Ibas à Marès le Persan", *RSR* 22 (1932), pp. 5–25.

Angenendt, A., *Heilige und Reliquien. Die Geschichte ihres Kultes vom frühen Christentum bis zur Gegenwart* (München, 1997²).

Ashbrook Harvey, Susan, "The Holy and the Poor: Models from Early Syriac Christianity", *Through the Eye of a Needle. Judeo-Christian Roots of Social Welfare*, eds. E. Albu Hanawalt, C. Lindberg (Kirksville, 1994), pp. 43–66.

Baumstark, A., *Geschichte der syrischen Literatur* (Bonn, 1992).

Bickell, G., *Ausgewählte Schriften der syrischen Kirchenväter Aphraates, Rabulas und Isaak von Ninive*, Bibliothek der Kirchenväter (Kempten, 1874), pp. 155–211.

Blum, G.G., *Rabbula von Edessa. Der Christ, der Bischof, der Theologe*, CSCO 300, Subs. 34 (Louvain, 1969).

Brockelmann, C., *Syrische Grammatik* (Berlin, 1912).

Brown, Peter, *Power and Persuasion in Late Antiquity. Towards a Christian Empire* (Madison, 1992).

Bruns, Peter, "Die Kanones des Rabbula (gest. 435) und ihr Beitrag zur Reform des kirchlichen Lebens in Edessa", *Theologia et Jus Canonicum. Festgabe für Heribert Heinemann*, ed. H.J.F. Reinhardt (Essen, 1995), pp. 471–80.

———, "Bischof Rabbula von Edessa—Dichter und Theologe", *Symposium Syriacum VII*, ed. R. Lavenant, OCA 256 (Rome, 1998), pp. 195–202.

Canivet, P., *Le monachisme syrien selon Théodoret de Cyr* (Paris, 1977).

Cox, Patricia, *Biography in Late Antiquity. A Quest for the Holy Man* (Berkeley/Los Angeles/London, 1983).

Downey, G., *A History of Antioch in Syria* (Princeton, 1961).

Drijvers, Han J.W., "The Persistence of Pagan Cults and Practices in Christian Syria", *East of Byzantium. Syria and Armenia in the Formative Period*, eds. N.G. Garsoïan, T.F. Mathews and R.W. Thompson (Washington D.C., 1982), pp. 35–43.

———, "The Syriac Romance of Julian. Its Function, Place of Origin and Original Language", *Symposium Syriacum VI*, ed. R. Lavenant, OCA 247 (Rome, 1994), pp. 201–14.

———, "The Man of God of Edessa, Bishop Rabbula, and the Urban Poor: Church and Society in the Fifth Century", *JECS* 4 (1996), pp. 235–48.

Drijvers, Jan Willem, "The Protonike legend and the Doctrina Addai", *Studia Patristica* 33, ed. E.A. Livingstone (Louvain, 1996), pp. 517–23.

———, "The Protonike Legend, the *Doctrina Addai* and Bishop Rabbula of Edessa", *Vig. Chr.* 51 (1997), pp. 298–315.

Duval, Rubens, *Histoire d'Édesse* (Paris, 1892).

Festugière, A.J., *Antioche païenne et chrétienne. Libanius, Chrysostome et les moines de Syrie* (Paris, 1959).

Flemming, J., *Akten der Ephesinischen Synode vom Jahre 449*, Abhandlungen der Akademie der Wissenschaften in Göttingen, phil.-hist. Kl., neue Folge 15.1 (Göttingen, 1917; repr. 1970).

Frazee, Charles A., "Late Roman and Byzantine Legislation on the Monastic Life from the Fourth to the Eighth Centuries", *Church History* 51 (1982), pp. 263–79.

Gregory, Timothy E., *Vox Populi. Violence and Popular Involvement in the Religious Controversies of the Fifth Century A.D.* (Columbus, 1979).

Grillmeier, A., *Christ in Christian Tradition*, vol. 1 (Atlanta, 1965).

Hayes, E.R., *L'école d'Édesse* (Paris, 1930).

Holum, Kenneth G., *Theodosian Empresses. Women and Imperial Dominion in Late Antiquity* (Berkeley/Los Angeles/London, 1982).

Honigmann, E., "Historische Topographie von Nordsyrien im Altertum", *ZDPV* 46 (Leipzig, 1923), pp. 149–93.

Hunt, E.D., *Holy Land Pilgrimage in the Later Roman Empire A.D. 312–460* (Oxford, 1982).

Lim, Richard, *Public Disputation, Power, and Social Order in Late Antiquity* (Berkeley/Los Angeles/London, 1995).

Jones, A.H.M., *The Cities of the Eastern Roman Provinces* (Oxford, 1971²).

———, *The Later Roman Empire 284–602. A Social Economic and Administrative Survey* (Oxford, 1964).

Kelly, J.N.D., *Early Christian Doctrines* (London, 1960).

Kennedy, H., Liebeschuetz, J.H.W.G., "Antioch and the Villages of Northern Syria in the Fifth and Sixth Centuries A.D.: Trends and Problems", *Nottingham Medieval Studies* 32 (1988), pp. 65–90.

MacMullen, R., *Christianity and Paganism in the Fourth to Eighth Centuries* (New Haven/ London, 1997).

Mann, M., *Sources of Social Power. A History of Power from the Beginning to A.D. 1760*, vol. 1 (Cambridge, 1986).

Mar Barhadbsabba 'Arbaya, *Cause de la fondation des Écoles*, PO IV.4.18 (Paris, 1907).

Millar, Fergus, *The Roman Near East 31 B.C.–A.D. 337* (Cambridge/London, 1993).

Monceaux, P., Brossé, L., "Chalcis ad Belum. Notes sur l'histoire et les ruines de la ville", *Syria. Revue d'art oriental et d'archéologie* 6 (1925), pp. 339–50.

Nagel, Peter, *Die Motivierung der Askese in der Alten Kirche und der Ursprung des Mönchtums*, Texte und Untersuchungen zur Geschichte der altchristlichen Literatur 95 (Berlin, 1966).

Nau, F., "Les 'belles actions' de Mar Rabboula, évêque d'Édesse de 412 au 7 août 435 (ou 436)", *RHR* 103 (1931), pp. 97–135.

Nedungatt, G., "The Covenanters of the Early Syriac-Speaking Church", *OCP* 49 (1973), pp. 191–215.

Norris, R.A., *Manhood and Christ. A Study in the Christology of Theodore of Mopsuestia* (Oxford, 1963).

Ortiz de Urbina, I., *Patrologia Syriaca* (Rome, 1965).

Overbeck, J.J., *S. Ephraemi Syri, Rabulae episcopi Edesseni, Balaeit aliorumque opera selecta* (Oxford, 1865), pp. 159–209.

Peeters, P., "La vie de Rabboula, évêque d'Édesse (+ 7 août 436)", *RSR* 18 (1928), pp. 170–204.

Quasten, J., *Patrology*, vol. 3 (Utrecht/Antwerp/Westminster, 1960).

Segal, J.B., *Edessa "the Blessed City"* (Oxford, 1970).

Vööbus, A., *La vie d'Alexandre en grec, un témoin d'une biographie inconnue de Rabbula, écrite en syriaque*, Contributions of the Baltic University 59 (Pinneberg, 1947).

———, *Literary Critical and Historical Studies in Ephrem the Syrian*, Papers of the Estonian Theological Society in Exile 10 (Stockholm, 1958).

———, *Syriac and Arabic Documents regarding Legislation relative to Syrian Asceticism*, Papers of the Estonian Theological Society in Exile 11 (Stockholm, 1960).

———, *History of the School of Nisibis*, CSCO 266, Subs. 26 (Louvain, 1965).

Wallace-Hadrill, D.S., *Christian Antioch. A Study of Early Christian Thought in the East* (Cambridge, 1982).

A PORTRAIT OF JOHN BAR APHTONIA, FOUNDER OF THE MONASTERY OF QENNESHRE

JOHN W. WATT

Cardiff University

The period of Late Antiquity is one of profound cultural and religious change. For all its apparent and in many respects real continuity with the "classical" world, significant developments were taking place which were to influence the future shape of Europe and the Near East. The spiritual authority exercised by outstanding figures in such a context, and the manner in which they were admired by their followers, gives us important insights into the mentality of the time. This contribution will be concerned with a portrait of a figure who could be said to stand on two boundaries, a "historical" and a "geographical". The historical is that between classical urban culture and medieval Christian monasticism, the geographical that between the Greek world and the Near East. It has of course been long recognized that neither of these boundaries is rigid or precise, but that the historical and geographical overlaps are broad and complex.

The narrower historical frame with which we are concerned is the fifth/sixth century, the geographical that from Antioch to Edessa, and the spiritual authority that exercised by John bar Aphtonia. This name does not spring to mind for a roll-call of the famous of late antiquity, but when we add "founder of the monastery of Qenneshre", the historical importance of this man's work becomes more apparent. One of the most significant intellectual developments during the later Roman empire was the embedding of Greek culture in sections of the Aramaic-speaking Near East and the rise of a Syriac literary culture which, both in its translations from Greek and its own original productions, preserved and continued the Greek heritage, not only throughout the Byzantine "Dark Ages", but beyond into the ninth and tenth centuries, eventually giving birth to the "renaissance" of classical culture in Islam.[1] This great process did not proceed

---

[1] On Graeco-Syriac bilingualism in late antiquity, cf., e.g., S.P. Brock, "Greek and Syriac in Late Antique Syria", *Literacy and Power in the Ancient World*, eds. A.K.

along just a single line of transmission. The idea, for example, of a
single line of philosophy proceeding "from Alexandria to Baghdad",
attributed to al-Farabi in Ibn abi Uṣaibiʿa, is an ideological construct
stemming from the Muslim ideal of the transmission of textbooks
within a tradition of oral instruction, not an accurate account of the
history of Greek philosophy in the late antique and early Islamic
East.[2] Yet the city of Edessa and the monastery of Qenneshre (on
the east bank of the Euphrates) were both significant locations within
the entire process, and in the person of John bar Aphtonia, a native
of Edessa and the founder of that monastery, these two locations
come together. Edessa was the home of classical Syriac, and at the
same time a center of Greek culture in the Near East.[3] In the seventh
and eighth centuries Qenneshre became one of the main centers of
Greek studies in the region and boasted such outstanding scholars
as Severus Sebokht, Jacob of Edessa, Athanasius of Balad, and probably George bishop of the Arabs.[4] It is even possible that from
Qenneshre much literature of Greek origin made its way first to
Syrian Orthodox monasteries further east and then to the East Syrian
scholars of the Abbasid period.[5] The network of grammatical and
rhetorical schools in the Hellenized cities of the East, and latterly
the convent-schools of the Syriac-speaking monasteries, were the
medium by which Greek culture was preserved and nurtured by

Bowman, G. Woolf (Cambridge, 1994), pp. 149–60, esp. 154–6; for the later period,
e.g., G. Strohmaier, "Hunain ibn Ishaq—an Arab Scholar translating into Syriac",
Aram 3 (1991), pp. 163–70. On bilingualism in hagiography, cf. P. Peeters, *Le tréfonds
oriental de l'hagiographie byzantine*, Subsidia Hagiographica 26 (Brussels, 1950), pp.
165–218.

    [2] Cf. G. Strohmaier, "'Von Alexandrien nach Bagdad'—eine fiktive Schultradition",
Aristoteles: Werk und Wirkung. Paul Moraux gewidmet II, ed. J. Wiesner (Berlin, 1987),
pp. 380–9.

    [3] Cf. H.J.W. Drijvers, "The School of Edessa: Greek Learning and Local Culture",
Centres of Learning. Learning and Location in Pre-Modern Europe and the Near East, eds.
J.W. Drijvers, A.A. MacDonald (Leiden, 1995), pp. 49–59.

    [4] Cf. S.P. Brock, "From Antagonism to Assimilation: Syriac Attitudes to Greek
Learning", *East of Byzantium. Syria and Armenia in the Formative Period*, eds. N.G.
Garsoian, T.F. Mathews and R.W. Thomson (Washington D.C., 1982), pp. 23–4.
On this group of scholars, cf. A. Baumstark, *Geschichte der syrischen Literatur* (Bonn,
1922), pp. 246–58. George is the only one of them who is not explicitly connected
in the Syriac sources to Qenneshre, but his personal or literary associations with
the others make a connection with Qenneshre very likely; cf. K.E. McVey, *George,
Bishop of the Arabs. A Homily on Blessed Mar Severus, Patriarch of Antioch*, CSCO 531
(Louvain, 1993), pp. xxii–xxiii.

    [5] Cf. Brock, "From Antagonism to Assimilation", pp. 23–4 (pointing to the activ-
ity of David bar Paulos, who was born near Mosul in the eighth century).

Syrians and eventually transmitted to Arabs.[6] In the portrait we are about to examine of the founder of Qenneshre, we have a fine example of the transmission of culture from the one type of school to the other.

When we speak of "portraits", we are of course employing an analogy between the visual and verbal arts which was well known to the literary culture of antiquity. The comparison of a portrait or statue was a commonplace of classical rhetoric, especially epideictic; it is found already in Quintilian and in later times was used, among others, by the Cappadocian Fathers.[7] In his influential oration *On the Forty Holy Martyrs*, Basil developed it in connection with the analogy of soldier and saint,

> . . . showing to all, as if in a picture, the prowess of these men. For the brave deeds of war often supply subjects for both speech writers and painters. Speech writers embellish them with their words, painters depict them on their panels, and both have led many on to acts of bravery. For what spoken narrative presents through hearing, this silent painting shows through imitation.[8]

Of especial interest in connection with the Syriac text which concerns us here is the use of the analogy by Procopius of Gaza (*c.* 465–528):

> Painting and poetry, the one with colors, the other with words—for words are the colors of poetry—both imitate the figures of gods and men, their passions and their loves. Poetry reports the drops of semen from Uranus falling upon the sea . . . Painting on the other hand gives a visual image to poetry's account . . .[9]

Roughly contemporary with the orations of Procopius is a Syriac text, published (with an introduction and French translation) by Nau,[10]

---

[6] Cf. C.H.M. Versteegh, "Hellenistic Education and the Origin of Arabic Grammar", in *Progress in Linguistic Historiography. Papers from the First International Conference on the History of the Language Sciences*, ed. E.F.K. Koerner (Amsterdam, 1979), pp. 333–7; idem, "The Origin of the Term 'Qiyas' in Arabic Grammar", *Zeitschrift für arabische Linguistik* 4 (1980), pp. 10–11; H. Daiber, *Aetius Arabus. Die Vorsokratiker in arabischer Überlieferung* (Wiesbaden, 1980), pp. 68–72.

[7] Quintilian II.13.8–14. See in general H. Maguire, *Art and Eloquence in Byzantium* (Princeton, 1981), pp. 9–12.

[8] Basil, *Or.* 19.2 (PG 31, 508C–509A), translated by Maguire, *Art and Eloquence*, p. 9.

[9] *Declamatio III*, eds. A. Garzya, R.-J. Loenertz, *Procopii Gazaei Epistolae et Declamationes*, Studia Patristica et Byzantina 9 (Ettal, 1963), p. 88, translated by G.A. Kennedy, *Greek Rhetoric under Christian Emperors* (Princeton, 1983), pp. 171–2.

[10] F. Nau, "Histoire de Jean bar Aphtonia", *Revue de l'Orient Chrétien* 7 (1902), pp. 97–135. References are to the section numbers of this edition.

entitled *A Narrative of the Master, John, Abbot of the Holy Monastery of Aphtonia, written by some disciple of his*. The author of this piece proclaims:

> Just as ink which is inferior to all pigments provides what is necessary to a painter who fashions a portrait of a king, for when it is applied first as required, it gives extra brilliance to the colors which are placed on top, so also these matters (of *patris* and *genos*) are regarded as minor, but when they are placed first and polished as appropriate, they add considerable force to what is said (§ 2).

We have here an explicit comparison of a royal (*basilikos*) portrait to the *logos/memra* which our author is composing in praise of the late superior of his monastery. In this and many other ways (to be presented in what follows), our author shows himself thoroughly familiar with the conventions of classical, epideictic rhetoric. Moreover, he begins with a clear affirmation of what we could call "continuity of form despite change of content" between the classical *basilikos logos* and his work in praise of a Christian "general", picking up the comparison, already seen in Basil, of soldier and saint:

> When I look at the soldiers who are deemed worthy of encomia, crowns, statues, and even an indelible memorial ... I rise above my stature and, deceiving myself (as to what) I am, I dare to proclaim our hero, even though I may be thought to be presumptuous, so that Christians may not appear more ungrateful than pagans. For it is absurd that pagans even now are [praised] on account of bodily might, but that we leave without a statue the soldiers of Christ who have demonstrated spiritual might and vanquished the sect of the devil. The end of the mighty goodness of the former is the shedding of blood and the killing of men, but by the triumph of the latter God is pleased, the angels rejoice, men marvel, and the immaterial sect of demons laments its defeat by material men. Come, therefore, let us celebrate (that) victory! Let us erect a mental monument of a mental battle and crown that victorious mind with fruits of its own kind, for speeches are fruits of the mind (§ 1).

Thus it is not only the historical activity of John bar Aphtonia himself which bridges the Classical-Christian transformation (and the Greek-Syriac boundary), but also this literary portrait of him by one of his disciples.

The adaptation of the structures and *topoi* of epideictic rhetoric to Christian hagiography is well known in Greek texts.[11] Our text, however, is of particular interest not only because it is in Syriac, but

---

[11] Cf. C. Mango, *Byzantium. The Empire of New Rome* (London, 1980), pp. 247–9.

also because of the importance of Qenneshre in cultural history. It is not all that significant whether we categorize it as rhetoric (speech) or literature (hagiography). Our author himself is well aware of the similarity when he writes:

What speech writer (*makteb memre*) can write or narrative writer (*makteb tashʿyata*) narrate his labors on behalf of the truth? (§ 7)[12]

Possibly more troubling for us is the question of the historical trustworthiness of the information it purveys concerning John, once we have recognized the essentially laudatory (whether rhetorical or hagiographic) character of the piece. If "these potted rules (of epideictic or hagiography) . . . could be applied to any monastic saint concerning whom nothing definite was known save for his name, place of origin and date of his liturgical commemoration",[13] pieces which fit the encomiastic scheme rather too well may become suspect in respect of historical veracity. However, the author indicates that he was among those who followed John from the monastery of St. Thomas at Seleucia to the new foundation at Qenneshre,[14] and his work, far from giving the impression of knowing nothing definite about the saint, seems on the contrary to be based on long acquaintance with him. While some incidents and facets of his life (to be discussed below) are worked up in a manner that may cause suspicion, the general outline appears to be quite sound.

However, if the broader cultural process rather than the detail of John's life is what primarily interests us, the portrait is significant in itself whatever may be the historical veracity of a number of details. It represents the way one of his "elite" disciples saw his life, and since it was the elite disciples who over the course of time made Qenneshre such an important center of Greek culture in the Near East, their viewpoint is itself a significant piece of cultural history.[15] This consideration applies particularly to the question of the transmission of

---

[12] The piece is entitled *tashʿita* (narrative), but in the text itself the author refers (§§ 1 and 2) to his *memra* (speech). Assimilation of epideictic to written compositions goes back to Aristotle, *Rhetoric* III.12.1414a, 17ff. The piece is transmitted in the unique manuscript, British Library Add. 12174, foll. 84r–87v, as part of a collection of saints' lives, mostly entitled *tashʿita*, and may have been given its title by this context. Cf. W. Wright, *Catalogue of the Syriac Manuscripts in the British Museum* (London, 1872), pp. 1123–39, no. 5.

[13] Mango, *Byzantium*, p. 248.

[14] § 8; cf. § 6. Cf. Nau, "Histoire", introduction, p. 100.

[15] Not all the monks of Qenneshre were "intellectuals"; some were more attracted to traditional monasticism. Cf. A. Palmer, *Monk and Mason on the Tigris Frontier. The Early History of Tur ʿAbdin* (Cambridge, 1990), pp. 88–9; and below, n. 51.

Greek rhetoric and general education (*enkyklios paideia*). An older scholarly consensus held that only the philosophical side of Greek culture
took firm hold in the Near East, while rhetoric—with the eventual
exception of the "logical" *Rhetoric* of Aristotle—passed into oblivion.
More recently, the view has been gaining ground that not only philosophy, but rhetoric also, was alive and well in the Orient for a long
time.[16] There is no doubt that Qenneshre was a center of philosophical study, but what our text has to tell us about the father of
its founder and the education of his brothers opens up another perspective. "His father partook of the secular wisdom, as not without
foresight it ends up with the art of rhetoric (*'ummanuta d-rhetruta*)",
while after the death of his father, his mother, "sending some (of his
brothers) to schools, fortified (them) with the wisdom of speeches and
laws (*memre wa-nmose*, i.e., rhetoric and law), while for others . . . she
procured imperial offices and appointments" (§ 2). It is true that the
author goes on to assert that John was brought up by his mother
herself at home "as in a sanctuary" (§ 3), but this (even if true) does
not imply that he received no "grammatical" education. At the age
of fifteen he was taken to the monastery of St. Thomas at Seleucia
near Antioch (§§ 3–4)—the very age from which boys could proceed
from the second ("grammatical") to the third stage of education (that
usually provided by the rhetor or sophist).[17] It is likely, in fact, that
he received a bilingual grammatical education, not only because that
monastery was known as a center for the study of Greek literature,
but also because his later literary output may have been entirely in
Greek.[18] Seven years later, when he was admitted to full membership of the monastery (§ 5), he was allegedly still not allowed to proceed immediately (*mehda*) to any art based on *logos* (*'ummanuta mlilta
meddem*)[19]—which implies, however, that he *was* allowed to do so

---

[16] Cf. R. Würsch, *Avicennas Bearbeitungen der aristotelischen Rhetorik. Ein Beitrag zum
Fortleben antiken Bildungsgutes in der islamischen Welt* (Berlin, 1991), pp. 1–10; J.W. Watt,
"Grammar, Rhetoric, and the Enkyklios Paideia in Syriac", *ZDMG* 143 (1993), pp.
45–71; idem, "Eastward and Westward Transmission of Classical Rhetoric", *Centres
of Learning. Learning and Location in Pre-Modern Europe and the Near East*, eds. J.W.
Drijvers, A.A. MacDonald (Leiden, 1995), pp. 63–75; idem, "Greek Historiography
and the 'Chronicle of Joshua the Stylite'", *After Bardaisan. Studies on Continuity and
Change in Syriac Christianity in Honour of Professor Han J.W. Drijvers*, eds. G.J. Reinink,
A.C. Klugkist (Louvain, 1999), pp. 317–28; and the works mentioned above, n. 6.
[17] Cf. H.-I. Marrou, *A History of Education in Antiquity* (London, 1956), p. 265;
W. Liebeschuetz, "Hochschule", *RAC* 15 (1991), cols. 862, 866.
[18] Cf. Baumstark, *Geschichte der syrischen Literatur*, p. 181.
[19] The *logikai technai* as opposed to the manual or practical arts (among which

eventually.[20] This information may be compared with what is said about John and about this monastery in the so-called *Historia Ecclesiastica* of Pseudo-Zachariah.[21] There Mare bar Qustant is said to have been

> ... eloquent (*mlil*) in the Greek language and learned, because he had been educated in the monastery of St. Thomas the Apostle at Seleucia, which migrated on account of zealous faith and was rebuilt when re-settled at Qenneshre on the river Euphrates by John bar Aphtonia, a learned man, abbot at the time, an advocate[22] (originating) from Edessa.[23]

Shortly thereafter the *Historia* notes that "the monastery of Thomas at Seleucia was brought with the fraternity to Qenneshre on the Euphrates and resettled (there) by the eloquent (*mlila*) abbot John bar Aphtonia",[24] and "the eloquent (*mlila*) abbot John bar Aphtonia" is mentioned again later in connection with a gathering of bishops before Justinian in 531.[25]

There can hardly therefore be any doubt that John received a full grammatical and rhetorical education at Edessa and the monastery of St. Thomas at Seleucia,[26] an education which he subsequently put to good use. In stressing so heavily the "saintly" aspects of his upbringing,

---

latter carpentry is mentioned both in Greek texts and in § 5 of this Syriac pane-gyric of John). Cf. I. Hadot, *Arts libéraux et philosophie dans la pensée antique* (Paris, 1984), pp. 269–70.

[20] Cf. Nau, "Histoire", introduction, pp. 98 and 111.

[21] *Historia Ecclesiastica Zachariah Rhetori vulgo adscripta*, vol. 2, ed. and transl. by E.W. Brooks, CSCO 84 [88], Script. Syri 39 [42] (Louvain, 1921 [1924]); German transl. by K. Ahrens, G. Krüger, *Die sogennante Kirchengeschichte des Zacharias Rhetor* (Leipzig, 1899).

[22] Syriac *'apdiqoniqon* is presumably Greek ἀπὸ δικανικῶν. Cf. VII.10 (Brooks, p. 51, 9–10 [35, 15–17]; Ahrens, Krüger, p. 131, 21–24): "... Severus, a certain monk, eloquent (*mlila*) (and) approved, from the monastery of Theodorus, an advo-cate (*'apdiqn'iqon*) from Gaza".

[23] VIII.5 (Brooks, p. 79, 14–19 [54, 15–20]; Ahrens, Krüger, *Die sogennante Kirchengeschichte*, p. 155, 17–24).

[24] Ibidem (Brooks, p. 80, 15–17 [55, 7–9]; Ahrens, Krüger, *Die sogennante Kirchengeschichte*, p. 156, 18–21).

[25] IX.15 (Brooks, p. 122, 22–23 [84, 18–19]; Ahrens, Krüger, *Die sogennante Kirchengeschichte*, p. 196, 11). Cf. Nau, "Histoire", introduction, pp. 106–7 and 112.

[26] No doubt it included training in judicial oratory (cf. above, n. 22), although there is no other evidence that John, like Severus, ever underwent a course of legal training. Nau, "Histoire", introduction, p. 98, n. 2 and p. 99, n. 2, takes *'apdiqoniqon* ("ex-avocat") as virtually synonymous with *mlila* ("rhéteur"). Although during the course of the fourth century the roles of sophist and *dikanikos* (advocate) had become separate, advocates still received a rhetorical education, and *rhetor* could signify not only someone who had received a rhetorical training, but also an advocate. Cf. P. Wolf, *Vom Schulwesen der Spätantike. Studien zu Libanius* (Baden-Baden, 1952), pp. 13–24.

the panegyrist has played down the "academic" side of his education, but he has not totally obscured or denied it. The fact remains that one of the early monks of Qenneshre reveals here in this portrait not only his own mastery of rhetoric, but also his view that the founder of his monastery was heir to the rhetorical tradition of urban Edessa and eventually became expert in rhetoric.[27] Both in the manner of its composition and in the information it transmits concerning its hero, this text brings before us in miniature the entry of general Greek culture into the Syriac-speaking monasteries. From its earliest period, therefore, Qenneshre was a center of rhetoric, and its elite, Greek-orientated students studied both philosophy and general culture (the *enkyklios paideia*). Two of its most famous students from later times were George bishop of the Arabs and Athanasius of Balad. Both were distinguished Aristotelians, but George could also write a fine Greek-style encomium (of Severus of Antioch),[28] and Athanasius knew his Homer.[29]

The structure of our portrait of John bar Aphtonia may be analyzed in the terms of epideictic rhetoric as follows:[30]

§ 1   Prooemium
§ 2   Native country and family (*patris* and *genos*).
§ 3   Birth and upbringing (*genesis* and *anatrophe*).
§§ 4–6   Education, nature, accomplishments (*paideia, physis, epitedeumata*).
§§ 7–8   Achievements (*praxeis*).
§§ 8–9   Death
§ 10   Epilogue

---

[27] The *Life of Severus* by John of Beth Aphtonia (ed. M.A. Kugener, PO 2.3 [1904], pp. 205–64) exhibits a degree of literary sophistication which, if John of Beth Aphtonia were to be identified with John bar Aphtonia, would provide further confirmation of the latter's literary education. However, although it has recently been argued that the identification is reasonable (cf. McVey, *George, Bishop of the Arabs*, p. xxii, n. 90), it remains quite uncertain (cf. Nau, "Histoire", introduction, pp. 100–8).

[28] Cf. McVey, *George, Bishop of the Arabs*, pp. v–xi.

[29] Cf. G. Furlani, "Una introduzione alla logica Aristotelica di Atanasio di Balad", *Rendiconti della Reale Academia dei Lincei. Classe di Scienze morali, storiche e filologiche*, Ser. V, vol. 25 (1917), pp. 732–3, p. 769; Watt, "Grammar, Rhetoric, and the Enkyklios Paideia", p. 60.

[30] For the structure of the classical *basilikos logos*, cf. especially Menander Rhetor 368–77 (ed. L. Spengel, *Rhetores Graeci*, vol. III [Leipzig, 1856]); edition and translation D.A. Russell, N.G. Wilson, *Menander Rhetor* (Oxford, 1981), pp. 76–95. For the way the Greek terms are rendered in Syriac in the later theoretical treatise on rhetoric by Antony of Tagrit, see J.W. Watt, "Syriac Panegyric in Theory and Practice. Antony of Tagrit and Eli of Qartamin", *Le Muséon* 102 (1989), pp. 271–98.

The prooemium (§ 1) would not have embarrassed Menander Rhetor,[31] save for the Christian rather than pagan content. As Menander prescribes, he "derives the prooemium from the amplification" and makes the obligatory declaration of his incapacity to rise to the challenge of the task ahead of him, making a *synkrisis* (comparison) between the pagan "soldiers deemed worthy of encomia" and the "soldiers of Christ who have demonstrated spiritual might".[32] Another *synkrisis* follows between the choice menu offered to him by all the noble deeds of John and that offered to lovers of fine food at a banquet. He gives grandeur to his work by alluding not to Homer, but to the Gospel (John 19:31), and by placing "the spiritual head of our community" among "the ranks (of ascetics and martyrs)". Rather than "expressing uncertainty about the point with which to begin the encomium",[33] he indicates that "we will begin the speech with the beginning of our salvation, the incarnation of God the Word", and makes the link to the next section with the remark, "Let us return to his *patris* and *genos* (*'atra* and *gensa*), for we do not grant a (merely) minor heading in the speech to these matters" (§ 2).

These *topoi* of *patris* and *genos* were of course sometimes rather an embarrassment even to pagan rhetors, let alone Christian orators. Basil poured scorn on them in a memorable manner when repudiating their significance for the praise of Christian martyrs:

> It is the fixed habit of encomia to search out the history of the native city, to find out the family exploits, and to relate the education of the subject of the encomium, but it is our custom to pass over in silence such details and to compose the encomium of each martyr from those facts which have a bearing on his martyrdom. How could I be an object of more reverence or be more illustrious from the fact that my native city once upon a time endured great and heavy battles and after routing her enemies erected famous trophies? What if she is so happily located that in summer and winter her climate is pleasant? If she is the mother of heroes and is capable of supporting cattle, what gain are these to me? In her herds of horses she surpasses all lands under the sun. How may these facts improve us in manly virtue?[34]

---

[31] Cf. Menander Rhetor 368–9 on the prooemium of a *basilikos logos*.
[32] The beginning of the prooemium is cited more fully above, p. 158.
[33] Menander Rhetor 369.16–7.
[34] *Or.* 18.2 (PG 31, 492C), translated by J.M. Campbell, *The Influence of the Second Sophistic on the Style of the Sermons of St. Basil the Great* (Washington D.C., 1922), p. 147. For pagan rhetors, cf. Menander Rhetor 370.9–28: "If neither his city nor his nation is conspicuously famous, you should omit this topic, and consider whether his family has prestige or not. If it has, work this up. If it is humble or without prestige, omit it likewise, and start with the emperor himself".

This embarrassment did not of course prevent Christian orators making use of these *topoi* when it suited them to do so.[35] Our author, clearly suffering a little of the same embarrassment, excuses himself, following the comparison of panegyrist and painter cited above,[36] by noting that these *topoi* appear "even in the scripture inspired by God", for it says, "There was a man in the land of Uz named Job" and "this man was of noble birth (*gensa*) and from the East and had great wealth".[37] Having therefore justified his employment of them, he proceeds to tell us that "if someone says about our father what was said about Job, he is not mistaken, for in truth he was of noble birth from the Easterners from across the river (Euphrates) and of a country (*'atra*) near to the patriarch Abraham", namely Edessa. His parents, in addition to "being rich in righteousness and piety", were from the governing class. His father "partook of the secular wisdom, as not without foresight it ends up with the art of rhetoric", while "speech is inadequate to depict the virtue of his mother Aphtonia".

The following section (§ 3) deals with John's birth and upbringing (*genesis* and *anatrophe*). His father died before he was born and his mother, "who bore handsome and good children, all boys", is said to have "consecrated him to God by a kind of prophecy while she still carried him in the womb". She is also asserted to have brought him up at home by herself "as in a sanctuary" to avoid contamination by the world, but as noted above, it is unlikely that this implies that he did not receive a good grammatical education. Here, and in the emphasis placed upon his years of humble servitude in the monastery before being allowed to proceed to higher studies and complete his education,[38] we can see the influence of Christian hagiography upon the classical, epideictic scheme.[39]

The following sections (§§ 4–6), tracing his life from his entry into the monastery of St. Thomas to his election as its abbot, may be viewed as the epideictic *paideia*, *physis*, and *epitedeumata* (education, nature, and accomplishments or occupation). Unlike the *praxeis* (deeds),

---

[35] Cf., e.g., Gregory Nazianzen, *Or.* 43.3–10. In this memorial oration on Basil, Gregory employs these *topoi* even while belittling them.

[36] Cf. above, p. 158.

[37] Job 1:1 and 3. On the text of the citation, cf. Nau, "Histoire", p. 122, n. 4.

[38] Cf. § 5 and above, p. 160.

[39] Cf. Mango, *Byzantium*, p. 248: in the hagiographic *schema* the saint would "either completely spurn all classical learning or else imbibe only as much of it as he considered necessary ... For several years he would execute with complete humility the most menial tasks ...".

the order is basically chronological. "If any divine sign occurred at the time of his birth", advised Menander, "compare the circumstances with those of Romulus, Cyrus, and similar stories, since in these cases also there were miraculous happenings . . . (such as) the dream of Cyrus' mother . . .".[40] In this text it is not so much the birth as the entry of the hero into a monastery at the tender age of fifteen which is worked up as a miraculous happening. Initially the abbot refused him admission because he had not yet grown a beard, but on being told by St. Thomas in a dream that this boy would one day be the savior of the monastery, he overturned the rules and accepted him. The abbot then acted towards him "as a tutor and teacher" (*tara' w-malpana*),[41] requiring him first to prove himself by manual labor and humble tasks. In this way the hero exhibited his nature and accomplishments and "became greatly admired for his profound humility, for his steadfast manner, for his seriousness, for his lowering and control of the eyes, for the disciplined measure of his speech, and for the admirable soberness of his walk". "How can I proclaim each of (his virtues)?" asks the writer. "In a short time he made right what others find difficult to make right up to the end (of their lives)."

Seven years on, when he had finally grown a beard, he received the monk's habit, though even then "they did not immediately give him a book or allow him to come to any art based on *logos*, but (only) to a toilsome and wearisome one, the art of carpentry" (§ 5).[42] When at Justin's succession after the death of Anastasius the empire passed "from bountiful good health to its opposite" (§ 6), the true *epitedeuma(ta)*[43] of John was eventually revealed: being placed between two difficulties and seeing the perils both of leaving the monks leaderless and accepting leadership despite his youthfulness, "he chose the lesser (evil) and assumed the headship of service". The section ends with a *synkrisis* of worldly and monastic authority: commandments in the world are effective through fear, but those in the monastery are only made effective by the personal conduct of the abbot. "For all the monks (John) was a rule and a mirror, an unwritten

---

[40] Menander Rhetor 371.5–9.

[41] In the schools of the rhetors, also, a pupil was attached to an individual teacher rather than to the institution. Cf. Liebeschuetz, "Hochschule", col. 866.

[42] On carpentry as a stock example of a manual art, cf. above, n. 19.

[43] On *epitedeuma(ta)* as "occupation" or "life-choice" (κρίσις ψυχῆς, ἡ τοῦ βίου αἵρεσις), see the texts cited in my "Syriac Panegyric", p. 280.

law and a living example, and they received his commands as divine revelations."

The heart of a panegyric is the *praxeis*, the laudation of the hero's virtues, usually according to some non-chronological scheme. "What speech writer can write or narrative writer narrate his labors on behalf of the truth?" is our panegyrist's introduction to this section (§ 7). He begins with John's journeys and appearances before emperors to testify against heresies, and after observing that "God first gave him the word of teaching, later enriching him with the gifts of fore-knowledge, miracles, and healing", he goes on to describe these miracles of healing and purification, inserting in this section John's foundation of the new monastery at Qenneshre: "That trusty pilot made allowance as for a torrential and violent storm and succeeded in bringing us to another monastery, situated in the desert" (§ 8). He ends John's miraculous deeds with the most exalted of comparisons: "In this he was like his Lord: he ordered them to keep silent about the things he had done".

The groupings of this section of the classical *basilikos logos*—by soul, body, and fortune; by war and peace; by the four cardinal virtues of courage, justice, temperance, and prudence—are generally less applicable to the praise of a Christian saint than many of the other *topoi* of the encomium. These divisions are therefore not usually discernible in Christian orations. Gregory's famous funeral oration on Basil, for example, deals with Basil's virtues in the order of poverty, temperance, chastity, philanthropy, modesty, eloquence, and theology.[44] That this panegyric of John bar Aphtonia is not very close to the classical *schema* at this point is therefore hardly surprising, and serves to remind us more forcefully then elsewhere in the oration that notwithstanding the adoption of the basic classical form, the cultural and religious context has changed. Some of John's other virtues, including many of those just mentioned for Basil, were lauded in the sections I have designated *physis* and *epitedeumata* (§§ 4–6). The final *topos* is his death (§§ 8–9), a standard item in an encomium for a person no longer alive. Our panegyrist works in here comparisons with Job, Lazarus, and Simeon, and he ends, as Menander suggests,[45] with an epilogue in the form of a prayer (§ 10).

"Uncommonly deficient in vivacity with strongly rhetorical pretense"

---

[44] Gregory Nazianzen, *Or.* 43.60–69. Cf. Kennedy, *Greek Rhetoric*, p. 236.
[45] Menander Rhetor 377.28; 422.2. Cf. Watt, "Syriac Panegyric", p. 283.

was Baumstark's characterization of this piece.[46] This somewhat harsh criticism, even if justified in its essentials, does not, however, capture the significance of the work. "Strongly rhetorical pretense" adheres to many literary works of late antiquity, but in this piece it serves as a valuable witness to a significant episode in cultural history. John himself wrote in Greek, his panegyrist in Syriac, and both were evidently well versed in rhetoric. John was a native of Edessa and founder of the monastery of Qenneshre; by the seventh century Qenneshre had become what Edessa had been for many years before: a center of Greek studies at the same time as a place for the cultivation of Syriac literature. There is no doubt that in Greek-speaking areas from about the fifth century onwards, the monasteries assumed an increasingly important role in the preservation and transmission of literary culture,[47] but a different picture has often been presented of the situation further east.[48] This portrait, however, of the founder of Qenneshre shows that the traditional rhetorical culture lived on also in a Syriac-speaking monastery as a vehicle for the presentation of the life of a Christian saint. We can see in this work the *Fortleben* of antiquity in Syriac-speaking Christianity—the predecessor of its *Fortleben* in Islam.

The lifetime of John bar Aphtonia was not only, however, a time of continuity, but also one of change. The traditional literary culture of higher education was now being challenged by the ascetic way of life of the monastery.[49] In this connection, the other prong of Baumstark's criticism ("deficient in vivacity") does not seem to hit the mark. The piece, to be sure, may not present us with a very lifelike portrait of John, but it gives us quite a vivid picture of the competition of asceticism and literary culture in the mind of the author. Frequently the full extent of his hero's classical educational background is underplayed in order to heighten his monastic virtues, but the antique heritage still shines through clearly. Yet the adoption, in the main, of the traditional epideictic form ultimately serves to

---

[46] "Eine bei stark rhetorischer Mache ungemein geringere Lebensfrische aufweisende Arbeit"; Baumstark, *Geschichte der syrischen Literatur*, p. 180.

[47] Cf. Liebeschuetz, "Hochschule", col. 904.

[48] Cf. P. Brown, *The World of Late Antiquity* (London, 1971), p. 186: "Christian clergymen eventually passed Aristotle, Plato and Galen on to the Arabs; but in the medieval Near East, Christian and Muslim alike chose to remain ignorant of Homer, of Thucydides, of Sophocles. It was the end of a millennium of literary culture." Contrast the works cited above, nn. 6 and 16.

[49] Cf. Liebeschuetz, "Hochschule", col. 888.

bring out all the more clearly the virtues of the monastic way of life. It is through the old rhetorical exercise of the *synkrisis* (comparison),[50] in this case comparing "the world" and the monastery, fear and love, that this disciple of John bar Aphtonia most effectively presents his portrait of spiritual authority:

> Secular authorities subdue by fear those subject to authority, either by sword or by punishment, but a leader of monks cannot subdue (them) unless he becomes a servant. He cannot persuade if he does not do what he teaches, inspire fear by a word widowed by conduct, or comfort by conduct not associated with a word. He has to have a soul which is a seer of the judgment of God and of the hidden faults of the brothers, so as to [utter] the one and conceal the other. These were the foremost and ruling (virtues) of our chief, (and) since our master had them in great abundance, he became an intermediary between God and us. Bringing the commandments from up there, he passed (them) to us down here. He was feared and loved at the same time by all. This is very easy (to understand), for each of them takes away the other: love dismisses fear, fear darkens love. For him both of them concurred: he was feared although he loved, and was loved although he was fearful, because he wisely provided for both of them. In this way he governed the monks in his charge, laying low those devoted to mental matters with bolts of prayers, and those devoted to visible matters with arrows of words.[51] For all the monks he was a rule and a mirror, an unwritten law and a living exemplar, and they accepted his judgments as divine revelations (§ 6).

BIBLIOGRAPHY

Ahrens, K., Krüger, G., *Die sogennante Kirchengeschichte des Zacharias Rhetor* (Leipzig, 1899).

Baumstark, A., *Geschichte der syrischen Literatur* (Bonn, 1922).

Brock, S.P., "From Antagonism to Assimilation: Syriac Attitudes to Greek Learning", *East of Byzantium. Syria and Armenia in the Formative Period*, eds. N.G. Garsoian, T.F. Mathews and R.W. Thomson (Washington D.C., 1982), pp. 17–34.

———, "Greek and Syriac in Late Antique Syria", *Literacy and Power in the Ancient World*, eds. A.K. Bowman, G. Woolf (Cambridge, 1994), pp. 149–60.

Brown, P., *The World of Late Antiquity* (London, 1971).

Campbell, J.M., *The Influence of the Second Sophistic on the Style of the Sermons of St. Basil the Great* (Washington D.C., 1922).

Daiber, H., *Aetius Arabus. Die Vorsokratiker in arabischer Überlieferung* (Wiesbaden, 1980).

---

[50] This was a basic exercise of the rhetorical *progymnasmata*. Cf. Kennedy, *Greek Rhetoric*, p. 64 and index s.v. *synkrisis*.

[51] An interesting remark which confirms that not all the monks of Qenneshre were "intellectuals". Cf. above, n. 15.

Drijvers, H.J.W., "The School of Edessa: Greek Learning and Local Culture", *Centres of Learning. Learning and Location in Pre-Modern Europe and the Near East*, eds. J.W. Drijvers, A.A. MacDonald (Leiden, 1995), pp. 49–59.

Furlani, G., "Una introduzione alla logica Aristotelica di Atanasio di Balad", *Rendiconti della Reale Academica dei Lincei. Classe di Scienze morali, storiche e filologiche*, Ser. V, vol. 25 (1917), pp. 717–78.

Garzya, A., Loenertz, R.-J., *Procopii Gazaei Epistolae et Declamationes*, Studia Patristica et Byzantina 9 (Ettal, 1963).

Hadot, I., *Arts libéraux et philosophie dans la pensée antique* (Paris, 1984).

Kennedy, G.A., *Greek Rhetoric under Christian Emperors* (Princeton, 1983).

Kugener, M.A., The *Life of Severus* by John of Beth Aphtonia, PO 2.3 (1904), pp. 205–64.

Liebeschuetz, W., "Hochschule", *RAC* 15 (1991), cols. 858–911.

Maguire, H., *Art and Eloquence in Byzantium* (Princeton, 1981).

Mango, C., *Byzantium. The Empire of New Rome* (London, 1980).

Marrou, H.-I., *A History of Education in Antiquity* (London, 1956).

McVey, K.E., *George, Bishop of the Arabs. A Homily on Blessed Mar Severus, Patriarch of Antioch*, CSCO 531 (Louvain, 1993).

Nau, F., "Histoire de Jean bar Aphtonia", *Revue de l'Orient Chrétien* 7 (1902), pp. 97–135.

Palmer, A.N., *Monk and Mason on the Tigris Frontier. The Early History of Tur 'Abdin* (Cambridge, 1990).

Peeters, P., *Le tréfonds oriental de l'hagiographie byzantine*, Subsidia Hagiographica 26 (Brussels, 1950).

Russell, D.A., Wilson, N.G., *Menander Rhetor* (Oxford, 1981).

Strohmaier, G., "'Von Alexandrien nach Bagdad'—eine fiktive Schultradition", in *Aristoteles: Werk und Wirkung. Paul Moraux gewidmet* II, ed. J. Wiesner (Berlin, 1987), pp. 380–9.

———, "Hunain ibn Ishaq—an Arab Scholar translating into Syriac", *Aram* 3 (1991), pp. 163–70.

Versteegh, C.H.M., "Hellenistic Education and the Origin of Arabic Grammar", *Progress in Linguistic Historiography. Papers from the First International Conference on the History of the Language Sciences*, ed. E.F.K. Koerner (Amsterdam, 1979), pp. 333–44.

———, "The Origin of the Term 'Qiyas' in Arabic Grammar", *Zeitschrift für arabische Linguistik* 4 (1980), pp. 7–30.

Watt, J.W., "Grammar, Rhetoric, and the Enkyklios Paideia in Syriac", *ZDMG* 143 (1993), pp. 45–71.

———, "Eastward and Westward Transmission of Classical Rhetoric", *Centres of Learning. Learning and Location in Pre-Modern Europe and the Near East*, eds. J.W. Drijvers, A.A. MacDonald (Leiden, 1995), pp. 63–75.

———, "Greek Historiography and the 'Chronicle of Joshua the Stylite'", *After Bardaisan. Studies on Continuity and Change in Syriac Christianity in Honour of Professor Han J.W. Drijvers*, eds. G.J. Reinink, A.C. Klugkist (Louvain, 1999), pp. 317–28.

———, "Syriac Panegyric in Theory and Practice. Antony of Tagrit and Eli of Qartamin", *Le Muséon* 102 (1989), pp. 271–98.

Wolf, P., *Vom Schulwesen der Spätantike. Studien zu Libanius* (Baden-Baden, 1952).

Wright, W., *Catalogue of the Syriac Manuscripts in the British Museum* (London, 1872).

Würsch, R., *Avicennas Bearbeitungen der aristotelischen Rhetorik. Ein Beitrag zum Fortleben antiken Bildungsgutes in der islamischen Welt* (Berlin, 1991).

Zacharias Rhetor, *Historia Ecclesiastica Zachariah Rhetori vulgo adscripta*, vol. II, ed. [tr.] E.W. Brooks, CSCO 84 [88], Script. Syri 39 [42] (Louvain, 1921 [1924]).

BABAI THE GREAT'S *LIFE OF GEORGE* AND THE PROPAGATION OF DOCTRINE IN THE LATE SASANIAN EMPIRE

GERRIT J. REININK
University of Groningen

Magundat-Anastasius, one of the last Christian martyrs in the Sasanian empire,[1] was executed by order of the shah Chosroes II on 22 January 628.[2] His biographer reports that the holy martyr at the time of his execution rendered thanks to God that his desire to suffer martyrdom for the sake of Christ was now fulfilled.[3] The seeds of his wish to become a martyr for Christianity were, in fact, already sown before his baptism. After his desertion from the Persian army, Magundat found shelter with a Persian Christian goldsmith in Hierapolis (Mabbug).[4] In this town he visited the Christian churches, where he saw the pictures of the holy martyrs,[5] and, having been informed about the meaning of these representations, Magundat's interest in these holy men was aroused.[6] Later on, after having received baptism in Jerusalem and having entered the monastery of Anastasius to the north of the Holy City,[7] Magundat, now called Anastasius, read the *Lives* of the holy martyrs of the Church and began secretly to cherish the desire to become likewise a martyr for

---

[1] For an introduction to the history and literature of the East Syrian martyrs, see now J. Rist, "Die Verfolgung der Christen im spätantiken Sasanidenreich: Ursachen, Verlauf und Folgen", *Oriens Christianus* 80 (1996), pp. 17–42.

[2] An excellent edition of Anastasius' *Life* and related texts now by B. Flusin, *Saint Anastase le Perse et l'histoire de la Palestine au début du VIIᵉ siècle*, I: Les textes; II: Commentaire (Paris, 1992). Henceforth I quote Flusin's edition/translation of Anastasius' *Life* (= les Actes anciens) by the abbreviation AL.

[3] AL 38; Flusin, *Saint Anastase* I, pp. 82–5.

[4] AL 8; Flusin, *Saint Anastase* I, pp. 48–9.

[5] ... τὰς ἱστορίας τῶν ἁγίων μαρτύρων ἑώρα ...; cf. Flusin, *Saint Anastase* II, p. 228, n. 45.

[6] AL 9; Flusin, *Saint Anastase* I, pp. 50–51.

[7] For this monastery, in which Anastasius stayed for seven years (620–627), see Flusin, *Saint Anastase* II, pp. 185–8; J. Patrich, *Sabas, Leader of Palestinian Monasticism. A Comparative Study in Eastern Monasticism, Fourth to Seventh Centuries*, Dumbarton Oaks Studies 32 (Washington D.C., 1995), pp. 327–8.

Christ.[8] Just how this wish of Anastasius was realized, forms the subject of the account given by his biographer.

Just as Anastasius' attention was drawn to the martyrs by looking at their pictures in the churches, and just as his wish for *imitatio* of their lives was kindled by reading their "written pictures" in the monastery, so the hagiographer by writing the *Life of Anastasius* is painting an icon of a holy man, a portrait of spiritual authority, in which the readers or auditors should recognize that the subject of this *Life* occupies a legitimate place in the choir of his holy predecessors.[9]

The *Life of Anastasius*, written in Greek in the Chalcedonian monastic milieu of Palestine, not long after the saint's death in 628,[10] is not the only surviving representantative of the genre to date from the late Sasanian period. Also in the East Syrian milieu of Persia there were composed *Lives* of converts from Zoroastrianism who suffered martyrdom under Chosroes II.[11] One of these works, the *Life of Mihr-Mah-Gushnasp-George*,[12] is of paramount importance, since it forms a first-class source of information for one of the most crucial periods in the history of the East Syrian Church.[13] Moreover, as compared with the other late Sasanian lives of the martyrs this *Life*

---

[8] AL 12; Flusin, *Saint Anastase* I, pp. 54–5.

[9] See in particular Flusin's remarks on the literary genre in *Saint Anastase* II, pp. 194–6.

[10] Flusin, *Saint Anastase* II, pp. 192–3.

[11] In addition to the *Life of Mihr-Mah-Gushnasp-George* (see below), Babai the Great wrote the *Martyrdom of Yazdoi-Christina* of Bet Garmai, of which only the *Preface* has been preserved; ed. by P. Bedjan, *Acta Martyrum et Sanctorum*, IV (Paris, 1894), pp. 201–7. The exact date of Christina's death is unknown. The work was probably written after the *Life of George*, since Babai does not mention it in the *Preface* of the latter (cf. below, n. 22). For a general view of the *Lives* written by Babai (most of them lost today), see G. Chediath, *The Christology of Mar Babai the Great*, Oriental Institute of Religious Studies 49 (Kottayam, 1982), pp. 35–8. The *Life of Mahanush-Isho'sabran* (died 620/1) was written by Isho'yahb of Adiabene, probably before his election as Catholicos in 649; edited with French summary by J.B. Chabot, "Histoire de Jésus-Sabran, écrite par Jésus-yab d'Adiabène", *Nouvelles archives des missions scientifiques et littéraires* 7 (1897), pp. 485–584. For a discussion of the martyrs under Chosroes II, see Flusin, *Saint Anastase* II, pp. 118–27.

[12] According to Ph. Gignoux, "Titres et fonctions religieuses sasanides d'après les sources syriaques hagiographiques", *Acta antiqua Academiae Scientiarum Hungaricae* 28 (1983), pp. 191–2, George's original Persian name was rather "Mihr-Mah-Gushnasp" than Mihramgushnasp", as he is usually called in the modern literature.

[13] Cf. J. Labourt, *Le christianisme dans l'empire perse sous la dynastie sasanide (224–632)* (Paris, 1904), pp. 217–31, esp. pp. 225–9; A. Guillaumont, *Les "Kephalaia Gnostica" d'Évagre le Pontique et l'histoire de l'Origénisme chez les Grecs et chez les Syriens*, Patristica Sorboniensia 5 (Paris, 1962), pp. 193–5.

occupies a special place, as has already been observed by Paul Devos: "La Passion de Mihramgušnasp-Georges, écrite par son supérieur, le célèbre Babaï le Grand, abbé du couvent nestorien du Mont Izla, est toute bruissante de querelles christologiques."[14] The question of the relation between the painter of this work of art, Babai the Great, and his portrait, the martyr George, will be subjected to closer examination in the present exposition.

The Syriac text of the *Life of George* was published in 1895 by Paul Bedjan,[15] who for his *manuscrit de base* used a modern copy of J.B. Abbeloos,[16] which he collated with the text preserved in the manuscript of the British Library Add.7200.[17] Before the publication of Bedjan's edition, Georg Hoffmann had published a German summary of the work from the London manuscript, in his *Auszüge aus syrischen Akten persischer Märtyrer*.[18] A French summary of the *Life* was published in 1902 by J.B. Chabot in his edition of the *Synodicon Orientale*, as a note to the assembly of East Syrian bishops at the court of Chosroes II in 612.[19] The only translation made to date is

---

[14] P. Devos, "Les martyrs persans à travers leurs actes syriaques", *Atti del Convegno sul tema. La Persia e il mondo greco-romano*, Academia Nazionale dei Lincei, anno 363 (Rome, 1966), p. 217.

[15] P. Bedjan (ed.), *Histoire de Mar-Jabalaha, de trois autres patriarches, d'un prêtre et de deux laïques nestoriens* (Paris, 1895), pp. 416–571 (henceforth quoted by the abbreviation LG).

[16] LG, pp. xv–xvi. The manuscript is described by J.B. Abbeloos, "Deux manuscrits chaldéens inexplorés", *Le Muséon* 2 (1883), pp. 143–4, and by J. Assfalg, *Verzeichnis der orientalischen Handschriften in Deutschland*, Bd.V: *Syrische Handschriften* (Wiesbaden, 1963), pp. 56–9. It is today known as *Ms.or.oct.1257* in the *Staatsbibliothek zu Berlin—Preussischer Kulturbesitz, Orientabteilung*; cf. H. Kaufhold, Review of *Répertoire des bibliothèques et des catalogues de manuscrits syriaques*, par Alain Desreumaux avec la collaboration de Françoise Briquel-Chatonnet (Paris, 1991), *Oriens Christianus* 76 (1992), p. 248. This manuscript was copied in 1869 by the deacon Gabriel of Mosul from an old manuscript of the Church of Mar Pethion in Diyarbakir, which may be identified with the manuscript *Diyarbakir 96* (now in Baghdad); cf. A. Scher, "Notice sur les manuscrits syriaques et arabes conservés à l'archevêché chaldéen de Diarbékir", *Journal Asiatique*, 10ᵉ sér., 10 (1907), pp. 398–401; J.-M. Vosté, "Notes sur les manuscrits syriaques de Diarbekir et autres localités d'Orient", *Le Muséon* 50 (1937), p. 349; W.F. Macomber, "New Finds of Syriac Manuscripts in the Middle East", *ZDMG*, Supplementa I, Teil 2 (Wiesbaden, 1969), p. 475.

[17] W. Wright, *Catalogue of the Syriac Manuscripts in the British Museum*, vol. III (London 1872), p. 1207.

[18] G. Hoffmann, *Auszüge aus syrischen Akten persischer Märtyrer*, Abhandlungen für die Kunde des Morgenlandes 7.3 (Leipzig, 1880), pp. 91–115.

[19] J.B. Chabot (ed., transl.), *Synodicon Orientale ou recueil de synodes nestoriens*, Notices et extraits des manuscrits de la Bibliothèque Nationale et autres bibliothèques publiés par l'Académie des Inscriptions et Belles-Lettres 37 (Paris, 1902), pp. 625–34.

Oskar Braun's German translation of 1915, in a volume of the *Bibliothek der Kirchenväter.*[20] However, although Braun translated the major part of George's *Life*, he omitted several sections which, in his view, were of minor importance for the essential narrative.[21] Since modern scholarship usually had recourse to Braun's translation, some important historical and literary data, in particular those preserved in Babai's *Preface*, have remained unnoticed. We still await a systematic study of the *Life of George*; and in the present contribution, it will only be possible to discuss a few problems connected with this rather complicated work.

Babai wrote the *Life of George* in the last years of his life (between 621 and 628),[22] and at the earliest about six years after George's martyrdom (615).[23] The work was meant to be read on the martyr's commemoration-day, as appears from the *Preface*. A certain deacon Shapur from the capital Seleucia-Ctesiphon had asked the abbot of the Great Monastery on mount Izla, above Nisibis, to write George's history,[24] undoubtedly with the intention that it should be read on the martyr's commemoration-day in the capital's churches and monasteries, in particular for the visitors to the martyr's tomb in the martyrion of Sergius.[25] This request was quite natural, since Babai had been acquainted with George for many years. After his conversion from Zoroastrianism, and his baptism by the bishop Simon of Hira in 596,[26] George entered the monastery on Izla in 601, when he

---

[20] O. Braun, *Ausgewählte Akten persischer Märtyrer*, Bibliothek der Kirchenväter 22 (Kempten/München, 1915), pp. 221–77 (henceforth quoted as Braun).

[21] Braun, p. 221, n. 1, and *passim*.

[22] In the *Preface* of LG, in which Babai gives a conspectus of the *Lives* written earlier by him, Babai says that he composed LG thirty-three years after he wrote the *History of Abraham of Kashkar*, the founder of the monastery on Izla (LG, p. 424; Braun, p. 221). If Abraham died in 588—cf. A. Baumstark, *Geschichte der syrischen Literatur* (Bonn, 1922), p. 130—, the *terminus a quo* of the composition of LG is about 621, whereas the *terminus ante quem* is determined by Babai's death in about 628; cf. Chediath, *Christology*, pp. 13–6.

[23] LG, p. 563; Braun, p. 277: George's martyrdom was on the fourteenth of Later Conun (January) in the year 926 of the Greeks (615 A.D.).

[24] LG, pp. 416–8; Braun, p. 221.

[25] In this *martyrion*, according to Babai, George's body was temporarily laid down, until a church could be built for George himself. This plan had not yet been realized when Babai wrote LG (cf. LG, pp. 558–9; Braun, pp. 274–5). This *martyrion* of Sergius was near the capital—cf. Hoffmann, *Auszüge*, p. 113, n. 1031—and has to be distinguished from the *martyrion* of Sergius in the neighbourhood of Hulwan (see below, n. 87).

[26] LG, p. 441; Braun, p. 226. For the date of George's baptism, see LG, p. 526;

was about twenty-five years of age.[27] There he met Babai as a fellow monk, who became his abbot in 604, when Babai succeeded
Dadisho' as head of the congregation.[28] From 601 until 612, the
year in which George undertook his fatal journey to the court of
Chosroes in Seleucia-Ctesiphon, the young monk stayed in Babai's
monastery.

In painting George's portrait, Babai follows the conventions of the
genre, in which not only the simple *passio* or *martyrion* (μαρτύριον) is
described, but also the martyr's *bios* (βίος) before his martyrdom.[29]
Like the other examples of the genre, Babai's *Life of George* is *stricto
sensu* neither biography nor historiography, but first of all hagiography. Not only should the saint's martyrdom, his arrest, the hard-
ships he suffered in prison, his courageous defence and confession
of the Christian religion before the pagan authorities, the conversions which he brought about by his impressive persistence and the
miracles that occurred at his execution and directly after his death,
not only these details but the whole of the saint's life should testify
to the legitimacy of the saint's holiness, which would thus draw the
faithful both to veneration and to imitation. One of the topics belonging to this concept is the saint's readiness for martyrdom from the
very beginning of his Christian life.

Just as the author of the *Life of Anastasius* stresses his hero's involvement in the figures of the holy martyrs *ab initio*, so Babai depicts
George's life before his *martyrion* as a life which is already enlightened

---

Braun, p. 262: George was baptized in the sixth year of Chosroes, when he was
twenty years of age. Chediath, *Christology*, p. 35, takes the year 596 as the year in
which George was baptized, whereas Fiey chooses the year 595; cf. J.M. Fiey, *Assyrie
chrétienne*, III, Recherches publiées sous la direction de l'Institut de Lettres Orientales
de Beyrouth 42 (Beirut, 1968), p. 164.

[27] In the *Preface* (LG, p. 431; not translated by Braun) Babai states that George
had been a monk for "two weeks of years" (fourteen years) before he suffered martyrdom in 615.

[28] Dadisho' ruled the community of Izla from 588 to 604; cf. A. Vööbus, *Syriac
and Arabic Documents Regarding Legislation Relative to Syrian Ascetism*, Papers of the Estonian
Theological Society in Exile 11 (Stockholm, 1960), pp. 163–75; M. Tamcke, *Der
Katholikos-Patriarch Sabrišo' I. (596–604) und das Mönchtum*, Europäische Hochschulschriften,
Reihe XXIII, Theologie 302 (Frankfurt aM/Bern/New York, 1988), pp. 41–50.

[29] See H. Delehaye, *Les passions des martyrs et les genres littéraires*, Studia Hagiographica 13B (Bruxelles, 1966), pp. 8–9. Since Delehaye did not consider the Syriac
legends of the martyrs, a systematic study of the Syriac material is still a *desideratum*;
cf. G. Wiessner, *Untersuchungen zur syrischen Literaturgeschichte* I: *Zur Märtyrerüberlieferung
aus der Christenverfolgung Schapurs II*. Abhandlungen der Akademie der Wissenschaften
in Göttingen, philol.-hist. Klasse, 3. Folge 67 (Göttingen, 1967), p. 218, n. 1.

by the glory of his future martyrdom. Even before his baptism, George, still called by his Persian name Mihr-Mah-Gushnasp, had already had some experience of hearing stories of martyrs and their lives. When he stayed for some time on one of his estates, escaping from the outbreak of an epidemic in the capital Seleucia-Ctesiphon, Mihr-Mah-Gushnasp had the opportunity to satisfy his curiosity about the Christian religion in his conversations with his Christian estate-steward. At his wish to hear something from a Christian text, it happened that the *Life of the martyr George* was read;[30] impressed by that story, Mihr-Mah-Gushnasp there and then decided to adopt the Christian name George, if he should ever become a Christian and be baptized.[31] Subsequently, from the moment of his baptism, George, in Babai's words, was always longing for and every day expecting his martyrdom.[32] In Babai's account, George's *martyrion* actually began when he left the safety of his monastery in 612.[33] But before that date, while he was still spending most days of his Christian life in the monastery, George was already preparing himself for martyrdom, since there was no contradiction between his wish to become a monk and his wish to become a martyr. The abbot Dadisho' readily admitted George into the congregation, according to Babai, "since also the monastic life and its labours are a kind of martyrdom through the labours, the readiness of the will, the application of the mind to death and the alienation from all transitory things".[34]

Babai portrays the monk George with all the features of an exemplary ascetic, as a paradigm which will attract auditors and readers of his life to imitation. However—and this seems to be a less traditional hagiographical motif—Babai portrays George even more as a religious doctor, whose teachings should be accepted as representing the only right and orthodox Christian doctrine. In his *Preface* Babai, addressing himself to the assembled monks, explains the divine design of George's martyrdom as follows:[35]

---

[30] The Syriac version of this martyrdom (BHO 312 + 313) is published by P. Bedjan, *Acta Martyrum et Sanctorum*, I (Paris, 1890), pp. 277–300. For this martyr, see *The Oxford Dictionary of Byzantium*, 2 (Oxford, 1991), pp. 834–5.

[31] LG, p. 440; Braun, p. 225.

[32] LG, p. 521; Braun, pp. 259–60.

[33] See below, p. 177.

[34] LG, p. 484; Braun, p. 242.

[35] LG, pp. 421–2; not translated by Braun.

O ye beloved of Christ, runners at the struggle for justice, who are assembled here today to honour the day of his martyrdom, to glorify Him who elected and called him and who judged right to give him the crown of martyrdom, in order to recompense him for his perfect love, and to encourage the weak, to strengthen the believers, to provoke the unbelievers, to strengthen the athletes, crucified unto the world,[36] and also to bring reproach upon and to put to shame and to scorn all children of error and the Theopaschite heresy, and to defeat all liars and people without hope: *may the prayers of this crowned martyr be for all those who continually live in his truth and follow in the footsteps of his orthodoxy, for which he suffered and which he signed by his cross and which he confirmed by his blood like his Lord and the rest of the holy Apostles whom he imitated and like whom he was made perfect,* and (may his prayers) particularly be for this monastic[37] congregation, in which he grew up spiritually and from which he was led to the victory of his marvelous martyrdom, and for all those who assembled today to honour his Lord on the day of his martyrdom, that we all may inherit the blessings which are prepared by Christ for his faithful. Amen.

Here Babai introduces George not as a martyr for Christianity as such—who, being a convert from Zoroastrianism fell a victim to the State's law of apostasy[38]—but rather presents him as primarily a martyr for orthodoxy. To understand the background of this presentation, we must first consider the historical circumstances which led to George's conviction and execution.

As we have already said, Babai considers George's departure from the monastery as the beginning of his *martyrion.*[39] The immediate cause of George's departure was a letter from the bishops, which arrived in the monastery on mount Izla in 612.[40] In this letter the bishops invited Babai's congregation to participate in an embassy to the court of Chosroes, expressing in particular the wish that George would become a member of this legation, since he—on account of his antecedents and parentage—had access to certain high-placed officials at the court.[41]

---

[36] Gal. 6:14.

[37] Lit. "strange", i.e. "being estranged from the things of this life"; cf. Hebr. 11:13.

[38] That was the actual charge against George; see below, p. 190. For the Persian law requiring capital punishment of the converts from Zoroastrianism, see A. Christensen, *L'Iran sous les Sassanides* (Copenhagen, 1944²), p. 64; M. Boyce, *The Letter of Tansar* (Rome, 1968), p. 42.

[39] LG, pp. 507–11; Braun, pp. 253–4.

[40] For a discussion of the date, see below n. 48.

[41] LG, p. 507; Braun, p. 252. Mihr-Mah-Gushnasp was a member of high nobility.

At first sight the sources do not seem to be quite unanimous about the reasons for this embassy. According to Babai, the influential Monophysite court-physician Gabriel of Sinjar got the shah's permission to look for a suitable candidate for the chair of Catholicos, which had been vacant since the death of the Catholicos Gregory I in 608/9.[42] When the report of that event reached the ears of the bishops, they immediately decided to send a delegation to the court to warn the shah against a possible "great commotion in the whole Church in the country of the Persians".[43] The bishops feared that the great opponent of the East Syrian Church, Gabriel of Sinjar, would present one of his sympathizers for the office, so that the Monophysite party could strengthen and extend further its influence in the Sasanian empire.[44] The purpose of the embassy was, according to Babai, to obtain the shah's permission for the appointment of a Catholicos according to the Church's habit and rule.[45] However, according to the *Khuzistan Chronicle* (probably composed in the 660s) the mission of the bishops was ordered by the shah at the instigation of Gabriel of Sinjar, who wished that a disputation should take place between the East Syrian bishops and his Monophysite co-religionists.[46] The *Synodicon Orientale* (eighth century), in which the account of the assembly is preserved, also speaks of a disputation which was ordered by the shah in 612 at Gabriel's instigation.[47] We cannot

His paternal grandfather was, according to Babai, "of royal lineage". For Mihr-Mah-Gushnasp's noble birth and his connection with the royal court during his youth, see LG, pp. 435–7; Braun, pp. 223–4; Christensen, *L'Iran sous les Sassanides*, pp. 413–4, 489–90.

[42] See below, n. 53.

[43] LG, pp. 506–7; Braun, p. 252.

[44] For the spread of Monophysitism in Iraq in the second half of the sixth century and the first decades of the seventh century, see Labourt, *Le christianisme dans l'empire perse*, pp. 217–31; J.M. Fiey, *Jalons pour une histoire de l'église en Iraq*, CSCO 310, Subs. 36 (Louvain, 1970), pp. 127–38; M.G. Morony, *Iraq after the Muslim Conquest* (Princeton, 1984), pp. 372–80.

[45] LG, p. 513; Braun, p. 255.

[46] Edition and Latin translation by I. Guidi, *Chronica Minora* I, CSCO 1–2, Script. Syri 1–2 (Paris, 1903), p. 23 (text), p. 20 (transl.). German transl. by Th. Nöldeke, "Die von Guidi herausgegebene Chronik", *Sitzungsberichte der kaiserlichen Akademie der Wissenschaften*, phil.-hist. Kl., 128/IX (Vienna, 1893), pp. 20–1. For a discussion of the date and provenance of this anonymous work, see now R.G. Hoyland, *Seeing Islam as Others Saw It. A Survey and Evaluation of Christian, Jewish and Zoroastrian Writings on Early Islam*, Studies in Late Antiquity and Early Islam 13 (Princeton, 1997), pp. 182–5.

[47] Chabot, *Synodicon Orientale*, pp. 562–3 (text), p. 580 (French transl.); German transl. by O. Braun, *Das Buch der Synhados oder Synodicon Orientale* (Wien, 1900), p. 307.

assume that there were two assemblies at Chosroes' court, one in 608/9 and one in 612.[48] The early sources, in which only one assembly is mentioned, refer both to the question of the vacancy of the Catholicate and the disputation. In the *Synodicon Orientale* the bishops, after having put in writing at the shah's request an official Confession of Faith, thereupon present a petition to the shah asking for permission to appoint a new Catholicos.[49] According to Babai the shah, after having been informed about the purpose of the delegation, made the condition that it should first of all be established "which belief is the true one".[50] According to Babai, it was not Gabriel of Sinjar, but Farrukhan, a dignitary of the king and George's contact at the court, who proposed to Chosroes the holding of a disputation (obviously between the East Syrian delegation and the Monophysites), a proposal to which the shah as yet did not agree.[51] Thereupon, as Babai reports, George proposed by the mouth of Farrukhan that the bishops should present a written Confession of Faith to Chosroes, a proposal that was accepted by the shah and subsequently carried out.[52] We may conclude, therefore, that there

---

[48] A. Vööbus, *History of the School of Nisibis*, CSCO 266, Subs. 26 (Louvain, 1965), pp. 315–7, assuming that Gabriel of Sinjar intended to nominate Henana of Adiabene or one of Henana's disciples for the chair of Catholicos after Gregory's death in 608/9 thinks that Henana was still alive at that time, whereas in 612, when the assembly at Chosroes' court took place, "Henana must have been dead for some time". However, it is clear that events moved swiftly: the bishops' organizing of the delegation to the shah's court, the delegation's journey to and arrival at the court— all these events must have occurred in the year 612. For the dubious report in the *Chronicle of Seert* concerning Gabriel's intention to make Henana Catholicos, see below, nn. 62–3.

[49] Chabot, *Synodicon Orientale*, p. 568 (text), pp. 585–6 (transl.); Braun, *Das Buch des Synhados*, p. 315.

[50] LG, p. 513; Braun, p. 255.

[51] According to Braun, p. 255, n. 1, Farrukhan is probably to be identified with Shahrbaraz, Chosroes' famous general, whose patronymic was Farrukhan (cf. Nöldeke, "Die von Guidi herausgegebene Chronik", p. 31, n. 4; Christensen, *L'Iran sous les Sassanides*, p. 448; Flusin, *Saint Anastase* II, p. 74, n. 32). Also Labourt, *Le christianisme dans l'empire perse*, p. 242, does not exclude the possibility of this identification. For this identification to stand up, we have to assume that Shahrbaraz in 612 had returned from his campaigns in the West to the royal court and for some time fulfilled the office of Chosroes' chamberlain (see below, n. 75). Is that a likely assumption? Anyhow, in 613 Shahrbaraz was back in the West, occupying Damascus in 613 and in 614 Jerusalem. For Shahrbaraz's campaigns in the Persian war against Byzantium, see A.N. Stratos, *Byzantium in the Seventh Century*, I: 602–634, transl. by M. Ogilvie-Grant (Amsterdam, 1968), pp. 63–4, 103–17; Flusin, *Saint Anastase* II, pp. 70–83, 152–64; C. Mango, "Deux études sur Byzance et la Perse sassanide: II. Héraclius, Šahrvaraz et la Vraie Croix", *Travaux et Mémoires* 9 (1985), pp. 105–18.

[52] LG, pp. 513–4; Braun, pp. 255–6.

was only one assembly of the East Syrian bishops and monks at
Chosroes' court, viz. that of the year 612. But how are the differences
between the sources to be explained? Was the delegation to the court
organized by the bishops at their own initiative, or were the bishops ordered by the shah to come to the capital? Moreover, if the
delegation came by order of Chosroes, what were the shah's actual
objectives in organizing a disputation between the rival parties? What
role did Gabriel of Sinjar actually play in all these things?

It should be noticed first of all that it is hardly possible to over-
rate the role which Chosroes' Monophysite physician played in all
these events. As the *Khuzistan Chronicle* also states, it was Gabriel of
Sinjar who was mainly responsable for the fact that the East Syrian
Church remained without a leader after the death of the Catholicos
Gregory in 608/9.[53] Since 603/4, the political climate had become
increasingly favourable to the Monophysites in the Sasanian empire.[54]
When the election of a new Catholicos was arrested, the East Syrian
Church was rendered vulnerable, since she was deprived of her most
important mouth-piece and guardian of her interests at the court.[55]

Babai's presentation of the course of events regarding the embassy
of 612 arouses one's suspicions, somewhat. The reader gains the
impression that Babai, in particular in connection with the disputation and the drafting of the Confession of Faith, wishes to make the
martyr George's role most prominent, and that, in accordance with
this intention, he is suppressing the role of Gabriel of Sinjar. It had
to be made very clear that it was not the cursed heretic Gabriel,
but the martyr George who took the initiative to present a written
Confession of Faith to the shah. After Chosroes' approval of George's
proposal, Babai suddenly introduces into his account the figure of
the monk Henanisho', whom he highly extols as "man of God, a
true orthodox believer, a teacher of the orthodox doctrine", and as

---

[53] Ed. Guidi, p. 22 (text), p. 20 (transl.); Nöldeke, "Die von Guidi herausgegebene
Chronik", p. 19; Fiey, *Jalons pour une histoire de l'église*, p. 135.

[54] In 603/4 Chosroes began his war against Byzantium, and this resulted in the
conquest of most eastern Byzantine provinces in 620. In the conquered territories
Chosroes for political reasons favoured the Monophysites; cf. W.H.C. Frend, *The
Rise of the Monophysite Movement* (Cambridge/London/New York/Melbourne, 1972),
pp. 335–9; Fiey, *Jalons pour une histoire de l'église*, p. 137; Morony, *Iraq*, p. 350; Flusin,
Saint Anastase II, pp. 112–8.

[55] Of course, a long vacancy of the Catholicate also had annoying consequences
for the internal affairs of the Church, such as the consecration of bishops and
metropolitans.

an exemplary monk and ascetic, almost as excellent as George, and like George "eagerly desiring the crown of martyrdom".[56] Since both men, Babai says, resembled each other in all divine things, they composed together, with the consent of the bishops, the orthodox Confession of Faith, viz. that of "two natures and two hypostases of divinity and humanity preserving their properties in one person of Christ, the Son of God".[57] One may wonder, however, whether it was not the monk Henanisho'—being a renowned polemicist and author in the field of Christology and also having connections with the monastery on Izla and Babai the Great[58]—who was primarily responsable for the drafting of the Confession of Faith as it is preserved in its extensive form in the *Synodicon Orientale*.[59] Henanisho'

---

[56] LG, pp. 514–5; Braun, p. 256.

[57] LG, pp. 515–6; Braun, p. 257; see below nn. 67 and 76.

[58] Isho'denah of Basra, *Book of Chastity* (c. 850), edition with French translation by J.B. Chabot, *Le livre de la chasteté composé par Jésusdenah, évêque de Baçrah*, Extrait des Mélanges d'archéologie et d'histoire 16 (Rome, 1896), p. 12 (text), p. 12 (transl.); *Chronicle of Seert* (10th–11th cent.), edition and French translation by A. Scher, *Histoire nestorienne (chronique de Séert)*, II/2, PO 13.4 (Paris, 1918), pp. 534–6 [214 6], Baumstark, *Geschichte*, p. 134; Vööbus, *History of the School of Nisibis*, pp. 276–7. Henanisho' defended the Christology of the two hypostases, as appears from his controversial chapters against a disciple of Henana of Adiabene, Isaiah of Tahal, who may have taught the doctrine of the one composite hypostasis (the neo-Chalcedonian formula); edition with English translation by L. Abramowski, A.F. Goodman, *A Nestorian Collection of Christological Texts*, University of Cambridge Oriental Publications 18–19 (Cambridge, 1972) I, pp. 170–9 (text); II, pp. 101–6 (transl.); cf. also Abramowski-Goodman's *Introduction* II, pp. xliv–xlvi. It is highly questionable whether the martyr George actually wrote controversial works in the field of Christology. The *Chronicle of Seert*, ed. Scher, II/2, p. 537 [217], only mentions a work against the Magians. This tradition may be taken seriously, since George was in his youth thoroughly instructed in Persian literature and religion (LG, pp. 436–7; Braun, pp. 223–4). According to Isho'denah George composed works on the monastic life and against the heretics who were the co-religionists of Gabriel of Sinjar, viz. the Theopaschites (ed. Chabot, *Le livre de la chasteté*, p. 36 (text), p. 31 (transl.)). However, the latter information probably is derived from LG, pp. 495–6; Braun, pp. 246–7, where Babai says that George not only by word, but also by writing confuted the Theopaschites and Henana of Adiabene "in partnership with a brother from the mountain" (the monastery on Izla). With this "brother" Babai himself is meant, and it is clear that Babai here for propagandistic reasons connects George with his own literary activity against the Monophysites and the followers of Henana of Adiabene (see below).

[59] Chabot, *Synodicon Orientale*, pp. 564–7 (text), pp. 581–4 (transl.); Braun, *Das Buch der Synhados*, pp. 309–15. English translation by S.P. Brock, "The Christology of the Church of the East in the Synods of the fifth to the early seventh centuries: preliminary considerations and materials", *Aksum-Thyateira. A Festschrift for Archbishop Methodios*, ed. G. Dragas (London, 1985), pp. 140–2; repr. in idem, *Studies in Syriac Christianity* (Aldershot, 1992). However, it is very likely that George, as the bishops'

was never a martyr and he could—in view of his parentage and past history—hardly be expected to become one.[60] Is not Babai here making Henanisho' an equal to the holy martyr George, in order that George could be made a participant in Henanisho''s work? However this may be, the bare fact that a renowned disputant such as Henanisho' was a member of the delegation makes the supposition obvious, that the disputation at Chosroes' court was not quite so unexpected as Babai would have us believe.

There is yet another element in Babai's account which raises some questions. At the beginning of the section dealing with the *martyrion* Babai says that the heresy of Henana of Adiabene found an advocate at the court in the person of the doctor Gabriel of Sinjar. Gabriel—it is implied—said to the shah: "Their teacher agrees with me, for behold his disciple came to me with his writings." "The shah believed him", Babai continues, "and therefore he ordered him to look for a suitable person, to make him Catholicos."[61] The interpretation of this section in the *Chronicle of Seert* (tenth-eleventh century)[62] has caused, in my opinion, considerable misunderstanding in the modern literature. According to the *Chronicle of Seert*, Gabriel of Sinjar proposed to the shah to make Henana or one of his disciples Catholicos.[63] However, in 612 Henana, the Director of the famous

---

mouth-piece before the shah, translated into Persian the Confession of Faith and the bishops' objections against the tenets of the Theopaschites (LG, p. 516; Braun, p. 257).

[60] Henanisho' was born into an Arab family in Hira, and he is reported to have been in the service of the Lakhmid king an-Nu'man ibn al-Mundhir (580–602), who converted to Christianity and was baptized by the Catholicos Sabrisho'; cf. F. Nau, *Les Arabes chrétiens de Mésopotamie et de Syrie du VIIe au VIIIe siècle*, Cahiers de la société asiatique, première série, I (Paris, 1933), p. 46; J. Spencer Trimingham, *Christianity among the Arabs in Pre-Islamic Times* (London/New York, 1979), pp. 198–200, 223; Tamcke, *Der Katholikos-Patriarch Sabrišo'*, pp. 22–3. The Christian martyrs under Chosroes II were usually Persians who converted from Zoroastrianism to Christianity and fell victim to the law of apostasy; cf. S.P. Brock, "Christians in the Sasanian Empire: A Case of Divided Loyalties", *Religion and National Identity*, Studies in Church History 18, ed. S. Mews (Oxford, 1982) p. 5; repr. in idem, *Syriac Perspectives on Late Antiquity* (London, 1984); Morony, *Iraq*, pp. 297–300, 332–3; Flusin, *Saint Anastase* II, pp. 120–7; Rist, "Die Verfolgung der Christen", pp. 37–41.

[61] LG, p. 506; Braun, p. 252.

[62] The author of the *Chronicle of Seert* undoubtedly knew Babai's *Life of George*, from which he used some data in the chapters concerning the lives of Henanisho' and George (ed. Scher, II/2, pp. 534–9 [214–9]); cf. for example, the quotation of the words of George and Shubhalmaran in ed. Scher, II/2, p. 538 [218] with the words of George and Henanisho' in LG, p. 519; Braun, p. 259.

[63] Ed. Scher, II/2, p. 537 [217]. Vööbus, *History of the School of Nisibis*, pp. 316–7,

East Syrian School of Nisibis,[64] was most probably already dead.[65] Moreover, if we read Babai's words carefully, we can only conclude that Gabriel is misleading the shah, using a fictitious story according to which a disciple of Henana demonstrated on the basis of some document allegedly written by Henana, that the Director of the School of Nisibis subscribed to the Theopaschite heresy. In reality, however, neither Henana nor his disciples ever adhered to the Monophysite (Severan) Christology of one nature and one hypostasis.[66]

---

concluded from these words that Gabriel of Sinjar really intended to make Chosroes appoint Henana or one of his disciples as Catholicos after the death of Gregory in 608/9 (see also above, n. 48). From the same section in the *Chronicle of Seert* Moffett concludes: "... his [Henana's] name figured prominently in the list of candidates when the patriarch Gregory died in 608"; S.H. Moffett, *A History of Christianity in Asia*, I: *Beginnings to 1500* (San Francisco, 1992), p. 240. Cf. also Flusin, *Saint Anastase II*, p. 111.

[64] For Henana's life and works, see Vööbus, *History of the School of Nisibis*, 234–317; G.J. Reinink, "'Edessa grew dim and Nisibis shone forth': The School of Nisibis at the transition of the sixth-seventh century", *Centres of Learning. Learning and Location in Pre-Modern Europe and the Near East*, eds. J.W. Drijvers, A.A. MacDonald (Leiden, 1995), pp. 77–89; L. van Rompay, "La littérature exégétique syriaque et le rapprochement des traditions syrienne-occidentale et syrienne-orientale", *Parole de l'Orient* 20 (1995), pp. 224–6.

[65] Henana probably died not long before the events of 612. Babai himself mentions this fact in the section which immediately precedes the second part of the *Life of George* (the *martyrion*). George would have published an anathema immediately "after the second death" of Henana, by which the followers of Henana would have been excluded from the Communion in the monastery on Izla, and the monks of Izla would have been forbidden to receive the Communion in a community in which the name of Henana is proclaimed (LG, pp. 503–4; Braun, pp. 250–1). By the "first death" of Henana his spiritual death as a heretic is meant, his "second death" refers to his natural death. Scher's (*Chronicle of Seert*, II/1, p. 537, n. 2) and Vööbus's (*History of the School of Nisibis*, p. 317, n. 28) explanations of the two deaths of Henana are unlikely and, in fact, unnecessary.

[66] In LG, pp. 496–7; Braun, p. 247, Babai says that Henana took part along with the followers of Severus in accepting the doctrine of one nature and one hypostasis in Christ. Directly after that, however, Babai imputes to the followers of the Director the Chalcedonian doctrine of two natures and one hypostasis. We know that Henana's disciple Isaiah of Tahal taught the Chalcedonian doctrine of the one hypostasis or perhaps the neo-Chalcedonian formula of the one composite hypostasis (see above, n. 57). The few preserved (fragments of) works of Henana show that Henana expresses a clear-cut Diophysite point of view; cf. G.J. Reinink, "Tradition and the Formation of the "Nestorian" Identity in 6th–7th Century Iraq", forthcoming in the *Proceedings of the Fourth Workshop on Late Antiquity and Early Islam. Patterns of Communal Identity in the Late Antique and Early Islamic Near East*, London, 5–7 May 1994. Most scholars today consider Babai's allegation that Henana was a "Theopaschite" to be sheer polemic, suggesting that Henana's Christology, rather, may have been close to the Chalcedonian standpoint—cf. Guillaumont, *Les "Kephalaia Gnostica"*, p. 195, n. 72; Brock, "The Christology of the Church of the East", p. 132, n. 41—or the neo-Chalcedonian formula (cf. L. Abramowski, "Die Christologie

Most probably we have to do here with Babai's polemical recast-
ing of the events. Babai, the great advocate of the "Nestorian" formula of two natures and two hypostases,[67] had spent a lifetime
combating Henana, accusing the Director and his supporters of cor-
rupting the orthodox doctrine of the East Syrian Church and having introduced the heresy of Origenism.[68] The *Life of George* is likewise
highly coloured by Babai's polemics against the "Henanians" (as he
calls Henana's disciples and supporters), who in the first decades of
the seventh century still represented a considerable stream of influence
within the East Syrian Church.[69] Only in 612, by virtue of the
Confession of Faith at Chosroes' court, did the "Nestorian" Christology
become the official position—"a hard-line one", to use Sebastian
Brock's wording, "expressed in a fairly uncompromising Antiochene
phraseology".[70] The reason why Babai closely connects George with
Henanisho' in writing the "Nestorian" Confession of Faith may be
the same as the reason why Babai twice connects himself with George
in the section concerning the martyr's stay in the monastery on
mount Izla. Both times, Babai associates himself with George, when
the teachings of Henana of Adiabene are confuted.[71] In the last section of George's *Life* before the *martyrion*, after stating that George,
in cooperation with himself, is zealously confuting Henana's heresy

Babais des Grossen", *Symposium Syriacum 1972*, OCA 197 (Rome, 1974), pp. 221–2),
or alternatively suggesting that Henana's Christology has to be considered as an
internal development of the East Syrian Diophysite tradition, based on (the Syriac
translation of) Theodore of Mopsuestia's work; cf. A. de Halleux, "La christologie
de Martyrios-Sahdona dans l'évolution du nestorianisme", *OCP* 23 (1957), p. 31.

[67] For Babai's Christology and its background, see V. Grumel, "Un théologien
nestorien: Babai le Grand (VIᵉ et VIIᵉ s.)", *Échos d'Orient* 22 (1923), pp. 153–81,
257–80; 23 (1924), pp. 9–33, 162–77, 257–74, 395–9; L. Scipioni, *Ricerche sulla
cristologia del "Libro di Eraclide di Nestorio"* (Freiburg, 1956), pp. 110–58; Abramowski,
"Die Christologie Babais des Grossen", pp. 219–44; idem, "Babai der Grosse:
Christologische Probleme und ihre Lösungen", *OCP* 41 (1975), pp. 289–343; Chediath,
Christology; idem, "La contribution théologique de Mar Babai le Grand", *Istina* 40
(1995), pp. 83–94.

[68] LG, pp. 477, 496; Braun, pp. 239, 247. For a well-balanced discussion of the
Origenist ideas which Babai in his *Life of George* and other writings—perhaps for
polemical reasons—imputes to Henana, see Guillaumont, *Les "Kephalaia Gnostica"*,
pp. 186–96.

[69] de Halleux, "La christologie de Martyrios-Sahdona", pp. 29–30; Abramowski,
"Die Christologie Babais des Grossen", p. 222; Reinink, "Tradition and the Formation
of 'Nestorian' Identity".

[70] Brock, "The Christology of the Church of the East", p. 127.

[71] LG, pp. 475, 459–96; Braun, pp. 238, 246–7. George's "brother" in the
monastery of Izla, who appears in these sections, is Babai himself.

through the spoken and the written word, Babai has George give an extensive *exposée*, in which George, using Babai's arguments, explains why the traditional East Syrian Christological formula of two natures and one person should henceforth be explained in the "Nestorian" sense of "two natures and two hypostases preserving their properties in one person of Christ, the Son of God, in one union and conjunction for ever".[72] Babai's reason for connecting George so closely with himself and Henanisho'—both being renowned controversialists and defenders of the "Nestorian" orthodoxy—is that he wishes to emphasize that George became a martyr not only for Christianity as such, but that he was the first martyr who suffered and died for "orthodoxy", viz. the Christology of which Babai was the most zealous defender.

The real reason for George's martyrdom, however, has, in our view, more to do with ecclesiastical and social power politics than with "Nestorian" orthodoxy. Let us attempt a reconstruction of the events in 612 and the following year. It is highly probable that the disputation at the court was indeed ordered by the shah at the instigation of Gabriel of Sinjar. The election of a new Catholicos for the Church of the East was used as a pretext to make the East Syrian bishops appear at the court. George's role in the delegation was above all else to act as the spokesman of the bishops. It is noteworthy that Babai mentions George's contact at the court by name: Farrukhan.[73] However, we can hardly believe that Farrukhan in every respect played the role which Babai assigns to him. For neither was the shah ignorant of the reason why the bishops came to the court,[74] nor was Farrukhan the one who proposed to the shah that there should take place a religious disputation. Farrukhan only fulfilled the office of the shah's doorkeeper/chamberlain, whose task it was to

---

[72] LG, pp. 495–502; Braun, pp. 246–50. Many arguments adduced by George can be found in Babai's main Christological work *On the Union*; edition and Latin translation by A. Vaschalde, *Babai magni liber de unione*, CSCO 79–80, Script. Syri 34–35 (Louvain, 1915); cf. Abramowski, "Die Christologie Babais des Grossen", p. 219: "In der Vita des Märtyrers Georg schildert Babai die Auseinandersetzung mit den Anhängern des Henana, die Argumente, die er seinem Helden in den Mund legt, sind mindestens in der Formulierung die des Autors."

[73] See above, n. 51.

[74] LG, p. 513; Braun, p. 255: Babai makes Farrukhan not only announce the arrival of the bishops, but also explain the purpose of the mission, viz. to acquire Chosroes' permission to appoint a Catholicos in conformity with the rules of the Church.

announce the arrival of the delegation and to act as intermediary
in the communication between the shah and the bishops (represented
by George).[75]

But why was Gabriel of Sinjar so greatly interested in a disputation between the delegation of the East Syrian Church and the
Monophysites and why should the delegation present a written
Confession of Faith to the shah? Reading the account of the assembly in the *Synodicon Orientale*, one gains the impression that the procedure at the court was well prepared and was enacted under a
strict direction. We may surmise that the bishops indeed presumed
that they had to defend the East Syrian standpoint over against the
Monophysites in order to get permission to elect a new Catholicos.
Once they had arrived at the court, however, they were told that
they had first of all to offer the shah a written Confession of Faith.
It is not difficult to make a guess at the reason for this. For more
than two decades the East Syrian Church had been seriously divided
on the subject of the correct formula of her Diophysite Christology.[76]
As a consequence of the demand for a written Confession of Faith
the bishops were forced to make a choice, and the result of their
choice would subsequently be in force as the official position of the
East Syrian Church. However, the position which would be chosen
was already clear beforehand. Gabriel of Sinjar may have had a
shrewd suspicion that the influence of Babai the Great—who since

---

[75] Cf. Morony, *Iraq*, p. 80.

[76] In my forthcoming article "Tradition and the Formation of 'Nestorian' Identity"
I have tried to explain why and how in the last decades of the sixth and the first
decades of the seventh century East Syrian scholars were divided on the question
of how a new Christological notion, namely the concept of hypostasis, could be
given a place in the Diophysite tradition of their Church. The discussion broke out
in the School of Nisibis, when Henana was the Director, and it culminated in a
serious and uncompromising controversy during the Catholicate of Isho'yahb I
(582–595). Babai and his supporters defended the position of the two natures and
two hypostases, whereas the Henanians adopted the formula of the two natures and
one hypostasis in Christ. Both groups could appeal to authorities considered as
orthodox in the East Syrian tradition. It is important to note in this context that
in none of the three synods that took place (585, 596 and 605) before 612 did the
East Syrian bishops formulate a creed, in which the traditional Antiochene formula
of the two natures was extended by the addition of the two hypostases in Christ,
in fact no mention is made of the term hypostasis at all; cf. Brock, "The Christology
of the Church of the East", p. 127. This circumstance may indicate how awkward
the question was for the preservation of the doctrinal unity of the East Syrian
Church at that time. For an ample discussion of these matters, the reader is referred
to my above-mentioned article.

the death of the Catholicos Gregory had run the affairs of the Church together with Aba, the archdeacon of Seleucia-Ctesiphon—would make the bishops adopt the "hard-line" position of the "Nestorian" Christology of the two natures and two hypostases over against the Monophysites. The consequence thereof would be that all those members of the East Syrian Church who refused to explain the traditional East Syrian formula in the new "Nestorian" sense would be officially declared heretical, would be anathematized by their own Church, and would possibly become an easy prey for Monophysite propaganda. Gabriel of Sinjar's design in making the shah convoke the assembly of 612 was perhaps not so much the unrealistic hope that a Monophysite would be appointed as Catholicos,[77] but rather a desire to weaken the position of the East Syrian Church still more by making the schism between the two currents within the East Syrian community official and definitive. After the Confession of Faith of 612 there no longer was available the possibility of a choice between an extreme Diophysite (represented by Babai and others) and a moderate Diophysite standpoint (represented by the adherents of Henana).[78] If the "Henanians" wished to remain members of their Church, they now had to accept the "Nestorian" Christology expressed in the Confession of Faith of 612.

Our hypothesis may find some support in the sources themselves. In the *Synodicon Orientale* the account of the assembly of 612 concludes with the following words of the secretary:

> After they had written and brought before the king this Confession of Faith together with the attached controversial treatise,[79] they received

---

[77] Labourt, *Le christianisme dans l'empire perse*, p. 224, suggests that Gabriel wished to impose a Monophysite Catholicos upon the East Syrian Church. However, it is hardly conceivable that Chosroes would have allowed the Church of the East, which represented a very important religious majority in the Sasanian empire, to be governed by a Catholicos belonging to the small Monophysite minority, since that would indeed have jeopardized the internal political stability of the empire.

[78] Cf. De Halleux, "La christologie de Martyrios-Sahdona", pp. 28–9; Abramowski, "Die Christologie Babais des Grossen", p. 222.

[79] The "controversial treatise" (*draša*) includes a number of "objections" (*pkare*) against the "Severan Theopaschites" (Chabot, *Synodicon Orientale*, pp. 568–73 (text), pp. 586–91 (transl.); Braun, *Das Buch des Synhados*, pp. 315–22; cf. LG, p. 516; Braun, p. 257). It is very likely that the bishops were not only asked to present a written Confession of Faith to the shah, but also—following the bishops' petition for the election of a Catholicos—to define their religious tenets over against the Monophysites. Babai makes it appear that also the controversial treatise was composed by George and Henanisho' at the delegation's own initiative.

no answer from him, either because paganism was unable to understand the doctrine of the knowledge of the fear of God and he (*i.e.* the king) for that reason showed disdain for it, or because the king of kings was favourable to Gabriel, the leader of the heretical faction of the Theopaschites.[80]

The second of these suggestions may be closer to the truth, for Gabriel had achieved his end, and the chair of Catholicos remained vacant as before.[81] Babai, furthermore, cannot conceal that the bishops were, in fact, misled: after having presented the Confession of Faith to Chosroes and having answered three additional written questions from the shah,[82] the shah did the same as before. As Babai says, "He kept silence and did not say anything".[83]

It is evident from the next section of the *Life of George* how much the bishops still hoped for a positive response from Chosroes on the subject of the election of a Catholicos. They decided to follow the shah, when, after some time, he made his usual departure for his summer-residence in the province of Bet Madaye.[84] During their stay

---

[80] Chabot, *Synodicon Orientale*, p. 580 (text), p. 598 (transl.); Braun, *Das Buch des Synhados*, p. 331.

[81] It remained so until Chosroes' death in 628. According to the *Khuzistan Chronicle* and the *Chronicle of Seert*, the disputation of 612 was most successful for the East Syrian delegation, since Gabriel of Sinjar and the Monophysites were worsted (*Khuzistan Chronicle*, ed. Guidi, p. 23 (text), p. 20 (transl.); Nöldeke, "Die von Guidi herausgegebene Chronik", p. 21) and the Nestorian tenets were declared as the only true ones by Chosroes, if Christianity were to be the true religion (*Chronicle of Seert*, ed. Scher, II/2, p. 538 [219]). If the report given by these sources were correct, Babai most certainly would have sounded the praises of the victory of "orthodoxy" over the heretics at Chosroes' court.

[82] According to Babai (LG, pp. 516–7; Braun, p. 257) Chosroes would seem to have written three questions which the bishops had to answer: (1) Who have first turned aside from the faith which was proclaimed by the Apostles and from that time forth: the monks (i.e. the Monophysites) or the Nestorians?; (2) To whom did Mary give birth: God or man?; (3) Previous to Nestorius, is there some teacher who said that Christ is two natures and two hypostases? The *Synodicon Orientale* (Chabot, p. 574 (text), p. 591 (transl.); Braun, *Das Buch des Synhados*, p. 322) does not have the second question. The last question in particular may reveal the actual intention behind Gabriel of Sinjar's instigating Chosroes to order the disputation at the court, for, by raising the question of the antiquity (and thus the legitimacy) of the tradition of the two hypostases in Christ fuel was added to the fire of the *internal* dissensions within the East Syrian Church; cf. Reinink, "Tradition and the Formation of 'Nestorian' Identity".

[83] LG, p. 517; Braun, p. 257.

[84] LG, pp. 517–8; Braun, p. 258. Chosroes' summer-residence in this province was most probably the castle Qasr-i Shirin in the neighbourhood of Hulwan, built by Chosroes for his Christian wife Shirin; cf. Christensen, *L'Iran sous les Sassanides*, pp. 455–6; Morony, *Iraq*, p. 72.

in that region something happened that would prove the actual cause of George's martyrdom.

From the time that the East Syrian Church was without a leader, Gabriel of Sinjar tried to favour the Monophysite position in the empire by expelling East Syrian monks from their monasteries and handing over the latter to the Monophysites.[85] When the bishops stayed at the shah's summer-residence, Gabriel, presumably with the backing of the Christian queen Shirin,[86] tried to expel the East Syrian monks from the *martyrion* of Sergius (probably in the neighbourhood of Hulwan).[87] When Shubhalmaran, the Metropolitan of Karka de Bet Slok and the head of the bishops' delegation,[88] together

---

[85] Cf. *Khuzistan Chronicle*, ed. Guidi, p. 22 (text), p. 20 (transl.); Nöldeke, "Die von Guidi herausgegebene Chronik", p. 19; Morony, *Iraq*, p. 377.

[86] For the relation between Gabriel and the queen Shirin, who probably followed the physician in his switch to the Monophysite party, see Labourt, *Le christianisme dans l'empire perse*, pp. 219, 221; Flusin, *Saint Anastase* II, p. 111; Moffett, *A History of Christianity in Asia* I, p. 240.

[87] This monastery was built together with the castle (above, n. 84) for Shirin (cf. *Chronicle of Seert*, ed. Scher, II/2, pp. 466–7 [146–7]; Thomas of Marga, *The Book of the Governors*, ed. E.A.W. Budge (London, 1893) I, p. 47 (text), II, pp. 80–1 (transl.)). J.M. Fiey, "Topography of al-Mada'in", *Sumer* 23 (1967), p. 33, n. 271, thinks that Shirin's monastery near Hulwan was not called the *martyrion* of Sergius. Fiey, therefore, suggests that Babai's *Life of George*, in connecting the *martyrion* of Sergius with the province of Bet Madaye, has to be considered as "a mistake (probably a marginal gloss, later incorporated in the text), since the same text says later that George was buried in the monastery he had fought for, and it is sure that this one was that of Mabrakhta" (near the capital; see above, n. 25). However, we can neither doubt that the monastery George was fighting for was near the shah's summer-residence in Bet Madaye, nor that it was (also) called the *martyrion* of Sergius. The fact that George suffered and died for "the house of Sergius" (near Hulwan) and that he was buried after his martyrdom in the "*martyrion* of Sergius" (near the capital) is for Babai one of the wonders which attest to the saint's holiness. When Babai in LG, p. 558 (Braun, p. 274) says that George was laid down "in the same house of Mar Sergius", he does not necessarily mean the same building, but may rather wish to emphasize in a more or less rhetorical way that George was buried in the same sort of building (viz. one of the *martyria* for the martyr Sergius). For the cult of saint Sergius of Rusafa (Sergiopolis) in the Sasanian empire and the popularity of this saint with Chosroes II and Shirin, see G. Wiessner, "Christlicher Heiligenkult im Umkreis eines sassanidischen Großkönigs", *Festgabe deutscher Iranisten zur 2500 Jahrfeier Irans*, ed. W. Eilers (Stuttgart, 1971), pp. 141–55.

[88] For Shubhalmaran's life and literary heritage (mainly in the field of monastic spirituality), see Baumstark, *Geschichte*, p. 133. D.J. Lane has published several articles on Shubhalmaran's works; cf. Lane, "Admonition and Analogy: 13 Chapters from Šubhalmaran", *Aram* 5 (1993), p. 277, n. 1. It is interesting to note that Shubhalmaran's expositions in the field of Christology do not show the influence of Babai's Christology of the two hypostases in Christ; cf. Lane, "A Nestorian Creed: The Creed of Šubhalmaran", *V Symposium Syriacum 1988*, OCA 236, ed. R. Lavenant (Rome, 1990), pp. 155–62.

with George, being the delegation's most prominent mouth-piece at
the court, jointly put up a vehement resistance against Gabriel's
action, the court-physician took revenge on George, denouncing him
as an apostate from Zoroastrianism.[89]

We do not propose here to enter into the sequel of the story of
George's *martyrion*,[90] but shall confine ourselves to some characteristics of Babai's picture. It is entirely clear that George was a victim
of ecclesiastical power politics. Gabriel of Sinjar, knowing George's
antecedents, took advantage of the latter's weak spot, and success-
fully tried to eliminate his opponent by resorting to the State's law
of apostasy. As such, George may be labelled as a martyr for his
(East Syrian) Church, perhaps the only martyr in the Sasanian empire
who fell victim to the intrigues of a fellow-Christian, who belonged
to the rival Monophysite community. But was George a martyr for
"Nestorian" orthodoxy? Babai clearly wishes to have the readers or
auditors of the *Life of George* believe that George was indeed a martyr for the "Nestorian" Christology. After George's rebuke of Gabriel,
Babai suddenly brings the "cursed Henanians" back upon the scene,
saying that they supported Gabriel in his striving to have George
crucified, and suggesting that the "Henanians" welcomed this opportunity of getting rid of such a formidable defender of "Nestorianism".[91]
The theme returns in the words through which Babai makes Gabriel
bring the charge against George before the shah:

> One of the priests, who is with them, has reviled the king. He once
> was a Magian, was even honoured by Your Majesty and was minis-
> tering before Thee. Behold! he abandoned (all) these things, went away
> and became a Christian. And it was not enough for him that he was
> left alive by Thee, but he returned with all presumption to the court
> of Your Majesty and he is *a fervent advocate of the Nestorians*, and he also
> exhorts the bishops and the others.[92]

However, as appears from the following account in Babai's work, it
is not George's "Nestorianism" which bothered the shah so much,

[89] LG, pp. 519–22; Braun, pp. 259–60. At the instigation of Gabriel of Sinjar
Shubhalmaran was imprisoned and subsequently exiled by Chosroes (he died in
exile); *Chronicle of Seert*, ed. Scher, II/2, p. 539 [219]; Isho'denah, ed. Chabot, *Le
livre de la chasteté*, p. 36 (text), p. 31 (transl.).
[90] For an English translation of the discussion between George and the Rad (chief
of the inquisitors), see A.V. Williams, "Zoroastrians and Christians in Sasanian
Iran", *Bulletin of the John Rylands University Library of Manchester* 78.3 (1996), p. 52.
[91] LG, pp. 520–1; Braun, p. 259.
[92] LG, p. 522; Braun, p. 260.

but rather the circumstances under which George had converted to Christianity, and the actual reason for the present conflict between George and his court-physician.[93]

Mihr-Mah-Gushnasp-George was most certainly a faithful follower of the orthodoxy of his teacher and abbot, Babai the Great, the painter of his portrait. However, the picture of George, in which the features of his martyrdom for "Nestorian" orthodoxy are strongly emphasized, betrays the hand of the master, who intended not only to convince the spectators of the martyr's sanctity, but also to incite them "to follow in the footsteps of his orthodoxy". Thus the *Life of George* was to become one of the literary vehicles by which Babai's Christology would be diffused and propagated in the late Sasanian empire.[94]

BIBLIOGRAPHY

Abbeloos, J.B., "Deux manuscrits chaldéens inexplorés", *Le Muséon* 2 (1883), pp. 143–4.

Abramowski, L., Goodman, A.E., *A Nestorian Collection of Christological Texts*, University of Cambridge Oriental Publications 18–19 (Cambridge, 1972).

———, "Die Christologie Babais des Grossen", *Symposium Syriacum 1972*, OCA 197 (Rome, 1974), pp. 219–44.

———, "Babai der Grosse: Christologische Probleme und ihre Lösungen", *OCP* 41 (1975), pp. 289–343.

———, "Die Reste der syrischen Übersetzung von Theodor von Mopsuestia, de Incarnatione, in Add. 14.669", *Aram* 5 (1993), pp. 23–32.

Assfalg, J., *Verzeichnis der orientalischen Handschriften in Deutschland*, Bd. V: *Syrische Handschriften* (Wiesbaden, 1963).

Baumstark, A., *Geschichte der syrischen Literatur* (Bonn, 1922).

Bedjan, P., *Acta Martyrum et Sanctorum*, 7 vols. (Paris, 1890–97; photomech. repr. Hildesheim, 1968).

———, (ed.), *Histoire de Mar-Jabalaha, de trois autres patriarches, d'un prêtre et de deux laïques nestoriens* (Paris, 1895).

Boyce, M., *The Letter of Tansar* (Rome, 1968).

Braun, O., *Das Buch der Synhados oder Synodicon Orientale* (Wien, 1900).

———, *Ausgewählte Akten persischer Märtyrer*, Bibliothek der Kirchenväter 22 (Kempten/München, 1915).

Brock, S.P., "Christians in the Sasanian Empire: A Case of Divided Loyalties", *Religion and National Identity*, Studies in Church History 18, ed. S. Mews (Oxford, 1982), pp. 1–19; repr. in idem, *Syriac Perspectives on Late Antiquity* (London, 1984).

---

[93] LG, pp. 524–5; Braun, p. 261.

[94] L. Abramowski, "Die Reste der syrischen Übersetzung von Theodor von Mopsuestia, de Incarnatione, in Add. 14.669", *Aram* 5 (1993), p. 29, aptly observes, concerning Babai's *Life of George*: ". . . eine Märtyrerbiographie war ein gutes Mittel, diese Theologie (i.e. Babai's Christology of the two hypostases) auch bei nicht gelehrten Christen zu verbreiten."

————, "The Christology of the Church of the East in the Synods of the fifth to the early seventh centuries: preliminary considerations and materials", *Aksum-Thyateira. A Festschrift for Archbishop Methodios*, ed. G. Dragas (London, 1985), pp. 125–42; repr. in idem, *Studies in Syriac Christianity* (Aldershot, 1992).

Budge, E.A.W. (ed.), *The Book of the Governors* (London, 1893).

Chabot, J.B., *Le livre de la chasteté composé par Jésusdenah, évêque de Baçrah*, Extrait des Mélanges d'archéologie et d'histoire 16 (Rome, 1896).

————, "Histoire de Jésus-Sabran, écrite par Jésus-yab d'Adiabène", *Nouvelles archives des missions scientifiques et littéraires* 7 (1897), pp. 485–584.

————, (ed., transl.), *Synodicon Orientale ou recueil de synodes nestoriens*, Notices et extraits des manuscrits de la Bibliothèque Nationale et autres bibliothèques publiés par l'Académie des Inscriptions et Belles-Lettres 37 (Paris, 1902).

Chediath, G., *The Christology of Mar Babai the Great*, Oriental Institute of Religious Studies 49 (Kottayam, 1982).

————, "La contribution théologique de Mar Babai le Grand", *Istina* 40 (1995), pp. 83–94.

Christensen, A., *L'Iran sous les Sassanides* (Copenhagen, 1944²).

Delehaye, H., *Les passions des martyrs et les genres littéraires*, Studia Hagiographica 13B (Bruxelles, 1966).

Devos, P., "Les martyrs persans à travers leurs actes syriaques", *Atti del Convegno sul tema. La Persia e il mondo greco-romano*, Academia Nazionale dei Lincei, anno 363 (Rome, 1966), pp. 213–25.

Fiey, J.M., "Topography of al-Mada'in", *Sumer* 23 (1967), pp. 3–38.

————, *Assyrie chrétienne*, III, Recherches publiées sous la direction de l'Institut de Lettres Orientales de Beyrouth 42 (Beirut, 1968).

————, *Jalons pour une histoire de l'église en Iraq*, CSCO 310, Subs. 36 (Louvain, 1970).

Flusin, B., *Saint Anastase le Perse et l'histoire de la Palestine au début du VIIᵉ siècle*, I: Les textes; II: Commentaire (Paris, 1992).

Frend, W.H.C., *The Rise of the Monophysite Movement* (Cambridge/London/New York/Melbourne, 1972).

Gignoux, Ph., "Titres et fonctions religieuses sasanides d'après les sources syriaques hagiographiques", *Acta antiqua Academiae Scientiarum Hungaricae* 28 (1983), pp. 191–203.

Grumel, V., "Un théologien nestorien: Babai le Grand (VIe et VIIe s.)", *Échos d'Orient* 22 (1923), pp. 153–81, pp. 257–80; 23 (1924), pp. 9–33, pp. 162–77, pp. 257–74, pp. 395–99.

Guidi, I., *Chronica minora*, I, CSCO 1–2, Script. Syri 1–2 (Paris, 1903).

Guillaumont, A., *Les "Kephalaia Gnostica" d'Évagre le Pontique et l'histoire de l'Origénisme chez les Grecs et chez les Syriens*, Patristica Sorboniensia 5 (Paris, 1962).

Halleux, A. de, "La christologie de Martyrios-Sahdona dans l'évolution du nestorianisme", *OCP* 23 (1957), pp. 5–32.

Hoffmann, G., *Auszüge aus syrischen Akten persischer Märtyrer*, Abhandlungen für die Kunde des Morgenlandes 7.3 (Leipzig, 1880).

Hoyland, R.G., *Seeing Islam as Others Saw It. A Survey and Evaluation of Christian, Jewish and Zoroastrian Writings on Early Islam*, Studies in Late Antiquity and Early Islam 13 (Princeton, 1997).

Kaufhold, H., Review of *Répertoire des bibliothèques et des catalogues de manuscrits syriaques*, par Alain Desreumaux avec la collaboration de Françoise Briquel-Chatonnet (Paris, 1991), *Oriens Christianus* 76 (1992), pp. 244–52.

Labourt, J., *Le christianisme dans l'empire perse sous la dynastie sassanide (224–632)* (Paris, 1904).

Lane, D.J., "A Nestorian Creed: The Creed of Šubhalmaran", *V Symposium Syriacum 1988*, OCA 236, ed. R. Lavenant (Rome, 1990), pp. 155–62.

————, "Admonition and Analogy: 13 Chapters from Šubhalmaran", *Aram* 5 (1993), pp. 277–84.

Macomber, W.F., "New Finds of Syriac Manuscripts in the Middle East", *ZDMG*, Supplementa I, Teil 2 (Wiesbaden, 1969), pp. 473–82.

Mango, C., "Deux études sur Byzance et la Perse sassanide: II. Héraclius, Šahrvaraz et la Vraie Croix", *Travaux et Mémoires* 9 (1985), pp. 105–18.

Moffett, S.H., *A History of Christianity in Asia*, I: *Beginnings to 1500* (San Francisco, 1992).

Morony, M.G., *Iraq after the Muslim Conquest* (Princeton, 1984).

Nau, F., *Les Arabes chrétiens de Mésopotamie et de Syrie du VIIe au VIIIe siècle*, Cahiers de la société asiatique, première série, I (Paris, 1933).

Nöldeke, Th., "Die von Guidi herausgegebene Chronik", *Sitzungsberichte der kaiserlichen Akademie der Wissenschaften*, phil.-hist. Kl., 128/IX (Vienna, 1893), pp. 1–48.

Patrich, J., *Sabas, Leader of Palestinian Monasticism. A Comparative Study in Eastern Monasticism, Fourth to Seventh Centuries*, Dumbarton Oaks Studies 32 (Washington D.C., 1995).

Reinink, G.J., "'Edessa grew dim and Nisibis shone forth': The School of Nisibis at the transition of the sixth-seventh century", *Centres of Learning. Learning and Location in Pre-Modern Europe and the Near East*, eds. J.W. Drijvers, A.A. MacDonald (Leiden, 1995), pp. 77–89.

————, "Tradition and the Formation of the "Nestorian" Identity in 6th–7th Century Iraq", forthcoming in the *Proceedings of the Fourth Workshop on Late Antiquity and Early Islam. Patterns of Communal Identity in the Late Antique and Early Islamic Near East*, London, 5–7 May 1994.

Rist, J., "Die Verfolgung der Christen im spätantiken Sasanidenreich: Ursachen, Verlauf und Folgen", *Oriens Christianus* 80 (1996), pp. 17–42.

Rompay, L. van, "La littérature exégétique syriaque et le rapprochement des traditions syrienne-occidentale et syrienne-orientale", *Parole de l'Orient* 20 (1995), pp. 221–35.

Scher, A., "Notice sur les manuscrits syriaques et arabes conservés à l'archevêché chaldéen de Diarbékir", *Journal Asiatique*, 10e sér., 10 (1907), pp. 331–62, pp. 385–431.

————, *Histoire nestorienne (chronique de Séert)*, II/2, PO 13.4 (Paris, 1918).

Scipioni, L., *Ricerche sulla cristologia del "Libro di Eraclide di Nestorio"* (Freiburg, 1956).

Spencer Trimingham, J., *Christianity among the Arabs in Pre-Islamic Times* (London/New York, 1979).

Stratos, A.N., *Byzantium in the Seventh Century*, I: 602–634, transl. by M. Ogilvie-Grant (Amsterdam, 1968).

Tamcke, M., *Der Katholikos-Patriarch Sabrišo' I. (596–604) und das Mönchtum*, Europäische Hochschulschriften, Reihe XXIII, Theologie 302 (Frankfurt aM./Bern/New York, 1988).

Vaschalde, A., *Babai magni liber de unione*, CSCO 79–80, Script. Syri 34–35 (Louvain, 1915).

Vööbus, A., *Syriac and Arabic Documents Regarding Legislation Relative to Syrian Ascetism*, Papers of the Estonian Theological Society in Exile 11 (Stockholm, 1960).

————, *History of the School of Nisibis*, CSCO 266, Subs. 26 (Louvain, 1965).

Vosté, J.-M., "Notes sur les manuscrits syriaques de Diarbekir et autres localités d'Orient", *Le Muséon* 50 (1937), pp. 345–51.

Wiessner, G., *Untersuchungen zur syrischen Literaturgeschichte* I: *Zur Märtyrerüberlieferung aus der Christenverfolgung Schapurs II*, Abhandlungen der Akademie der Wissenschaften in Göttingen, philol.-hist. Klasse, 3. Folge 67 (Göttingen, 1967).

————, "Christlicher Heiligenkult im Umkreis eines sassanidischen Großkönigs", *Festgabe deutscher Iranisten zur 2500 Jahrfeier Irans*, ed. W. Eilers (Stuttgart, 1971), pp. 141–55.

Williams, A.V., "Zoroastrians and Christians in Sasanian Iran", *Bulletin of the John Rylands University Library of Manchester* 78.3 (1996), pp. 37–53.

Wright, W., *Catalogue of the Syriac Manuscripts in the British Museum* (London, 1872).

SPIRITUAL AUTHORITY AND MONASTICISM IN CONSTANTINOPLE DURING THE DARK AGES (650–800)

Peter Hatlie

University of Groningen

Although spiritual authority and "the holy" remain fertile topics for discussion among early Christian and late antique scholars, it receives considerably less attention from Byzantinists working in the generations to follow.[1] What has become a powerful tool of historical analysis for one scholarly community is therefore largely relegated to the tool-chest in the other—a curious incongruity to be sure. But what might lie behind it? The relative dearth of sources in general and hagiography in particular for the later period in the East may serve to explain some loss of focus. Nor can it be denied that with the advent of the seventh century in the East we have crossed a decisive historical boundary of sorts, between Antiquity and the Middle Ages, and one civilization and its world views to the next.[2] If such a transition occurred at all, however, it must have been somewhat gradual. Indeed, as far as "the holy" is concerned, the tenacity of the older tradition still seems alive and well as late as the third quarter of the seventh century in the person of Maximos the Confessor, a monk and holy man *par excellence* throughout his younger years who meets a tragic death at the hands of the official church and state only very late in life.[3] Perhaps it should be argued that the case of Maximos, notably his journey from renowned holy man to condemned criminal, brings us to the very border-crossing itself between the late antique "holy" and whatever form(s) of holiness

---

[1] For the purposes of this study, I take such terms as spiritual authority, religious charisma, and the much-used "the holy" to be roughly synonymous. All primary sources cited below observe the following format: page(s). line(s) or column(s).

[2] Cf. Robert A. Markus, *The End of Ancient Christianity* (Cambridge, 1990); John F. Haldon, *Byzantium in the Seventh Century. The Transformation of a Culture* (Cambridge, 1990).

[3] For Maximos' life, see Andrew Louth, *Maximus the Confessor* (London/New York, 1996), esp. pp. 3–18. For contemporary descriptions of Maximos as "servant of God" (*doulos theou*) and "holy man" (*haghios anthropos*), see *Relatio motionis*, in PG 90, 112A–B.

that came to follow? This may be an interesting idea, though not
one shared by scholars at large. The truth is that figures such as
Maximos and other holy men and women like him do not normally
figure into the annals of spiritual authority in contemporary scholarship.[4] The question—now perhaps as much a historiographic as
historical one—is why.

The modern historian Peter Brown is widely credited with fram-
ing modern discussions on late antique holiness. His influence in this
subfield of studies has been keenly felt for the better part of the last
quarter century, beginning with his now famous essay of 1971, "The
Rise and Function of the Holy Man in Late Antiquity".[5] This essay
examined the extraordinary phenomenon of holy men in Mediterranean
society and religion from the third through the sixth centuries. In
hindsight, it seems obvious to ask whether the phenomenon documented for earlier centuries could be seen to have continued into
the Byzantine age proper, i.e. the seventh century and beyond.[6] Yet
Byzantine scholars working in later periods seem to have taken little immediate notice of the implications of Brown's findings for their
own studies. Preoccupied with a host of seemingly more pressing historiographic issues—be it the theological struggles and social and
economic transformation of the seventh century, or the advent of
Iconoclasm in the eighth—they were not inclined to put his insights
to the test in greater depth.[7] Nor was Brown himself immediately
interested in treating this problem systematically. In the 1971 article he remained fairly tentative about what was to come, noting only
that in subsequent centuries, "his [the holy man's] decline—or rather
the levelling off of the trajectory of his ascent—coincides with the
reassertion of a new sense of the majesty of the community".[8] About
the holy man in the later East we learn very little more from Brown

---

[4] See the series of commemorative articles about the early Christian and Late
Antiquity "holy" published in *JECS* 6.3 (Fall 1998).

[5] Peter Brown, "The Rise and Function of the Holy Man in Late Antiquity",
JRS 61 (1971), pp. 80–101.

[6] Earlier boundaries explored by Robert Kirschner, "The Vocation of Holiness
in Late Antiquity", *Vig. Chr.* 38 (1984), pp. 105–24; Garth Fowden, "The Pagan
Holy Man in Late Antique Society", *JHS* 102 (1982), pp. 33–59.

[7] Yet see Han J.W. Drijvers, "Hellenistic and Oriental Origins", *The Byzantine
Saint. The University of Birmingham Fourteenth Spring Symposium of Byzantine Studies*, ed.
Sergei Hackel (London, 1981), pp. 25–33; Evelyn Patlagean, "Sainteté et Pouvoir",
ibidem, pp. 88–105.

[8] "Rise and Function", p. 100. See also Peter Brown, "Eastern and Western
Christendom in Late Antiquity: A Parting of the Ways?", *The Orthodox Churches and*

until another article appeared in 1973, the somewhat controversial "A Dark Age Crisis: Aspects of the Iconoclast Controversy."[9] Abandoning his early reticence, Brown's 1973 article now treated the seventh and eighth centuries directly. His aim was evidently nothing less than to solve the long-standing problem over the origins and development of Iconoclasm, a problem he saw as intimately connected with the issues of holiness and its perception that he had taken up for earlier centuries.

How intimate was this connection in Brown's mind? Reduced to its barest form, his method was seemingly to export his late antique holy man into the Byzantine empire on the eve of Iconoclasm—that is, to the late seventh and early eighth centuries—and trace the new contours and eventual implications of that event. As we see them now, some one or two hundred years after their heyday, our holy men are no longer the stunning charismatics of old. They are still individualists of a sort, but in order to accomplish their famed mediation between God and humanity they now rely on icons and relics. These holy objects now command the high ground of spiritual authority, also doing the often necessary if controversial social, political and relief work that the famed holy men of old once did in times of need and trouble.[10] Accordingly our holy men—who are now mostly conventional monks—have come down just slightly in the world. No longer powerful in their own right, they have had to settle for the role of being the guardians, purveyors and promoters of these objects.[11] Worse still, even this very status will soon be challenged with the advent of Iconoclasm when, through a complex set of circumstances, holy men, together with the holy objects they cherish and protect, become the putative scapegoats for an almost universal sense of anxiety and demoralization pervading seventh-century Byzantium.

---

the West, Studies in Church History 13 (Oxford, 1976), pp. 1–24; repr. in idem, Society and the Holy in Late Antiquity (London, 1982), pp. 166–95.

[9] Peter Brown, "A Dark Age Crisis. Aspects of the Iconoclast Controversy", The English Historical Review 346 (1973), pp. 1–34.

[10] A case in point, the defence of Constantinople against the Perso-Avar siege of 626. See Chronicon Paschale, ed. L. Dindorf (Bonn, 1832), p. 725; transl. by Michael and Mary Whitby, Chronicon Paschale 284–628 A.D. Translated with Notes and Introduction, Translated Texts for Historians 7 (Liverpool, 1989), pp. 179–80. Theophanes, Chronographia, 2 vols., ed. C. de Boor (Leipzig, 1883–5), p. 316; transl. by C. Mango and R. Scott, The Chronicle of Theophanes Confessor (Oxford, 1997), p. 447.

[11] Brown, "Dark Age Crisis", pp. 9–23, esp. p. 14: "The holy man, therefore, was the impresario of the piety that focuses on the icon, as it had focused on himself, as the tangible presence of an intercessor before God."

What follows in the eighth century is first the destruction of icons and then the persecution against monks, a process which Brown characterized as a "cleaning away of undergrowth in a well-established forest". Put more plainly, the ambitious eighth-century Isaurian emperors Leo III and Constantine V wage war against both icons (*iconomachê*) and monks (*monachomachê*) as part of a plan to solidify their power base within the empire and return security and prosperity to the Byzantine citizenry.[12]

Brown's celebrated interpretations of earlier holy men notwithstanding, the ideas put forth in this 1973 article received decidedly mixed reviews within Byzantine scholarly circles. At the heart of these reviews was the matter of his identification of the destruction of icons (*iconomachê*) with that of monks (*monomachê*). Some of the criticism and qualifications were fair, others rather overblown. On the whole, though, specialists in the field were seemingly taken with surprise by this sudden intrusion of Late Antiquity on to their Byzantine soil and consequently found constructive, sustained engagement with Brown's ideas difficult.[13] In short, the basic problem of holy men and their interactions with society in the period after Late Antiquity was left in suspense, renewed in a daring way by Brown on the one hand, yet all but buried by his critics on the other. Seemingly deferring to both sides, subsequent scholarship tended to steer clear of this thorny question.[14]

---

[12] Ibidem, pp. 28–34, and (for the quotation) p. 28.

[13] Compare Leslie W. Barnard, *The Graeco-Roman and Oriental Background of the Iconoclast Controversy* (Leiden, 1974), pp. 63–5; Patrick Henry, "What was the Iconoclast Controversy all about?", *Church History* 45 (1976), pp. 21–2, 28–31; Peter Schreiner, "Legende und Wirklichheit in der Darstellung des byzantinischen Bilderstreites", *Saeculum* 27 (1976), p. 174, esp. n. 62; John F. Haldon, "Some Remarks on the Background to the Iconoclast Controversy", *Byzantinoslavica* 38 (1977), pp. 161–3; Sebastian P. Brock, "Iconoclasm and the Monophysites", *Iconoclasm. Papers given at the Ninth Spring Symposium of Byzantine Studies, University of Birmingham, March 1975*, eds. A. Bryer, J. Herrin (Birmingham, 1977), p. 57 n. 47; Hélène Ahrweiler, "The Geography of the Iconoclast World", *Iconoclasm*, pp. 25–6; David Freedburg, "The Structure of Byzantine and European Iconoclasm", *Iconoclasm*, p. 173; Stephen Gero, *Byzantine Iconoclasm during the Reign of Constantine V* (Louvain, 1977), p. 140, esp. n. 115; idem, "Byzantine Iconoclasm and Monachomachy", *JEH* 28 (1977), pp. 247–8.

[14] Though see for the sixth and seventh centuries, Haldon, *Byzantium in the Seventh Century*, pp. 293–5, pp. 348–53; Gilbert Dagron, "L'église et la chrétienté byzantines entre les invasions et l'iconoclasme (vii*e*–début viii*e* siècle)", *Histoire du Christianisme des origines à nos jours*, Tome III: *Évêques, Moines et Empereurs (610–1054)*, eds. J.-M. Mayeur, C. et L. Piétri, A. Vauchez, M. Venard (Paris, 1993), pp. 80–4; for the eighth and ninth centuries, Kathryn M. Ringrose, "Monks and Society in Iconoclast Byzantium", *Byzantine Studies/Études Byzantines* 6 (1979), pp. 130–51.

The purpose of this paper is to revisit the issue of spiritual authority in the post late antique period. Its point of departure, shared with Brown, is the proposition that "the holy" is also a useful category of analysis for our understanding of Byzantine society and religion during the iconoclast age. This treatment will be different from Brown's, however, in one crucial respect: it will seek to avoid linking the issue of spiritual authority too closely to that of the phenomenon we have come to call Iconoclasm, the seemingly all-consuming problem of icons and the immediate struggles over them during the eighth and early ninth centuries.[15] The tendency to make Iconoclast reforms the central if not exclusive concern of the age is one that many have succumbed to, not merely in their examination of religion and society,[16] but also in such areas as the economy, internal politics and international relations.[17] What is required instead are examinations of eighth and early ninth-century society in its own right, removed from considerations of Iconoclasm to such an extent as is possible and appropriate. To be sure the nature of existing sources presents enormous problems of interpretation. In their studies of the era scholars are invariably constrained to sift through ideologically-loaded material, generated from one of the two parties in the Iconoclast debate, rather than dealing with sources which reflect the realities and concerns of society more directly.[18] The challenge of separating developments in Iconoclasm from other events in the age is therefore a real and difficult one. Still a shift away from the axiom, "Iconoclasm is everything, and everything is Iconoclasm", is slowly taking place.[19] Military and economic historians,[20] as well as

---

[15] For purposes of clarity, this article will adopted the words "Iconoclasm/Iconoclast" to refer to the historiographic phenomenon, the words "iconoclasm/iconoclast" for the chronological period in question, i.e. the years 726–787.

[16] See in particular, Eleonora Kountoura-Galakê, *The Byzantine Clergy and Society in the Dark Centuries* (Athens, 1996) (in Greek).

[17] E.g. George Ostrogorsky, *History of the Byzantine State*, transl. by Joan Hussey (New Brunswick, 1969), pp. 160ff.; Milton Anastos, "Iconoclasm and Imperial Rule 717–842", *The Cambridge Medieval History*, ed. Joan M. Hussey, vol. 4.1 (Cambridge, 1966), pp. 61–105.

[18] J. Karayannopoulos-Günter Weiss, *Quellenkunde zur Geschichte von Byzanz (324–1453)*, 2 vols. (Wiesbaden, 1982), vol. 2, esp. pp. 319–66. See also, e.g. Schreiner, "Legende und Wirklichkeit"; F. Winkelmann, W. Brandes (eds.), *Quellen zur Geschichte des frühen Byzanz (4.–9. Jahrhundert)* (Berlin, 1987; reprint Amsterdam, 1990).

[19] For example, recent scholarship has identified many Byzantines from the iconoclast age who travelled seemingly effortlessly between Iconoclast and Iconodule circles. For this view, see esp. Paul Speck, *Kaiser Konstantin VI. Die Legitimation einer fremden und der Versuch einer eigenen Herrschaft* (München, 1978), pp. 63–72.

[20] Mark Whittow, *The Making of Orthodox Byzantium, 600–1025* (Basingstoke/

scholars concerned with education and learning,[21] are among the outstanding examples, whereas social and religious history arguably continues to lag behind.[22] When it comes to Byzantine monasticism, in particular, few scholars have managed to separate themselves from larger Iconoclast debates. To the extent that monasticism is treated at all—institutionally, socially, economically, even religiously, including the question of "spiritual authority"—it is usually in the learned footnotes of a work heading in another direction.[23]

In what follows I will attempt to follow the successors of Brown's "holy men" into the later seventh and eighth centuries, to trace, if not their rise, then at least their function. The basic goal is to broaden our understanding of the specific context in which holy men and women endeavored to exercise spiritual authority, and then document the results of their efforts. The focus will mainly be on Constantinople during the first stage of Iconoclasm (until the Council of Nicaea, 787), and some attention will be focused upon the larger debate about monks and the Iconoclast controversy itself. For I do think that what we find out about the function of monks in the period, especially the nature and degree of spiritual authority they seem to have commanded, does ultimately help to clarify events and tendencies within the wider world of religion and politics.

Let me begin with two anecdotes from the period relevant to the problem of spiritual authority. The first regards a certain Philaretos

---

Hampshire, 1996); Michel Kaplan, *Les hommes et la terre à Byzance du vi⁰ au xi⁰ siècle. Propriété et exploitation du sol* (Paris, 1992).

[21] Paul Lemerle, *Byzantine Humanism. The First Phase*, transl. by H. Lindsay and A. Moffat (Canberra, 1986), pp. 81–169; Cyril Mango, "The Availability of Books in the Byzantine Empire, A.D. 750–850", *Byzantine Books and Bookmen. A Dumbarton Oaks Colloquium* (Washington D.C., 1975), pp. 29–45; Patricia Karlin-Hayter, "Où l'abeille butine. La culture littéraire monastique à Byzance aux viiie et ixe siècles", *Revue Bénédictine* 109 (1993), pp. 99–116.

[22] Evelyn Patlagean, "Vers une nouvelle Byzance? (milieux viie–ixe siècles)", *Le Moyen Age*, ed. R. Fossier, vol. 1 (Paris, 1982–3), pp. 283–330.

[23] Recent notable exceptions in Denise Papachryssanthou, "La vie monastique dans les campagnes byzantines du viiie au xe siècle. Ermitages, groupes, et communautés", *Byzantion* 43 (1973), pp. 158–80; Michel Kaplan, "Les moines et leurs biens fonciers à Byzance du viiie au xe siècle: acquisition, conservation et mise en valeur", *Revue Bénédictine* 109 (1993), pp. 209–23; Gilbert Dagron, "Économie et société chrétienne (viiie–xe siècles)", *Histoire du Christianisme des origines à nos jours*, Tome III: *Évêques, Moines et Empereurs (610–1054)*, eds. J.-M. Mayeur, C. et L. Piétri, A. Vauchez, M. Venard (Paris, 1993), pp. 241–95. The recent book of Michel Kaplan, *La Chrétienté byzantine du début du viie siècle au milieu du xie siècle. Images et reliques, moines et moniales, Constantinople et Rome* (Paris, 1997), came to my attention too late to be considered for this article.

the Merciful, a man born of rich parents near the city of Amnia in Paphlagonia in the year 702.[24] He inherited great wealth, including lands, servants, animals. Then, after a successful marriage and children, his increasing concern for the difficult lot of his neighbors in the face of frequent Arab military raids in the area together with the inner stirrings of Christian piety led him to give away his worldly goods at an alarming rate. Before long he had given away absolutely everything—down to the last goat, the beehives and honey, as well as his last tunic—and his wife, children and now grandchildren were not amused. Then divine good fortune struck. Philaretos' granddaughter Maria won a nation-wide beauty contest, elevating her to the status of imperial empress no less, and also bringing the entire family to Constantinople.[25] The once impoverished grandfather Philaretos thus became rich again. Still mindful of his Christian duties, however, he gave regularly to the needy of the City and apparently had a good influence on the emperor in this regard. He died in 792 at the age of ninety with either insignificant or no miracles to his credit. At his own request his body was interred in a women's monastery in Constantinople which had earlier been the object of his patronage.

A virtual contemporary of Philarctos is Stephen the Younger.[26] Stephen was born in Constantinople of comfortable but non-noble parents around the year 714.[27] During his infancy the parents kept an eye out for an attractive monastery, having concluded that his birth was miraculous and that dedicating their son to God's service was the least they could do. By the time he had come of age, around 730, Iconoclasm had begun and the City's monasteries were reportedly "in disarray",[28] so they decided to send him to a monastery

---

[24] "The Life of Philaretos", in *La Vie de S. Philarete*, eds. M.-H. Fourmy, M. Leroy, *Byzantion* 9 (1934), pp. 85–111 (introduction), pp. 112–170 (text and French translation). For Philaretos' family background, ibidem, pp. 113.4–115.8. See also Marie-France Auzépy, "De Philarète, de sa famille et de certains monastères de Constantinople", *Les saints et leur sanctuaire à Byzance. Textes, images et monuments*, Byzantina Sorbonensia 11 (Paris, 1993), pp. 117–35.

[25] Speck, *Kaiser Konstantin VI*, pp. 203–10, pp. 252–3.

[26] "The Life of Stephen the Younger", in *La Vie d' Étienne le Jeune par Étienne le Diacre, introduction, édition et traduction*, ed. Marie-France Auzépy (Aldershot, 1997), pp. 1–84 (introduction), pp. 85–178 (Greek text), pp. 179–277 (annotated French translation).

[27] On Stephen's parents, "Life of Stephen", p. 91.14–21. Cf. Kountoura-Galakê, *Clergy and Society*, pp. 191–2.

[28] "Life of Stephen", p. 101.21.

away from Constantinople. For a number of years, Stephen studied
with a hermit named John on Mt. Auxentios (modern Kash Daği)
in the diocese of Chalcedon before succeeding him as chief hermit
of the Mountain. Between his arrival in 730 and the explosive events
of the early 760s nothing of great note seems to have happened.
Predictably, Stephen's ascetic prowess won him a small following of
disciples, he oversaw the activities of the nearby female monastery,
he sponsored some building projects, and entertained occasional visitors to the Mountain. Miracles are conspicuous by their absence:
only his training of a rather miraculous messenger dog and his cure
of a neighboring abbot through prayer and strong drink seem to
qualify. Before long, however, Stephen was—rather surprisingly, it
must be admitted—the empire's worst criminal. Sometime around
763 his trials began, and when it was all over he had been exiled,
interrogated incessantly, and finally dragged through the streets of
Constantinople and ritually murdered by a mob. His enemies threw
what remained of his decapitated body into a grave for political
criminals. His head, an important relic, disappeared under mysteri-
ous circumstances.

While the above stories might be called anecdotes, in fact they
are much more than that. Sources for the eighth century are fairly
rare, and the *vitae* from which these two stories are drawn are among
a handful of accounts available for Constantinople.[29] Importantly,
they also turn out to be among the very few direct narrative accounts
of spiritual authority in action.[30] So, given their importance, it is
worth asking what the message is of these *vitae*, and is it a representative one?

It will be observed first that one of the men is a noble and the
other a commoner, which suggests the possibility of some social diversity in the pool of spiritual authority.[31] This evidence gains particu-

---

[29] Compare Patlagean, "Sainteté et Pouvoir", pp. 92–101; Ihor Sevcenko, "Hagiography of the Iconoclast Period", *Iconoclasm, Papers given at the Ninth Spring Symposium
of Byzantine Studies, University of Birmingham, March 1975*, eds. A. Bryer, J. Herrin
(Birmingham, 1977), pp. 113–33; repr. in idem, *Ideology, Letters and Culture in the
Byzantine World* (London, 1986), pp. 1–42; Marie-France Auzépy, "L'analyse littéraire
et l'historien: l'example des vies de saints iconoclastes", *Byzantinoslavica* 53 (1992),
pp. 57–67. For a comprehensive bibliographic review of the *vitae* of practically all
eighth-century holy men and women, Kountoura-Galakê, *Clergy and Society*, pp. 14–22.
[30] On Stephen, Auzépy, *Vie d'Étienne*, esp. pp. 17–8, pp. 38–42. On Philaretos,
Sevcenko, "Hagiography", p. 126; Patlagean, "Sainteté et Pouvoir", pp. 100–1.
[31] Evidence for the social backgrounds of monks and nuns in the early eighth

lar significance when we consider the social profiles of some of the more prominent spiritual heroes in Constantinople's earlier history.[32] Very few humbly-born figures appear in that history. Among the few is a certain Barnabas of the important Monastery of Bassianos in the late fifth and early sixth century who prior to becoming a monk was a theatre performer, a notoriously lower-class form of employment.[33] Another is Andrew the Fool, a Scythian and former slave by birth, who reportedly lived during the same age, though as we know his *vita* seems to have been written much later—in the mid tenth century—and is widely considered to be a work of pure fiction. It therefore may better reflect upon tenth—or even eighth and ninth—century prides and prejudices than those of the early Byzantine age.[34] When we look beyond these two examples of humbly-born men who did well for themselves, the profiles become uniformly upper-class. For the seventh century, the noble social background of Maximos the Confessor is noteworthy.[35] For the fifth through sixth centuries the situation looks fairly similar, including such nobly born figures as Hypatios of the Rufinianae monastery,[36] Alexander of the "Non-Sleepers" monastery,[37] the famous cross-dresser Matrona,[38] St. Elizabeth

---

century is scanty. In addition to the mother and sister of Stephen ("Life of Stephen", p. 107.5–19), for another probable non-noble see "The Life of Anna the Younger (alt. Euphemianos)", in *Synaxarium Ecclesiae Constantinopolae, Propylaeum ad Acta Sanctorum Novembris*, ed. II. Delehaye, October 29, pp. 173–4.16–23. For a nobly born nun of *c*. 755, note Anne of the Trichinarea Monastery, see "Life of Stephen", pp. 115.8–116.31. Toward *c*. 760 onwards monastic leaders both from Constantinople and elsewhere, with some exceptions, increasingly came from privileged backgrounds, a fact observed by Kountoura-Galakê, *Clergy and Society*, pp. 163–74, pp. 186–9, pp. 196–202, p. 222.

[32] For an introduction to this problem for the earlier centuries, see Michel Kaplan, "L'hinterland religieux de Constantinople: moines et saints de banlieue d'après l'hagiographie", *Constantinople and Its Hinterland. Papers from the Twenty-Seventh Spring Symposium of Byzantine Studies, Oxford, April 1993*, Society for the Promotion of Byzantine Studies Publications 3, eds. Cyril Mango, Gilbert Dagron (Aldershot, 1995), pp. 191–205; Helen Saradi, "Constantinople and Its Saints (IVth–Vth c.). The Image of the City and Social Considerations", *Studi medievale* 36 (1995), pp. 87–110.

[33] "The Life of St. Matrona", in *Acta Sanctorum Novembris* 3 (Brussels, 1910), p. 792.

[34] Nikephoros the Priest, "The Life of Andrew the Fool", in *The Life of St. Andrew the Fool. Text, Translation, and Notes*, Acta Universitatis Uppsaliensis 4.2, ed. L. Rydén (Uppsala, 1995), prologue, p. 11.12–15 and p. 304 n. 1.

[35] "Life of Maximus", PG 90, 69A–B.

[36] Kallinikos the Monk, "The Life of Hypatios", in *Vie d'Hypatios*, ed. G.J.M. Bartelink, SC 177 (Paris, 1971), p. 72.

[37] "Life of Alexander of the Non-Sleepers", in "Vie d'Alexandre l'Acémète. Texte grec et traduction latine", ed. E. de Stoop, PO 6.5 (1911), pp. 660.14–661.7.

[38] "Life of Matrona", *Acta Sanctorum Novembris* 3 (Brussels, 1910), 792a.

the Wonder-Worker,[39] John Kalybites,[40] Theodore of Chora,[41] and finally St. Sampson of the great Constantinopolitan hospital.[42] They all came from very good families, well placed in the higher ranks of the military and civil bureaucracy or senatorial aristocracy. The chronographer Theophanes gives us a final illuminating glimpse of the mid fifth-century holy man:

> John, a man of consular rank surnamed Vincomalus, having implored the holy Bassianos, became a monk with him. He continued to go on processions in the palace as one of the senators and when he left [the palace] he was escorted as a consular as far as the monastery of Bassianos. But once inside the monastery, he immediately put on the monastic goat's-hair cloak and fulfilled his duties in the kitchen and the stable and in other work of this kind.[43]

John Vincomalus was a person of his times, at home in the conspicuously high-born world of Constantinopolitan monasticism. In search of other examples we have purposely refrained from underscoring the backgrounds of St. Daniel the Stylite (late fifth to early sixth centuries) and the third abbot of the "Non-Sleepers" monastery, Markellos—both of humble birth, apparently—,[44] as their cases bring up another interesting social question: the geographic and ethnic origins of early Byzantine saints. The latter individuals are therefore not upper-class individuals but neither are they home-grown Constantinopolitan material,[45] a point to return to below.

---

[39] "Life of Elizabeth the Wonder-Worker", in "Sainte Elisabeth d' Héraclée, abbesse à Constantinople", ed. François Halkin, *Anal. Boll.* 91 (1973), p. 252.1–2.

[40] "Life of John Kalybites", in "Ho Hagios Ioannes Ho Kalybites (Anekdota Keimena ek Parisinon Kodikon)", ed. Odysseus Lampsides, *Platon* 16 (1964), p. 262.1–17.

[41] "Life of Theodore of Chora", in "De S. Theodoro Monacho Hegumenoque Chorensi", ed. Chrysantho Loparev, *Zapiski klassicheskago otdel. imperatorskago russkago arkeologischeskago obschestva* 1 (1904), p. 3.1–15. Theodore is a semi-legendary figure, reportedly a relative of the empress Theodora, who was promoted to the senate and served out a distinguished career in the army before becoming a monk.

[42] "Life of Samson", in "Saint Samson le Xénodoque de Constantinople (VIe siècle)", ed. François Halkin, *Rivista di studi bizantini e neoellenici* n.s. 14–16 (1977–1979), pp. 8–9.

[43] Theophanes, *Chronographia*, p. 114; transl. Mango, *Chronicle*, p. 177.

[44] On Daniel, "Life of Daniel", in "The Life and Works of Our Holy Father, St. Daniel the Stylite", transl. by Elizabeth Dawes and Norman H. Baynes, *Three Byzantine Saints* (London/Oxford 1948; repr. 1977), p. 8; "Life of Markellos of the Non-Sleepers", in "La vie ancienne de Saint Marcel l'Acémète", ed. Gilbert Dagron, *Anal. Boll.* 86 (1968), p. 288.

[45] "Constantinople", in the event, defined as the city and its hinterland, esp.

Returning to their *vitae* for other clues about Stephen and Philaretos, another striking feature is that neither man spends much quality-time in Constantinople.[46] Both men—the one a monk, the other a lay holy man—opt instead to nurture their spiritual authority quite far away from the capital, whether by benefaction (Philaretos) or asceticism coupled with spiritual counselling and outreach (Stephen). Both men return to the city only in the very last years of their lives, and both—but especially Stephen—in some sense against their will. In light of what we have just seen above—that is, a number of spiritually gifted monks who populated the city and exerted authority in the fifth through mid seventh centuries—this trend appears strange, even disturbing. Of course there had always been plenty of monastic worthies who did what Philaretos and Stephen did, in effect bring their talents to Constantinople, for a limited period of time, whether it be out of Greece, out of deep Asia Minor or indeed from the Orient. These included St. Jonas of Thrace and St. Auxentios in the later fourth and fifth century,[47] and Theodore of Sykeon, Antiochos the African and David of Thessaloniki in the sixth.[48] One might add at this point the even more celebrated visits of Symeon the Stylite in the fifth century (by letter of course),[49] as well as those of Severus and Sabas in the early sixth.[50] These sorts of "provincial"

Thrace and Bithynia. For the various geographic "zones" of the empire, see the useful observations of Ihor Sevcenko, "Constantinople viewed from the Eastern Provinces in the Middle Byzantine Period", *Harvard Ukrainian Studies* 3–4 (1979–80), pp. 717–47, esp. pp. 717–21.

[46] On the background to this phenomenon, Kountoura-Galakê, *Clergy and Society*, pp. 167–72, pp. 213–8.

[47] "The Life of Hypatios", 80 (Jonas' origins in Armenia), 94 (trip to Constantinople); "Life of Auxentios", PG 114, 1380A (origins in Armenia), 1405A–D, 1411A (mediation at the Council of Chalcedon).

[48] "Life of Theodore of Sykeon", in *Vie de Théodore de Sykéôn*, ed. A.J. Festugiére, *Subsidia Hagiographica* 48 (Brussels, 1970) pp. 69.51ff.; transl. in *Three Byzantine Saints*, p. 145 (requesting aid to his monastic community); ibidem, pp. 60.56–61.6, transl. p. 137 (Antiochos' request for aid for his hometown, sacked by barbarians); "Life of David of Thessaloniki [BHG³ 493]", in *Leben des heiligen David*, ed. Valentine Rose (Berlin, 1887), pp. 9.17–13.2 and "Life of David [BHG³ 493d]", in "Anekdoton egkomion eis ton hosion David", ed. Basil Laourdes, *Makedonika* 10 (1970), pp. 249.15–251.33 (on David's request for aid from Justinian).

[49] Evagrius Scholasticus, *The Ecclesiastical History of Evagrius*, eds. J. Bidez, L. Parmentier (London, 1898; reprint Amsterdam, 1964), p. 22.11–29; p. 61.32–62.4.

[50] On Sabas: "Live of Sabas", in *Kyrillos von Skythopolis*, ed. E. Schwartz (Leipzig, 1939), pp. 139.20–147.9; *Parastaseis Syntomoi Chronikai*, in *Constantinople in the Early Eighth Century*, eds. Averil Cameron, Judith Herrin (Leiden, 1984), p. 60.2–3; "Life of Theodore of Chora", *De S. Theodoro Monacho Hegumenoque Chorensi*, ed. Chrysantho

holy men had always existed and sometimes managed to exert real influence in the City, and would continue to do so for centuries. They would not necessarily have been out of place in the eighth century.[51] What is more perplexing, however, is the apparent scarcity of any prominent holy men permanently at work in Constantinople for the later seventh and most of the eighth century.[52]

When we look for further signs of life in the City beyond the brief appearances of Philaretos and Stephen there is unfortunately not much to go on. Such evidence as there is for spiritual authority in action remains fairly ambiguous. At the turn of the seventh and advent of the eighth century, for example, there are no less than three monks—Paul of the Kallistratos monastery; Kyros, a hermit from Amastris; and Gregory of the Florus Monastery—who prophesied and then neatly facilitated the overthrow of one emperor and the succession of another; indeed, the above named Paul (or his replacement at the Kallistratos) performed this service twice, for two different emperors (Leontios, 695–8; Phillipikos, 711–13).[53] To be sure, these cases may strike the modern observer as a fairly cynical use of spiritual authority for political ends, especially when we hear that Paul was also an astronomer and Gregory formerly a high ranking military officer, and that both of them were "friends" with at least one of the usurping emperors prior to the deed in question (Leontios).[54] Is this indeed a picture of spiritual authority at work, then, or something else? The fact that religious issues seem to have

---

Loparev, *Zapiski klassichekago otdel. imperatorskago russkago arkeologischeskago obschestva* 1 (1904), p. xxiv, pp. 10.29–11.7. On Severus: Theophanes, *Chronographia*, p. 152.6–16, pp. 154.3ff.; Zachariah Rhetor, "Life of Severus", in *Vita Severi*, ed. M.-A. Kugener, PO 2.1 (1907), pp. 103–8.

[51] Though, see below, pp. 211–3.

[52] I find very little support in the sources for, and therefore take issue with, Kountoura-Galakê's picture (*Clergy and Society*, pp. 45–55) of an "uninterrupted presence" (*tên adialeiptê parousia*) of monasticism in the early to middle eighth-century Constantinople. Monks there certainly were, though neither in significant numbers nor in force.

[53] Theophanes, *Chronographia*, pp. 381.6ff. (on Paul, or another Kallistratou monk, alone); ibidem, p. 375.14–15 (on Kyros); ibidem, pp. 368.22ff., Nikephoros, Patriarch of Constantinople, *The Short History*, ed. Cyril Mango, *Corpus Fontium Historiae Byzantinae* 13 (Washington, 1990), pp. 94.7ff. (on Paul and Gregory). This evidence is discussed by Kountoura-Galakê, *Clergy and Society*, pp. 62–70 *passim*, pp. 93–4.

[54] For friendship in this age, see Peter Hatlie, "Friendship and the Byzantine Iconoclast Age", *Friendship and Friendship Networks in Medieval Europe*, ed. Julian Haseldine (London, 1998), forthcoming.

played a part in at least one of the cases,[55] and the good of the community and empire in the others,[56] may suggest that these prophet-monks were authentic leaders of a silent majority in Constantinople, possibly by virtue of their spiritual gifts. Other sources fail to cor-roborate this hypothesis, however, nor are there other manifest signs of spiritual authority at work among monks who were politically active in Constantinople in subsequent decades. On the contrary, the three other known case histories from the later eighth century prove to be equally ambiguous, with a certain monk Anastasios, Peter the Stylite or Peter of Blachernae, and Andrew Kalybites, all ending up as victims of state-sponsored persecution.[57] The question is whether there is a truly spiritual, charismatic man walking in the shoes of these victims of political murder. Just as in the above-men-tioned cases of Paul and Gregory, it would be instructive to know whether their entrance into the political arena derived from genuine charisma or merely the cheapest kind of self-interest and cronyism.

One final and indeed related question about the case-histories of Philaretos and Stephen—about whom, by contrast, we seem to know a great deal—remains. The question is why did men with such demonstrable charismatic gifts and such an obvious following each, in his own way, end so badly? When we last see Philaretos, he is comfortably housed in the imperial palace giving away his pocket money to beggars but otherwise living a fairly privileged life. Then, near to death, this benefactor *par excellence* prepares a very privileged burial for himself in a private tomb. His wife Theosebo followed Philaretos to the same tomb, making this a family foundation.[58] Moving to Stephen, a clear example of the political saint in Byzantium,

---

[55] The succession of Philippikos in 711 is followed by an imperial council con-demning the anti-monothelete legislation of the Council of 680–1.

[56] I.e. the unseating of the unstable Justinian II, both by Leontios (695) and Phillipikos (711).

[57] On Anastasios, *Parastaseis Syntomoi Chronikai*, in *Constantinople in the Early Eighth Century*, p. 140.7–10. For doubts about this account, see Mango and Scott, *Chronicle of Theophanes Confessor*, p. 598 n. 6. On Peter, Theophanes, *Chronographia*, p. 442.18–24; Stephen the Deacon, "Life of Stephen the Younger", in *La Vie d'Étienne le Jeune par Étienne le Diacre. Introduction, édition et traduction*, ed. M.-F. Auzépy (Aldershot, 1997), p. 162.10–15. On Andrew, Theophanes, p. 432.16–19. For doubts about the verac-ity of later accounts about Andrew, see Auzépy, "De Philarète", pp. 128–31 *passim*. For the hypothesis that Peter and Andrew may be the same person, cf. ibidem, pp. 130–1; Auzépy, *Vie d'Étienne*, p. 260 n. 384; Mango and Scott, *Chronicle of Theophanes Confessor*, p. 598 n. 6.

[58] Auzépy, "De Philarète", p. 122.7–34.

when we last see him he has lost his battle against imperial power and suffered the savage wrath of the people of Constantinople; his body lay in pieces on the street. There is precious little of his corpse left upon which to found a cult in his memory.[59]

A striking feature of these hagiographical details is the extent to which the authors of both works seem to betray their heroes in the closing chapters of their lives. When genre demands dictated that political saints should end up victorious (or at least still fighting) and benefactors die penniless, why is it that authors subvert the natural course of the narrative? The simplest answer—far too simple, of course[60]—is that the *vitae* may relate what really happened, or nearly so. The political saint Stephen the Younger came to Constantinople with a chance to defeat the emperor and win over the masses, just as many famous individual monks had done in the past. Yet contemporary realities thwarted this plan. Similarly, Philaretos witnessed the death of his hard-won vocation when his gift-giving efforts suddenly became formalistic and stale late in life. In both cases, the spiritual life proved far too weak to sustain itself in the later eighth century city. The lesson of these hagiographic tales, provided they are true or even partly true, is that there had been a decided shift in quality of holy men and the status of "the holy" since the early Byzantine period.[61]

In order to understand why this shift had taken place, the temptation is great of course to introduce Iconoclasm at this point, for

---

[59] On the fate of Stephen's head, for a while a known relic, "Life of Stephen the Younger", pp. 170.25–171.9, pp. 172.21–173.7, pp. 173.16–174.16. On this problem, Auzépy, *Vie d' Étienne*, p. 274 n. 448.

[60] For ideas on the motives and pretexts for the composition of these *vitae*, cf. (for Philaretos) Patlagean, "Sainteté et Pouvoir", pp. 100–1; Sevcenko, "Hagiography", p. 126; Auzépy, "De Philarète", p. 117; (for Stephen), George Huxley, "On the *Vita* of St. Stephen the Younger", *GRBS* 18 (1977), pp. 97–108; Vincenzo Ruggieri, "Note su schemi simbolic e letterari nella *Vita S. Stephani Junioris*", *Byzantion* 63 (1993), pp. 196–212; Auzépy, *Vie d' Étienne*, pp. 9–18, pp. 41–2; Peter Hatlie, "Some Intertexts of the *Vita Stephani Junioris*", *Modern Greek and Byzantine Studies* 22 (1998), pp. 200–14.

[61] For the earlier period, cf. Heinrich Bacht, "Die Rolle des orientalischen Mönchtums in den kirchenpolitisichen Auseinandersetzungen um Chalkedon (431–519)", *Das Konzil Von Chalkedon* II, eds. Aloys Grillmeier, Heinrich Bacht (Würzburg, 1954), pp. 193–314; Gilbert Dagron, "Les moines et la ville. Le monachisme à Constantinople jusqu'au concile de Chalcédoine (451)", *Travaux et Mémoires* 4 (1970), pp. 229–76 (repr. in *La romanité chrétienne en Orient. Héritages et mutations* [London, 1984]); Susan Ashbrook Harvey, *Asceticism and Society in Crisis. John of Ephesus and the Lives of the Eastern Saints* (Berkeley/Los Angeles/London, 1990), pp. 80–91.

either of two reasons. One reason, source considerations, would serve to explain the shifts I have identified simply as the result of a lack of testimonies: that is to say, the extant literature—*vitae*, chronographies, sermons, and so forth—does not tell the whole story. The whole story, according to this view, would instead have resided in the literature known to have been destroyed by iconodules after iconoclasm was concluded, and accordingly "the holy" may have been alive and well among iconoclasts in eighth-century Constantinople but we will never know about it.[62] A second way to approach the case histories of Stephen and Philaretos would be to go the way of Peter Brown and others in explaining that iconoclast emperors had themselves systematically rooted out all vital forms of "the holy" in the city, starting with the most powerful religious leaders and working their way down, and henceforth leaving no room for the activities of holy men. To accept this position one need not be so particular as to insist upon Brown's equivalency between the destruction of icons (*iconomachê*) and the destruction of monks (*monachomachê*). For the hypothesis still works if one accepts that monks and spiritual leaders of all sorts were simply unwelcome, for whatever reason, though not necessarily because of their attachment to icons. Stephen Gero, for example, one of Brown's most vocal critics, attributed the attacks on monks simply to the emperors' belief that monasticism was an unnatural and perverse way of life.[63] In the same vein, others have put forth economic arguments for the persecution of monks.[64] But whatever the motive, according to this view, the goal in persecuting holy men and women was to clear the undergrowth of a relatively flourishing monastic regime in the capital.

---

[62] The story of the early-eighth century monk and "astronomer" Paul (above, n. 53), who is characterized as a "heretic" possessing charismatic gifts, may be instructive in this regard even though it predates the iconoclast age by a few years. Equally intriguing and more to the point are the associates and advisors of the iconoclast emperors, some of whom are or were monks. See, e.g., the cases of Leo Kontzodaktylos, in Theophanes, *Chronographia*, p. 445.30; Pt. Constantine II, ibidem, p. 428.3–4; Nikephoros, *Short History*, p. 142.10; Sergios, "Life of Stephen the Younger", p. 131.14–18; George, ibidem, p. 139.16–24, pp. 140.12–141.4; Stephen, ibidem, pp. 145.25–148.11.

[63] Gero, *Byzantine Iconoclasm*, pp. 141–2; "Byzantine Iconoclasm and Monachomachy", pp. 246–7.

[64] N. Iorga, "Les origines de l'iconoclasme", *Études Byzantines* 2 (1940), pp. 225–45; François Masai, "La politique du Isauriens et la naissance de l'Europe", *Byzantion* 33 (1963), esp. pp. 193–210; Giorgio Ravegnani, "Motivi propogandistici iconoduli nel regno di Leone III e Constantino V in due cronache marciane inedite", *Studi Veneziani* 15:1973 (1975), esp. pp. 3–4, p. 16.

Such "Iconoclast" readings of the failures and tragedies of holy
men during the era have received the extensive attention of scholars, both prior and subsequent to Brown's 1973 article (noted above)
on the subject.[65] What these discussions generally have in common
is the proposition that Constantinopolitan holy men stood in a relatively privileged and strong position in eighth-century society, and
that their troubles during the age were in some sense the product
of their success: their very status as a clearly identifiable and successful group—however that is measured—made them a target for
the predatory tendencies of contemporary emperors as part of the
latter's extensive Iconoclast reforms. Given more space, it would be
useful to investigate the above claims more carefully. For the moment,
however, it seems useful to propose an alternative which seeks to
explain the plight of Constantinople's eighth-century holy men without reference to Iconoclasm.[66] According to this view the falling fortune of monks during the era was less the result of the action and
aggression of Iconoclasts as it was the product of some decisive and
on the whole debilitating developments within the monastic estate
itself. More specifically, "the holy" in eighth-century Constantinople,
whether it be iconodule or iconoclast, had simply become irrelevant.
It lay dormant and prostrate owing to the absence of either great
individual charismatic monastic leaders and well-organized, dynamic
monastic groups or a larger social and religious context capable of
sustaining and appreciating even average holy men for their merits.
It should be added that this state of affairs had not developed all
of the sudden, and by no means are Byzantium's eighth-century
emperors to blame. Rather the monks themselves and historical
changes were.

Let me very briefly suggest three explanations for this state of
affairs: one, social; the other, economic; and the last, institutional.

About eighth-century society, it is worth repeating the information garnered above from the *vitae* of Stephen and Philaretos which
suggested a shift in the social profiles of prominent eighth-century

---

[65] See, e.g., Alfred Lombard, *Constantin V, Empereur des Romains (740–775)* (Paris,
1902), esp. pp. 149–51; Schreiner, "Legende und Wirklichkeit"; Gero, "Byzantine
Iconoclasm and Monachomachy", pp. 241–8; Kountoura-Galakê, *Clergy and Society*,
esp. pp. 174–80.
[66] This article represents the preliminary sketch of a larger monograph on
Iconoclasm and society incorporating such a perspective on the period.

holy men in comparison to those who frequented Constantinople in earlier centuries.[67] Yet if it is true that monasticism no longer attracted dynamic members of upper-class society—at least not early in their careers—it also appears that it no longer drew any benefit or had any drawing power from being a rank of "outsiders". The ranks of prominent early Byzantine holy men had come to the City normally from foreign or exotic lands. These include those who adopted Constantinople as a permanent residence, such as Daniel the Stylite and the two abbots of the "Non-Sleepers" monastery, Alexander and Markellos,[68] as well as those famous holy men from the provinces who visited the city from time to time to great acclaim.[69] The early centuries of Constantinopolitan monasticism had been deeply marked by these and other "outsiders", immigrants from Egypt, Syria, Mesopotamia, Phrygria, Armenia, and other such exotic locations.[70]

So what had changed? For one thing, by the eighth century foreigners were everywhere, whether they be barbarian Goths, Slavo-Bulgarians and Armenians assimilated into the population over the course of earlier centuries, and notably those integrated into Byzantine armies,[71] or eastern monks, churchmen, and laity fleeing ignominiously for their lives in advance of the Persian and Arab invasions of the seventh century.[72] The effect of these demographic developments must have been to make the foreigner look more ordinary

---

[67] See above, pp. 202–4.

[68] On Daniel, "The Life of Daniel the Stylite", in *Les saints stylites*, ed. H. Delehaye, *Subsidia Hagiographica* 14 (Brussels, 1923), pp. ii–iii, 2.11–14, x, 10.13ff., transl. Elizabeth Dawes and Norman H. Baynes, *Three Byzantine Saints* (London/Oxford, 1948; repr. 1977), p. 8, pp. 12ff. On Alexander, "Life of Alexander", ed. E. de Stoop, v, 660.14–15. On Markellos: "Life of Markellos of the Non-Sleepers", ed. Gilbert Dagron, ii, 288, iii, 289.

[69] E.g. on Jonas the Thracian: Kallinikos the Monk, *Vie d'Hypatios*, ed. Bartelink, p. 80. On Hypatios of the Rufinianae: ibidem, p. 72. On Auxentios (who visits Chalcedon, not the City proper), "Life of St. Auxentios (BHG³ 199)", in PG 114, 1380A. On David of Thessaloniki: John Moschos, "Pratum spirituale", PG 87, 2321B; transl. by John Wortley, *The Spiritual Meadow of John Moschos*, Cistercian Studies Series 139 (Kalamazoo, 1992), pp. 52–3.

[70] Ashbrook Harvey, *Asceticism and Society*, pp. 80–91.

[71] See the series of studies on this theme by Peter Charanis, reprinted collectively in his *Studies on the Demography of the Byzantine Empire* (London, 1972), esp. essays I–V, XX–XXII. For the seventh century in particular, Haldon, *Byzantium in the Seventh Century*, pp. 355–60, pp. 387–99, esp. p. 390.

[72] For monks, in particular, cf. Derwas J. Chitty, *The Desert a City* (Oxford, 1966), pp. 145–63 *passim*; A. Vööbus, *History of Asceticism in the Syrian Orient*, CSCO 500, Subs. 81 (Louvain, 1988), pp. 303–24.

than he or she had in the past. Furthermore, and a corollary perhaps, the citizens of the empire and their more assimilated emperors were increasingly introverted in their own right, more comfortable with cultural conformity than diversity.[73] Hence the curiosity of the foreigner arguably no longer provoked the positive reception it once had, and indeed in some instances it may have sparked feelings of suspicion. Even the most holy Daniel the Stylite reportedly had troubles in this regard upon his arrival to the city in the later fifth century before winning over one and all to his side.[74] Subsequent centuries no doubt produced similar if not stronger reactions. Sources which mention such matters, though not always referring specifically to affairs in Constantinople and notoriously difficult to interpret, suggest the growing mood of intolerance nonetheless. They are full of frequent and biting allusions to, *inter alia*, demonic and slavish Ethiopians, rapacious Huns and Goths, trouble-making Scythians or Slavs, pleasure-loving Phrygians and Isaurians, and crafty Syrians. The Syrians come off the worst because of their strong associations with heresy.[75] But in all events it is clear that these general racial attitudes found their way into discourses about religion, and it is therefore reasonable to suppose that they also trickled into popular attitudes toward "the holy". The effect of this, we might suppose, was an unspoken taboo on foreign-born holy men and women by the eighth century. The implication of this new standard was of course the fact that outstanding eighth-century holy men and women needed to be home-

---

[73] Haldon, *Byzantium in the Seventh Century*, pp. 348–55, pp. 382–87.

[74] "Life of Daniel", pp. 17.1ff., pp. 27.17ff.; transl. Dawes and Baynes, *Three Byzantine Saints*, p. 16, 22–3.

[75] On Scythians: Nikephoros the Priest, *The Life of St. Andrew the Fool*, ed. Lennart Rydén, prologue, p. 11.12–15; *CSEL* (Wien, 1866), xxxv, pp. 644–5, pp. 648–9. On Ethiopians (a *locus classicus*): "Life of Andrew", p. 1.14–18; Leontios of Neapolis, "Life of Symeon the Fool", ed. Lennart Rydén, *Das Leben des heiligen Narren Symeon* (Uppsala, 1963), pp. 153–4, transl. by Derek Krueger, *Symeon the Holy Fool. Leontius' Life and the Late Antique City*, (Berkeley/Los Angeles/London, 1996), pp. 157–8. On Goths and Huns: "Life of Daniel the Stylite", p. 53; Joshua the Stylite, *The Chronicle of Joshua the Stylite*, transl. by W. Wright (Cambridge, 1882), p. 67, p. 72, pp. 72–3; Theophanes, *Chronographia*, pp. 386.5ff. On Isaurians and Phrygians (esp. the figure of Zeno), cf., with references, Pauline Allen, *Evagrius Scholasticus the Church Historian* (Louvain, 1981), pp. 121–2; Whitby and Whitby, *Chronicon Paschale*, p. 93 n. 303; see also Ps. Zachariah of Mitylene, *The Syriac Chronicle Known as that of Zachariah of Mitylene*, transl. by F.J. Hamilton and E.W. Brooks (London, 1899), pp. 150–1; "Life of Eustratios the Patriarch", PG 86, 2280A. On Syrians: Evagrius, *Ecclesiastical History*, p. 146.13–20; Theophanes, *Chronographia*, p. 402, p. 414, p. 429 *passim*; "Life of Stephen the Younger", p. 119.5–10, p. 132.1

grown—they needed in a sense to be prophets in their own country, with all the inherent difficulties involved in that enterprise.

Prophets there might eventually have been, if not for the marked shift in the monastic ideal over the last two centuries both within Constantinople and in the empire as a whole. The shifts in discipline that had taken place were truly momentous, so momentous that they cannot be documented in full here.[76] Suffice it to say, however, that among the many dynamics and variables at work in the era none seems to point to a mere decline in day-to-day discipline. The Council of Chalcedon (451) banned monks from involvement in business, and the Council at Trullo in 692 followed up with prohibitions on attendance at horseraces and the theater, warnings against public bathing with women as well as a more serious measure against monks who fornicate and marry.[77] Similar lapses in discipline surely occurred in the eighth century,[78] but there is nothing to suggest that individual discipline was any more of a problem than before. Abbots who were themselves not involved in such activities no doubt condemned them at all times. More interesting and to the point is the considerable body of evidence suggesting major shifts—economically and institutionally—in the monastic profession itself. Much of this evidence is in the form of canons and imperial legislation which regulate the way monasteries conducted their internal business, especially their economic affairs. The image of monasticism as big business is indeed unmistakable, right through to a mid eighth-century law book, the *Ecloga*, with its regulations over monks in property-lease and guardianship agreements.[79]

The structural changes in monasticism did not end there. Another remarkable shift was the evident drift of the monastic order from either the intensely private or the emphatically public vocation of centuries past. The fact that from the sixth century onward monasteries

---

[76] For basic bibliography, see above n. 23.

[77] Chalcedon, canon 3. Trullo, canons 6, 24, 77. Some of these canons cite the secular clergy as well.

[78] Cf. the Council of Nicaea (787), canons 4, 20, 21, 22.

[79] For monks cited in the *Ecloga*, see *Ecloga. Das Gesetzbuch Leons III und Konstantinos' V*, ed. L. Burgmann (Frankfurt am Main, 1983), esp. chs. 7 and 12. For general information see above n. 23, and Peter Charanis, "The Monastic Properties and the State in the Byzantine Empire", *DOP* 4 (1948), pp. 53–118; idem, "The Monk as an Element in Byzantine Society", *DOP* 25 (1971), pp. 63–84; both repr. in idem, *Social, Economic and Political Life in the Byzantine Empire* (London, 1973). John Thomas, *Private Religious Foundations* (Washington, 1987), pp. 37–58, pp. 111ff.

were seemingly as often used as prisons and especially places of
retirement as they were the locus of monastic discipline and action
points to the general tendency of the times.[80] A certain laxity had
set in. Gone, apparently—though we cannot be absolutely sure—
were the great coenobitic houses of times past which had dedicated
themselves to all-night psalming, manual labor, or other communal
projects serving the needs and interests of the monastery. Yet gone,
too, were the days in which armies of monks came to Constantinople
and other imperial cities in search of confrontation, be it with the
unconverted pagan and Jew or their opponents in a heated religious
debate.[81] By the late seventh and eighth centuries such dramatic
demonstrations of collective monastic activism had practically disappeared, and there is little to suggest that new forms of monastic
power politics had come to take their place. Quite to the contrary,
monks seem now to have lost (or been dispossessed of) even the
more subtle, indirect organs of power that they had once enjoyed.
For example, the office of exarch (or archimandrite) of Constantinopolitan monasticism had long since ceased to exist after enjoying a
measure of power and influence at least as late as the mid fifth century. The passing of this institution in subsequent centuries seems to
indicate a real reduction in official monastic representation at the
imperial court and patriarchate, or at the very least it suggests a
decline in the spirit of cooperation and coordinated action among
Constantinopolitan monasteries themselves in the face of external
challenges.[82] Furthermore, their formal associations within the official
church had been signficantly reduced. Far fewer numbers of monks

---

[80] A rough count of monasteries used as places of political imprisonment in the
early Byzantine centuries (prior to 787) reveals at least six names: the Dalmatos,
Theodote (alt. Isidore), Stoudios, Theodore in the Rhesion, Chora, and the
Chorakoudion. For these see R. Janin, *La géographie ecclésiastique de l'empire byzantin*,
I: *Le siège de Constantinople et le patriarcat oecuménique*, 3: *Les églises et les monastères* (Paris,
1969²), *passim*. For more on this question, see Kountoura-Galakê, *Clergy and Society*,
p. 57.

[81] Frank R. Trombley, *Hellenic Religion and Christianization, c. 370–529*, 2 vols.
(Leiden, 1993–94), vol. 2, esp. pp. 183–199.

[82] On the office of archimandrite/exarch in earlier centuries, Gilbert Dagron,
"Les moines et la ville. Le monachisme à Constantinople jusqu'au concile de
Chalcédoine (451)", *Travaux et Mémoires* 4 (1970), pp. 269–70, 274; repr. in idem,
La romanité chrétienne en Orient. Héritages et mutations (London, 1984). On the seeming
lack of any principle of organization and hierarchy within the world of eighth-
century monasticism, see R. Janin, *Les églises et les monastères des grand centres byzantines* (Paris, 1975), pp. 427–9.

and abbots were ordained as clergy in the eighth century than had been the case in an earlier era,[83] a development that arguably reduced their participation in the daily workings of local churches in general and possibly also placed an obstacle in the way of monastic appointments to positions of power and responsibility within the church hierarchy.

In making these comparisons between early Byzantine and eighth-century monks it would be a mistake to overstate the inherent power and influence of monks in the earlier age. For it is doubtful whether Constantinople's monks ever achieved the same status as did their counterparts in other major cities such as Antioch, Jerusalem and Alexandria. Be that as it may, it is nevertheless clear from the evidence presented above that monks in succeeding centuries suffered a real setback within the highest social and political circles of the capital, both objectively and in relation to the fortunes of other social groups. Furthermore, it may even be possible to detect the impact of this progressive decline at lower levels on the ladder of monastic experience.

Two pieces of evidence suggest as much. The first is a canon from Trullo in which hermits living on the streets with long hair and black robes are required to settle in a monastery or else be forcibly evicted from imperial cities.[84] The canon makes clear therefore that certain monks are in fact a public nuisance to urban society because of their unseemly conduct. Such evidence no doubt hearkens back to concerns over monastic stability voiced so often before in canons and legislation. Yet it is also worth noting that the nuisance represented by these late seventh-century hermits stands in quite sharp contrast to the problems posed by fifth- and sixth-century monks, who were threatened with eviction from cities for disrupting urban life at its very roots through their mass gatherings in the streets and frequent violence. They were trouble-makers writ large, arguably as disruptive to city life as the circus factions were.[85] By the later seventh and early eighth centuries things had apparently changed. The days which witnessed armies of monks coming to imperial cities in search of confrontation were simply gone. Good, well-behaved monks were

---

[83] Janin, *Les églises et les monastères*, p. 428.
[84] Canon 42.
[85] See, e.g., Council of Chalcedon, canons 4, 18, 23.

seemingly in the majority. But even the nuisance which their counterparts, "bad monks", now posed was banal in comparison to centuries past, now a mere *brutta figura* upon the urban landscape rather than the brute force they once were.[86]

The second piece of evidence reinforces this image of eighth-century monks as more or less regular people, blending into the background of daily life and without the strong public vocation of centuries past. It comes from the years 742–743 during a siege of Constantinople, amidst a civil war. The besieged emperor refused to allow all but a few of the starving and desperate citizens to leave the city, obviously for fear that they would join the other side. He made exceptions only with women, monks and poor people.[87] For these groups were apparently considered to be, if not above suspicion, then at least unempowered and consequently irrelevant. This episode together with the Trullo canon suggests therefore that average monks in the eighth century had been relegated to the margins of city life and politics at the same times as their betters—urban abbots and their high-ranking assistants—had lost ground within the church. This would be a pitiful picture of the monastic estate on the whole if not for the fact that monks are known to have played a considerable role in urban charities. Indeed it is tempting to identify this activity, more than any other, as the defining vocation of our eighth-century monks. It is true that they did not have a monopoly on the market, sharing it with the episcopate which was directly involved and the urban nobility who participated vicariously through their grants to monastic and episcopal institutions. But monks in general, and female religious in particular, seem to have played a major role in charitable institutions nonetheless.[88]

To conclude, allow me to return to the case histories of Stephen the Younger and Philaretos, whom I earlier described as failures (if we believe their hagiographers) in their respective vocations of political saint and benefactor. Having reviewed some aspects of the social and religious context in which these men lived and worked, it will

---

[86] Cf. Timothy Gregory, *Vox Populi. Popular Opinion and Violence in Religious Controversies of the Fifth Century A.D.* (Columbus, 1979).

[87] Theophanes, *Chronographia*, pp. 419.7–420.4.

[88] Evelyn Patlagean, *Pauvreté économique et pauvreté sociale à Byzance, 4ᵉ–7ᵉ siècles* (Paris, 1977); Demetrios Constantelos, *Byzantine Philanthropy and Social Welfare* (New Brunswick, 1968), 88–110 and *passim*; Timothy Miller, *The Birth of the Hospital in the Byzantine Empire* (Baltimore/London, 1985), esp. 118–140.

be necessary to qualify that opinion, adding a few words about the phenomenon called Iconoclasm in this connection. These two men were not so much failures in their chosen fields as people far out of their depths, vocationally speaking. Stephen entered a city where monasticism had become almost banal in its tendency toward social and cultural assimilation, economic introversion, and a distinct distaste for the political. He would have done well to join the armies of monastic social workers—perhaps even lead them—in which case he may have died a penniless but fulfilled man. Instead he challenged the emperor, a role he was manifestly unqualified for and for which he had no following. In other words, despite being a famous ascetic in his day, he lacked spiritual authority and a command over "the holy" in Peter Brown's sense of the word precisely because this sort of thing simply did not exist anymore. To that extent his persecution and death were not part of a "cleaning away of undergrowth in a well-established forest" so much as the isolated murder of an upstart subject who just happened to be—and most surprisingly at that—a monk. In this reading it matters very little whether Stephen's challenge was a public expression of his genuine attachment to icons or part of a veiled political conspiracy; for in either case he had gone far out of his depths and needed to be corrected. As for Philaretos, the same logic holds true. Whether to identify him confessionally as an iconoclast, iconodule or something in-between seems therefore a minor consideration in comparison to that of the peculiar vocational choices he makes under the circumstances afforded him.[89] When Philaretos came to Constantinople as the rich noble he was, with good connections in the countryside, he would have been expected to enter the political intrigues of the court. This was the sort of thing nobles were supposed to do after all. Or, failing at that, and in view of his philanthropic tendencies, Philaretos might have come to town, mules loaded down with gold, and founded a charitable organization run by monks and nuns. He might even have become a monk and abbot himself. But instead Philaretos actually got his hands dirty; for a while he stood ankle-deep in the muddy streets of Constantinople right alongside the poor. This would of course have been too much for the husband of his granddaughter, the emperor, to take. Philaretos needed to be fished out from the

---

[89] For Philarete as iconoclast, see Sevcenko, "Hagiography", p. 126; Auzépy, "De Philarète", p. 121.

vocational depths of the holy man to which he had drifted and present himself in a more dignified if still charitable light, which is indeed what happened. Until this point, however, he had succumbed to a similar temptation as Stephen. The two indeed had a lot in common. The old nobleman Philaretos adopted a monastic posture and attitudes without ever donning the monastic dress, just as Stephen developed a taste and voice for politics all the while enigmatically dressed in black. Clearly neither was a man of his times, a world in which spiritual authority had quite clearly lost its direction when measured against "the holy" of old.

BIBLIOGRAPHY

Sources

Chronicon Paschale, ed. L. Dindorf (Bonn, 1832); transl. by Michael and Mary Whitby, *Chronicon Paschale 284–628 A.D. Translated with notes and Introduction*, Translated Texts for Historians 7 (Liverpool, 1989).
Ecloga. Das Gesetzbuch Leons III und Konstantinos' V, ed. L. Burgmann (Frankfurt am Main, 1983).
Evagrius Scholasticus, *The Ecclesiastical History of Evagrius*, eds. J. Bidez, L. Parmentier (London, 1898; reprint Amsterdam, 1964).
Joshua the Stylite, *The Chronicle of Joshua the Stylite*, transl. by W. Wright (Cambridge, 1882).
Kallinikos the Monk, "The Life of Hypatios", in *Vie d'Hypatios*, ed. G.J.M. Bartelink, SC 177 (Paris, 1971).
Leontios of Neapolis, "Life of Symeon the Fool", ed. Lennart Rydén, *Das Leben des heiligen Narren Symeon* (Uppsala, 1963); transl. by Derek Krueger, *Symeon the Holy Fool. Leontius' Life and the Late Antique City* (Berkeley/Los Angeles/London, 1996).
"Life of Alexander of the Non-Sleepers", in "Vie d'Alexandre l'Acémète. Texte grec et traduction latine", ed. E. de Stoop, PO 6.5 (1911), pp. 658–704.
"Life of Anna the Younger (alt. Euphemianos)", in *Synaxarium Ecclesiae Constantinopolae, Propylaeum ad Acta Sanctorum Novembris*, ed. H. Delehaye, October 29.
"Life of Daniel the Stylite", in "The Life and Works of Our Holy Father, St. Daniel the Stylite", transl. by Elizabeth Dawes and Norman H. Baynes, *Three Byzantine Saints* (London/Oxford, 1948; repr. 1977), pp. 7–71.
"Life of Daniel the Stylite", in *Les saints stylites*, ed. H. Delehaye, *Subsidia Hagiographica* 14 (Brussels, 1923), pp. 1–94; transl. by Elizabeth Dawes, *Three Byzantine Saints* (London/Oxford, 1948; repr. 1977).
"Life of David of Thessaloniki [BHG³ 493d]", in "Anekdoton egkomion eis ton hosion David", ed. Basil Laourdes, *Makedonika* 10 (1970), pp. 234–52.
"Life of David of Thessaloniki [BHG³ 493]", in *Leben des heiligen David*, ed. Valentine Rose (Berlin, 1887), pp. 1–15.
"Life of Elizabeth the Wonder-Worker", in "Sainte Elisabeth d' Héraclée, abbesse à Constantinople", ed. François Halkin, *Anal. Boll.* 91 (1973), pp. 251–64.
"Life of John Kalybites", in "Ho Hagios Ioannes Ho Kalybites (Anekdota Keimena ek Parisinon Kodikon)", ed. Odysseus Lampsides, *Platon* 16 (1964), pp. 288–99.
"Life of Markellos of the Non-Sleepers", in "La vie ancienne de Saint Marcel l'Acémète", ed. Gilbert Dagron, *Anal. Boll.* 86 (1968), pp. 287–321.
"Life of St. Matrona", in *Acta Sanctorum Novembris* 3 (Brussels, 1910).

"Life of Philaretos", in *La Vie de S. Philarete*, eds. M.-H. Fourmy and M. Leroy, *Byzantion* 9 (1934), pp. 112–70.

"Life of Sabas", in *Kyrillos von Skythopolis*, ed. E. Schwartz (Leipzig, 1939).

"Life of Samson", in "Saint Samson le Xénodoque de Constantinople (VIᵉ siècle)", ed. François Halkin, *Rivista di studi bizantini e neoellenici* n.s. 14–16 (1977–1979), pp. 6–17.

"Life of Stephen the Younger", in *La Vie d' Étienne le Jeune par Étienne le Diacre. Introduction, édition et traduction*, ed. Marie-France Auzépy (Aldershot, 1997).

"Life of Theodore of Chora", in "De S. Theodoro Monacho Hegumenoque Chorensi", ed. Chrysantho Loparev, *Zapiski klassicheskago otdel. imperatorskago russkago arkeologischeskago obschestva* 1 (1904), pp. 1–16.

"Life of Theodore of Sykeon", in *Vie de Théodore de Sykéôn*, ed. A.J. Festugiére, *Subsidia Hagiographica* 48 (Brussels, 1970); transl. by Elizabeth Dawes and Norman H. Baynes, *Three Byzantine Saints* (London/Oxford, 1948; repr. 1977), pp. 88–192.

Moschos, John, *Patrum Spirituale*, in PG 87, 2851–3112; transl. by John Wortley, *The Spiritual Meadow of John Moschos*, Cistercian Studies Series 139 (Kalamazoo, 1992).

Nikephoros, Patriarch of Constantinople, *The Short History*, ed. Cyril Mango, *Corpus Fontium Historiae Byzantinae* 13 (Washington, 1990).

Nikephoros the Priest, "The Life of Andrew the Fool", in *The Life of St. Andrew the Fool. Text, Translation, and Notes*, Acta Universitatis Uppsaliensis 4.2, ed. L. Rydén (Uppsala, 1995).

Parastaseis Syntomoi Chronikai, in *Constantinople in the Early Eighth Century*, eds. Averil Cameron, Judith Herrin (Leiden, 1984).

Theophanes, *Chronographia*, 2 vols., ed. C. de Boor (Leipzig, 1883–5); transl. by C. Mango and R. Scott, *The Chronicle of Theophanes Confessor* (Oxford, 1997).

Ps. Zachariah of Mitylene, *The Syriac Chronicle Known as that of Zachariah of Mitylene*, transl. by F.J. Hamilton and E.W. Brooks (London, 1899).

Zachariah Rhetor, "Life of Severus", in *Vita Severi*, ed. M.-A. Kugener, PO 2.1 (1907), pp. 103–8.

Secondary Literature

Ahrweiler, Hélène, "The Geography of the Iconoclast World", *Iconoclasm, Papers given at the Ninth Spring Symposium of Byzantine Studies, University of Birmingham, March 1975*, eds. A. Bryer, J. Herrin (Birmingham, 1977), pp. 21–7.

Allen, Pauline, *Evagrius Scholasticus the Church Historian* (Louvain, 1981).

Anastos, Milton, "Iconoclasm and Imperial Rule 717–842", *The Cambridge Medieval History*, ed. Joan M. Hussey, vol. 4.1 (Cambridge, 1966), pp. 61–105.

Ashbrook Harvey, Susan, *Asceticism and Society in Crisis. John of Ephesus and the Lives of the Eastern Saints* (Berkeley/Los Angeles/London, 1990).

Auzépy, Marie-France, "L'analyse littéraire et l'historien: l'exemple des vies de saints iconoclastes", *Byzantinoslavica* 53 (1992), pp. 57–67.

———, "De Philarète, de sa famille et de certains monastères de Constantinople", *Les saints et leur sanctuaire à Byzance. Textes, images et monuments*, Byzantina Sorbonensia 11 (Paris, 1993), pp. 117–35.

Bacht, Heinrich, "Die Rolle des orientalischen Mönchtums in den kirchenpolitisichen Auseinandersetzungen um Chalkedon (431–519)", *Das Konzil Von Chalkedon* II, eds. Aloys Grillmeier, Heinrich Bacht (Würzburg, 1954), pp. 193–314.

Barnard, Leslie W., *The Graeco-Roman and Oriental Background of the Iconoclast Controversy* (Leiden, 1974).

Brock, Sebastian P., "Iconoclasm and the Monophysites", *Iconoclasm, Papers given at the Ninth Spring Symposium of Byzantine Studies, University of Birmingham, March 1975*, eds. A. Bryer, J. Herrin (Birmingham, 1977), pp. 53–7.

Brown, Peter, "The Rise and Function of the Holy Man in Late Antiquity", *JRS* 61 (1971), pp. 80–101.

————, "A Dark Age Crisis. Aspects of the Iconoclast Controversy", *The English Historical Review* 346 (1973), pp. 1–34.

————, "Eastern and Western Christendom in Late Antiquity: A Parting of the Ways?", *The Orthodox Churches and the West*, Studies in Church History 13 (Oxford, 1976), pp. 1–24; reprinted in his *Society and the Holy in Late Antiquity* (London, 1982), pp. 166–95.

Charanis, Peter, "The Monastic Properties and the State in the Byzantine Empire", *DOP* 4 (1948), pp. 53–118; repr. in idem, *Social, Economic and Political Life in the Byzantine Empire* (London, 1973).

————, "The Monk as an Element in Byzantine Society", *DOP* 25 (1971), pp. 63–84; repr. in idem, *Social, Economic and Political Life in the Byzantine Empire* (London, 1973).

————, *Studies on the Demography of the Byzantine Empire* (London, 1972).

Chitty, Derwas J., *The Desert a City* (Oxford, 1966).

Constantelos, Demetrios, *Byzantine Philanthropy and Social Welfare* (New Brunswick, 1968).

Dagron, Gilbert, "Les moines et la ville. Le monachisme à Constantinople jusqu'au concile de Chalcédoine (451)", *Travaux et Mémoires* 4 (1970), pp. 229–76; repr. in idem, *La romanité chrétienne en Orient. Héritages et mutations* (London, 1984), pp. 229–76.

————, "L' église et la chrétienté byzantines entre les invasions et l'iconoclasme (viie–début viiie siècle)", *Histoire du Christianisme des origines à nos jours*, Tome III: *Évêques, Moines et Empereurs (610–1054)*, eds. J.-M. Mayeur, C. et L. Piétri, A. Vauchez, M. Venard (Paris, 1993), pp. 9–91.

————, "Économie et société chrétienne (viiie–xe siècles)", *Histoire du Christianisme des origines à nos jours*, Tome III: *Évêques, Moines et Empereurs (610–1054)*, eds. J.-M. Mayeur, C. et L. Piétri, A. Vauchez, M. Venard (Paris, 1993), pp. 241–95.

Drijvers, Han J.W., "Hellenistic and Oriental Origins", *The Byzantine Saint. The University of Birmingham Fourteenth Spring Symposium of Byzantine Studies*, ed. Sergei Hackel (London, 1981), pp. 25–33.

Garth Fowden, "The Pagan Holy Man in Late Antique Society", *JHS* 102 (1982), pp. 33–59.

Freedburg, David, "The Structure of Byzantine and European Iconoclasm", in *Iconoclasm, Papers given at the Ninth Spring Symposium of Byzantine Studies, University of Birmingham, March 1975*, eds. A. Bryer, J. Herrin (Birmingham, 1977), pp. 165–77.

Gero, Stephen, *Byzantine Iconoclasm during the Reign of Constantine V* (Louvain, 1977).

————, "Byzantine Iconoclasm and Monachomachy", *JEH* 28 (1977), pp. 241–8.

Gregory, Timothy, *Vox Populi. Popular Opinion and Violence in Religious Controversies of the Fifth Century A.D.* (Columbus, 1979).

Haldon, John F., "Some Remarks on the Background to the Iconoclast Controversy", *Byzantinoslavica* 38 (1977), pp. 161–84.

————, *Byzantium in the Seventh Century. The Transformation of a Culture* (Cambridge, 1990).

Hatlie, Peter, "Some Intertexts of the *Vita Stephani Junioris*", *Modern Greek and Byzantine Studies* 22 (1998), pp. 200–14.

————, "Friendship and the Byzantine Iconoclast Age", *Friendship and Friendship Networks in Medieval Europe*, ed. Julian Haseldine (London, 1998), forthcoming.

Henry, Patrick, "What was the Iconoclast Controversy all about", *Church History* 45 (1976), pp. 16–31.

Huxley, George, "On the *Vita* of St. Stephen the Younger", *GRBS* 18 (1977), pp. 97–108.

Iorga, N., "Les origines de l'iconoclasme", *Études Byzantines* 2 (1940), pp. 225–45.

Janin, R., *La géographie ecclésiastique de l'empire byzantin*, I: *Le siège de Constantinople et le patriarcat oecuménique*, 3: *Les églises et les monastères* (Paris, 1969²).

————, *Les églises et les monastères des grand centres byzantines* (Paris, 1975).

Kaplan, Michel, *Les hommes et la terre à Byzance du vi^e au xie siècle. Propriété et exploitation du sol* (Paris, 1992).

————, "Les moines et leurs biens fonciers à Byzance du VIIIe au Xe siècle: acquisition, conservation et mise en valeur", *Revue Bénédictine* 109 (1993), pp. 209–223.

————, "L'hinterland religieux de Constantinople: moines et saints de banlieue d'après l'hagiographie", *Constantinople and Its Hinterland. Papers from the Twenty-Seventh Spring Symposium of Byzantine Studies, Oxford, April 1993*, Society for the Promotion of Byzantine Studies Publications 3, eds. Cyril Mango, Gilbert Dagron (Aldershot, 1995), pp. 191–205.

————, *La Chrétienté byzantine du début du viie siècle au milieu du xie siècle. Images et reliques, moines et moniales, Constantinople et Rome* (Paris, 1997).

Karayannopoulos, J., Weiss, Günter, *Quellenkunde zur Geschichte von Byzanz (324–1453)*, 2 vols. (Wiesbaden, 1982).

Karlin-Hayter, Patricia, "Où l'abeille butine. La culture littéraire monastique à Byzance aux viiie et ixe siècles", *Revue Bénédictine* 109 (1993), pp. 99–116.

Kirschner, Robert, "The Vocation of Holiness in Late Antiquity", *Vig. Chr.* 38 (1984), pp. 105–24.

Kountoura-Galakê, Eleonora, *The Byzantine Clergy and Society in the Dark Centuries* (Athens, 1996) (in Greek).

Lombard, Alfred, *Constantin V, Empereur des Romains (740–775)* (Paris, 1902).

Lemerle, Paul, *Byzantine Humanism. The First Phase*, transl. by H. Lindsay and A. Moffat (Canberra, 1986).

Louth, Andrew, *Maximus the Confessor* (London/New York, 1996).

Mango, Cyril, "The Availability of Books in the Byzantine Empire, A.D. 750–850", *Byzantine Books and Bookmen. A Dumbarton Oaks Colloquium* (Washington D.C., 1975), pp. 29–45.

Markus, Robert A., *The End of Ancient Christianity* (Cambridge, 1990).

Masai, François, "La politique du Isauriens et la naissance de l'Europe", *Byzantion* 33 (1963), pp. 191–223.

Miller, Timothy, *The Birth of the Hospital in the Byzantine Empire* (Baltimore/London, 1985).

Ostrogorsky, George, *History of the Byzantine State*, transl. by Joan Hussey (New Brunswick, 1969).

Papachryssanthou, Denise, "La vie monastique dans les campagnes byzantines du viiie au xe siècle. Ermitages, groupes, et communautés", *Byzantion* 43 (1973), pp. 158–80.

Patlagean, Evelyn, *Pauvreté économique et pauvreté sociale à Byzance, 4e–7e siècles* (Paris, 1977).

————, "Sainteté et Pouvoir", *The Byzantine Saint. The University of Birmingham Fourteenth Spring Symposium of Byzantine Studies*, ed. Sergei Hackel (London, 1981), pp. 88–105.

————, "Vers une nouvelle Byzance? (milieux viie–ixe siècles)", *Le Moyen Age*, ed. R. Fossier, vol. 1 (Paris, 1982–3), pp. 283–330.

Ravegnani, Giorgio, "Motivi propogandistici iconoduli nel regno di Leone III e Constantino V in due cronache marciane inedite", *Studi Veneziani* 15:1973 (1975), pp. 3–20.

Ringrose, Kathryn M., "Monks and Society in Iconoclast Byzantium", *Byzantine Studies/Études Byzantines* 6 (1979), pp. 130–51.

Ruggieri, Vincenzo, "Note su schemi simbolic e letterari nella *Vita S. Stephani Junioris*", *Byzantion* 63 (1993), pp. 196–212.

Saradi, Helen, "Constantinople and Its Saints (IVth–Vth c.). The Image of the City and Social Considerations", *Studi medievale* 36 (1995), pp. 87–110.

Schreiner, Peter, "Legende und Wirklichkeit in der Darstellung des byzantinischen Bilderstreites", *Saeculum* 27 (1976), pp. 165–79.

Sevcenko, Ihor, "Hagiography of the Iconoclast Period", *Iconoclasm, Papers given at the Ninth Spring Symposium of Byzantine Studies, University of Birmingham, March 1975,* eds. A. Bryer, J. Herrin (Birmingham, 1977), pp. 113–33; repr. in idem, *Ideology, Letters and Culture in the Byzantine World* (London, 1986), pp. 1–42.

———, "Constantinople viewed from the Eastern Provinces in the Middle Byzantine Period", *Harvard Ukrainian Studies* 3–4 (1979–80), pp. 717–47.

Speck, Paul, *Kaiser Konstantin VI. Die Legitimation einer Fremden und der Versuch einer eigenen Herrschaft* (München, 1978).

Thomas, John, *Private Religious Foundations* (Washington, 1987).

Trombley, Frank R., *Hellenic Religion and Christianization, c. 370–529,* 2 vols. (Leiden, 1993–94).

Vööbus, A., *History of Asceticism in the Syrian Orient,* CSCO 500, Subs. 81 (Louvain, 1988).

Whittow, Mark, *The Making of Orthodox Byzantium, 600–1025* (Basingstoke/Hampshire, 1996).

Winkelmann, F., Brandes, W., (eds.), *Quellen zur Geschichte des frühen Byzanz (4.–9. Jahrhundert)* (Berlin, 1987; reprint Amsterdam, 1990).

INDEX

RELIGIONS IN
THE GRAECO-ROMAN WORLD

Recent publications:

114. Green, T.M. *The City of the Moon God.* Religious Traditions of Harran. 1992. ISBN 90 04 09513 6
115. Trombley, F.R. *Hellenic Religion and Christianization c. 370-529.* Volume 1. Reprint 1995. ISBN 90 04 09624 8 Volume 2. Reprint 1995. ISBN 90 04 09691 4
116. Friesen, S.J. *Twice Neokoros.* Ephesus, Asia and the Cult of the Flavian Imperial Family. 1993. ISBN 90 04 09689 2
117. Hornum, M.B. *Nemesis, the Roman State, and the Games.* 1993. ISBN 90 04 09745 7
118. Lieu, S.N.C. *Manichaeism in Mesopotamia and the Roman East.* 1994. ISBN 90 04 09742 2 Reprint 1998.
119. Pietersma, A. *The Apocryphon of Jannes and Jambres the Magicians.* P. Chester Beatty XVI (with New Editions of Papyrus Vindobonensis Greek inv. 29456 + 29828 verso and British Library Cotton Tiberius B. v f. 87). Edited with Introduction, Translation and Commentary. With full facsimile of all three texts. 1994. ISBN 90 04 09938 7
120. Blok, J.H. *The Early Amazons.* Modern and Ancient Perspectives on a Persistent Myth. 1994. ISBN 90 04 10077 6
121. Meyboom, P.G.P. *The Nile Mosaic of Palestrina.* Early Evidence of Egyptian Religion in Italy. 1994. ISBN 90 04 10137 3
122. McKay, H.A. *Sabbath and Synagogue.* The Question of Sabbath Worship in Ancient Judaism. 1994. ISBN 90 04 10060 1
123. Thom, J.C. *The Pythagorean Golden Verses.* With Introduction and Commentary. 1994. ISBN 90 04 10105 5
124. Takács, S.A. *Isis and Sarapis in the Roman World.* 1994. ISBN 90 04 10121 7
125. Fauth, W. *Helios Megistos.* Zur synkretistischen Theologie der Spätantike. 1995. ISBN 90 04 10194 2
126. Rutgers, L.V. *The Jews in Late Ancient Rome.* Evidence of Cultural Interaction in the Roman Diaspora. 1995. ISBN 90 04 10269 8

127. Straten, F.T. van. *Hierà kalá*. Images of Animal Sacrifice in Archaic and Classical Greece. 1995. ISBN 90 04 10292 2

128. Dijkstra, K. *Life and Loyalty*. A Study in the Socio-Religious Culture of Syria and Mesopotamia in the Graeco-Roman Period Based on Epigraphical Evidence. 1995. ISBN 90 04 09996 4

129. Meyer, M. & Mirccki P. (eds.). *Ancient Magic and Ritual Power*. 1995. ISBN 90 04 10406 2

130. Smith, M. & Cohen, S.J.D. (ed.). *Studies in the Cult of Yahweh*. 2 volumes. 1996. ISBN 90 04 10372 4 (set)
Vol. 1: *Studies in Historical Method, Ancient Israel, Ancient Ju-daism*. 1996. ISBN 90 04 10477 1
Vol. 2: *Studies in New Testament, Early Christianity, and Magic*. 1996. ISBN 90 04 10479 8

131. Lane, E.N. (ed.). *Cybele, Attis and Related Cults*. Essays in Memory of M.J. Vermaseren. 1996. ISBN 90 04 10196 9

132. Lukian von Samosata. *Alexandros oder der Lügenprophet*. Eingeleitet, herausgegeben, übersetzt und erklärt von U. Victor. 1997. ISBN 90 04 10792 4

133. Jong, A. de. *Traditions of the Magi*. Zoroastrianism in Greek and Latin Literature. 1997. ISBN 90 04 10844 0

134. Frankfurter, D. *Pilgrimage and Holy Space in Late Antique Egypt*. 1998. ISBN 90 04 11127 1

135. Ustinova, Y. *The Supreme Gods of the Bosporan Kingdom*. Celestial Aphrodite and the Most High God. 1998. ISBN 90 04 11231 6

137. Drijvers, J.W. & Watt, J.W. *Portraits of Spiritual Authority*. Religious Power in Early Christianity, Byzantium and the Christian Orient. 1999. ISBN 90 04 11459 9

138. Dirven, L. *The Palmyrenes of Dura-Europos*. A Study of Religious Interaction in Roman Syria. 1999. ISBN 90 04 11589 7